INTELLIGENT CONTROL:
DEVELOPMENTS IN PUBLIC ORDER POLICING IN CANADA

WILLEM DE LINT AND ALAN HALL

Intelligent Control

Developments in Public Order Policing in Canada

UNIVERSITY OF TORONTO PRESS
Toronto Buffalo London

© University of Toronto Press Incorporated 2009
Toronto Buffalo London
www.utppublishing.com
Printed in Canada

ISBN 978-0-8020-3846-3

Printed on acid-free paper

Library and Archives Canada Cataloguing in Publication

De Lint, Willem, 1959–
Intelligent control: developments in public order policing in Canada/
Willem de Lint and Alan Hall.

Includes bibliographical references and index.
ISBN 978-0-8020-3846-3

1. Police – Canada.   I. Hall, Alan   II. Title.

HV8157.D435 2009   363.20971   C2008-907730-X

This book has been published with the help of a grant from the Canadian
Federation for the Humanities and Social Sciences, through the Aid to
Scholarly Publications Programme, using funds provided by the Social
Sciences and Humanities Research Council of Canada.

University of Toronto Press acknowledges the financial assistance to its
publishing program of the Canada Council for the Arts and the Ontario Arts
Council.

University of Toronto Press acknowledges the financial support for its
publishing activities of the Government of Canada through the Book
Publishing Industry Development Program (BPIDP).

Contents

Acknowledgments

We would like to acknowledge the Social Sciences and Humanities Research Council of Canada, Standard Research Grants program for funding that supported the collection of data and contributed to support for analysis and dissemination at conferences and journal articles. We would also like to thank the excellent work of graduate students who helped us with the surveys, coding, and interview transcription: Dale Balluci, Ryan Gostlow, Celine Marin Halford, and Rob McLennan. We also wish to recognize the contributions of other graduate students who have helped keep us on course over the years especially Christian Pasiak, Ryan Cotter, and Shannon Speed. We want to express our appreciation to the two anonymous reviewers for University of Toronto Press, Jim Leahy and Anne Laughlin for expert editing and sound advice, Mary Newberry for outstanding indexing, and Virgil Duff for believing in the project. Both authors also express their admiration and thanks to the liaison and other police officers, union, and company officials who gave their time to this effort and made it all possible. Special thanks go out to those police services who contributed so much to our case studies – the Windsor Police Services, Hamilton–Wentforth Police, the Toronto Metropolitan Police, the Vancouver Police, the RCMP BC Division, and the Vancouver Police.

Willem de Lint would like to thank Vaughen for her support and love and for standing by him during his bouts of stormy rage and despair, and his mother for the same at earlier stages of 'development.' Also, he would like to thank, for scholarly engagement over the years, Pat O'Malley, 'Tank' Waddington, David Waddington, John Noakes, Pete Gill, Stuart Farson, Robert Reiner, Peter Carrington, James Sheptycki, Kevin Stenson, Philip Stenning, and Commissioner Sydney Linden.

Alan Hall wishes to thank Lynne Phillips for her never-ending support and invaluable guidance over the rough spots. A special thanks to

Rachel Phillips Hall for her love and understanding. Thanks go out as well to my loving parents, Kenneth and Margaret Hall. It makes all the difference in the world to have loved ones who encourage and believe in you.

The authors express their appreciation to the following journals for their permission to reproduce small portions of published material:

Part of chapter 4 appeared in Willem de Lint and A. Hall, 'Making Pickets Responsible: Policing Labour at a Distance in Windsor, Ontario,' *Canadian Review of Sociology and Anthropology* 39/1 (2002): 1–27. Parts of chapter 5 appeared in Alan Hall and W. de Lint, 'Policing Labour in Canada,' *Policing and Society: An International Journal of Research and Policy* 13/3 (2003): 219–34, and in Willem de Lint, R. Gostlow, and A. Hall, 'Judgement by Deferral: The Interlocutory Injunction in Labour Disputes Involving Picketing,' *Canadian Journal of Law and Society* 20/2 (2005): 67–93. Parts of chapters 2 and 7 appeared in Willem de Lint, 'Public Order Policing: A Tough Act to Follow?' *International Journal of the Sociology of Law* 33/4 (2005): 179–99. Part of chapter 8 appeared in Willem de Lint, S. Virta, and J. Deukmedjian, 'Simulating Control: A Shift in Policing,' *American Behavioral Scientist* 50/7 (2007).

This book is a collaborative project in which both authors shared equally in developing the original conception for the book and its organization; collecting, recording, and coding the interviews; conducting the research of primary data; outlining and writing the chapter drafts; and completing the manuscript in its final form.

INTELLIGENT CONTROL:
DEVELOPMENTS IN PUBLIC ORDER POLICING IN CANADA

1 Policing Labour / Policing Protest

Introduction

Among the most powerful symbols of liberal democracy are a worker's right to strike and a citizen's right to engage in protest. Democratic or authoritarian political systems are often distinguished by police tactics in these situations, seen as reflecting the nature of the relationship between citizens, workers, and governing authorities. Accordingly, spectacles of riot police clubbing, pepper spraying, or arresting protesters or pickets are among the most widely appreciated bellwethers that liberal democracies are degenerating into authoritarian or police states.

What, then, can we make of neo-liberal democracies? Have labour and human rights persisted in importance as nation after nation has narrowed the sphere of welfare state provisions, national economic regulations, and the public interest? Are police still constrained by public and political sensibilities regarding the use of force? These are crucial questions because, as Sung (2006) argues, police have been faced with an intensified dilemma with the rise of neo-liberalism. By many accounts, most neo-liberal governments have enhanced the potential for serious labour confrontations through regressive labour reforms, increased use of back-to-work legislation, privatization of unionized public sector jobs, and massive job cuts (Panitch and Swartz, 2003; Harvey, 2007). Industrial restructuring prompted by trade liberalization has had profound effects on many labour unions, with significant increases in plant closures and job insecurity leading often to major concessions in working rules and conditions (Adams, 2003; Broad, 1995; Fairbrother and Yates, 2006; Ogmundsen and Doyle, 2002).

Viewed in this way, neo-liberalism can be seen as a significant assault on labour and social movements (Adams, 2003; Broad, 1995; McBride, 1992; Panitch and Swartz, 2003). Arguably, it was from the fruits of this assault that mass demonstrations proliferated around the turn of the millennium, converging pro-labour, pro-environment, and politically disenfranchised groups into a common cause against neo-liberal globalization initiatives. While weakening the capacity of organized labour to mount meaningful resistance at the points of production (as evidenced by the general declines in unionization levels [Jackson, 2006; Ogmundsen and Doyle, 2002] and the number of strikes in most Western countries), union movements in many countries, often through alliances with other social movements, have had some success in mounting significant opposition to neo-liberal restructuring and reforms (Kumar and Murray, 2002; Kumar and Schenk, 2006; Peters, 2002; Yates, 2000; Stinson and Ballantyne, 2006). At the same time, major cuts to welfare, increasing wage gaps, foot dragging on Native land claims, and weak attention to a rapidly deteriorating environment have all contributed to increased social and economic tensions. The ongoing negative public (and policy) reaction to police use of force against these and other protesters (ACLU, 2000; RCMP, 2001; Ipperwash Commission, 2007; Warwyck, 2007) provide ample illustration that public dis/order remains a signal dilemma for police and the state or liberal governance more generally. How such displays of discontent are contained, deterred, or managed continues to refract the values and intentions of politics and polity.

Public policing has been experiencing dramatic restructuring pressures at the local, provincial, and national levels, which include fiscal constraints as well as demands for greater accountability, citizenry oversight, and transparency (Murphy, 1998). Along with increasing specialization, professionalization, and community relation orientations, police are being encouraged to redefine their 'core' areas of responsibility with concomitant restrictions on their 'public' mandate. As Christopher Murphy (1998) points out, the neo-liberal market concepts of 'private responsibility, user pay, cost efficiency, market based services and self-policing' have become increasingly popular.[1] At the same time, a 'new managerialism' grounded in 'post-Fordist' management techniques has also fuelled an increasing emphasis on formal policy development, program evaluation, and risk analysis – along with an associated growth in intelligence-based policing (de Lint, 1998; Ericson and Haggerty, 1997; Maguire, 2000; Maguire and John, 2006).

These developments suggest that police have been confronted with countering heightened public disorder at the same time as they are experiencing pressure to sanitize their public order imagery and/or responsibilities. In this context, perhaps it should come as no surprise to find private security, at one time centrestage in the countering of labour challenges (Jamieson, 1968; Lipton, 1967; Silver, 1966; Johnson, 1976; Rigakos, 2002), returning to play a more important role. Still, given heightened sensitivities about the spectacle of public coercion, it is not only the lateral movement or shift to private providers, but also the distribution of the public order mandate among different agencies and agents, including the primary parties to the grievance themselves (labour unions and demonstrators), that might be expected. As we shall show, large demonstrations are today countered or managed by joint task forces or operations consisting of sometimes a dozen or more different public agencies. As this also implies, the imagery of private security forces putting down a popular demonstration has thus far been avoided, and there is little evidence to suggest that the public police have relinquished the authority or readiness to put down disorder or protect public safety through shows or exercises of force.

The main question which this book addresses then is: how have public police in Canada attempted to negotiate public order relationships between labour, capital, civil society, and governing authorities within the context of neo-liberalism? In addressing this question, we seek to recognize the contested and dynamic nature of these efforts, focusing on emerging trends in labour and public order policing – particularly the growth in intelligence-based, paramilitary, and community policing applications (Johnston, 2000; King, 1997; Hall and de Lint, 2003; Stenning et al., 2007). While we recognize some continuing struggles with police over these strategic and tactical approaches (King, 1997), our examination of public order reveals these trends as complementary developments representing a shift from reactive ad hoc forms of coercion and accommodation to a more strategic integrated approach we call 'intelligent control.'

As we illustrate in what follows, most Canadian police services have developed sophisticated and regularized 'liaison' strategies and capacities that are used to pre-empt or minimize the need for force, police monitoring, or more covert intelligence gathering. Relationships of trust, responsibility, and accommodation form the foundation for the prevention of 'trouble' and the reduced need for control through force. As we also try to show, this development did not appear without a great deal of iterative introspection. As Tilly (2004) has demonstrated, trust is a quantity that is often stored up and squandered depending on the recent record of public authorities' use of valued resources. For police in liberal (and neo-liberal) democracies, it is the accumulation of public confidence that allows labour or protest self-regulation as the expected norm; but as we demonstrate, specialized 'liaison' police personnel also actively work to maintain their relations of trust with labour and other groups through communication and education, by establishing their neutrality in strike and protest situations, and by restraining institutional and corporate impulses to use force to resolve picket line or protest disputes.

Along with the liaison strategy, we document enhanced technical, organizational, and professional paramilitary and intelligence capabilities, which allow the police to use overwhelming and/or precise force against large and small demonstrations or groups – in particular those groups which are unwilling to play by the rules of the liaison approach. The intensification of intelligence gathering, the development of containment strategies such as the use of preventative detention and security fences, and the siting of political conferences in isolated areas, are all recognized as important elements of the current public order enforcement toolkit. Consonant with the liaison approach more generally, we argue that many of these strategies are aimed at avoiding confrontation and concealing coercion. The use of covert intelligence and pre-emptive or targeted arrests are particularly key features of this effort. As this implies, we see an increasing convergence of ideas around the integration of consensual and coercive strategies. This integration is key to what we mean by 'intelligent control': the graduated application of countering applications through real-time information management.

In what follows, we see the liaison approach and a more circumspect use of force as indications of continued political sensitivities surrounding police confrontations with strikers and protesters. But we also argue that 'intelligent control' is an evolving effort by police to modulate the optics of political expression. In the context of neo-liberalism and neo-conservatism and its welfare cost containment, reduced public or state provisions, and crime and security angst, police are on the front lines confronting harder social conditions (Harvey, 2007). Police strategies and tactics are also sharpened by cultural and political-economic changes stemming from police development itself and its experience of successive iterations of protest movements (della Porta and Reiter

1998). Altogether, public police in societies like that of Canada today are seen as playing a difficult role by managing public order without aggravating tensions or fertilizing a more radical politics. They attempt to accomplish the task by modulating the dosage of intelligence, prevention, and counter-measures. They identify, isolate, and target those they consider to be significant threats while the remainder are invited to cooperate or partner with the police liaison advice and information service. This helps to minimize the use of police resources, limits the potential for confrontations, and reinforces immediate and broader commitments to the rule of law.

The police don't always get it right. Protest conditions and tactics are not static. There is great ambiguity and dynamism in any protest and strike situation. However, the process we document here speaks to a major effort on the part of police to systematically restructure their approach to public order. The singular aim of intelligent control, if it has one, is to take out as much ambiguity and dynamism and exert as much control and predictability as possible. Our main task in this book is to show how and why this happened in the Canadian context.

Seeing Police through Labour

For critical labour historians, thinking about the policing of strikes most often conjures images of riot or mounted police charging through pickets with batons ready and shields raised. Indeed, many historical descriptions of labour unions or labour movements are reminiscent of war accounts with police playing the unambiguous role of the aggressive enemy (Frank, 1987; Mitchell and Naylor, 1998; Heron and Palmer, 1977; Kealey, 1986, 1992). In this frame of thinking, police frequently appear as little more than the coercive arm of the state, a governing authority acting more often than not in the direct interests of capital. Although it is recognized that police are not deployed in all situations, the decision to do so is often understood at least implicitly as a government prerogative motivated by direct political or economic interests (Gordon, 2005; Hall et al. 1978; Panitch and Swartz, 2003).

This model of coercive state-centred policing has been representative of the role and impact of police in the early labour histories of most industrialized countries. Although it is sometimes claimed that Canada has a relatively benign record of police actions as compared with countries such as the United States, the development of the Canadian labour movement, leading well into the twentieth century, was marked by numerous examples of violent clashes between pickets and police, often resulting in mass or targeted arrests of striking workers, the imposition of debilitating fines, and forced deportations of union leaders (Fudge and Tucker, 2001; Brown and Brown 1973; Hewitt, 1997). In the early stages of industrialization, aggressive police actions were grounded in an extensive arsenal of criminal, common, and immigration laws that mandated the use of police force and intimidation as the primary response to workers' demands and organizing efforts. Even after public police forces were widely established, it was not uncommon to see the use of the military or locally organized militia alongside private security forces. Most major police and military actions appeared to be operating under the direct orders of the ruling national or provincial governments of the day, and, as such, the state frequently appeared in full view as an ally of capital.

Yet a frequent theme even in early labour history is the contradictory impact of coercion on both the development of the labour movement and the subsequent conduct of policing. On the one hand, strikes and unions were often reportedly broken by the heavy hand of the law, and indeed, there were significant periods of time where the combination of police repression and economic factors appeared to have profound negative effects on labour organizations and their political strength (Heron, 1998; Palmer, 1992). On the other, police violence was often recognized as contributing to the radicalization and politicization of workers and workers' organizations, and as a consequence workers became increasingly effective by appealing to a growing distaste for displays of authorized violence and by challenging police coercion as a legitimate and primary means of control on labour (Russell, 1995). As these and other political pressures shaped the contours of liberal governance, and particularly as the laws and norms governing labour relations moderated, police use of force became politically charged. Unions were legalized and critical union activities such as organizing, picketing, and boycotting were not only decriminalized, but, by the second half of the twentieth century, given formal legal standing and protection under a new body of labour relations legislation (e.g., PC 1003 in 1944; see McCrorie, 1995). While most of these new laws imposed some significant restrictions on labour unions – including a ban on strikes during the life of a collective agreement – and were limited in important ways, such as failing to prohibit the use of replacement workers during strikes, they reduced violence and helped to usher in a period of relative labour peace in Canadian industrial relations (McCrorie, 1995; Russell, 1995). The often violent 'recognition strikes' of the 1930s and 1940s were replaced in the mid-1940s by an orderly government-supervised voting and certification process. Moreover, within a postwar period of major economic expansion, many of the larger capital-intensive firms adopted more cooperative negotiating models that provided workers with significant economic gains, what some refer to as the 'Fordist' exchange or compromise (Heron and Storey, 1986; Jessop, 1995; Russell, 1991). While there were still major strikes and some significant incidents of police/labour confrontations, especially in the mid-1960s, on the whole police intervention and incidents of violence appeared to be in decline (Jamieson, 1971; Marquis, 1993).

As picket violence waned in the 1950s, police began to disappear from the critical labour history of this period. For many critical analysts, particularly those operating from a political economy perspective, police simply became less important as a controlling force. Following Gramsci's (1971) notion of Fordism as a 'hegemonic regime,' union actions were constructed within a framework of 'responsible unionism' and 'self-policing' under the rule of law. Accordingly, conflict was increasingly ritualized and institutionalized in collective bargaining and quasi-legal processes of grievance arbitration (Burawoy, 1985; Fudge and Tucker, 2001; de Lint, Gostlow, and Hall, 2005). From this perspective of labour mobilization, the role and tactics of the police were seen as decreasingly relevant. However, when serious strains began to show in the mid-1960s, becoming large ruptures or fissures in the 1970s and 1980s or what many analysts call the 'Fordist crisis' (Jessop, 1995), public police re-emerged in historical accounts in their traditional role, albeit with a more modern arsenal of paramilitary tactics, specialized personnel, training, and equipment (Waddington, 1992).

This interpretation was particularly evident in Britain, where observers analysed a series of major confrontations between police and British labour unions, including the infamous 1985 coal strikes. Beginning with Hall et al.'s (1978) authoritarian thesis, a body of British research found that police had moved to a much more aggressive posture aimed at controlling the breakdown in consent arising from Thatcher's neo-conservative attack on labour unions and worker rights (Fielding, 1991; Uglow, 1988; D. Waddington, 1992; Reiner, 1998; Vogler, 1991; Jefferson, 1990). Stemming from Marxist regulation and political economy views of 'relatively autonomous' police function and symbolism, this argument followed the line that the style and method of intervention of the public police is dependent on shifts in the contest between capital and labour; thus, sometimes police must accommodate labour in order to maintain state legitimacy; at other times police will accommodate capital. The flexibility of police mobilization is drawn from the impossibility of purely private or purely public monopolizations of violence (or 'repressive apparatus') and between purely local or extra-local applications of 'justice.' As the state gets more authoritarian, police are less accommodating to labour, and this will be reflected in the strategies and techniques of protest policing.

As regards British civil society, as D. Waddington (1992) notes, since the mid-1960s the postwar consensus politics has been breached and a 'right to work' has replaced a right of trade unions to a partnership role. Some have suggested that the change began when police 'lost' a series of industrial disputes leading ultimately to the fall of the Heath government (Reiner, 1998: 45).[2] Others have linked changes directly to both the political culture that elected Margaret Thatcher to power as well the anti-labour and home security policies of Thatcher's neo-conservative government. Under Thatcher, police response to public disorder was a national policy that saw the freeing up and defence of business interests alongside the repression of crime and disorder. According to D. Waddington (1998), Thatcher was extremely hostile to the pickets, calling them an 'enemy within,' perhaps ensuring the distortion of police priorities. As he and others argue, picket line violence and arrests were consequently more frequent (see also Scraton, 1985).

Similar trends were perceived somewhat earlier in the unfolding of American public order experience. There, unemployment, poor housing conditions, and aggressive police practice (Kerner, 1968; Fielding, 1991) were associated with many of the late-1960s American riots. The lack of inclusion or incorporation of black minorities (given the widespread conscription of blacks into military service) was also widely viewed as contributory, and this again was subject at the micro-level to the hair-trigger of reactive police deployment, often following a pattern of aggressive countering of a minor violation leading to a large-scale public order confrontation (e.g., Watts, Detroit; also perceived in Britain by Lord Scarman, 1981). Indeed, the term 'police riot' captures this problem. Stemming from the social and political unease in the civil rights movement of the early 1960s and the demands by black minorities of a greater part of the political (as well as social and economic) franchise, public disorder was exacerbated by the behaviour of police against protesters. Commissions of inquiry into major riots fingered police response as too rigid and detached, resulting in calls for major overhauls in the way policing was delivered, leading particularly to the connection between public relations and community policing.

In Canada, there was also a 'return to coercion thesis,' most notably in the work of Panitch and Swartz (1993; 2003), which portrayed federal and provincial governments, backed by the traditional coercive support of the police and the courts, as attacking unions and workers in the 1980s and 1990s. Others such as Gordon (2005; 2006) have focused on the repressive aspects of recent Canadian law-and-order policies within neo-liberalism, with particular reference to the policing of the poor and minority groups and the policing of anti-globalization protests (Ericson and Doyle, 1999; Palmer, 2003). However, as we will demonstrate, there is a need for a more nuanced hypothesis. It is true that accusations of a ramped up coercive police state and public expressions of concern about the decline of liberal democracy have only intensified in the aftermath of the 11 September 2001 attacks in the United States (e.g., Palmer, 2003). Yet, in Canada as elsewhere, 9/11 has also reinforced the drive towards intelligence-based policing, with its trademark solution of trading less visible or exemplary coercion for less scrutiny of law enforcement decision making. As we will see, this is not simply a return to coercion, nor can it be explained fully by perceiving the maturation of 'secret state' provisions in the management of the internal security of liberal democracies.

Contesting Neo-coercion

The simple hypothesis of reinvigorated legitimate violence in the 'lean, mean' neo-liberal state has not gone unchallenged (Geary, 1985; della Porta and Reiter, 1998; McPhail, Schweingruber, and McCarthy, 1998). European and American literature suggests that the primary changes during the 1980s and 1990s have actually been oriented towards *minimizing* the use of force by placing more emphasis on communication, negotiation, and flexible law enforcement. This has been the reported pattern in many countries where police confrontation and strike or protest violence have been historically more common than in Britain, including Spain, France, Germany, and the United States (della Porta and Reiter, 1998; Fillieule and Jobard, 1998; Jaime-Jimenez and Reinares, 1998; King, 1997; McPhail, Schweingruber, and McCarthy, 1998). In describing this historical trend, della Porta and Reiter (1998: 6) suggest three emerging tactical tendencies: under-enforcement of the law, an emphasis on negotiation and mediation, and large-scale collection of information. In terms of under-enforcement, they suggest that police seek to avoid coercive intervention as much as possible, often by tolerating a certain level of law-breaking and emphasizing peacemaking over law enforcement. In an effort to prevent confrontations, police also routinely engage in protracted and complex negotiation procedures as well as ongoing public relations and education efforts. They point especially to the work of McPhail, Schweingruber, and McCarthy (1998) in the United States, della Porta and Reiter (1998) in Europe, and Waddington (1994a, b) in Britain which suggests that protest compliance is gained principally through negotiations and efforts to accommodate protester needs. With respect to information collection, more extensive intelligence gathering is credited as a crucial development as the police seek to determine how to approach a variety of public order situations and actors (della Porta and de Biasi, 1998).

While suggesting that the overall trend in the 1990s was towards consensual policing, della Porta and Reiter (1998) recognize that police were selective in how they approached different groups and situations. For example, pointing to the work of Fillieule and Jobard (1998), they note that French police will tolerate levels of violence from some groups such as farmers or unions in some situations and not others, for both tactical and political reasons. In her own work, della Porta (1998) notes that within the general trend towards more tolerance in Italy, there is still a continuum of policing styles which stretch from a cooperative, collaborative approach to a heavier reliance on mass paramilitary police presence and control principally through uses and shows of force. Moreover, McPhail, Schweingruber, and McCarthy (1998) observe that while a similar trend towards what they call a 'negotiated management' approach is evident in the United States, the majority of police services do not adhere to this kind of conciliatory model, while Reiner (1998) argues that authoritarian regimes have lasting effects well after a shift to democratic systems.

In one of the few studies on public-order policing in Canada, King (1997) suggests that there are actually two distinct opposing trends emerging at the same time. Along with the more conciliatory and consultative approach, he points to an increasingly militarized potential for confrontation that the police stand ready to use. In later work on the policing of protest in Canada, King (2004) generally reaffirms this perspective, albeit with more emphasis on intelligence, contingency planning, and crowd management. A similar observation has been made more broadly about the contradictions of community policing models and the parallel emphasis on heavily armed tactical squads in criminal investigations (Kraska and Kappeler, 1997). While King's earlier study was focused largely on the policing of Natives by the RCMP, the implication was that these competing trends were evident more broadly in public order policing.

While King (1997) presents consensual and coercive policing as 'diametrically opposed' developments, P. Waddington (1998) challenges the very idea that there has been a significant shift in public order policing – arguing that there is a long-standing, continuing strategy in which police prefer to use carrots while reserving their capacity to use an impressive arsenal of non-lethal and lethal sticks when the circumstances call for them to 'die in the ditch.' For Waddington, at least with reference to British case, there was no substantial shift in policing orientations to labour or social protests since the police have long used both coercive and non-coercive control tactics. He argues that, on the whole, police have continued to seek ways of accommodating labour and protesters, often in defiance of government wishes, but he also recognizes that police have certain 'lines in the sand' that they are committed to protect and beyond which they will not move. In those situations, often not of their choosing, police are well prepared to deploy force (P. Waddington, 1998: 378). Thus, for Waddington (1998), as for many other analysts (see also Latornell, 1993), the key question is not whether there have been major changes in policing practices, but rather how can we better understand the conditions under which protest violence and the use of police force occurs.

Taken as a whole, the consensual policing literature poses a number of interesting challenges to the images of the police conveyed by critical labour history and political economy. For one, it introduces the idea that the role and impact of the police in labour relations are not confined to the use or threat of force. This further suggests that it is important to recognize the multi-modal nature of policing control tactics and strategies. The legitimate use of force remains critical as a relatively privileged police tool. P. Waddington's work properly cautions us against assuming a major break from the past in current public order policing. The notion that there have been substantial historical changes in these tactics and strategies and not just a simple increase or decrease in coercion over time is also an important addition to our thinking about public order policing. The idea that policing tactics may be variable, selective, situational, and strategic also forces us to consider and be prepared to explain the policing of labour and strikes as one instance of the policing of mass or public demonstrations of grievance. However, what is particularly challenging theoretically to the 'authoritarian' or 'return to coercion' thesis is the claim that this trend towards a consensual approach to control was emerging within the context of the Fordist crisis and the neo-liberal response – that is, precisely when the state and capital were supposedly attacking labour, the poor, and other social movements. This points to the need to better understand the autonomous character of police and the different elements within and beyond neo-liberalism shaping its development as an institution of public order. It also suggests that we need to theorize more effectively the relationship between neo-liberalism, restructuring, and the reproduction of consent.

Methodology and Organization of This Book

This book is aimed at understanding developments of public order policing in Canada. Public order policing is understood here as the use of police authority and capacity to establish a legitimate equilibrium between governmental and societal, collective and individual rights and interests in a mass or collective demonstration of grievance (de Lint, 2005). A mass or collective demonstration of grievance occurs when a group of individuals gather for the purpose of communicating a spurned claim via a medium or venue which is appropriated under questionable authority. There are two types of demonstrations that concern us here: the policing of strikes and the policing of protests. Following Turner (1968), protest can be defined as an act which expresses a grievance and a conviction of a wrong or injustice. Since protesters are unable to correct the condition directly through their own efforts (e.g., negotiations, arbitrations, court orders), the protest action is intended to draw attention to the grievances and is further meant to provoke ameliorative steps by some target group: protesters depend on some combination of sympathy and fear to move the target group on their behalf (Turner, 1968: 816). A labour strike is understood as a particular form of protest aimed specifically at employment grievances which involves the collective withdrawal of labour from targeted employers (Peirce, 2000).

The analysis is based on a number of data sources collected over a five-year period.[3] The research began with a detailed case history of strike policing in Windsor, Ontario, drawn from interviews with current and past labour and police officials and archival research (N=30). Subsequently, over a three-year period (1999–2002), phone interviews were conducted with representatives from all police forces in Canadian municipalities of 100,000 or more (N=40), which also included provincial and RCMP detachments in all the provinces.[4] Interviews included closed and open questions on both strike and protest policing policies and practices. The chief constables of each police service were contacted, informed of the study purposes, and asked to approve interviews with staff currently responsible for strike and public order policing. In some cases, a single interview was conducted, while in others, where the initial contact's knowledge of history or public order was found to be limited, additional staff were interviewed.

Four additional case studies were selected, including the Hamilton Regional Police, the Toronto Police, and the Vancouver Police. Hamilton was selected in large part because the survey interview had indicated that the service had moved very early on to adopt aspects of the liaison approach. It was also seen as an excellent comparison with Windsor given its relatively similar size and strong industrial labour history. Evidence from the survey indicated that Vancouver and Toronto were also very early innovators, but particularly important in our decision to select them was the finding that they had fully integrated their approaches to strikes and public order. As the two largest Canadian cities and municipal police services in Canada with long histories of both labour and social protest activity, these were also seen as providing valuable bases for comparison. The British Columbia (BC) RCMP provincial service was added when it became clear in the survey and in the initial Vancouver interviews that it had been instrumental in changing the direction of strike policing in Vancouver and in the province as a whole. We then intended to include the Ontario Provincial Police as a comparator for the BC RCMP and completed some interviews with this in mind. However, we did not complete a full case study due to resource limitations.

The case study designs consisted of interviews with all front-line and senior police staff working in the areas of strike and public order policing and the collection and review of any historical documents, newspaper articles, and policy documents relating to strike and protests. Former (usually retired) police staff with knowledge of the early history of the service were identified through the current staff interviews and interviewed on the history of policing tactics and strategies and the shift to the liaison policies. A list of strikes in the four cities and in BC over a five-year period was then compiled, and both management and the union locals were contacted. A total of forty-six labour representatives and twenty-one management representatives consented to phone interviews, which consisted of closed and open questions regarding their accounts of police practices and their assessment of those practices. Open-ended interviews were also conducted with union officials, management and employer group representatives, local community activists, and labour lawyers in Windsor, Hamilton, Toronto, and Vancouver with the focus of the interviews varying with the experience of the interviewees (N=65). Although some of these interviews were follow-up interviews on the labour/management survey – that is, where the survey responses had indicated an interesting or distinct experience or perspective – most of these interviewees had either been recommended through other interviews or their organizations were identified through recent newspaper accounts or other documents.

Observations were also conducted at selected strikes and protests over the four-year period, including the 2000 OAS protest in Windsor, Ontario, and the 2001 Quebec Summit protest. A small number of OAS and Quebec City protesters (N=12) were also interviewed during and after the protest. Most of these interviews were taped and transcribed, although some were on site during the protests where taping was not possible. On-the-spot, unstructured interviews were also conducted with a small number of strikers (N=22) at five different strikes aimed at assessing their views of police actions during the strike. These were largely opportunistic selections, although in some cases there was an explicit effort to identify the union executive members, and picket captains or marshals, for more detailed interviews on the current and any previous picket line history. Archival information was collected from all the services in the survey and the case studies. Detailed archival research was also conducted throughout this period and into 2004, involving several inquiry and complaint commission reports, court judgments, and related media articles. Unfortunately, our efforts to obtain more recent historical statistics on strike- and protest-related arrests and incidents from the police had limited success.

After reviewing the significant literature on public order and neoliberalism, and offering our own particular reference points in chapter 2, the book is organized to loosely follow the changing practices of public order policing chronologically, with chapter 3 providing an account of the early policing of labour and bringing the narrative through the gradual, iterative institutionalization and segmentation of labour within Fordism. In our brief account of the development of Canadian state policy and labour union and collective bargaining law through to the 1960s, we follow the roles and actions of police as different factions within labour develop distinct political and institutional identities, structures, and tactics. Our main purpose is to unpack how legalization or the rule of law was established over industrial relations in Canada, while also identifying the limits and changing nature of this control over union and worker struggles in responsible unionism discipline.

In chapters 4 and 5, we examine the 1960s through 1980s as a time of crisis for Fordism and state welfarism. In chapter 4 we focus on the emergence of liaison policing as an outcrop of dissatisfaction and political necessity. We review the initial increases in labour strikes during the late 1960s, the 1970s, and early 1980s and changes to public order as predicated in part by experience south of the border, where race riots and anti-war protests exploded onto the scene. Through three case studies of police services, we show how a combination of internal and external labour and policing dynamics shape both the persistence of an institutionalized unionism committed to the rule of law as well as an alternative policy of public order that could not previously have been imagined – that is, the cultivation of cooperative relations between labour and the police.

In chapter 5, we examine the constituent parts of the labour liaison approach, including accounts of its development from those who participated in spearheading it. We identify five main operating principles underlying the approach and discuss origins and impacts of the principles. We conclude the chapter by stressing declining union strength and militancy, proactive courts, and the persistence of responsibilization as the key contexts in which police finally adopted formal policies of liaison policing.

In chapter 6, we retrace the emergence of liaison policing as part of a more concerted effort to deepen the response of police to public order and public relations crises. While highlighting the extension of liaison to protest policing more generally, we also recognize differences in the police perception and treatment of protests. This chapter also examines the role of other changes within policing including the development of new managerial techniques and public relations and community policing.

In chapter 7, we outline the distinctive character of anti-globalization and land claims as tests of the liaison model that required further strategic adaptations on the part of police. The chapter reviews recent political protest policing against the aim to restrict the deployment of violence against identified transgressor cohorts. Here we argue that liaison (gentler) policing opens the gate for the entry of a harder knowledge (expressive violence and security intelligence).

In chapter 8, we situate liaison policing in the broader movement towards intelligent control. We offer an analysis of our data as evidence that the recursive capacities of intelligent coercion represent an adaptation by police to the special circumstances of labour and protest sites.

The final chapter summarizes our findings and concludes by addressing the impact of police strategies and tactics on both labour and social dissent. We offer a broad assessment of how this analysis aids understanding of the relationship between labour, government, law, and police.

2 Interpreting Public Order Policing

Introduction

In the last chapter we hinted that a more nuanced approach to the policing of public order might require further explanation, given the neo-liberal context of the 'lean, mean state.' If it is true that the 'return to coercion' thesis is found wanting, we still need to explain the rise of the paramilitarism and the intensification of intelligence-based policing. If the use of force is more restrained and selective, as della Porta, Waddington, and others suggest, how can we account for the restraint and selection? This chapter looks for tentative answers to these questions by providing a review of the broader literatures on neo-liberalism, policing, and social movements.

We begin with the perspective that policing strategies and tactics are closely tied to the development of liberalism and liberal institutions and to the persistence and transformation of these ideas and institutions within neo-liberalism. We draw particular attention to the tensions identified in the literature between liberalization and privatization and civilianization, tensions that are also stressed in more recent examinations of neo-liberal policing (Loader and Walker, 2007; Loader and Walker, 2001; Ericson, 1981). We then move on to consider theories of institutionalization that are focused more specifically on explaining the processes and consequences underlying the institutional development of both the police and labour and social movements. A key point to emerge from this review is the importance of conflict routinization and ritualization that underlies normative performances by police, labour, and social movement actors. We are particularly keen to consider here the persistence of a commitment to the rule of law among these actors within neo-liberalism, but also whether institutional changes within neo-liberalism help explain the limits of that commitment on the part of both protesters and the police. Finally, after reviewing some salient points about the development of domestic policing offered via the governmentality literature, we offer a framework for categorizing and analysing different types of public order policing.

Liberalization and Privatization

Among analysts who challenge the authoritarian state or return to coercion thesis, one alternative view is that both the state and the police continue to operate within a cultural and political framework of liberal values which constrain the use of force and coercion against rights-bearing citizens (Geary, 1985; P. Waddington, 1998). This perspective tends to see common trends or directions in the development of policing within democratic states that stretch from the turn of the twentieth century to the turn of the twenty-first, albeit with some important variations and changes along the way. In this view, liberalization includes a number of dimensions, including the importance of the rule of law and democratic institutions, the separation of powers, public accountability, and the privatization of violence. This view draws primarily on the observed tradition of modern policing deriving out of its 'birth' in metropolitan London, a concrete event that insisted on the reviewability of the police function by 'the public' but also grounded in the doctrine of police independence and the civilization thesis of Norbert Elias. It is this latter point that is consistent with the trend, as della Porta and Reiter (1998: 6) summarize it, toward 'soft, tolerant, selective, legal, preventative, flexible, and professional' delivery.

From a liberal perspective, values influence structure – that is, liberal democratic societies are built materially on normative values. Of particular importance to the argument has been the Montesquieuian separation of power model of governance. This mainstay of constitutional argument in many Western democracies including Canada has been the notion of separation, redundancy, and balance between the various branches of government in order to provide a check on monarchist tendencies and executive overreach. Perhaps the American constitutional expert Lawrence Tribe put it best when he argued that 'the oldest and most central tenet of American constitutionalism is that all lawful power derives from the people and must be held in check to preserve their freedom' (2000: 6).

With respect to the police, a powerful antidote to centralized power has been the notion of self-government in the office of the constable, which underlies the push to professionalize the police. Indeed, to some, power separation is itself incorporated into the very 'idea of police' (Klockars 1988). That police were to be accountable to the rule of law and not the rule of [elite] men, and that they must be institutionally situated to carry out this mandate, was most dramatically formulated in Robert Peel's 'nine principles' document. Offered as the seedbed of the London Metropolitan Police in 1829, police were not to follow the French model in which they were instruments of the department of the interior, but were to be accountable to the lower judiciary, the public at large, and municipal and central authorities. Police discretion, already part of the office of constable, was retained with common law jurisprudence and, consequently, has aided in the realization of legitimacy in liberal democracies as to some degree fluid between bottom-up and top-down determinations. At the same time, police were at the entry point of the adversarial system, given the important role, particularly in enforcing public order, of deciding whether or not to apply or invoke criminal process. In police reforms in Britain, the United States, and Canada throughout the nineteenth and most of the twentieth century, the aim has been to situate police carefully between local and state authorities and executive and judicial accountabilities. As Skolnick (1966) has argued, police have had to incorporate democratic order and the rule of law.

The dependence of policing on democratic institutions is another feature of this view. Modern police in liberal democracies are reliant for their own institutional elaboration on the co-development or maintenance of other contiguous liberal democratic institutions, like public accountability and rights to free speech, assembly, non-discrimination, privacy, and so forth. Against those who would essentialize political economy or the needs of capital, advocates of the liberalization hypothesis argue that capital relations afford these values and are dependent on them and that police, in particular, must continuously demonstrate refreshment in liberal democratic forums, sometimes even where these threaten economic and political bases. For example, according to Geary (1985), change in police response to industrial disputes can be explained by the increasing constitutionalization of trade unions, the impact of media, and the progressive democratization of civil liberties. For P. Waddington (1991) as previously mentioned, this is also demonstrated when police sometimes act against the clear immediate interests of a political regime.

As this implies, the effects of liberalization are not confined to police. The media, unions, and various social movements also become sensitized to these same values – looking to the police to reflect their expectations and reacting somewhat predictably when they do (Snyder and Tilly, 1974; McCarthy and McPhail, 1998). A central point here, which Marxist political economy also recognizes (Fudge and Tucker, 2001), is the developing commitment to a rule of law which circumscribes strike and protest activities within narrow legal parameters. The 'look of lawfulness' is here not readily distinguishable from manifest practices, and the centrality of appearances of lawful propriety continuously rejuvenates police, institutionally, on democratic values.

For Grimshaw and Jefferson (1987), liberalization places operational independence at the heart of the problem of public order policing. Operational independence means that political authorities are restricted from micromanaging police at the operational level or directing, for example, how police are to handle a particular situation. But this cuts both ways. As much as governments benefit from the cover of operational independence of police, so do police benefit from claiming independence from government on operational questions. Police are independently interested in their legitimacy, which makes them independently interested in operational autonomy. In Canada, this was illustrated most recently in incidents of public protest in BC and Ontario[1] that produced strong negative public relations repercussions for the federal Liberal and provincial Progressive Conservative governments, specifically on the point that they were negating the rule of law by covertly directing the actions of the police to address political interests (see chapter 6).

Another feature of the liberalization argument stems from the association between modern liberal democratic institutions and the privatization of violence. While in modern political theory, the democratic state monopolizes legitimate violence and police are seen to carry out the consent of the governed to micromanage violence expression, the larger trajectory identified by Elias (1978), Beattie (1984), and Spierenburg (1984) is in the elimination of public violence and the identification of expressive state violence with pre-modern civilization. Consequently, although police 'monopolize violence,' in return they must do so in the context of civilization in very rationalized, limited, and inexpressive ways. Public displays of gross violence will identify them with the failure of civilization. Police therefore seek to modify and moderate their expertise and to prevent occasions where they are placed in the 'no-win' situation of public expressions of gross violence. As police develop practices consistent with liberal values and principles and as they develop their craft skills (and technology) pertaining to the use of force, law, and information (de Lint, 2003), they are better able to avoid destructive public spectacles of violence. They become professional with regard to their core institutional mandates, and this involves civilization and rationalization.

It is partially from this perspective that we can also understand why police institutions seek to off-load or render less visible controversial elements of coercive practice. Since the observance of public answerability and the drive to privatize violence tend to push in opposite directions, the public police are encouraged to off-load the spectacular displays of the 'petty sovereign' (cf. Agamben, 1998). Indeed, much current thinking on policing within neo-liberalism is also about its transformation as a 'public' institution. Work here includes what Jones and Newburn (2002) have called the 'transformation thesis' of Bayley and Shearing (1996) that currently there is 'a watershed' in which the old public monopoly is or has ended, replaced by private provision and also pluralization involving the provision of security services by a host of other state or non-state actors including a revival of vigilantism and self-policing. Close to this is the 'fragmentation thesis,' which holds that police and security provision has split up across public and private, voluntary and for-profit sectors, creating the need to think of security provision in terms of network metaphors and multiple, loosely coordinated authorities. Important here is the revitalization of the view of sectoral slippage between public and private administration of the coercive (and informational) mandate, a slippage that Cohen (1985) was hypothesizing in the early 1980s. In the more recent work of Shearing and associates (Johnston and Shearing, 2003; Shearing and Wood, 2003), the notion of nodal governance has been deployed to account for security relations empowered and tilted more favourably towards advantaged security clients or consumers. Such work contextualizes both the state and public police in a wider array of legitimate security providers and follows the notion that neo-liberal governance within late capitalism has much in common with feudal governance practices and less in common with the cumbersome, bureaucratic public services particularly of the postwar welfare state. The policing of industrial disputes and protests is just one of many domains in which the so-called decline of the 'public interest' is notable (cf. Loader and Walker, 2001; Loader and Walker 2007). Given the rise of private and civilian forms of policing, it would appear that an analysis of almost any locus of police action will need to pay heed to this idea that social and public spaces and rights are vanishing or in jeopardy.[2]

Continuing public interest in the rule of law and democratic interests in media (of political expression) would suggest, however, that there are limits to the exclusion both of the public and of public police from politically significant sites and venues. As noted, the measure of a society's democratic institutions (to which various constitutional sections like the right of assembly and the right of expression refer) is still found in participation rates or in the degree to which common folk are excluded from such sites and venues (cf. Ewick and Silbey, 1998). At the same time, it can be observed that the public ownership and accountability of regulation and enforcement of such sites are necessary to ensure they are not stripped of political (and cultural) significance. As we show in this book, this is important in the area of public protest but also in the area of industrial dispute. The policing and regulation of the latter is also a litmus test of the democratization of the police function, as has been well studied in, for instance, Turk (1982). To return to the point by Johnson (1976), the relative embeddedness of police (in either their locality or extra-locality) is important in that it predicts to some extent their receptiveness to local entreaties in the determination of law.

That being said, a number of analysts have argued that in the post-industrial information age, the relative importance of the constabulary office and police discretion has been receding with the waning of a rights-based discourse. Sociologists like Manuel Castells (1998) and Anthony Giddens (1990; 1991) have suggested that in late modernity social control is maintained less by the moral suasion of officials or specialists situated physically in the interstices and more by managerial policy that establishes flows of population and checks identities into territories (Ericson and Haggerty, 1997). In what Deleuze (2000) has called 'societies of control,' these flows should not be viewed as concerned primarily with the reform of individuals but rather with the movement of data and information. The growth of preventive and pre-emptive policing is illustrative of this wider phenomenon, but so too is the re-emergence of centralized and bureaucratic police delivery. As Ericson and Haggerty (1997) and de Lint (2000) have argued, with new communications systems there is an exponential increase in the quantity, quality, and timeliness of information flows (mainly about risk) down to and up from beat officers, allowing for real-time decision-making and micromanaging from the centre. Although this would appear to match larger trends, the policing field may be more complicated still: in particular, does the evidence show that police independence and police discretion are on the wane and that policy formation is again more top-down? Much of the recent scholarship would appear to predict it, with terms like 'control,' 'information management,' and 'risk' rather than 'justice,' 'morality,' and 'democracy.' With respect to public order policing, we also perceive much micromanagement from the centre. However, a more complete evaluation of the site will suggest more nuance. For instance, in the countering of Native protests at least, police practice continues to be highly sensitive to charges of political interference and absorptive to a variety of democratizing impulses.

The question of police operational independence in the area of public order is best captured by P. Waddington's (1998) description of a 'line in the sand.' As he found from fieldwork with police in England, police are highly sensitive to the question of where the protection of sovereign space (as ambiguous as this is) begins to require push-back against rights of speech and assembly. During the early to mid-1980s, as per the clear wishes of the British prime minister, Margaret Thatcher, pressure on that line was immense. Accordingly, labour as a movement found itself pushed back forcibly. Periods of re-politicization of public order policing are discernible, the most notorious being the miners' strike of 1984–5. Geary (1985) notes that police chiefs were left in no doubt in the message from political quarters that they were to pursue their actions vigorously against the strikers, and for many analysts including Geary, this helped to explain the rise in police brutality on the picket lines. Research on the Canadian experience also suggests that where there is a high-stakes contest between political authority and a challenger, there will be a concerted effort by representatives of that political authority to ensure that the outcome of the contest is favourable (King, 1997). This includes attempting to pressure influence on high-level police (Ipperwash, 2005). A brief look also appears to indicate that whereas throughout much of the twentieth century labour has been at the centre of many of those high-stakes contests, more recently it is key 'issue-based' (Willis, 2001) protest agendas that have given public order policing the most controversy concerning political 'interference.'

Others have also contended that in the United States and Canada the 'separation of powers' doctrine is often practised in the breach, a point referred to above and elaborated in the troublesome questions of exceptionalism and security (Panitch and Swartz, 2003). In the

post-9/11 public policy discourse in particular, scrutiny and challenge of executive action by the judiciary and the legislative branches
have been recast as threatening security by providing 'aid or comfort
to the state's enemies' (Baker, 2002). However, this argument is by no
means unique to post-9/11 events. The rationale has been used many
times during earlier wars and other crises that the executive must be
given extraordinary powers to defend and protect 'the homeland'
from external and internal threats. On this logically (and empirically)
weak but emotionally powerful premise (cf. Lustgarten and Leigh,
1996), extraordinary tools, usually coercive ones, are given to law
enforcement officials, including police. Whether the police use them
or not, how and on whom, as Waddington (1998) warns us, are very
important empirical and theoretical questions. But as has been suggested, having the capacity to use force often sets up pressures to use
that force, if for no other reason to justify its provision (cf. Ipperwash
Commission 2007). Certainly, if the substance of executive power includes greater secrecy, administrative fiat, and the manipulation of
information and coercive resources generally, then there is more
room for concern. One thing that has been well documented as a
consequence of a renewed vitality of executive power is the normalization of intelligence in the regular mandate of the public police
(de Lint, Virta, and Deukmedjian, 2007).

    What our discussion suggests thus far then is that neither the au-
thoritarian state nor progressive liberalization fully describes the
current setting. We see enhanced Hobbesian sovereignty or 'petty sovereigns' (Chappell, 2006) at the same time that elements of liberalization are also adapted. Privacy, for instance, becomes secrecy and the
right not to disclose sensitive information on the one hand, and the exclusion of public interest from frames of contest or conflict on the other.
That violence becomes more private is consistent with the neo-liberal
diminution of the scope of public interest, but police – arguably continued stakeholders of that public interest – also seek to reduce the
dynamic unpredictabilities associated with expressive displays of coercion. As has also been noted in the policing literature, accountability
even with the moniker 'public' comes more and more to mean answerability to 'stakeholders,' 'clients,' and 'customers,' thus also forcing
(the wider implication of) universal consent from the operable objective. As we will demonstrate in this study, the combination of these
trends suggests that the industrial dispute will be treated by police less
as a public spectacle demonstrating the capacity and legitimacy of the

state and more as a private dispute. However, as the literature also suggests, where political or administrative authority itself is the target of grievances in unpredictable expressions of public protest, the sovereignty dimension will continue to outmuscle privatization inclinations. In that context, police continue to seek innovations that help them to manage the dilemmas of using force.

Fordism, Institutionalization, and Liberal Hegemony

To better understand the impact of liberalization and neo-liberalism, one option is to focus more fully on the associated institutional and political economic developments. According to Scott and Meyer (1994: 10), institutionalization refers to the process in which a 'given set of units and a pattern of activities come to be normatively and cognitively held in place, and practically taken for granted as lawful (whether as a matter of formal law, custom, or knowledge).' The liberalization argument relies heavily on this view of institutionalization in the sense that police within democracies are seen as internalizing certain normative, moral, and legal imperatives that guide and give meaning to their practices and discourses. Police procedures, command structures, training, and technologies are all supposed to reflect an *internal* institutional commitment to liberal values as well as responses to *external* expectations and pressures coming from the public and other liberalized institutions, including, of course, the judiciary and legislatures. Police are also 'granted' within the liberal democracies the legitimate authority to use force in circumstances where liberal values and institutions are seen as being threatened. It is this authority to use force that helps to shape contrary authoritarian origins and tendencies, a tension that King (1997) recognized in his work. At the same time, these threats are Waddington's 'lines in the sand' that are seen as underlying the strategic *choices* of the police to use consensual and/or coercive tactics. While liberal and institutional theory place considerable emphasis on the autonomy of police, strategic choices are understood as being conditioned by local and national characteristics of the political opportunity structure, in particular the existing dominant culture and institutions (see also della Porta and Reiter, 1998). With respect to public order policing, this suggests a need to focus attention on the broader realms of [neo]liberal institutional development and their effects on the way in which conflict is conceptualized and managed.

Given the importance of the rule of law within liberalism, a key area to consider is the development of laws and legal institutions that govern labour and employment relations. With reference to labour law in Canada, there are a number of critical historical developments which historians widely understand as representing a liberal expansion of worker and labour union rights, including the legalization of labour unions, the repeal of criminal statutes, the early factory, employment standards and related legislation governing working conditions, and, of course, the more recent postwar labour relations legislation which spells out a process and procedure for certifying unions and governing collective bargaining (Fudge and Tucker, 2001; Heron, 1996; McCrorie, 1995). As we show in chapter 3, most of these major changes in Canadian labour law occurred over the twentieth century, particularly the immediate post–Second World War period that also coincided with a shift to welfare programs and policies. The period between the 1960s and the 1980s also witnessed other legislative and constitutional developments with respect to other social movements and issues, including the introduction of human and civil rights laws, the improvement of welfare legislation and programs, the creation of the Canadian Charter of Rights and Freedoms, major modifications in the federal Indian Act, and the expansion of environmental law including such legislation as the Ontario Environmental Bill of Rights. Along with these laws, federal and provincial governments established and expanded state and quasi-state institutions (e.g., labour relations boards, ministries or departments of labour) charged with responsibility for administering and enforcing these laws. With those administrative and enforcement institutions we also begin to see a whole new body of law created in quasi-judicial administrative contexts (e.g., labour arbitration law, human rights law).

Liberal and institutional accounts tend to see these legislative, administrative, and enforcement developments as evidence of liberal accommodations to demands for greater social and political participation and respect for labour and human rights reflecting a reciprocity between interests and power (Pierce, 2000). Control within liberalism is consent-based and consent is grounded in the actual sharing of power and wealth. For neo-Marxists, in particular Gramscian and regulation theorists (Burawoy, 1985; Fudge and Tucker, 2001; Hall, 1999; Kebede, 2005; Shields, 1990), there is also some recognition of reciprocity, but here the rule of law and the consent it achieves are seen as providing cover for continued and, within neo-liberalism, intensified capitalist exploitation of workers, the environment, and other constituencies (Ewick and Silbey, 1998; Harvey, 2007). Although the necessity of preserving appearances may also be trumpeted as proof of the persistence of liberal ethics in society at large, or at least among groups that have enough power to matter, most neo-Marxists, owing much to Gramsci's concept of hegemony, insist that consent is not achieved simply through legal democratic performances, but through real accommodations to those ideals. From a Marxist political economic perspective, accommodation performances do not come close to approaching political, social, or economic equality. More troubling still, liberalism provides rationales (exceptionalism, for example) for the use of force *without necessarily* denying state and police authorities the capacity to manipulate the conditions under which these may be justified. This being said, this view of hegemony is not completely inconsistent with the institutional view that the ups and downs of labour strikes and labour violence cannot be understood without considering the historical accommodations that have been made to labour by capital, the state, and, ultimately, police. Similar points have been made with respect to accommodations to other political constituencies including the women's movement, environmental movements, and Native and civil rights movements (Carroll, 1992; Adkin, 1992).

For many labour and social historians, some of whom were concerned with the reproduction of class hegemony, the postwar wave of labour and welfare legislation signalled some substantive material improvements for the working class in exchange for their cooperation and in some cases collaboration in the expansion and transformation of national and international capitalist development (Heron, 1996). More concretely, this Fordist exchange meant that unions worked with their employers to achieve worker acceptance of technological and other labour process changes while agreeing to achieve circumscribed local union goals, through legally prescribed certification, collective bargaining, and grievance procedures. Of course, as we see in chapter 3, this also meant a wholesale rejection of socialism or communism and an endorsement of capitalism as the means to achieving progress for workers.

According to the classical model on social movement decline, all movements can lose their dynamism in this way, when an elite emerges to exercise disproportionate control over its organization, when liberal law imposes legal responsibilities, when its original goals are displaced with more conservative ones, and when its division of labour becomes more hierarchical, professionalized, and explicit (McAdam, 1999: 325–6).

As Turner (1968) argues, a routinized bargaining relationship develops between unions and employers which ultimately erodes protest meanings and de-politicizes grievance expression. Routinized bargaining and the protest interpretation become increasingly incompatible because protest tends to define open-ended commitments, but bargaining can only occur with respect to specific and delimited demands. What also happens is that the injustice at back of the grievance becomes more invisible, as the official approach is the impersonal approach of bargaining. This also means that certain normative and legal practices are established as agreed-upon rules of the game (in strikes and protest), which subsequently limit confrontation and violence. Moreover, public sanction of the protest interpretation weakens as this happens. The public is desensitized to the injustice and re-sensitized to the disturbance as an inconvenience, creating a backlash which labour or police may experience if they are seen as being too aggressive or too lenient or as losing control (Turner, 1968: 828–9; Gillham and Marx, 2000). From this perspective, the post–Second World War development of labour relations law, welfare programs, and human rights legislation is widely seen as pacifying and shifting labour from its more radical socialist objectives as well as circumscribing the use of public protests as a central political tool. Labour unions, while still often operating within an adversarial model (McCarthy and McPhail, 1998: 84; Panitch and Swartz, 2003), are seen as quintessential examples of hegemony through institutionalization – where organized labour and its relations with capital become corporatized, legalistic, bureaucratic, and hierarchical within a liberal legal framework which binds the unions to certain confining procedures, rules, and structures.

Routinization is seen in the conduct of strikes and protests in the sense that institutionalized organized labour and protest groups seek to control the display of protest within the narrow confines of the law. The taken-for-granted rules are that violence must be limited if not eliminated, and if used at all, in a very controlled way, what Geary (1985) refers to as 'pushing and shoving.' From this perspective, changes to police strategies and tactics are at least partly a response to the moderation of conflict and physical confrontations that reflect the changing tactics and capabilities of the protest movements. Complementary, consensually-based police practices eventually become institutionalized and routinized *because* labour and social protests have been pacified through material gains, liberal ideology, and a labour and human rights regime, rendering more aggressive tactics not only unnecessary, but also politically problematic. In this context, the institutionalized rationale that governs much of the conduct of police, labour, and protest group relations is the taken-for-granted view that there is a *common interest* in the law and accordingly in conducting protests in a non-violent lawful manner.

However, institutionalization is a two-sided sword. On one hand police and union/protest institutionalization has limited the recourse to violence. On the other hand, it has aided in stripping the mass or collective demonstration of grievance of much of its political potency. As the mechanics and the organization of demonstration become ritualized and as labour and protest organization becomes institutionalized (full-time boards, executives, etc.), does it then become bereft of the threat found in the play of uncertainty or ambiguity (cf. McCarthy and McPhail, 1998: 96–102)? If so, demonstrations and protests as 'politics by other means' are made 'banal and less remarkable' by institutionalization and, in so becoming, rendered less effective as a politics of progressive change.

The Fordist Crisis and the Neo-Liberal Response

While liberal, institutionalization, and regulation arguments carry some weight as potential explanations for the development of more conciliatory public order policing in much of the twentieth century in Canada, they tend to run into some difficulty in explaining what happens when the 'Fordist' accommodations are no longer being made. As we have already seen, the 'return to coercion' or 'authoritarian state' theses of Panitch and Swartz and Hall et al. attribute the rise of neo-conservative, neo-liberal governments to the Fordist crisis, which comprises both state withdrawal from a labour market regulation and welfare protections regime[3] and capital's capacity to barter for increasingly regressive concessions from labour and other groups. From a regulation perspective, this withdrawal from the substantive accommodations established within the postwar consensus places the critical bases of consent and control in question and, by some accounts at least, yields both increasing levels of strike and protest activity and, in response to this, a police return to more coercive tactics (Hall et al., 1978; McBride, 1991). In regulation theory terms, the [Fordist] crisis in accumulation yields a crisis of regulation that prompts a reactionary response on the part of the state and police.

Yet as noted in chapter 1, and as will be shown for the Canadian case in this book, much of the empirical evidence on public order policing suggests that the opposite has happened: as neo-liberalism began to gain traction around the world, and even as strike and protest levels increased, most police services adopted more consensual approaches. Granted, the literature also demonstrates that paramilitary and covert intelligence capacities have been expanding over this same period, but if we are correct, again following della Porta and others, that these capacities are used more selectively within an overall framework of communication, negotiation, and conciliation, then we still need to explain when, how, and why these varying policing strategies are applied within the broader neo-liberal context.

Part of the answer may lie in a better understanding of neo-liberalism *in praxis*. First, it could be argued that neo-liberalism has not substantially altered (as yet at least) the core liberal values and the accommodations underlying those values. The commitment of police, courts, government, and corporate, labour, and civil society institutions to the rule of law and to certain collective as well as individual rights remains entrenched, while material conditions have been plentiful enough to provide for widespread public commitment to these institutions and values. Losses that have been experienced in terms of employment and financial security, income inequality, and work intensification have been neutralized through a discursive ramping-up of individual responsibility, hard work, and personal success.[4] To extend the argument further in regulation theory terms, it is largely on this basis that neo-liberalism can be seen as operating quite effectively as a dominant or hegemonic ideology by reducing questions of freedom, equality, and rights to crude notions of consumer choice, individual rights, and 'free markets' (Laclau and Mouffe, 1985).

A second line of argument is that liberalism is continuing to evolve through the accommodation of its market distributive goals. Many governments have largely maintained, and in some cases have extended, their postwar labour and employment law regimes, continuing to place some restraints on employers while ensuring overall labour union commitment to the rule of law (Russell, 1991). It is worth noting, for example, that the Canadian Supreme Court recently recognized collective bargaining as being protected under the country's Charter of Rights and Freedoms, contradicting over twenty years of court decisions which denied this right (Tyler, 2007). At the same time, free trade policies and agreements, industry deregulation, and massive industrial restructuring have substantially weakened the bargaining power of unions and, arguably, the power of the strike weapon (Jackson, 2006; Wells, 1997). Many companies have also sought to restructure their relations with organized labour and workers with an eye to limiting labour's resistance through the introduction of profit-sharing schemes, participative management approaches, generous severance and early retirement plans, and split wage contracts that grandparent existing staff (Russell, 1999).

Whether via the continuity of liberal practices or the adaptation of liberalism to perceived market conditions, there is considerable evidence that labour and many protest groups have been seriously weakened or compromised under neo-liberalism. From the early 1980s to the present, labour union strike activity and union density have declined markedly across the developed world. In Canada, strike activity was much higher in the 1960s and 1970s than in the 1980s and 1990s. Although union density has not declined in Canada to the extent of other countries, particularly the United States, this has been due largely to government extension of liberal labour laws to government workers. Still, in Canada as elsewhere, union wage and benefit differentials have been declining in a context of overall stagnant compensation. Concession and conciliatory forms of bargaining (such as interest bargaining) and deferral to team production are indications of union weakness and/or co-optation (Wells, 1997). The absence of any resurgent radicalism within labour movements in most developed nations is a point often made to support the argument that liberal/neo-liberal ideology and political-economic regimes have relatively few significant challengers at least in North America. Indeed, it would appear ironic that it was at a time of relative strength for unions, and particularly for lower-middle-class employment and upward mobility profiles, that we saw the most vigorous public agitation for more inclusivity in the social and political franchise.[5]

The evidence also speaks to differences between countries in the way and extent to which neo-liberalism and restructuring have been introduced. New Zealand, Australia, the United States, and Britain, for example, are often seen as moving earlier and much more aggressively to deregulate and privatize than Canada and much of continental Europe with a consonant greater decrease in union density and activity levels (Fairbrother and Yates, 2003). Certainly, several analysts have suggested that the neo-conservatism of Thatcher and Reagan moved to deregulate and privatize Britain and the United States much more rapidly and extensively in the 1980s than the Mulroney Conservative government in Canada or the liberal or social democratic governments of many continental European countries (McBride, 1991; Russell, 1990). As we show in the Canadian case in chapters 4 and 5, regional and provincial differences within countries have also been well documented, with much more explicit neo-conservative attacks on labour in BC in the 1980s and Ontario in the 1990s than was evident in the other provinces or in the federal government approach, although even these were much milder than the changes introduced in countries such as New Zealand. Similarly, it has been widely noted that since Thatcher, British Prime Minister Tony Blair's 'third way' represented a gentler approach to neo-liberalism, which made modest concessions to the public interest without substantially altering the march towards the flexibilization and liberalization of British and U.S. markets (Peck and Tickell, 2002). And quite apart from national and regional differences, researchers continue to find major differences between the ideals of neo-liberalism and the practices on the ground, many of which again relate to levels of actual privatization, individualization, deregulation, and de-welfarization (Cohen and Centeno, 2006).

These observations suggest that considerable caution needs to be exercised in assuming that neo-liberalism in practice is a uniformly radical break from welfare liberalism, or that consent is breaking down within the context of the changes that have been introduced. However, as noted in chapter 1, there is also ample evidence that new and in some cases intensified social tensions have emerged both globally and in Canada that may be attributed in part to capital, labour, and its regulation within neo-liberalism. The large-scale labour protests of the 1980s in BC and 1990s in Ontario, the intensified environmental confrontations with corporate loggers and fishers in the 1990s, the spread of Native land occupations in Canada over the last twenty years, and, of course, the large-scale anti-globalization protests across the globe in the late 1990s, can all be linked in significant ways to neo-liberal policies and practices, demonstrating persistent collective contestation and significant challenges to and weaknesses in neo-liberal hegemony. At the same time, the sources of many of these conflicts are not confined to neo-liberal policies. For example, while the intensification of Native land occupations over the course of the 1990s can be tied to neo-liberalism in various ways, the relationship between the Native strategies and tactics and police responses speaks to a more complicated series of external and internal political pressures (see chapter 6).

That police respond differently to different groups is well demonstrated in the public order literature, just as we also know that other situational factors, such as the political stakes involved, will alter the way police view and treat any given group. Police appreciation of acceptable and appropriate responses by particular groups are subject to changing political and technical assessments, perceptions, and pressures, but not all of these changes are reducible to neo-liberalism.

As these latter points suggest, we need to be aware that there are other political and cultural influences operating at the local, provincial, and national levels that are not neo-liberal in origin or form. Just as clearly, we need to know that it is often difficult in the context of expansive definitions of neo-liberalism to draw a line with respect to relying on neo-liberalism as an all-inclusive explanation for change. In that regard, it might be useful to reiterate here the distinction between the more discursive-leaning and materialist-leaning explanations of neo-liberalism. As a way of speaking how to do things that must be done, neo-liberalism stresses consumer choice and the connection between the choosing consumer and free markets. But neo-liberalism is also about constraining the sovereign choosing of whole countries, as evidenced in structural adjustment and even 'shock therapy' (Klien, 2007). If the problem is to understand shifts in labour or social protest or police practices and organization, this suggests the need to be more precise in the account of major political or economic change. For example, many institutional and regulation analysts are quick to stress that the Fordist crisis did not lead just to neo-liberal ideologies and forms of state governance, but also much more extensively to post-Fordist regimes of production, accumulation, and regulation grounded in enhanced consumer and labour market flexibility, lean and just-in-time production, and labour–management cooperation (Jessop, 1994). For these analysts, post-Fordism as a hegemonic regime replacing Fordism speaks in particular to questions of labour consent and conflict, as noted above, but it can also speak to our understanding of cultural and structural changes *within* police organizations, as in the enhanced emphasis on managerialism and communication technologies (cf. de Lint, 1998; O'Malley, 1997; O'Malley and Palmer, 1996). Granted, many analysts would describe the application of managerialism in the form of new public management as a feature of neo-liberalism, but as in the case of neo-liberalism, there is considerable disagreement even among Marxists as to the definition and parameters of post-Fordism, and indeed even on the question of whether the concept of post-Fordism has any value as an analytical or descriptive referent for advanced capitalism (Elam, 1994; Jessop, 1994).

Yet, from our reading of this literature, the more critical point is not whether Fordism has turned into post-Fordism or neo-Fordism, but rather whether we can identify and link shifts in particular *practices* of accumulation (e.g., high-wage, nationally based mass production and consumption to low-wage flexible or specialized production and consumption) to changes in particular *strategies* of social regulation *within* the workplace, the community, and the state (i.e., repression or legitimation). This suggests then that we need to connect the reduction in police–labour confrontations not only to changes in police structures, policies, and practices, but also to the interconnections between police and industrial relations developments over time, while linking those in turn to changes in labour processes and labour markets. Clearly, both liberalism and neo-liberalism are integral aspects of this transformation, both as ideologies and political regimes, but what is often missing from the police literature on neo-liberalism is any analysis of the dynamics and strategies of capital and labour. By drawing on political *economic* concepts such as post-industrialism, Fordism, and post-Fordism, we not only draw class relations into the centre of our analysis of labour consent and conflict, and the emergence of new social movements, but can also see the police themselves in terms of their class positions, both as workers and as mediators of class conflict. As well, by recognizing related technological and cultural shifts such as the development of the so-called 'information society,' we can better locate our analysis of police and protest innovations and rationales in a framework that avoids reducing control relations to simple economic and political interests.

Governmentality

While the analysis of neo-liberalism as hegemony offers important insights for understanding the development of public order policing, another significant line of analysis which draws more substantially on cultural analysis falls under the general realm of governance theory. From this perspective, it is important to go beyond political economy and liberalization by understanding changes to the policing of labour and protest as changes in the rationalities of rule. Relations of power are not fully captured either by political economy or by the normative evaluations of the liberal project. Here we return to questions introduced earlier such as whether policing reflects information age concerns with knowledge of populations and risk rather than modern age concerns with rights and politics. Is today's police officer better described as an information broker and knowledge worker than as a law enforcement officer or peacekeeper?

Governmentality offers a rich toolkit of concepts to probe the site of policing and security work. A focus on 'governmental technology,' or the ways that information, for example, may shape how to think about a problem or rule or order, evokes sensitivity to dynamic processes in these relations of power and arguably allows for a better sense of how consent is actually secured within neo-liberalism. What governmentality work on policing also offers is a view of power and governance beyond the 'limits of the sovereign state' (Garland 1996). In a sense, it re-articulates the old liberal notion that politics is wider than state-determined governance or the rule offered by state governments. Recent re-evaluations of institutions of governance (informed by the work of Foucault and Nikolas Rose, in particular) have challenged vertical relationships and reinterpreted the manner in which subjects and authorities have been capacitated in various constellations of rule (O'Malley, 1992; 1993; O'Malley and Palmer, 1996; Garland, 1996; Shearing, 2004, 1993; Johnston and Shearing, 2003). Work stemming from Simon (1988), O'Malley (1993) and Beck (1992) has also noted a shift to actuarial rule and the pre-eminence of predictive rather than prescriptive technologies. These studies suggest that in reference both to sovereignty and violence and to discipline and surveillance, there needs to be a reworking of how police and their relationship with labour or protesters should be viewed. That reworking emphasizes the knowledge work of police (Ericson and Haggerty, 1997) in the production of actuarial subjects and a preventative, depoliticized approach in which recourse to violence and persuasion is delimited through a re-articulation of government (beyond liberalism) dedicated to risk communications.

This overlaps in some respects with the institutional literature and the argument that protest countering is a key index of police professional self-definition (della Porta and Reiter, 1998: 1). Here, strategy is contingent upon *police knowledge*, which consists of police perceptions of the disturbances, the techniques at their disposal, and the requests that come from outside their ranks. Police knowledge refers to the images held by police about their role as mediated by the external challenges they are asked to face. The environmental culture or the totality of assumptions held about their external reality is also influenced by the professional culture, or a mediation of prior activity within the totality of assumptions about their own cause or role. In other words, police knowledge derives from institutional police organization and power and from police culture, and is also influenced by public opinion and government (which, in turn, are influenced by law-and-order and civil rights coalitions). The view is not so much an underestimation of the importance of wider political opportunities and constraints, but rather a privileging of (albeit dependent) institutional knowledge.[6]

Recent analyses of Foucault's previously unpublished lectures (Valverde, 2007; Dillon 2007) also provide an understanding of the current relationship between public police and labour and the historical role of police in liberal governance more generally. Foucault distinguished what he called 'liberal governmentality,' as the domain of markets particularly and the political economy generally, from *polizeiwissenschaft* or 'police' as concerned with 'the internal refinement of "reason of state"' (Foucault, 2004: 29) and subject to external restraint through public law grounded in constitutional rights. According to Foucault's understanding of the term police governance, it is a necessarily particularistic and discretionary application of authority to meet specific necessities that cannot be determined through a straightforward overlay of law. If the 'police' domain was 'the regulatory and preventive governance of the internal order of the kingdom' (Valverde, 2007: 11) then the differentiations of public order in police regulations and deployments can be perceived as exemplary. The intersection of commercial, residential, and recreational spaces in town squares, railway lands, harbours, riverways, markets, and roads were hot points for the articulation of public/private distinctions in the micro-politics of the emerging liberal order. Police power as enforced regulations is aimed at exclusionable groups such as vagrants and streetwalkers according to space/time designations, the exact same device that was developed to monitor police constables themselves on their beats (de Lint 2000; Gordon, 2005).

Many authors argue that the regulatory practices now may toggle beyond sovereign and disciplinary strategies to shift into place strategies of control. Work by Deleuze (1992) has problematized a 'society of control' as post-disciplinary, which is to say unconcerned with normalizing subjects and the sovereign–subject relation. Not interested in changing people or insisting on their compliance, regulatory strategies in the society of control manage the circuits of government and civil society by designating and attributing risk and by monitoring and preventing: preventing breaching of the integrity of information and place and ensuring the proper course for data deposits. In this there is a largely preventative or pre-emptive function practised by regulatory powers, an argument which fits nicely with explaining the development of community and what we are calling liaison policing, but also, interestingly enough, the use of preventative detention. As the argument goes, it is not necessary to rely on the sovereign in determinations of threat. On the contrary, de facto status is dependent on relative access to the circuits of credit and relative absence from the exclusion lists. Both labour and media of communications of grievances or political disagreement may be seen more or less as scarce resources. If access to labour or media are blocked, this produces economic and political crises. In this context, police may be seen as access brokers (de Lint, 2003), protecting the avenues of commerce and to some extent communication from being stymied, occupied, or colonized by what is construed as illegitimate use by illegitimate users. In a society of control, institutions of governance seek greater predictability through enhanced pre-emption and action on action is at the level of the code and the simulation rather than on the behaviour of individuals or in the disciplining of cohorts.

Although governmentality places needed emphasis on the practices of rule rather than on 'ultimate' determinants, whether structural or normative, it leaves the material context perhaps too insignificant. For instance, in the widely discussed 'governance beyond the state' literature, the fly in the ointment is that liberal state practices have been, to use Gramscian terms, hegemonic *precisely because* they have demonstrated a (liberal) reticence about deploying an immediate or direct reliance on coercive authority in response to political economic crises. And in so doing, they reinforce a claim of independence while the powerful capital interests work diligently in other ways to reproduce the conditions for capital accumulation. While early liberal governments incorporated much from feudal practices like Frankpledge to minimize the cumbersome and clumsy reliance on militia or standing armies, there is now more sophistication in the use of private or para-policing (Rigakos, 2002), where it is possible to off-load the coercive responsibility. At the same time, the overall pattern of police professionalization has followed the course of least resistance by making the use of force increasingly selective, effective, and targeted (cf. Klockars, 1985).[7] Yet none of these developments or their consequences with respect to control are independent of the emerging and changing material conditions of workers, employers, citizens, or the police themselves.

In addition, current governmentality views of policing need to account more fully for its political components. Policing as Turk (1982) and Huggins (1998) have argued is already a kind of politics. That policing is devoted to reconciling the engine of the economy to civil society or the rule of power to the rule of law is not saying too much that any security or police officer does not already intuit. That the tactics and strategies deployed to achieve this must be sufficiently adaptable is also a familiar point. As Fillieule and Jobard (1998) argue, it is more sensible to speak of political antagonism (to labour or protesters) than police antagonism where political leadership sets out to direct or influence police response. But even here, the relationship between left and right politics and antagonism to public expression of grievances is not clear-cut. Some politicians identified on the left of centre, as della Porta and Reiter (1998: 16) point out, need to appease business interests by showing they can be tough on challengers. Indeed, the early 1980s saw the last major disturbances where, as Willis (2001: 19) says, 'the degrees of disorder could be interpreted either as assaults on social order itself, or as means by which significantly large minority groups were seeking to establish or preserve their stake in civil order.' This included the Brixton disorders of 1981 and the 1984–5 miners' strike.

For Willis (2001: 119), what has been occurring more recently in public order policing is a response to a lesser profile of public disorder in that events are not delivered or received as constituting a threat to the state or its legitimacy, but tend to be 'issue-specific, politically-bounded and (mostly) time-limited expression of disaffection.' What has occurred then in terms of police response is less adequately described as freedom restricting (coercive, 'hard,' dissent-crushing policing) and more as rights-driven. Willis also notes that police administrators, rank and file police, and the public give a low priority to public order policing and thus little support for investing public monies in this area. Together with the neo-liberalization of the police institution, in which many traditional police roles are reassessed and reassigned to other providers (i.e., private security), the prognosis for this is likewise that regular duty constables may be able to move out of primary delivery.[8]

In the end, we suggest that the governance literature takes our view of public order policing in an important direction. While Liberal theorists have tended to see police as accommodating protest within a framework of due process and consent (Waddington, 1992; Geary, 1985; Loader and Walker, 2001), critical criminologists and labour historians have emphasized the coercive deployment of the public police in the interests of capital accumulation and/or political repression whenever consent breaks down (Brogden, 1982; Harring and McMullin, 1975; Johnson, 1976; Silver, 1967; Turk, 1982). A post-critical account recognizes a more complex relationship between capital, labour, and public and private regulation, also taking into account how neo-liberalism reconfigures the regulatory tableau (deconstructing subjects and sovereigns) to privilege private interests and responsibilities over social rights and public obligations. That this reconfiguration has been uneven both within and between states has already been observed, but nevertheless it has had profound influences on key aspects of police operations and orientations, including the general thrust to redefine the boundaries and conditions of public order and the role of the public police in regulating this order (Murphy, 1998; Rigakos, 2002).

Neo-Liberal Governance and Public Order

The notion that institutional, Marxist, and governance accounts of control within neo-liberalism, or 'advanced liberalism' as Rose (1996) calls it, can be reconciled has been soundly criticized by some (Barnett, 2004) and praised by others (Jessop, 1995). In this book, we follow the latter line of thinking by seeking to draw on insights from all three perspectives. Much of this integration comes within our effort to pull together three central questions: in Canadian society, what is the relative power of labour and other social movements and the state within the context of liberalism, neo-liberalism, and post-Fordism; how is that power managed and consent reproduced within the context of public order policing; and what is the relative power of 'the public' or 'the social' in the designation of public order policing and the policing of industrial disputes and protest? The third question recognizes the tremendous interest in private and civilian forms of policing and the so-called vanishing 'social' and 'public' throughout police scholarship. This demands an analysis of policing reforms and philosophies as expressions of the changing nature of governance but also with reference to institutional change and continuity. The first and second questions require plotting changes to the relative advantages between state, labour, social, and business interests in the context of capitalist development. In thinking about how administrative authorities respond and have altered response to public disorder, it is first necessary to identify the key constituent terms. Only then is the distinction between private and public domains and between civil and criminal response made meaningful.[9]

According to a relatively straightforward institutional and liberal-pluralist reading, the liberal project has long been accomplished through institutions of consent or self-governance. Given the pre-eminence of classic liberal values at the time of the establishment of modern policing, there was a tractable insistence that police were to be integrative, visible, impartial, and limited. Liberal governance was also grounded in an adversarial model that pitted the private individual against public authority and programmed wide review in accountability exercises to balance the heft of the state. Police service, or active integrative efforts on the part of police, was in part designed to bridge the gap of authoritarian control and individual autonomy. In the idea of the modern salaried police, conceived in the late eighteenth century by Patrick Colquhoun and established for Greater London by Sir Robert Peel in 1829, volunteer militias, voluntary felons associations, and an amateur constabulary were substituted with full-time public employees answerable to the lower judiciary, local government, and parliament and regulated through paramilitary discipline. Colquhoun and Peel knew that the acceptance of the new police depended on their being seen, especially by the merchant class, in a variety of actions, including public assistance. Such visibility and monitoring were intentionally redundant, incorporating a variety of extant interests, including the lower judiciary in evaluating their use of law, ex-military men in structuring their work performance, and lawmakers in reviewing the organization through ministerial answer in parliament. These provisions provided a chain of delegation between government authority and citizens, with police situated between republican and authoritarian rule.

Self-governance also required dimensions of impartiality and limit. That police could be impartial was predicated on the notion that politics and policing were distinct enterprises that could remain mutually exclusive, a view owing to Enlightenment influence. For Colquhoun and later for Peel, the new police were differentiated from long-standing forms of dispute resolution and their tarnished records of influence peddling, arbitrariness, and profiteering. Police professionalization or 'modernization' was envisioned as a progressive project, not weighted down by traditional power relations. Peel saw impartiality as a way of overcoming political differences. With respect to limitation, police were embedded and spatially restricted by dominion; they were made accountable to events in place and made responsible in this way according to the peace that they kept in their patrol areas (de Lint, 2000). This generated and fed their visibility, representation, and limitation. It constrained also the measure of success: the relative absence of crime and disorder and the presence of good conduct (Reiner, 2000). In short, the new police were integrative, visible, impartial, and limited. This was how knowledge of populations could be reconciled to liberalism.

From political economy, it is important to extract that policing is dependent on broader historical and material changes that influence the position of the state and the administration of legitimate coercion. It is well known that consent policing was neither achieved nor perhaps intended in 'far-away' British colonies or on frontiers. 'Home' policing had to be more circumspect than 'away' policing, where police tasks, according to Cain (1996: 400), included maintaining external boundaries, collecting customs duties and poll taxes, 'pacifying' opposition groups, rounding up conscript labour, and suppressing indigenous religious or cultural practices. In divided societies similarly (Johnston and Shearing, 2003; Weitzer, 1995), the countering of constitutional divisions is understood to trump service delivery.

Even at home, consent policing was always more the way things were talked about than done. For instance, as Turk (1982: 22) argues, policing after Peel firmly established 'that the objective of policing is not to terrorize people, but to tranquilize them.' With Peel's modern police, the 'less explicit the threat of violence and the more explicit the concern for public safety the more [the appearance of] effective policing' (23). As we noted at the outset, policing is fundamental to the ideology of liberal democracy so that as legitimate violence is privatized in profound ways, so is the expression of public order policing. As Turk (1982: 24) also notes, 'policing is the mechanism by which authorities, whether or not they realize it, establish the framework and gain the time needed for the development of even more subtle and powerful modes of political socialization.'

It is also crucial to recognize that policing institutions are relatively autonomous in ways that go beyond the typical Marxist reading. True, they develop in ways that derive from political, economic, and cultural contexts. However, they draw from their setting a power-knowledge that is distinctive and self-generating. Security, in being both means and ends, provides the ground for development that is both dependent on *and* competitive with the practices and interests of various political authorities. In evaluating changes to police deployment and strategies we can see how the occupational culture reads various targets as appropriate or not and how this reading is linked to wider ideological fears within the political culture, including antipathy to foreigners, communists, terrorists, and the underclass. Consistent with both the interactionist and the institutional development theses, one also cannot generalize too readily between local and state police and undercut the variation between and across constituencies, regions, and states. Things become significant historical events because they are located and meaningful or because they represent a site of conflict or contest and/or have become a narrative juncture point (see, e.g., Waddington, Jones, and Critcher 1989).

Finally, from governmentality, it is important to recognize the independent force of rationalities of rule. 'Police rationality' depended directly on the take-up of liberalism or government articulated in terms of sovereign limits (Dillon, 2007; Valverde, 2007). The domestic function was already from the outset conceived or at least practised in a kind of princely pact that allowed that incipient international relations depended upon a duty of each for their own internal order and economy: only by assurances that such internal orders were being upheld could there be a proper plane for a transnational order.

Given the pre-eminent context, and recognizing that force monopoly was alone insufficient for durable rule, modern liberal democracies cultivated institutions of civil society not as an end but as a means to informational resource control (Dandeker, 1990; Holquist, 1997). In this reading, a relatively autonomous civil society was an epiphenomenon of a more robust administration of populations through evaluation tools (Giddens, 1985; Dean, 2002). The needs of states to carry out unpopular wars required better understanding of popular opinion or beliefs and thus the better production of domestic persuasion enterprises, including propaganda and public relations (Holquist, 1997). Knowledge about families, markets, religious views, and political opinion was gleaned through census data, polling, espionage, and analysis. Of course, technology played a critical role here, but as the public relations capacity of governments thus developed, governments sought to exploit the institutions of civil society for the continuity of control. Accordingly, the local constable was a conduit or insertion point, providing the two-way data flow of government administration. Thus, talk of consent has never been merely symbolic for modern police. Boundaries, visibilities, and politics play a significant role in shaping the qualitative and performative aspect of policing.

Successive iterations of liberal democratic policing would continue to refer to this original doctrine of consent (in various twentieth-century reforms, particularly). These references could become increasingly presumptive. Consent was not only instantiated in bureaucratic exigencies, but presumed as a backstop as other immediate problems of role, mission, or mandate eased their way out of the bureaucracy or sub-political arenas. And as consent became a legacy and reified as a *fait accompli*, transparency, liberty, equality, efficiency, and justice more generically are being displaced in police reference with elements consistent with a 'culture of control' (Garland, 2001), 'exclusive society' (Young, 1999), or 'societies of control' (Deleuze, 2000) (e.g., prediction, prevention, risk, protection, difference). This trend has been most remarkable particularly in the sub-political arenas that police have been engaged in, including, today, the various 'projects' through which police, often representing different constituencies, share tasks and solve security problems. The regionalization and, following this, the transnational integration and interoperability of police countering capacity more dramatically force the question of domestic, national, and transnational interests. After 9/11, internal and external security, law enforcement and security intelligence, and pre-emptive or preventive intervention were three key elements of a new security regime, seen also in Canada's national security plan, 'Canada's Approach to National Security.'

Consequently, one debate within policing research concerns the degree to which policing in the information age is characterized more by preventative and pre-emptive strategies and risk aversion and less by the coercive authority of state agents representing established interests. Police action may be seen as proactive or reactive, intelligence-led or law enforcement driven. During the 1950s and 1960s, as we will show, the police relation with industrial disputes and public order protests may be seen as governed more by law enforcement reaction and less by the long view of population management that informs intelligence-based policing today. Nonetheless, the take-up of community and now intelligence-based policing still only operates in the context of normative and territorial jurisdictions in which coercive displays and law enforcement sometimes take discursive priority. In sites we will examine it will be shown that multiple orders act simultaneously in the overlap of multiple police agencies. As we show at the OAS protest in Windsor, for example, the Windsor police offered conciliation, while the OPP showed coercion and the RCMP gathered intelligence. But even this masks how each agency is flexible with respect to selecting mandate and orientation.

Our view, however, is that what is behind the changing dynamics of public order policing is more than adaptations within the state or administrative authorities, more than independent technical, professional, or institutional developments, and more also than the liberalization of policing. Policing is an exquisitely political undertaking; that is, it is always understood in how that politics is rebuffed, adapted, or absorbed wholesale. It is for this reason that we concentrate on the contours of the relation between politics and economy in the development of official or coercive responses to labour or political strife. But, as we will also show here, that development is not only responsive to extant objective material conditions. In addition, what also develops is a way of understanding liberalism, freedoms, and regulatory responses in an almost self-fulfilling discourse that police and others are both caught up in and drive forward. Thus, today, we may increasingly understand the liberal democratic order as idealized in the constantly deferred or pre-empted consent of the self-governed, trumped routinely in the necessity of control and containment. Accordingly, intelligence, secrecy, and knowledge exclusions rather than visibility, consent, and accountability become the standard-bearing practices.

Types of Public Order Policing

To aid understanding in how we apply these various arguments to explaining the Canadian case, our final task in this chapter is to present a typology of public order policing. We use this typology to locate both past and current developments and to draw together the different combinations of factors which shape those developments. This framework also provides a basis for explaining the use of force in particular situations, as well as understanding why the increased capacity to use force and coercive tactics does not represent an increased *use* of such tactics.

The notion that public order events, and by association public order policing, can be usefully divided according to type of cause has been proposed by various researchers, including King and Brearley (1996: 37–69), Baxter (2001: 247), Button et al. (2002), and King (2004). King and Brearley, followed by Baxter, suggest three typologies (political, industrial, single-issue conflict) while King (2004) suggests as many as seven types (political, industrial, festival and urban, environmental protest, animal rights, anti-capitalism, and anti-globalization). Button et al. (2002) also view environmental protest as a unique type of political pressure or activism, with 'militant activist groups' on the rise perhaps because of the effectiveness in shunning bureaucratic structure and their pursuit of 'direct-action' tactics. Wiles (1999) sees the emergence of single-issue protests in recent decades as demanding less symbolic repression on the part of police. Ericson and Doyle (1999) add that the policing of protest at an international event is a distinctive type of public order problem: such protests are dramatizations for various audiences.

This links to police approaches when we consider the evidence that police view protesters according to the record of those participating, comprised mainly of their experience with or intelligence on them (della Porta and Reiter, 1998; King, 2004). Police experience with various groups or types of groups is either direct or comes through police communications' conduits. It is necessary here to preview a major finding of our research accordance with Turner's (1968) expectation on social movements and mobilization that police view various groups according to their relative institutionalization. In Canada, police view anti-poverty activists and anarchists and perhaps even young people more generally as requiring more forceful – or law-enforcement-grounded – crowd management techniques because they are not sufficiently institutionalized. They have no – or an unfavourable – record of lawful self-regulation. Conversely, where mass demonstrations of grievances are planned by established unions, police will view the event as requiring liaison and limited, non-coercive strategies.[10] Many protests and public order events involve a mélange of actors, actions, and causes that complicate their typecasting. As Button et al. (2002: 27) point out, policing agencies are often confronted with a wide range of actors, actions, and issues even in a single public order event.

However, following our earlier lines of argument on liberalism, classifying or typologizing protest policing includes reference to the legal, political, and social context of liberal democracies (Geary, 1985; Waddington, 1992; P. Waddington, 1994a; P. Waddington, 1994b; P. Waddington, 1998; Baxter, 2001). For instance, Baxter (2001: 265–81) sees three foundation principles within democracy that must be given equal weighting if the balance between powers of the state and rights of citizens is to be maintained. These are: constitutional or state legitimacy, the legitimacy of the law, and the legitimacy of institutions of the state including police. The state, the law, and police are thus three points of a 'pyramid of legitimacy,' each of which must be balanced by the other. It is on this pyramid base that the police approach to public order is balanced. Baxter suggests a conflict management approach which situates the 'power-coercion' role of police as instruments of the state with their community service role. But this management is also structured by other influences, including cultural, human rights, legal, and ethical/moral issues. Again, the type of intervention considered is weighted according to the type of conflict and the danger to the state itself that is posed by it.

Drawing from this, it may be said that a range of tactics will be applied differentially according to police experience of a range of protest types. This may be clarified further and a more clean division of protest types provided if, like police, we view protest in terms of its relative political challenge to authority. As Turk (1982) and P. Waddington (1993) have noted, police are concerned about public order events qua public order events to the degree that they are perceived to have consequences to the extant political order. Or to follow more recent work, one may divide the 'government monopoly' between the authorization function and the implementation function (Bayley and Shearing, 2001). In liberal democracies, public police must be concerned about the authorization function in the way of defending the order that permits the law that in turn authorizes them as order enforcers.

Consequently, we may plot police responses according to a range of public order policing events, from those in which protesters and/or observers share basic agreement regarding the authority of police – as representing legitimate government – to those that stem from explicit or tacit dispute over police and government authority. Some grievances are more or less countered as dangerous flashpoints of festering political or even constitutional grievances (P. Waddington, Jones, and Critcher, 1989); others are periodic expressions of narrower cultural, identity, or local differences; still others are a (milder) form of sponsored outrage against a single-issue policy. Following Baxter (2001), this gives us three intersecting dimensions of order production: the politics of law, the politics of enforcement, and the politics of consent:

- *The politics of law* refers to the legitimacy of rule-making or the legislative function. Is the law-making function well-grounded constitutionally, representative, and founded in liberal democratic values?
- *The politics of consent* refers to the legitimacy of rule following or the value of strong compliance with the polity. The orientation

may be more or less consensual; that is to say, the politico-legal environment may take the relation between institutions and individuals as reinforcing.

- *The politics of enforcement* refers to the legitimacy of the enforcement function. Is enforcement of law more or less integrative? Is it carried out according to liberal democratic values, respecting constitutional rights and freedoms? Is it reflective of best practices, representative of the polity, and effective in its mandate to diffuse disorder or political disintegration?

Within this framework, consent is more strained the more unrepresentative and unauthorized the rule-making and the less integrative the enforcing of the law. This may be ameliorated or exacerbated in the recursivity between the executive and legislative function. For instance, the executive often seeks changes in law that will legitimate police practices and provide a greater range of options in the politics of order. On the other hand, legislators and courts also provide a check on the executive function, attempting to ensure that the range of options matches public expectations. Police attempt to reorder conflicts by brokering new consensual arrangements. Where the rules appear to be illegitimate or weakly grounded, police may still create a local order by producing temporary peaces. If, however, law-making is weakly grounded and order enforcing is weakly imaginative, productive, or diffusing, then disputants will be discouraged from consensual engagements. Members of the polity take cues from the legitimacy of law and the integrative capacity of ordering. Police are adaptive to the requirements of liberal democratic rule, yet liberal democratic rule is manifested in the behaviour of police.

Plotting the politics of law across and the politics of enforcement down a grid produces five ideal public order policing types: crisis policing, disordered policing, control policing, service policing, and hybrid policing (see figure 2.1):

- *Crisis policing* is disintegrative policing in a disputed ground context. Bowden (1978) calls harsh reactions to perceived threats to the state order 'crisis politics.' Crisis policing is disordered or de-legitimated policing in a context of political fracture. It resorts to explicit protection of the executive function of the government of the day. It is expressed in routine violations of civil rights beyond even the exceptions provided by martial law.

- *Disordered policing* is under-professionalized, under-representative, inexpert, and ineffective order maintenance in a politico-legal context of integrative consent or in circumstances favourable for integrative policing. Police are de-legitimated because they introduce disintegration through faulty or unprofessional enforcement practices, including quick resort to coercive force and rule breaking, organizational and operational misalignments, turf contests, improper command, and so forth.
- *Control policing* is professional, knowledgeable, effective, but authoritarian order maintenance in a politico-legal context of exclusivity and division. Policing here is not so much the keeping of order as it is the attempted production of order out of exceptional circumstances or divided rule.
- *Service policing* is professional, knowledgeable, representative, and effective order maintenance in a politico-legal context of integrative consent. The order-keeping is appropriate to the circumstances, and the circumstances are favourable for integrative policing. It may be said that service policing adds value across the socio-economic spectrum.
- *Hybrid policing* is a utilization of dual control strategies (information and hard countering [paramilitary, intelligence]). On the one hand, it finesses the appearance of service policing and its limitation on violence and adding of value. This requires the exploitation of informational or communications resources particularly. On the other hand, it readies hard countering behind the absorptive layer of accommodation.

In this framework, police practice and knowledge are perceived as designed to be polity integrative. That is to say, police are evaluated according to liberal democracy values as more or less committed to the ideal and practice of an inclusive polity, and are more or less integrationist in advancing this cause. Public order policing is a particularly visible expression of police compliance with liberal democratic values and the emphasis on inclusion; it is almost its best indicator. This is not to say, however, that the legal terrain may not inhibit or enhance exclusionary police practice or that police practice may not exhibit less coercive and more persuasive methods still aimed at the maintenance of order and continuity. In moving from a forceful reaction to threatening behaviour to pre-empting the possibility of disorder, intelligence-led policing minimizes the social and political risks of order maintenance

Figure 2.1 Types of Public Order Policing

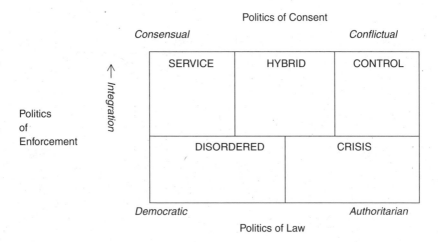

without sacrificing intensity, scope, and completeness. Integrationist order enforcing maximizes police efficacy in order maintenance with minimum recourse to exclusionary practices.

The uniqueness of police experience and of political and social environments, each of which is subtly altered by perceptions of intentions, policies, and manifest or abstract threats, makes comparative work difficult because such work depends on constant measures. Although there is a great deal of agreement in police literature on best practices in public order, practices are also shaped by the political and social environments and by police knowledge and experience in those environments. This analytical tool intends to provide some of the range necessary to plot individual public order events and to guide interpretation of public order policing across jurisdictions and time. It is also worth noting that the legal order is not the only available backdrop against which police activity is staged. Security work, in which public police play a part, has accrued institutional interests and mandates from sources beyond the state and the polity. That is to say, the more police are institutionally enabled to depend on professional expertise and technical knowledge for decision-making regarding the deployment of public order resources, the less they can still claim be practising democratic policing (cf. Roach, 2004).[11]

Although we would like to believe that there is a clear trajectory which pulls police and by which police push themselves towards a civilizing process of violence reduction, perhaps the key vulnerability of police is their responsivity to changing political cultures. Just as police may adopt a mission which takes violence reduction as the chief objective in a political culture which is indulgent of this motivation, so too can a changing tide of cultural sensibilities place pressure on police to retreat back to law enforcement priorities (Gordon, 2005).

3 Liberalism and Labour/Police Development

Introduction

Before we can appreciate recent changes to Canadian public order policing within neo-liberalism and post-Fordism, it is necessary to offer a broader historical overview of the relationship between labour, industry, and policing within Canada. We do this by highlighting the key features of policing within Canada's historical development as a liberal welfare state and a Fordist industrial economy. In particular, we document the early engagement of private security and intelligence in labour countering, and the gradual institutionalization of labour. We show that while labour protest is initially not well organized and put down violently by militia and special constables, changes to the legitimacy of labour and the organization and professionalism of policing help to account for increasing police adaptations to the character of labour strikes. In particular, as the labour movement begins to radicalize and factionalize, a dual strategy emerges in which repression of more radical elements is augmented by somewhat more conciliatory approaches toward moderate, responsible unions.

While we wish to essentialize neither capital nor the liberal democratic state in accounting for changes to police policy regarding the regulation of labour strikes, we suggest that changes to political rationality do not simply appear as a result of changes to how government is conceived, as if concrete interests were not relevant to such adaptations. On the contrary, policy changes are seen as a result of an overlap of governmental and economic interests and emergent political rationalities or discourses. The changes to police policy can be understood, although never completely, as adaptations which attempt to maximize police legitimacy and utility in the context of changing economic and political relations. Even more broadly, adaptations in the securing of economic relations by both private and public institutions or agencies reflect the relative strength of state resources and discourses.

Labour and the Development of Public Order in Canada

Labour Disputes in the 1800s

At the beginning of the nineteenth century in Canada, wage labour was largely unorganized in the sense that most labour disputes were temporary, spontaneous protests, formed around limited, immediate demands or complaints and – given hiring practices – frequently organized along ethnic rather than class lines (Forsey, 1982; Kealey, 1986; Jamieson, 1968; Lipton, 1967). Although historians such as Craig Heron (1996: 4) have argued that protesters were often well organized and any violence 'controlled and directed at specific targets,' the colonial authorities tended to characterize such labour actions as 'riots,' often using troops and militia and the full weight of criminal law to suppress both the protests and workers' demands. These early interpretations of labour protests as 'threats to public order' informed a critical justification for the use of force against strikers even as workers were becoming more formally organized.

Craft-based unions began to emerge in the 1820s and 1830s as more and more entrepreneurial employers began to realize the profit potential of larger workshops, but many of these early unions were focused more on providing mutual support and benefits, and relatively few at this point were involved in strike activity. The less-skilled work in the mines, construction, and forestry camps were the other main sources of early wage labour and most of the labour disputes, but here, too, class relations were enmeshed and partially hidden in a paternalistic system based on personal relations and high levels of dependency for all the workers' basic needs, including housing, schooling, food, and other goods (Heron, 1996; 1998; Pentland, 1981). Similar to apprentices, many of these workers were indentured, which meant that they saw this relationship as temporary, for a time mitigating the development of more permanent organizations and a more organized approach to labour protest.

However, as factory-based industrial capitalism developed in the latter half of the nineteenth century, work and employment relationships were altered significantly (Palmer, 1992). More and more workers were drawn into full-time wage labour in larger and more mechanized workplaces, which were increasingly located in urban centres such as Montreal, Toronto, Hamilton, and Halifax. As workers and their families became entirely dependent on wage labour for their survival and increasing competition drove employers to seek the advantages of greater productivity through factory discipline and machine-based production, class tensions escalated. Initially, attempts by the emerging industrialists to reduce their reliance on crafts labour were largely unsuccessful, and, if anything, craft unions were strengthened and grew in numbers. Many new crafts unions formed around industries which continued to be highly dependent on traditional crafts such as tailors, shipbuilders, printers, and shoemakers, but new industrial crafts also became important, including machinists and locomotive engineers (Palmer, 1992; Heron, 1996).

By the 1860s, the first construction, forestry, and mining unions were also being formed, followed very quickly by the early signs of a central labour movement. In 1867, Montreal workers organized around an association called the Grand Association of Canadian Workingmen, while in 1871, the Toronto Trades Assembly was established in an effort to draw together all unions in the city. This assembly was instrumental in organizing a march and protest rally in 1872 in support of a printers' strike and their demand for a nine-hour work day, drawing 10,000 people to Queen's Park (Lipton, 1966: 30). This development was part of the nine-hour movement which had spread across Ontario and Quebec as a unifying symbol and one of the earlier examples of an emerging labour movement organized around a common working-class issue.

As labour organizations became more formalized, strikes and other actions such as boycotts against specific employers became more common and more organized. Most employers responded to these efforts in a repressive manner, firing and blacklisting leaders, using strike-breakers, and forcing workers to sign iron-clad or 'yellow dog' contracts that banned their participation in any union activity (Jamieson, 1968; Lipton, 1966). Through well into the twentieth century, employers relied mainly on the military and local militia and 'specials' appointed by the local magistrates to police strike activities. They also relied heavily on private police, such as the infamous detective agency the Pinkertons, both as spies and as security forces. The violence used by these private police was often extreme, including beatings and even summary executions.

Visible Countering: Municipal, Provincial and Federal Police

Manwaring-White (1983: 5) suggests that the establishment of public police is intimately connected to public disorder. As he points out, the history of policing is one 'which all along the line has been modified by parliamentary and police reaction to violent disturbance – just as it is today.' As has been well documented, one of the spurs to policing reform in Great Britain leading to the establishment of the New Police was the disharmony evident in the Gordon riots and a notable rise in mass occasions of public protest and visible disorder. In Canada, a similar theme is apparent in nineteenth-century and early twentieth-century police establishment.[1] As Gregory Kealey (1985) argues, the twenty-nine riots between 1839 and 1864 were primary vehicles of political expression launched to test (like a nineteenth-century trial balloon) the relative advantage of established versus emergent sectional interests. Serendipitously, it was how police responded to public demonstrations or riots that led to the first major government inquiries into British North America policing systems and calls for reforms. For instance, in Toronto a commission of inquiry into the 1841 riots disclosed that a substantial portion of Toronto police were recruited from the Orange lodges through the high bailiff George Kingsmill (Rogers, 1984: 118). Two further riots (the Circus riot in Toronto and the Chalmer's Church riot in Montreal,both in 1854) also served to mobilize inquiries (Lelievre and McNab inquiries) and spearheaded the long process of authorizing provincial and federal police forces (Lelievre, Felton, and Johnson, 1854; MacNab et al. 1855; de Lint 1999). As demonstrated by these inquiries, blatant sectarian repression by police or militia was becoming increasingly unpalatable to leaders wishing to establish rule of law legitimacy.

Part of the response was the movement to establish permanent public police services. Over the course of the last two-thirds of the 1800s, public police forces began to appear in the larger urban centres. In Quebec City (1833), Toronto (1835), Montreal (1843), Hamilton (1846), London (1855), and gradually other large municipalities, police departments were established as part of municipal governments that had the capacity to regulate and tax local citizens. By mid-century, the development was first institutionalized with the Municipal Corporations Act (or Baldwin Act) of 1849. It stipulated that towns were required to operate a police office at which a police magistrate or a mayor regularly dealt with police matters as a justice of the peace. The magistrate or mayor could suspend chief constables or constables for cause 'for any period in his discretion' and the city council had the power of dismissal. In towns with no police magistrate, the mayor and councillors were responsible for preserving the peace. As municipalization spread, many smaller towns established their own permanent police forces.

In 1856, John A. Macdonald, then attorney general of the United Canadas, introduced legislation for a province-wide police force. It was based on the recommendations of a provincial commission led by Allan McNab which had been struck to investigate the existing problems of local patronage and influence and the unwillingness or inability of the municipal forces to handle big public order disturbances. The bill proposed to amalgamate existing municipal forces into one large force consisting of 350 constables and 150 sub-constables. It proposed that municipalities would have to foot two-thirds of the cost. The bill was opposed in Toronto and denounced in that city's Council, where it failed, having been perceived as a political interjection by Roman Catholics in 'Protestant' Upper Canada.[2] However, the debate contributed to the establishment of municipal police boards under the 1858 Municipal Institutions of Upper Canada Act (Rogers, 1984: 122–3; Stenning, 1981: 51). It also encouraged municipal police practices, one of which became a purposive appointing of officers 'from outside' of the locality in an effort to establish 'a more centralized, paramilitary force' (Rogers, 1984: 136).

As mining developed in northern Ontario in the late nineteenth century and early 1900s, there was also increasing interest in policing remote areas, in particular in securing extractive industries from labour disputes. The Ontario provincial police services began to grow in size and importance, and by 1908 there were about seventy provincial constables serving as small police forces in several parts of the province. In 1909, these were all formally centralized under a newly created Ontario Provincial Police (OPP) force. The often-stated precipitator to the OPP's establishment was the discovery of gold and silver in northern Ontario and the flow of population to previously unsettled areas (McDougall, 1971: 16). Underneath that, however, was the knowledge that extractive work at the edges of the dominion was a regulatory problem that required coordinated administration. Again, federalists following John A. Macdonald saw the maintenance and deepening of internal order, particularly at the fringes, as a necessary component of nation-building, and police regularization was a key part of this process.

Out west, the British Columbia Provincial Police (BCPP) was similarly conceived. The BCPP was established following the merging of colonies in Vancouver Island and mainland British Columbia and was predicated on providing law and order following a flood of gold miners, many of whom were American, and settlers in 1858. In 1866, two forces were amalgamated under a superintendent of police (Chartres Brew), and this became the Provincial Police following the entry of British Columbia into Confederation in 1871 (Horrall, 1975). In short, Brew was transferred from the Royal Irish Constabulary to help protect mining extraction and to counter the disorder of extraction and the threat of American expansionism. A mounted troop was also established by the BCPP during the depression years 'to quell serious demonstrations' (Jamieson, 1968: 14). Quebec had moved in the 1870s to establish a provincial constabulary, largely to protect the legislature, but like Ontario, and along with some western provinces, Quebec moved increasingly to expand the provincial police across the province during this same period.

The North West Mounted Police (NWMP) was also established in 1873 in large part not only to rebuff American expansionism and provide security to Canadian settlers, but also to defend the Canadian Pacific Railway (CPR)(Macleod, 1976). Commissioner George Arthur French, in organizing the force, 'placed great stress on the non-military role of police, suggesting that along with other duties they should build roads and establish postal and telegraph communications.' (Macleod, 1976: 23). One of the core functions of the NWMP was to open up the west for agricultural development, which initially meant pacifying and assimilating the Natives through a treaty and reservation system. The NWMP made defending the Canadian Pacific Railway part of their mandate, guarding it 'against Indians, settlers and *their own employees*' (Brown and Brown 1973: 24). Within a fairly short period of time, labour became a more critical area of concern.

The Hidden Hand: Intelligence and Labour Countering

Labour unrest and the institutional division of labour and industry were not only springboards of public police development; they also figured in the emergence of political policing, or what would become security intelligence. In the mid-nineteenth century, and as early as the 1850s in the United States, the protection of railroad lands, lines, and goods from pickpockets, employee theft, and robbery spurred the railway companies to hire private detectives to prevent loss. Allan Pinkerton, who had drawn praise for his work as a special assistant to the sheriff of Chicago and the first detective in the history of that city, established an agency exclusively contracted to the service of what was to become the Chicago and North Western and Illinois Central railways (Shulz 1987: 90). As Weiss reports, Pinkerton worked for the Union during the American Civil War as the first chief of the United States Secret Service, creating a detective force that was the 'federal government's earliest intelligence agency' (Weiss 1986: 88). At the same time, he worked, until emancipation, at preventing the escape of slaves and initiated 'the first labour spy service in the United States' by using 'spotters' to detect thieving and lazing among employees (88). He developed employee 'testing' to track employee performance, attitudes, and dishonesty. In Canada, train security developed a little later, but by 1860, the Railway Act of Canada empowered railways to appoint officers throughout the country, and by1885 the larger yards of the Grand Trunk Railway System had a number of private officers dedicated to their protection (91–2).

These initiatives went further in the early 1870s. Following the 'Molly Maguires' template, Pinkerton offered employers detectives who could provide internal surveillance by infiltrating political groups and the labour organizations themselves, providing companies with valuable information to prevent work stoppages and undermine labour demands (Weiss, 1986: 89–90). As Weiss argues, Pinkerton's success at countering labour, particularly groups like the Workingmen's Benevolent Association, which its agents infiltrated and against which it deputized Coal and Iron Police and provided evidence for successful prosecutions, made him useful to extraction and railway corporations (91–2). As O'Reilly and Ellison (2006: 647) note:

> The emphasis placed upon high policing techniques of covert surveillance by the Pinkerton National Detective Agency in the nineteenth and early twentieth centuries provides something of a missing link in high policing genealogy. Through its deployment of vast networks of informants and agents provocateurs, the Agency demonstrated an ideological affinity with the French haute police system ... and also provided the template for North American state security agencies.

Pinkerton was successful in part because local law enforcement, including deputies and sheriffs, had often demurred from acting harshly against other local residents. Nonetheless, too much success also began to produce strong reaction among the public at large against the misuses of private police authority, particularly following the 1892 Carnegie Steel Company strike in Homestead, Pennsylvania. In this case, the U.S. House of Representatives issued a report critical of private policing of labour by Pinkerton detectives (Weiss, 1986: 93). Indeed, as Weiss recounts, it was because of the offensive practices of Pinkerton's rather than their objectives (i.e., maintaining industrial profitability) that states moved toward state police, which were capable of mobilizing for larger strikes. As already noted, this was a precursor to that level of policing also seen in the Canadian experience. In a parallel development, state capacity in intelligence and surveillance also emerged from the private domain.

Canada's early development established a wide overlap between state and industrial interests, with the federal government in particular asserting sovereignty through economic development and its protection, and by building up infrastructures such as water and rail transportation. For example, in Quebec City and Montreal in the 1840s, and a key element of police duties included policing the waterfront labour. In 1849, the Elgin riots in Montreal resulted in the establishment of a mounted force, the Montreal Water Police, to look after Eastern Canada. Canal police were also created to police the canal system in Upper Canada. As Marquis (1993: 34) notes, following labour stoppages in 1843–4, the United Canadas legislature passed the Act for the Preservation of the Peace Near Public Works to control the canal workers and establish a dedicated constabulary.

Similar policing arrangements were later extended to the railways when, in the 1850s, they became the main mode of transportation. According to a Canadian official quoted in Parnaby and Kealey (2003: 215), the Order-in-Council that created the Western Frontier Constabulary stipulated a 'detective and preventive police force, for the purpose of watching and patrolling the whole frontier from Toronto to Sarnia.' Its purpose was to 'find out any attempt to disturb the public peace, the existence of any plot, conspiracy, or organization whereby peace would be endangered, the Queen's Majesty insulted, or her proclamation of neutrality infringed' (Parnaby and Kealy, 2003: 215). Gilbert McKinnon was appointed the stipendiary magistrate with this jurisdiction, and he in turn hired five detectives to comprise that force until he became one of the two commissioners for the whole Dominion of Canada (Dominion Police) (PAC RG1 E8 v. 84).[3] The constabulary operated along the Upper Canada borders and rail lines, reporting on activities related to the the Fenians, the American Civil War, and American incursions into British North America. According to Parnaby and Kealey (2003: 215), by 1870 'approximately fifty agents, working both in the United States and in Canada, were attending Fenian meetings, hanging out at "Irish Saloons," and shadowing suspected "Irish Rebbles."'

As Parnaby and Kealey (2003) have shown, Fenian counter-insurgency was a springboard for the establishment of a permanent Canadian security service; it provided the earliest use of government informants in a systemic effort to stem threats to government. In 1866, the Canadian government amended treason legislation to permit it to try by military court martial and suspend habeas corpus (for a year) 'any foreigner or British subject who took up arms in the province' (Parnaby and Kealey, 2003: 219). In 1866 and again in 1868, using legislation and informants, police arrested men listed under suspicion of Fenian sympathies, with fifty taken in the former year and some seventy in the latter. When another Fenian crisis emerged in 1869 and 1870, government officials were able to counter it with almost complete knowledge of Fenian planning (Parnaby and Kealey, 213: 219).

Under authority of the Police of Canada Act S.C. 1868 31 Vict. c. 73, the federal government established in May 1868 a twelve-member Dominion Police with a mandate to protect government buildings, investigate federal crimes such as mail theft, and, more broadly, undertake the political policing previously carried out by the Western Frontier Constabulary. Officers were assigned to a security intelligence function when necessary, returning to regular duties afterwards. They opened mail, established dossiers, and made secret reports to the prime minister and ministers using a secret service fund which was invisible to government audit. By the beginning of the First World War, the constabulary had 140 members.

Although formed initially as a semi-military force aimed at colonizing and taming the wild northwest, with particular reference to the Aboriginal populations, the NWMP also became more and more active in policing strike activity in the mines and lumber camps. In their state-capacitating role, these territorial police pacified the 'Indians' and attempted with a good deal of success to keep labour disorder from impeding infrastructure development, particularly in railways and natural resource extraction. According to Brown and Brown (1973), the NWMP began breaking strikes for the CPR during the 1880s, and by the 1920s and 1930s the NWMP were the most notorious strikebreakers

in Canada. This developed somewhat predictably, given that Commissioner French, in organizing the force, had placed great stress on the
non-military role of the police, suggesting that along with other duties
they should build transportation and communications infrastructure.

At this time, police were used not just to escort strikebreakers or to
prevent damage and sabotage, but often to intimidate the strikers and
in some cases to actually run the trains. Brown and Brown (1973: 29)
quote F.J.E. Fitzpatrick, one of the officers in charge of the NWMP operation: 'Our men took charge of the mail trains and ran them from
Winnipeg clear to the Rockies. It was strange, but our force seemed to
possess men who could do almost anything when the occasion demanded it.' Brown and Brown (1973: 36) also note that the NWMP, in
its annual report of 1883, credited itself with putting down a strike of
the railway, reflecting the close links between the NWMP and the CPR
and with magnates like Donald Smith, governor of the Hudson's Bay
Company, and illustrating an open anti-labour bias that would last
fifty years or more.

The relationship between key industry and federal police was also
evident in the development of public security from private security.
Greg Kealey (2000) has highlighted the tight relationship between the
waterway and railways, private intelligence, and the development of
Canada's largest public policing institutions. J.W. Murray, the former
head of detectives for Canadian Southern Railway, was employed as
an investigator to assist the untrained county constabulary in the investigation of serious crimes. Murray was employed as a 'government
detective,' and the Order-in-Council appointing him stipulated that he
was not to be paid for 'the discovery, apprehension, or conviction of of-
fenders' but given a salary of $1500 per annum (Higley, 1984: 43). The
NWMP also moved into security service activity beginning with the
use of Pinkerton's agents. Pinkerton's most lucrative Canadian client
before it established a criminal investigation capacity in the 1920s was
the BCPP, which since its inception contracted the private detective
agency for criminal investigation and surveillance of radical groups.

Policing Labour: The Public Interest

In Canada the call for wider-jurisdiction police such as the NWMP and
provincial services was, as we have indicated, predicated on the need
for disembedded or extra-local regulatory and countering capacity. As

we have seen, the call for provincial and federal police forces was partly stimulated by the need to exhibit and exercise a coherent and cohesive government authority at the fringes of the dominion. It was also supported in the need to institutionalize the relationship between industry, labour, and social order. Throughout most of the nineteenth century, security and intelligence services that protected the larger industries were private. Public security and intelligence services emerged in the latter half of the nineteenth and early part of the twentieth centuries as Canadian institutions began to require the transparencies of the rule of law.

As Spitzer and Scull (1977: 22) and Weiss (1986: 88) note, by the 1930s there had been a marked decline of the role of private police in the 'extra-local' countering of labour. Government departments and agencies that had employed private detective agencies like Pinkerton's began to find it cheaper and more convenient to use the Mounted Police (cf. Spitzer and Scull, 1977; McCleod, 2000). Given that by the 1920s the new responsibilities of government were already mostly regulatory, involving a routine investigations capacity (McCleod 2000), it was neither expedient nor cost-effective to employ private investigators. Again, this was attributed to the rise of public police capacity and the normalization or regulation of strikes.

Nonetheless, and as Johnson (1976: 97) points out, labour spying was still carried out on a massive scale up to the 1930s in the United States and was dubbed by one industrialist as part of the 'big stick system' (Brandes 1976: 2). Even in 1936, one-third of Pinkerton's business still consisted of providing confidential information to employers on employee unrest and the presence or actions of 'outside agitators' (Spitzer and Scull, 1977: 22n2, citing Horan 1967). Between 1934 and 1936, General Motors paid out nearly $1 million for spies and strikebreakers, most of them provided by Pinkerton's (Zwelling, 1972: 30).

When state policing capable of intelligence work emerged in the late nineteenth and early twentieth century, the reliance on private detection became a collaboration between public police and private detective agencies. Both government and employers used police spies and private detective agencies like Pinkerton's. As Kealey (2000) documents, detective agencies did double time working both for an employer and the government during strikes, often simultaneously, sometimes under direct contract with the RCMP. This collaboration continued through to the 1930s at least. In 1922, for example, J.S. Woodsworth, a labour party

MP, and later the leader of the Co-operative Commonwealth Federation, cited some of the anti-labour expenses incurred by the RCMP over that year, including large payments to Pinkerton's and the Thiel Detective agencies as well as expenses for employer's detective agencies, and many other costs related to 'One Big Union activities' and even special duties in cities such as Boston and Springfield (Brown and Brown, 1972: 52). Pinkerton spies were used to gather information against labour leaders but also to sow confusion and dissension and to provoke acts of violence that could then justify legal action by police. So pervasive was the practice of infiltrating labour by the early 1920s that Woodsworth told the House of Commons that 'in labour circles when any man stands up at a meeting and talks of violence, he is immediately suspected by the labour people of being a spy' (51).

Despite the concurrent existence of the Dominion Police until 1920, the NWMP began recruiting its own secret agents and detectives from the early days of the First World War. They had eight secret agents and six detectives across western Canada by 1918. They had been infiltrating labour organizations, as in the example of F.W. Zaneth, who testified against the leaders of the Winnipeg General Strike at their trial, although this had been going on for some time before the 1919 strike (Kealey, 2000: 44). The Security and Intelligence Branch of the RCMP was formed immediately following incorporation of the Dominion Police. This branch infiltrated labour organizations and developed an extensive undercover network. Corporal Zaneth was one of these infiltrators, who sold banned literature to union leaders so that he could later charge the people who had bought it (51). Police also raided union leaders and prominent unionist homes during this time, as well as the offices of several left-wing papers, such as the *Federationist*, the *Camp Worker*, and the *Red Flag*, and the offices of the British Columbia Federation of Labour.

Similarly, in Toronto in the 1920 and 1930s, Chief Constable Dennis Draper's Red Squad, a branch of the municipal police department, would club and jail labourers for distributing pro-communist newsletters. Given that it was understood that much of the more vibrant labour and political agitation stemmed from new immigrant communities, it also prohibited meetings in foreign languages, prevented campaigning during elections, used tear gas to break up meetings, and collaborated with the Catholic Church to discover and counter insurgents. In 1931, it arrested nine leaders of the Communist Party of Canada (CPC) under section 98 of the Criminal Code (Maurutto, 2000).

Incipient Liberalism: Respectable Unionism, Radicalism, and the Rule of Law

Although strike violence was certainly not infrequent during the late 1800s and early 1900s (Jamieson, 1971), historians suggest that unions were quick to become conscious of the need to gain public support through more controlled actions, both economically and politically. As Craig Heron (1996: 12) put it, 'the sober strike parade and the quiet picket became the respectable means of accomplishing both purposes' – that is, placing pressure on the employer through both the withdrawal of production and community opinion. Indeed, many craft unions retained a strong commitment to this ethic of 'respectability,' which frequently discouraged strike action. As unions also became more conscious of the potential value of action at the ballot box, there were further concerns about the need to present a controlled and organized public face in all forms of social action (Lipton, 1968).

The rising concern about the need to influence the state and public perception arose in part as workers struggled under the considerable restraints of nineteenth-century criminal and common law. Throughout most of the 1800s, employers and governments had relied on a legislative and common law framework modelled after the British Combinations Act (1800), which effectively criminalized membership in unions, organizing, and collective bargaining (Fudge and Tucker, 2001; Mitchell and Naylor, 1998). However, as unions grew in numbers, but also in part as liberalism became increasingly established as the dominant political ideology, labour made considerable headway in achieving public acceptance of the need for worker organization and action, and as such, was increasingly successful in mobilizing public disapproval against anti-union laws.

For many historians, a key watershed was the Toronto printers' strike of 1872, when twenty-four members of the strike committee were arrested on criminal conspiracy charges after a general protest at the legislature in Toronto (Heron, 1996, Palmer, 1992). The resulting public outcry prompted the federal government to alter the legal status of unions by passing the federal Trade Union Act that formally legalized labour unions in Canada. In the same year, 1873, the Criminal Law Amendments Act was also passed which freed unions from conspiracy charges and allowed strikes and peaceful picketing for certain legitimate objectives.

While these reforms decriminalized union and union activities in important ways, the Criminal Law Amendment Act also created a number of ambiguous criminal activities including obstructing, watching, and besetting. The labour movement was able to gain improvements in a further 1876 reform which allowed peaceful picketing, but a later enactment of the Criminal Code in 1892 omitted the peaceful picketing proviso (Arthurs et al., 1993), and until the Criminal Code was finally reformed again in 1934 to restore the right, the courts and police were able to use the criminal charges of 'watching and besetting' to restrict virtually every form of picketing (Fudge and Tucker, 2001).

Although symbolic of an increasing union legitimacy, the 1870s' reforms did not stabilize the growth of the labour movement as both unionization and strike activity 'roller coasted' over the period from the 1870s to early 1900s, reflecting in part the extraordinary instability of the industrial economy, but also the substantial failures of the fledgling union movement to develop a united and coherent framework for pulling together working-class interests (Palmer, 1992). One aspect of this was the heavy emphasis of the dominant crafts unions on organizing and acting on narrow craft lines as well as their considerable cultural emphasis on 'respectability' (Fudge and Tucker, 2001: 61). As noted, this often meant that many union leaders were reluctant to use the strike weapon, and even less so in an organized general strike.

Still, there were some important unifying movements during this period, including the birth of the Knights of Labour and the Nine Hour Movement, which, although they failed to achieve their goals, demonstrated through a number of substantial general strikes and protests, as well as through more direct election politics, the capacity of workers to organize and take peaceful action across the spectrum of crafts and workplaces. These broader protest activities often drew the attention of the militia and, increasingly, the emerging municipal and state police forces, but, reflecting the increasing political importance of this movement, political parties and the state often acted in a conciliatory fashion, granting at least some of the workers' demands.

Indeed, as we move into the 1900s, there is evidence to suggest that police and courts were increasingly selective in their use of criminal law, often permitting peaceful picketing (Fudge and Tucker, 2001: 31 Hewitt, 1997). As Hewitt (1997: 165) argues, this often depended on whether the police saw the strikers' demands as reasonable relative to their own working conditions. Concerns about 'radical foreigners' were also critical in explaining the more aggressive actions of the

RCMP (165). At the same time, courts and police continued to offer labour little if any protection against hostile company tactics that included selected or mass firings, the tactical use of violence, threats, and disciplinary penalties. There were also few indications in the historical record that police or courts were willing to charge employers or their hired guns for their part in violence (Fudge and Tucker, 2001: 31).

As the twentieth century began, union and strike activities were also subject to considerable restraints through the civil courts (Fudge and Tucker, 2001: 18.). In particular, employers began to make frequent and effective use of the injunction to place major restrictions on picketing in all its forms, as well as seeking to attach liability by filing damages suits against individuals and unions for employer losses associated with strike and other union activities (Lipton, 1968; Jamieson, 1968). For the most part, the courts were responsive to these requests, and the civil proceedings became a vital new tool for undermining the capacity of workers to pressure employers through strikes and other activities.

While the increasing emphasis on civil over criminal law suggests a greater acknowledgment of strikes as private or civil matters, this was not reflected in any withdrawal of public police involvement or a resurgence of private policing. Quite the contrary: the public police became increasingly involved in policing strikes in general and enforcing civil court orders and injunctions, the latter becoming another source of tension between labour and police. Moreover, as employers strengthened their resistance to labour unions and labour demands, there was little sustained progress in working conditions (Lipton, 1968). As the emerging industrial working class struggled to survive and the crafts and increasing numbers of less-skilled workers came under increasing attack, more radical and militant stances emerged within the labour movements, which included overt calls to overthrow the government by force. This development of radical factions within and around labour was instrumental in shifting police and government discourse away from the control of strikes to the view of labour unions as ongoing security risks, justifying an increase in intelligence activities, as well as supporting the continued use of force by the state and police in strike situations (Fudge and Tucker, 2001; Hewitt, 1997).

Carrot and Stick

While the state deepened its coercive efforts in some ways, a number of major strikes and labour protests during the early years of the twentieth century, including a number of violent incidents during the cross-country CPR strike in 1901 and the Grand Trunk Railway strike of 1905, were instrumental in pushing the federal government to seek alternatives to coercion (Russell, 1990). Faced with significant challenges to its national dream of a country linked by rail from sea to sea, the government introduced conciliation and arbitration legislation, initially in the form of the Conciliation Act, 1900, and Railway Labour Disputes Act, 1903, and then in the more far-reaching Industrial Disputes Investigation Act (IDIA) of 1907. These legislations were at least a partial recognition by the federal government that force and the persistent denial of worker demands were not working, a position which was expressed clearly in the 1903 Royal Commission on Industrial Relations, which recommended the introduction of mandatory conciliation. As the minister of justice stated in the House of Commons in 1906:

> True, a few strikes here and there in a large territory may be of little conse-
> quence for the time being but as the country grows, as the area covered by
> these strikes increases, then the danger becomes greater and greater every
> day. The troops are called out, bitterness and class hatred is created and
> we find that after labour agitation, the country resembles a house divided
> against itself. The duties and obligations of citizenship are sometimes for-
> gotten and the supreme authority of the state is ignored. (quoted in Fudge
> and Tucker, 2001: 51)

Bob Russell (1990) also points out that while the IDIA placed some new significant restrictions on unions in the form of compulsory conciliation and requirements for delays and cooling-off periods before strikes were permitted, this kind of legislation signalled a new, more conciliatory role for the state. In so doing it also offered a greater degree of political legitimacy to collective bargaining and unions more generally. While government efforts to be more conciliatory were evident earlier in the late 1800s, the IDIA can be seen as the beginning of a more systematic 'carrot and stick' approach to labour relations which developed, albeit slowly and in fits and starts, through the first half of the twentieth century (Heron, 1996; Russell, 1990; Panitch and Swartz, 2003; Fudge and Tucker, 2001).

   In its initial form, many unions, especially the emerging industrial unions, rejected the legal IDIA restraints that went with this new relationship, in part because it was soon revealed that the 'carrot' was on the small side, offering unions and workers very few substantive protections against company reprisals, while placing significant restrictions on the right to strike, to picket, and to boycott. As such, Canadian employers remained quite free to refuse to recognize and negotiate with unions, to fire and blacklist workers, and to hire strikebreakers with impunity, while at the same time continuing to make frequent and effective use of the legal apparatus, both civil and criminal, to undermine unions and collective action. As such, up to the 1940s, most strikes continued to be about recognition of the unions, an issue which conciliation often failed to address simply because many companies refused to accept unions (Russell, 1990).

It is also crucial to note that despite the continuing limitations of these early reforms, and the emergence of radical factions within labour, most union leaders continued to stress the need for peaceful and lawful actions, decrying the lack of fairness in the law but rarely advocating a direct challenge. On the other hand, the inadequacies of the law in the face of continued employer intransigence also reinforced the conditions for continued radicalization within the labour movement. The emergence of socialist and communist organizations such as the Socialist Party of Canada and the International Workers of the World in the early 1900s, both of which rejected the possibilities of political reform and openly advocated overthrowing the government, were particularly critical indications of growing radicalism in Canada and the United States (Palmer, 1992).

It is within this emerging radicalization of elements of labour in the early 1900s that we begin to see the more strategic differentiation of responsible unions and leaders from radical unions and leaders by police and the state more generally, with the government employing covert and increasingly coercive measures against the radicals while seeking within limits to work with the more responsible unions through conciliation and corporatist arrangements (Fudge and Tucker, 2001). For example, while government and some unions engaged in various forms of discussions, the government also moved amendments to the Immigration Act in 1910 aimed at weeding out the radicals by allowing the government to deport any immigrants who advocated a violent overthrow of the government or who were involved in provoking a riot. Since many labour leaders were immigrants, and strikes were still often characterized as riots, this was frequently an effective coercive tool.

This dual approach was especially evident in the context of the First World War, as dissatisfaction with the 'liberal regime of industrial legality' spread to more and more workers and unions. Initially, the government generally tried to control the rising militancy through specific efforts to broker compromises using investigations, mediations, and even the occasional government seizure of control over operations (Fudge and Tucker, 2001: 95). Again, early forms of corporatism also emerged as the federal government sought to bring a labour representative from the Trades and Labour Congress (TLC) into its war cabinet, and later in the war the government appointed labour representatives to a full range of government councils and commissions and began hiring former trade union officials in the Department of Labour. And, as Marquis (1993) suggests, the municipal police often had agreements with legal strikers as to 'how picketing would be conducted' (112), suggesting a conciliatory turn at the policing level as well. But then again, these gentler approaches were not as evident among the NWMP or the OPP as they were continued to be called on by governments and employers specifically whenever a stick was needed.

Post–First World War

The 1918 armistice brought an end to many of the more repressive wartime legislative measures while the federal government sought to continue a policy of 'rapprochement' with the 'responsible unions' by convening a National Industrial Conference in 1919 (Fudge and Tucker, 2001: 120). However, in the face of major inflation, high postwar expectations, and major unemployment, this failed to produce any consensus on trade union resolutions, in large part because the government was still unwilling to move to challenge employer positions on unionization. Here we see a good illustration of Tilly's (2004) point about what happens when there is a withdrawal from trust relations as unions began to see through the state's early wartime corporatist arrangements. So as militancy continued to grow among the rank and file, and union members and strike numbers grew, the government again sought to expand its efforts to repress the militants and radicals. It did this in part by directing the Dominion Police to set up a special IWW (Industrial Works of the World) unit that launched a concerted effort to infiltrate radical organizations across the country (Fudge and Tucker, 2001; Heron, 1996). On the legislative front, the government introduced PC 815, which made it an offence for an adult male not to be engaged in a useful occupation and was used against union organizers and radicals, and PC 915, restricting anti-war comments. Repressive measures continued into 1918 as strike activity increased, including a number of general strikes. A report investigating radicalism commissioned by the federal governments argued that a Bolshevik conspiracy to take over the government was behind the labour unrest. PC 2381 banned enemy-language publications, affecting a significant number of ethnically based labour publications, while PC 2384 banned a number of radical organizations outright. Then the government went even further, after a general strike in Calgary, by banning all strikes and lockouts in industries covered under the IDIA. This alienated the conservative as well as the radical unions. However, in many of the resulting strike and protest events, the federal government also demonstrated its willingness to compromise, and quite frequently did not act vigorously against unions or union-supported organizations that ignored the bans (Fudge and Tucker, 2001).

When labour militancy reached a peak in 1919, both in the context of the Winnipeg General Strike and other major actions elsewhere in the country (McKay and Morton, 1998; Mitchell and Naylor, 1998), it was put down by considerable use of force. Again, the use of force was widely justified by fears of a broader conspiracy to overthrow the government. For example, despite all the evidence to the contrary, the speeches of the NWMP Commissioner Perry during the Winnipeg strike labelled the strike a 'One Big Union' conspiracy aimed at confiscating all private property and establishing a communist form of government (Brown and Brown, 1978: 44). Following the strike, the Robson Commission vindicated the strikers by finding that the strike was about recognition of collective bargaining and the achievement of economic concessions rather than a communist conspiracy (44), but the violent actions of the NWMP during the strike underscored the commissioner's view.

For its part, police sought to reflect government policy by distinguishing radicals from responsible unions (Marquis, 1993: 113). For example, the chief commissioner of the Dominion Police stated in 1918 that the 'great object to be accomplished now is vigorous enforcement but "with discretion," that is avoiding interfering unnecessarily with organizations that are legitimately desirous of helping the working class' (as quoted by (Fudge and Tucker, 2001: 101). For police in general, distinguishing between responsible and radical unions meant to some extent that police attention also shifted from the policing of strikes to the more intelligence-driven focus on revealing the 'enemy within' the labour movements, and it was in this context that federal and provincial police further expanded their intelligence operations. The Chief Constables Association of Canada (CCAC) also passed a resolution seeking enhanced federal and provincial sanctions against such subversive groups. In 1919, the country's police chiefs were increasingly afraid of a war between labour and capital and identified Winnipeg, Edmonton, and Vancouver as possible centres of revolution (Marquis, 1993). In large centres even as early as the First World War, formal policies for dealing with strikes were developed which reflected the increasing suspicion that labour's legitimate objectives were concealing a much more subversive project; consequently, there was a greater emphasis on intelligence, ongoing monitoring of strikes, and a readiness to mobilize a forceful response.

As labour market conditions shifted against workers in the early 1920s, and employers continued to enjoy the support of the courts, the federal and provincial police forces, and the militia, unions experienced a major decline in the mid- to late 1920s. During most of the 1920s, there were few signs that labour disputes would lead to any broader class-based action, and even when the economy improved in the late 1920s, unionization remained weak. The approaches of some companies shifted to corporate welfare schemes, and strikes and union drives declined, but police continued to place a special emphasis on targeting more radical labour groups including members of the Communist Party of Canada (Fudge and Tucker, 2001; Marquis, 1990).

However, the pressures of the depression in the 1930s led to increasing social tensions, and while unions remained relatively weak in Canada, radical groups such as the communists made considerable headway in organizing the unemployed, which drew further attention from the federal and provincial police. Unions affiliated with the communist Workers Unity League also made significant progress during this period. Identified in this way, governments, courts, and police continued to deal with the leaders and members of these groups in a harsh manner, often employing the Immigration Act to deport people. May Day marches and protests were suppressed by force and many cities refused to grant unions and unemployed groups the right to march, using force to break up any marches that were attempted (Fudge and Tucker, 2001). A new relief law established in 1931 gave cabinet sweeping powers to intervene against any and all threats to the public order. And when the government established relief camp programs for unemployed males, this also led to considerable unrest, including the famous 'On to Ottawa' trek that ended badly with numerous arrests and injuries at the Regina riot, provoked when RCMP and city police charged the trekkers with tear gas and batons (Palmer, 1992; Fudge and Tucker, 2001). On orders from Ottawa, the RCMP and city police had attempted to arrest the strike leaders, but when the protesters resisted, police used clubs, tear gas, and revolvers (Jamieson, 1968: 247). One city detective was killed and numerous injuries were reported on both sides. Eight strike leaders and 122 others were arrested. Eventually, the charges against the leaders were dropped, but 9 of the total 130 persons arrested were convicted (248).

By the mid-1930s, sympathies for the unemployed and workers more generally led to the defeat of many provincial Conservative governments and the emergence and growing electoral success of the labour-friendly Co-operative Commonwealth Federation (CCF). In the United States, President Roosevelt introduced his national industrial recovery program that included new labour legislation, the so-called Wagner Act, giving workers the protected right to choose a union without employer interference. These developments further complicated the federal government's readiness to use coercive tactics (Fudge and Tucker, 2001: 159). While the Bennett federal government steadfastly resisted demands for a Canadian version of the 1935–7 NIRA and U.S. Wagner Act, which recognized and protected collective bargaining rights, it did attempt to introduce its own version of the 'new deal,' including the Minimum Wages Act, the Weekly Rest in Industrial Undertakings Act, and the Limitations of Hours of Work Act. As Fudge and Tucker (2001: 167) point out, these acts did nothing to address the issues of unionization, union security, and collective, but a number of developments at the provincial level indicated an increasing openness to supportive labour union legislation. However, it would not be until the latter part of the Second World War that labour unions would gain the kind of protection afforded to American unions under the Wagner Act.

The Significance of Municipal Police Unionization and Local Politics

While municipal police became more and more involved in policing strikes as urban industry developed in the early 1900s, their primary purpose was to prevent and control common criminal occurrences such as drunkenness, disorderly conduct, and vagrancy. Unlike the larger territorial forces which owed their lineage to the Royal Irish Constabulary and more militaristic, mounted colonial policing, the municipal police embodied, as Greer (1992: 1) argues, a mobilization of sovereign power to keep down vice and 'dangerous classes.' Since municipal police developed along Peelian lines to emphasize service and urban order maintenance, there was very little detective or forensic work and most policing activities involved either preventive foot patrols or very physical interventions, literally carting individual drunks and vagrants to lock-up. Although this implied a readiness and capacity to use physical force, municipal forces were not set up in terms of numbers or training to deal with large-scale protests or strikes, which helps to explain why the local militia continued to be used and then over time increasingly replaced by federal and provincial police forces.

In addition to this, perhaps the more important limiting factor in the role of the municipal police in putting down labour is the fact that police themselves began to unionize, with the union drives being most pervasive at the local rather than national level. The police union movement grew out of police benefit funds, established, according to the Toronto Police, to 'grant gratuities and pensions for long service, and to assist members who may be disabled in the actual execution of their duty, or incapacitated from duty by long sickness, and to make provision for old age, and for families in case of death' (Toronto Police Museum). The Toronto Police Benefit Fund was established in 1881 and was under management and control of a committee of the force, subject to approval of the commissioners. Such funds were established in other police forces and were the kernel from which occupational police associations and unions developed.

The wider unionization movement began as early as 1913, and the first clear police strikes occurred in Montreal and Toronto in 1918. In Montreal, the city was racked by public disorder, crime, and vandalism, while in Toronto, several hundred constables went on a four-day strike, which included picketing at police stations, before the provincial government agreed to set up a royal commission to investigate police administration. However, the full implications of police unionization for the policing of labour became clearer in Winnipeg in 1919, when the majority of the municipal force took part in the General Strike. As a consequence, save for a few top officers and two constables, the entire department was fired en masse after they refused to sign a 'yellow dog contract' (Jamieson, 1968). Special constables were sworn in and the NWMP were brought in to police the strike, leading almost immediately to its violent suppression.

In this regard, the Winnipeg General Strike is usually highlighted in Canadian history because it signalled not only the potential of union solidarity and union militancy (Palmer, 1992; Heron, 1996) but also a possible crisis in the control of the union movement by those empowered to put it down – the police. The general strike also meant a recognition of the common interests of private *and* government employees including police. It would take some time before this recognition of the private and public interest in strikes became firmly established in executive as well as rank and file police thinking, yet this can be seen as a critical historical point in the move in this direction. For Marquis (1993), it was the concern about allegiances of municipal police and the role of the federal police during the Winnipeg strike that was instrumental in persuading the federal government to create the Royal Canadian Mounted Police in November 1919. (The amended order, including absorption of the Dominion Police, took effect on 1 February 1920.)

However, Marquis (1993) also argues that most municipal police chiefs, even in the early 1900s, were not opposed in general to trade unions, collective bargaining, strikes, and other demands of mainstream labour. This acceptance of their legitimacy was consistent not only with the increasingly prevalent views of the rank and file police but also with the public discourse and the state's legal recognition of and involvement in collective bargaining through such legislation as the Conciliation Act of 1900 and the Industrial Disputes Investigation Act of 1907. On the other hand, initially at least, police administrators were concerned about police unionization, and certainly events such as the Winnipeg strike must have raised some concern among political and corporate leaders. As Marquis (1993) found in his examination of the records of the CCAC, municipal police chiefs were well aware even at this early stage that keeping order at strikes and at lockouts was increasingly unpopular with the rank and file officers (Marquis, 1993: 112). This point is also made by Torrance (1986), who observes that the activity of clearing sidewalks and factory gates frequently left police open to being denounced as strikebreakers, a charge which many rank and file police found distasteful as they themselves unionized. Still, as Fudge and Tucker (2001) point out, police chiefs sought in 1918 to get the federal government to ban all police unions, but, interestingly, the government moved to prohibit only the federal mounted police from doing so. As such, not only was municipal police unionization a key turning point in the historical development of the federal and provincial police forces as enforcers of industrial order, but it may also have been instrumental in weakening the resolve of municipal police to use force in strike situations.

Indeed, although there are many historical accounts of violent confrontations between police and strikers from the 1920s to the 1940s, these confrontations were largely due not to any initial municipal police response, but tended to follow the intervention of militia, private police, or federal or provincial police (Jamieson, 1968). Police involvement in major events seems to follow a pattern in which employers used special constables and private security to protect strikebreakers. This was followed by escalated violence requiring additional provincial or federal police. As Jamieson (1968: 54) argues, the all-too-frequent deployment of the RCMP and provincial police en masse was usually enough to tip the scale in the hundreds of strikes and labour demonstrations during the first half of the 1900s.

At the same time, there is also evidence that the lack of local public support for such actions was often a problem that discouraged Mackenzie King and other politicians from using federal and provincial police. There were also emergent jurisdictional tensions between municipal, provincial, and federal authorities over the legitimacy of strike actions and police use of force. For example, in 1937 workers walked out at the General Motors plant in Oshawa in an effort to force the company to recognize their newly organized union. The premier of Ontario, Mitchell Hepburn, called the strike a conspiracy of foreign agitators and mobilized a formidable force of police and military personnel to deal with it (Jamieson, 1968: 252). The premier had decided that he did not want to recognize the trade union confederation the Congress of Industrial Organizations (CIO) in a mediation of the dispute and that a show of force was needed, for which he requested a dispatch of RCMP from the federal minister of justice. The federal government reluctantly provided 100 RCMP officers, but when Hepburn asked for an additional 100 officers, this was refused. Outraged, Hepburn wired the minister to take back his original 100 RCMP and instead formed a 'special task force' of 400 special constables to reinforce the provincial police, which were also placed on alert (Jamieson, 1968: 257–8). In the end, the strike itself was very peaceful and not a single arrest was made, but divisions between federal and provincial views on the best response had clearly been exposed.

Four other instances of municipal and provincial jurisdictional disagreements signal the increasing political costs associated with federal or provincial police involvement in local strikes. The first involves the historic Ford strike in Windsor, Ontario, in 1945. When Ford Canada appealed to the Windsor Police Commission to order the Windsor police through the pickets for company officials, the appeals were dismissed, the Windsor Police Commission instructing the police on duty to 'use their discretion.' According to our police and labour informants, and the archival record, very little happened with respect to picket line confrontation. The union had its own marshalling system to keep picket line order, and the Windsor police, who were widely supportive, were largely left to direct traffic. The police seemed to reflect the community as a whole, which offered significant support by joining the workers in a twenty-four-hour vigil at the plant while the mayor supported city relief for those in need. When Ford appealed for provincial and federal assistance, Mayor Art Reaume promised 8000 striking Ford workers that no police would be imported (Moulton, 1974). However, more than seven weeks later, the Windsor Police Commission, with the mayor still opposing, ordered the city police to enter the Ford gates to allow the opening up of the power plant. But police made only a half-hearted attempt to enter. There was some pushing and shoving but this was the only significant police/picket-line confrontation of the strike and resulted in minor injuries (Moulton, 1974: 140). One of our retired police informants, a rookie constable at the time, recalls the incident:

I: Did you have any specific instructions during the strike?
R: Only to protect property and to enable; there were enabling tasks for people to enter the premises who were legally entitled to enter the property.
I: How did the picketers behave?
R: They for the most part were not too bad. Of course, they had their moments. Especially early in the morning when others would be attempting to get into their offices or even the security police trying to get in to do their job ... When persons were trying to get through, they were unruly ... I know on one occasion when we sought to conduct special people through the line – and I'm talking special people maybe the president of Ford, but I know the chief and senior officers led a small contingent of Windsor police, maybe 30–40, through the picket lines ... The chief was assaulted and the deputy chief was punched and internally speaking the boys were roughed up. I think the police chief of the time got a black eye out of it.
I: Were any arrests made here?

R: No, it would have been practically impossible unless you knew somebody by sight to identify the person responsible for the assault ... it
would have only incited the crowd further. (R44)

However, against the wishes of Mayor Reaume, the Windsor Police
Commission followed up this incident by wiring Ontario Attorney
General Leslie Blackwell for police reinforcements to maintain law and
order. Blackwell quickly dispatched 125 provincial police and obtained
authorization for equal numbers of RCMP from the federal government. With considerable community support, the union set up a massive car barricade around the plant that effectively kept the integrity of
the picket line and also kept the police reinforcements out of effective
action. While public announcements by Attorney General Blackwell
were highly critical of the union, going so far as to accuse them of open
insurrection against the crown, the local community had spoken, and
the government, company, and union reached a compromise without
ever employing the provincial or federal police. An arbitrator, Justice
Ivan Rand, was appointed, and out of this arbitration came the now-
standard dues check-off process, the so-called Rand formula, which
ensures the direct deduction of dues to unions for all workers in a
unionized plant.

A similar situation occurred in Hamilton in 1946, with a huge strike
at the Steel Company of Canada involving thousands of workers.
Again, the community and the local city council were highly supportive of the strikers, while the company and the provincial government
insisted that there was a need for federal intervention in the form of
police. Substantial support came from local businesses and the community as a whole. Provincial pressures on the Mackenzie King
government to intervene with the RCMP were resisted; perhaps as a
consequence, there were relatively few incidents of violence. As in
Windsor, the union enjoyed a level of success, the company agreeing
to adopt the Rand formula and to grant major improvements in wages
(see Heron and Storey, 1986a, b).

The seamen's strike of 1946 is also instructive. It involved about
5000 members of the Canadian Seaman's Union who worked on
Great Lakes ships. In this dispute, the government sent in the RCMP
immediately and used its wartime powers to take over the docks and
the shipping companies. Although the government tried to characterize the strike as communist-incited, the workers received considerable public support and more moderate unions decried the efforts of

the government to engage in 'red baiting' (Lipton, 1968). Local community and political support was again critical in undermining the provincial and federal governments' use of state police services. The mayors of two Ontario communities, Cornwall and Thorold, strongly condemned OPP tactics, while 5000 union members protested the use of RCMP and OPP to protect 'scabs.' In Collingwood, townspeople gathered at the local train station to convince strikebreakers to leave town. Eventually the government imposed a favourable settlement, meeting two of the strikers' major demands.

The Quebec asbestos miners' strike of 1949 further demonstrates the political tensions and costs involved in repressive actions by the government and the limited capacity of the state to police strikes in this manner. In this case, the provincial police were dispatched by the Duplessis government to the scene very early despite a lack of striker violence, disorder, or property damage. While the provincial police patrolled the streets, the company brought in strikebreakers, eventually staffing up to one-third of the original levels. As was standard practice, police escorted the strikebreakers to and from company premises (Isbester, 1975: 174). This led to an altercation between the provincial police and the strikers in the basement of a church in which several strikers were badly beaten in front of *Life* and *Time* reporters (Isbester, 1975: 183). Once more, the municipal council passed a resolution condemning the provincial police on grounds that a large number of them were under influence of alcohol, were guilty of indecent acts in the streets of the city, and had caused disorder in public places with unprovoked acts of violence against employees of the company with the evident purpose of provoking trouble.

Great bitterness against the provincial police remained in the town, the incident being called one of the 'most infamous episodes in the labour-relations history of the province of Quebec.' While there is disagreement as to whether this was a victory for the strikers, police brutality became the lasting issue in *Le Devoir* and other Quebec newspapers (Isbester, 1975: 184), helping to fuel a shift in Quebec labour politics in the 1950s. In particular, the strike highlighted grievances between French and English Quebec and rising antipathy towards the Protestant elite. Catholic Church representatives came out in support of the strikers. The future prime minister of Canada, Pierre Trudeau, also achieved some early fame by roundly criticizing the government and police tactics in his edited book *Asbestos Strike* (Trudeau, 1974).

The Second World War and the Postwar Settlement

The increasing tensions surrounding police use of force against organized labour reflected a number of significant developments during
and just after the Second World War. As Canada moved out of the depression and into the war, increasing electoral strength in the pro-
labour CCF and complementary grassroots organizational power reinvigorated the labour movement. Much as during the First World War,
government responses from 1939 to 1943 simply aggravated the situation as the federal government and most provincial governments continued to resist demands for meaningful protections for unions.
Jamieson (1968) characterizes the government's performance in labour
relations: 'The first four years of the war was one of weakness, inde-
cision and absence of planning and foresight' (292). Employers also
persisted in resisting unions and, in combination with virtually full
employment, this led to a major increase in strikes and labour protests.

Emergency measures imposed wage controls and new restrictions
on the right to strike, which enraged even the more conservative
unions. Most of the strikes were in the major industries critical to the
war effort: coal, steel, auto, aircraft, and shipyards. Although many of
these strikes were short-term, many were also spontaneous wildcats in
direct violation of emergency-measure bans on strikes and represented
increasing challenges to the conservative leadership of many unions.
Thus, for the first four years of the war, police were faced with an enormous increase in public order challenges (Jamieson, 1971). One indication that they were more than a little overwhelmed is that neither they
nor the government moved to enforce the penalties against the union
leaders when the law was broken.

For their part, police had shifted much of their attention from controlling the unemployed to responding to the fascist threat. Although
this took some heat off 'the usual suspects,' communists and other left
radical organizations remained a concern. In 1943, the OPP organized
a special branch to keep tabs on a wide range of radical and ethnic organizations, including Germans, Italians, and Japanese, but also anti-
war groups such as the Jehovahs. However, since most communists
had also disavowed the war following the Moscow line, the party and
its members were declared illegal at the beginning of the war and
many communists within and outside labour were interned as a consequence (Marquis, 1993: 197). While it is commonly argued that the
RCMP turned their attention away from communists once the Soviet
Union joined the war against the Nazis, Marquis's (1993) review of

CACP documents shows that police continued to monitor the activities of communists and other radical left groups.

In response to worsening labour relations, the government finally acted in 1943 to implement some of the first substantive protections for unions (Russell, 1995). Provincial and federal legislation was introduced in 1943 and early 1944, the most significant being PC 1003. Modelled to a significant extent after the U.S. Wagner model (1937), PC 1003 provided unions with substantive collective bargaining rights and protections for the first time (McCrorie, 1995). Unions were expected to ensure that their members respected the law both during the life of a collective agreement and during strike/lockout situations. This meant abiding by the ban on strikes during the term of a collective agreement, which meant in turn that conflicts were to be routinely dealt with in the highly individualized and legalistic context of grievance procedures and arbitrations. When collective bargaining failed to reach agreement, strikes were to be called only after a vote and an effort to conciliate, and then when all else had failed, strikes must be conducted strictly within the limits of the law. At a more fundamental ideological level, private property rights and the legitimacy of profit-making enterprises were being accepted. With reference to strikes, unions placed an increasing emphasis on self-policing and controlling the conduct of their members, while increasingly viewing strikes in public relations terms.

The legislation formed the framework for a postwar labour law regime that largely continues to the current day. PC 1003 and the related post–Second World War legal developments (e.g., the Ontario Labour Relations Act) provided a substantive legal foundation for the liberalization of labour and its relationship with the state, which included much more pervasive commitment by labour to the rule of law. Moreover, as Russell (1995) suggests, unlike the United States, which moved to limit the Wagner model through regressive amendments (the Taft-Hartley Bill, 1947) and politically conservative appointments to the National Labour Relations Board, the original PC 1003 provisions were, if anything, further liberalized over the next thirty years with lower thresholds for certification, the introduction of automatic certifications, first-contract arbitration, the Rand formula, and other changes.

'Responsible Unionism' and the Decline of Radicalism

The initial effect of PC 1003 in 1944–5 was a sharp drop in the number of strikes. Immediately after the war, in 1946–7, strike frequency

Table 3.1
Work Stoppages, Canada, 1940–1959

Year	Frequency	Duration	Person days lost	Year	Frequency	Duration	Person days lost
1940	168	4.4	266,318	1950	160	7.2	1,387,500
1941	231	5.0	433,914	1951	258	8.9	901,620
1942	354	4.0	450,202	1952	219	24.6	2,765,510
1943	402	4.8	1,041,198	1953	173	24.1	1,312,000
1944	199	6.5	490,139	1954	173	25.3	1,430,000
1945	197	15.2	1,457,420	1955	159	31.2	1,875,400
1946	226	32.4	4,515,030	1956	229	14.1	1,246,000
1947	234	22.9	2,366,340	1957	245	18.3	1,477,000
1948	154	20.7	885,790	1958	259	24.4	2,816,850
1949	135	22.1	1,036,820	1959	216	15.0	738,700

Source: Labour Canada, *Strikes and Lockouts in Canada.*

rebounded to all-time highs, which was ominously reminiscent of the post–First World War period. However, unlike that earlier period, many of these strikes were successful for labour, buffered as they were by the protections offered by the federal PC 1003, which was still in effect (Fudge and Tucker, 2001). Consequently, although some major strikes occurred in certain industries during 1948–50 period, overall strike activity began to decline steadily after 1947 in most of Canada, a trend which then stretched through much of the 1950s (see table 3.1). Aided by their strengthened legal status and the inclusion of cost-of-living allowances in collective agreements, unions increasingly reached agreements without strikes (Heron, 1996: 88), while strikes themselves became more tame in part because fewer larger companies made any attempt to use replacement workers during strikes (Jamieson, 1971: 297).

As Jamieson (1971) demonstrates, both strike activity and violence dropped substantially in the 1950s. Certainly, there were some notably violent strikes and labour defeats during this period, particularly the Murdochville copper mines strike of 1957, again in Quebec, which involved over 100 provincial police and 40 armed 'detectives' hired by the company. Mining and forestry were also relatively hot strike spots in BC. But on the whole, and particularly in industrial Canada, the 1950s was a relatively 'golden' age of positive industrial relations (Heron, 1996), when wages and working conditions, and productivity generally improved, with relatively little conflict (see table 3.1). This political and economic context of widespread prosperity, and perhaps consequently, the declining use of strikebreakers by many of the larger employers, are widely seen as contributing to this reduction of picket-line violence during the 1950s (Jamieson, 1971). Although the use of scabs was legal in all provinces during this period, the capacity of employers to use strikebreakers was compromised given low unemployment, high levels of economic growth, and the size and complexity of many production settings. The success of unions in some industries in introducing provincial or national bargaining agreements also likely played a critical role in reducing confrontations in many of the major industries such as the automobile sector.

Still others argue that the lack of labour conflict was more accurately interpreted as an indication of declining combativeness and militancy within the union leadership and membership rather than a true indication of union success (Panitch and Swartz, 2003). From this perspective, postwar unions became increasingly conservative, committed to a 'business unionism' which was focused narrowly on improving wages, benefits, and job security for its particular groups of members, who had little interest in broader social issues and virtually no concern with challenging management rights or powers regarding the labour process. This also meant that the movement as a whole devoted relatively little energy to organizing outside their particular industries, which is demonstrated by the lack of meaningful growth in union coverage beyond the core manufacturing and primary resource sector industries over the course of the 1950s (Forrest, 1995).

For many historians, the move to a more conservative unionism was not a simple product of postwar material gains or legal legitimacy (Palmer, 1992). There was also a concerted campaign within the context of the broader emerging Cold War environment to explicitly root out the radical factions within the labour movement. Also, while the 1946–7 strike wave was short-lived, the strike activity was used to fuel new government and business efforts to differentiate responsible unionism from radicalism. Business leaders complained that certain unions and leaders were not willing to accept the responsibility that went with their new power. As McInnis (2002) quotes a 1947 editorial in *Canadian Business*, 'Today unions are accepted institutions. As such they enjoy certain privileges, yet they still lack responsibility' (177). Of course, blame for this lack of responsibility fell largely on communist unions and activists. As such, after a hiatus during the last part of the war, the state focus turned once again to the communist threat. Provincial governments, often with the enthusiastic support of the NDP, were extremely hostile to unions identified as communist or communist-influenced, such as the United Electrical Radio and Machine Workers of America (UE), Mine Mill, Canadian Seaman's Union, and the Industrial Wood and Allied Workers (IWA). In Quebec and Ontario, the provincial governments of Duplessis and Hepburn made frequent use of the provincial police to close down communist union offices and harass union leaders, while also using the communist threat whenever it was expedient to justify police action against strikers (McInnis, 2002: 177). In 1948, the Quebec government also introduced Bill 5, which replicated the regressive U.S. Taft-Hartley amendments, which banned closed shops, secondary boycotts, and 'communist unions.' Businesses were also extremely vocal in stressing the threat presented by communist unions and communist union activists.

The government and police were often complicit in aiding the takeover of communist-led unions by conservative 'international' unions, with particular reference to takeover of the Canadian Seaman's Union and Mine Mill (Solski and Smaller, 1984). These concerns about communism and other forms of radicalism within the union movement persisted through to the 1950s, fuelled by other developments in the Cold War, such as the revelations of a communist espionage ring arising from the defection of a Russian embassy clerk, Igor Gouzenko, in 1946, a Royal Commission on Espionage, and the prosecution and conviction of various Canadian 'spies,' including the only sitting Communist MP, Fred Rose. While governments, corporations, and police did their utmost to repress radicalism in the labour movement, much of the anti-communism campaign was fought by labour itself, as international (i.e., U.S.) unions and the central union bodies in Canada engaged in highly explicit and ultimately successful purging campaigns to rid unions of communists (Abella, 1975; Heron, 1996). Within most of Canada, as in the United States, the radical factions within the union movement suffered almost virtual elimination over the course of the 1950s and 1960s.

While there was a concerted effort to root out communism, it can also be argued that the success of these purges owes much to the impact of PC 1003 and the related post–Second World War legal developments. The laws and institutions established to administer the law provided a much more substantive legal foundation for the liberalization of labour and its relationship with the state and capital. The resulting concrete improvements in unionized workers' conditions and union security helped to strengthen the liberal and social democratic forces within the labour movement, fuelling and reinforcing the purge in part by de-legitimizing the claims of the more radical elements. Overthrowing the state was no longer even a point of debate within the labour movement as the capacity to realize labour's interests within a 'rule of law capitalism' was increasingly accepted as the only valid labour union position.

What is particularly significant from the perspective of police is that by the end of the 1950s, very few communists or socialists were left in the Canadian labour movement. The phrase 'class struggle' became increasingly absent from union discourse, replaced by newfound commitment to labour law and legal process. At a fundamental ideological level, this meant that unions accepted private property rights and the legitimacy of profit-making enterprises. More specifically, with reference to strikes, it also meant that unions carried an onus for self-policing and controlling the conduct of their members, which in turn made the visible expression of labour grievances more meaningful as a demonstration of legitimate power, rather than proof of effective capacity to shut down enterprises. Employers had long been pushing to impose legal liability on unions for their actions, but very little had been offered to unions in exchange for their acceptance of certain fundamental responsibilities (see also McCrorie, 1995; Russell, 1995). As Fudge and Tucker (2001: 305) put it, the 'quid pro quo' for the substantive collective bargaining protections offered in PC 1003 was the imposition of legal obligations on unions regarding the way in which labour interests and disputes would be addressed. Unions were expected to ensure that their members respected the law both during the life of a collective agreement and during strike/lockout situations. This also meant abiding by the ban on strikes during the term of a collective agreement, which meant in turn that conflicts were to be routinely dealt with in the highly individualized, bureaucratic, and legalistic contexts of grievance procedures and arbitrations. When collective bargaining failed to reach agreement, strikes were to be called only after a vote and an effort to conciliate, and then when all else had failed, strikes were to be strictly conducted within the limits of the law. Such detailed protocols resulted in a new concern for the rigid observance of process and the appearance of legality on the picket line.

Although some analysts have suggested that these restrictions eventually yielded a pattern of longer strikes in Canada (Huxley, 1979), others have emphasized the role of the grievance and arbitration process in individualizing and routinizing the resolution of labour–management conflicts around bureaucratic rules in the collective agreement while contributing to the professionalism and careerism within the leadership and serving to distance the leadership from the membership (Glasbeek, 1987; Panitch and Swartz, 2003). Again, in regulation theory terms (Jessop, 1995; Burawoy, 1985), the legal protections for union certification and collective bargaining, the low levels of unemployment, the increasing inclusion of cost-of-living allowances in collective agreements, and a more corporatist approach to labour relations all constituted the finishing touches of a 'Fordist regime' of industrial relations which was grounded in a level of substantive consensual exchange. It is in this context that strikes declined as agreements were increasingly reached without work stoppages and, when they did occur, were increasingly tame, since few of the larger companies made any attempt to use replacement workers during strikes (Jamieson, 1968: 297; Heron, 1996: 88).

The introduction of a majority-vote-based certification process for unionizing was also instrumental in eliminating one of the major sources of strike activity prior to PC 1003, the recognition strike. This meant that strikes were no longer about getting the employer to recognize and negotiate with the union, while the employer's capacity to intimidate was restrained at least to an extent by provisions and penalties for unfair labour practices. Many of the most violent strikes had been recognition strikes, often because the stakes were so high, but also because the employers were largely unfettered in the tactics they could employ. Indeed, where violence did occur during the 1950s and early 1960s, it was usually in a context where the employer was stubbornly resisting recent unionization, often in some of the more rural primary resource contexts (Heron, 1996: 83). For example, the violent 1957 copper strike in Quebec was fought over the issue of recognition. The Quebec Labour Relations Board had refused to recognize the union based on highly questionable company claims regarding its employee rolls (Jamieson, 1968: 362). But, as noted, for the most part, the stakes had changed significantly for the workers, who were increasingly secure and attached to their employer in a longer-term relationship, thus discouraging aggressive confrontations. Within the context of the Rand formula and the bureaucratization and professionalization of the union leadership, there was also a growing leadership commitment to operating within the terms of the law, and unions were concerned with the need for orderly and lawful picketing. With the protections of the law came the responsibility to operate within the law.

From this perspective, then, the PC 1003 model of industrial relations stifled militancy by encouraging a more bureaucratic approach to unionism, a more legalistic approach to labour conflict, and a more routinized approach to labour protest. The creation of a union hierarchy of full-time executive members, staff reps, and stewards, helped along by the Rand formula, which guaranteed dues collection, meant an increasing distance from their membership and encouraged self-interest in maintaining power, with accordingly less emphasis on shop-floor politics and organization. This also meant that labour–management relations became normalized within highly formalized negotiations, which for some analysts translated into ritualized conduct, even ritualized strike violence (Geary, 1985).

While the workers' stakes in strikes had also been moderated by the state's introduction of an improved social security blanket such as social housing and unemployment insurance, it is also worth noting that there were important changes in the tactics and strategies of many of the larger corporations. On the bargaining front, many of the larger capital-intensive industrial firms adopted the 1948 GM model of offering regular improvements in employment conditions in exchange for union and worker cooperation in achieving productivity improvements. The introduction of cost-of-living allowances, seniority provisions, and pensions also greatly enhanced the workers' commitment to the firm and the tying of union and company interests. Many companies also developed increasingly sophisticated personnel policies and human resource philosophies which discouraged the kind of authoritarian and arbitrary supervision and management practices that would often underlie labour–employer disputes and enhance the potential for violence during disputes (Burawoy, 1985; Heron, 1996).

The implications for the relationship between the police and labour are quite profound. With the communists and socialists largely gone, and the remaining labour leadership focused almost exclusively on narrow economic interests, police had less and less to do on the intelligence front and less political ammunition to use in justifying the forceful countering of labour. And although police continued to use force in strikes for another two decades in most parts of Canada, it was not long before an increasing number of police services began to question the need, cost, and legitimacy of such actions.

Policing Strikes in the 1950s: More of the Same?

The declining frequency and intensity of strike confrontations in the 1950s reduced the demands and pressures on police. As our retired police and union informants in Windsor insisted, most strikes were very tame affairs with little happening to touch off significant police involvement or violence (see also Jamieson, 1971). At the same time, unions were enjoying increased popularity as legitimate and responsible organizations successfully making a difference in workers' lives. Indeed, the combination of low unemployment, rising standards of living, high productivity, and low inflation contributed to a broadly positive perception of the union movement as working with government and employers to achieve a classless, affluent society within capitalism. All this served to further reinforce the claim that unions were accepted institutions with legal rights and valid interests within capitalism – views that were clearly percolating within police, the general public, and politicians.

While setting the conditions for changing police strategies, there are no indications during the 1950s of any formal changes or reforms in police policies or philosophies in strike situations. In terms of practices, there were no specialized police personnel dealing with strikes, pre-strike communications between police and strikers were rare, regular officers were being posted to monitor strikes around the clock, and, perhaps most importantly, the police were still routinely responding to management requests to use significant force to open picket lines. This lack of change in police tactics was particularly evident in those strikes involving first-contract negotiations, which was one of the key remaining areas of significant tension within the PC 1003 regime. In its early form, labour relations legislation did not offer adequate protection against intransigent employers when negotiating first contracts. It was in these kinds of charged circumstances that police continued to show little hesitation to use force when called upon to do so by these employers or local authorities. We have already described the 1949 asbestos strike and mentioned the 1957 copper strike in Murdochville, Quebec, both of which involved first-contract negotiations. The Murdochville strike was extremely violent, with provincial police and armed private detectives playing the traditional role of helping the company to break the strike (Jamieson, 1968: 363). There were also a number of other strikes in various parts of the country, in one of which police fired on picketers, leading to a number of deaths, the first to occur in almost twenty years (Marquis, 1993; Jamieson, 1968). These incidents helped to illustrate that while police–union confrontations on the picket line declined generally over the course of the 1950s, police themselves were still not thinking differently about their role and still saw the use of force to open picket lines as a fundamental aspect of their policing function, much as they had through the first half of twentieth century.

Conclusion

We have tried to show in this chapter that public order policing from the 1850s to the 1950s was largely focused on policing labour unions and related radical political organizations (e.g., anarchists, various communist and socialist factions). While other activist groups and protest events were in evidence, including Native movements such as the Louis Riel revolt, public order policing developed over this period mainly in response to emerging labour movement activism and the rise of communism and socialism as a key force within labour.

This chapter has also demonstrated that the state's efforts to control labour strikes and protests have changed in important ways, moving from what we characterized as 'disordered policing' to 'control policing.' During this period, the public responsibility to police both strikes and labour more generally developed in tandem with the development and growth of the public police – with the provincial and federal forces replacing militia and private security – but also the growth of municipal police services. This movement toward professionalized public policing was fostered, in no small part, by an effort to socialize or externalize the cost of industrial security. Canadian labour and police histories demonstrate the tight relationship between the security needs of large industry and the development of provincial and federal police services. We characterize the overall police approach to social order as control policing because it is generally authoritarian and non-integrative. As such, we see police, especially state police, being used in quite overt ways throughout the first half of the twentieth century to support in every possible manner the employers' efforts to resist unionization and to continue production during strikes, often using deadly force, while also seeking to undermine and disrupt union development more broadly through espionage and sabotage.

At the same time, we observe a growing strategic distinction among politicians and police and between conservative unions and radical unions and activists influenced by communist and socialist ideology, distinctions that reflected some significant and growing splits within the labour movement as industrial capitalism exerted its various contradictory influences on different areas of work and employment and class structure more generally. Here we see a system of divided rule where the segments of labour are provided with at least moderate accommodations apparently aimed at encouraging a more integrative politics as evidenced by the Conciliations Acts of the early 1900s. While we detect an uneven but gradual liberalization in state policies and accommodations regarding unions beginning in the early 1900s, again aimed in part at strengthening the less radical impulses of organizing labour, it is not until the 1940s and 1950s that substantive legal protections and economic gains are achieved.

Reflecting this liberalization, we also observed some growing tensions over the use of police force in strike situations, coming from both within and outside the police. Most significantly, questions were raised about the justification for using force against strikers who were increasingly seen as legitimate actors demanding nothing more than a higher wage or more job security from uncaring, wealthy employers. We see this sentiment expressed not just in the broader public discourse but also among members of municipal forces as both police unionization and local politics complicated the claims of legitimate intervention. As radicalism declined more generally and quite significantly in the 1950s, it became even harder to sustain rationales in support of police force.

As this implies, we understand the notion of self-government in liberal democracies as being dependent on consent, which means, at a minimum, the presentation of legality or the non-partisan application of the law. As politics of law and consent shift, so do the politics of enforcement. In particular, police go through periods of professionalization in response to these macro-political and cultural changes in an effort to recapture police legitimacy at times of disordering strain. Those professionalizing moments are marked by sometimes dramatic shifts in emphasis and may be understood in one dimension as the adaptive utilization of police in maintaining a secure democracy. Thus, while employers and the government relied quite heavily on the military and private security to control labour disputes throughout the 1800s and into the 1900s, the twentieth-century development of policing at the municipal, provincial, and federal levels represented not only a growth but a shift in the definition of the public interest. That interest, once defined closely with government and police support of industry, came to be seen with the burgeoning welfare state as inclusive of labour and rights.

While the early push for unionization of the police is a critical development here, it is also important to recognize the contradictory role of law in shaping these tensions. As the federal government sought to limit its involvement by encouraging a regime of 'voluntarism' through the early 1900s (Fudge and Tucker, 2001), it was also undermining the legitimacy of the claim that police intervention is a public matter. Moreover, while the division of unions into responsible and radical factions was effective in weakening the labour movement and limiting the demands of the labour movement to 'business matters,' as more and more unions opted to follow the rule of the law by the book, certain union activities including strikes were legitimated within this process, making it more and more difficult to sustain a generalized, forceful approach to policing strikes. As noted, police had also begun quite early on to differentiate, treating some unions with a softer glove, albeit often in a very unsystematic and uncontrolled manner. However, the point remains that police were beginning to see the value of greater tolerance and cooperation, while also beginning to experience the political and moral fallout from the use of violence.

In sum, strikebreaking begins to run up against a number of mediating factors: the unionization and professionalization of police, the growing legitimacy of unions and strikes, the impact of local politics and community, and the general liberalization and welfarization of the state. Granted, these pressures yielded few formal changes in police tactics and strategy right up until the 1970s, but that may well be in part because the Cold War rhetoric was still running its course through this period, while the reduction in strike numbers and conflicts due to PC 1003 and other factors sharply reduced the number of confrontations. This relative calm was broken in the 1960s and 1970s when strike numbers began to increase once again. Our main point is that these tensions form the root of conciliatory policing policies that begin to take shape, not only as police are faced with increasingly active labour union activity, but also as new social movements and other public order issues take the stage.

4 The Emergence of Labour Liaison: The Crisis in Fordism and Welfare Liberalism?

Introduction

In the previous chapter we argued that the development of the liberal state, police unionization, and union legitimacy had increasingly problematized the use of militia and police force in strike situations. By the late 1940s, a new legislative framework had effectively institutionalized labour conflict by responsibilizing and institutionalizing labour unions within a regime of industrial legality. But, as noted, while this greatly reduced the number of confrontations between police and labour through the 1950s and into the 1960s, police themselves were still formally approaching their role and their tactics much as they had through the first half of the century, that is, within a coercive 'control' framework.

In this chapter, we seek to show that as we move into the more turbulent late sixties and early seventies, there is evidence that police began to rethink their approaches in much more substantial and formal ways with respect to public order in general and strikes in particular. Here we see the beginnings of the 'service' approach to public order, where the public order emphasis shifts from authoritative control to integrative consensual strategies. We identify the early changes in policing while locating the larger-scale shift within the broader context of major developments in labour relations, state policies, law, and new social movements. The rise of new social movements is presented as a central development which we also understand in part as being linked to the development of liberalism, post-industrialism, Fordism, and welfarism. We suggest that both the crises in Fordism and welfarism and later the emerging post-Fordist, neo-Fordist, and neo-liberal solutions to these crises were instrumental in creating the conditions for major changes in police practices. As Nikolas Rose (1996: 53) put it, 'advanced liberalism' does not abandon the 'will to govern' but instead maintains the view that failure of the government to achieve its objectives is to be overcome by inventing new strategies of government that will succeed.

The Changing Terrain of Labour Conflict and Protest

After a decade of relative labour peace, the 1960s brought with it a new round of demands on police public order resources. From 1960 to 1966 the annual number of strikes doubled from 274 to 617, remaining at close to this level through to the 1970s, with a 500 per cent increase in the amount of work days lost involving eight times the number of workers as compared with the 1950s (see table 4.1). A record number of these strikes (369) were illegal wildcat stoppages led by rank and file workers and shop-floor activists explicitly defying union leadership (Palmer, 1992: 315). As the number of strikes increased over the decade, so too did the level of violence, police arrests, and property damage. As Jamieson (1968) reports, citing an unpublished study by Francois Cote, from 1960 to 1966, seventy-five disputes involved physical violence, intimidation, property damage, and/or arrests, with seventeen in 1964 alone (403). Bryan Palmer (1992: 316), following the work of Joy McBride, argues that there was a significant subversive element to the mid-1960s strikes in that the strikers were often younger workers rejecting state, management, and union authority while expressing a deep alienation and dissatisfaction with the lack of management respect for workers (see also Jamieson, 1968; Marquis 1993).

In Ontario and BC, the strike activity in the 1960s also developed into a broader controversy around the employers' use of injunctions to undermine strikes. There were a number of mass pickets and arrests at a number of strikes in defiance of the injunctions against mass pickets (Fudge and Tucker, 2001). In Oshawa, a strike in a smaller plant had led to supporting pickets that were then challenged in court, and an injunction was attained largely banning support picketing. This became a *cause célèbre* as local UAW unions turned out in defiance of the courts. In that case the government backed down, but in another well-known case, the Tilco strike in Peterborough, twenty-six strike supporters were imprisoned, some for up to two months, for failing to abide by a similar injunction order. This and an increasing use of injunctions by employers outraged many workers, leading to calls for a general

Table 4.1
Work stoppages, Canada, 1960–1983

Year	Frequency	Duration	Person days lost	Year	Frequency	Duration	Person days lost
1960	274	15.0	738,700	1972	598	10.0	7,753,350
1961	287	13.6	1,335,080	1973	724	16.4	5,776,080
1962	311	19.1	1,417,900	1974	1218	15.6	9,221,890
1963	332	11.0	917,140	1975	1171	21.6	10,908,810
1964	343	15.7	1,580,550	1976	1040	7.3	11,544,170
1965	501	13.4	2,349,870	1977	806	15.3	3,320,050
1966	617	12.6	5,178,170	1978	1057	18.4	7,357,180
1967	522	15.8	3,974,760	1979	1049	16.9	7,819,350
1968	582	22.7	5,082,732	1980	1028	20.8	9,129,960
1969	595	25.2	7,751,880	1981	1049	25.9	8,850,040
1970	542	25.0	6,539,560	1982	679	12.3	5,702,370
1971	569	11.9	2,866,590	1983	645	13.5	4,440,900

Source: Labour Canada, *Strikes and Lockouts in Canada.*

campaign of disobedience at the Canadian Labour Congress (CLC) and the Ontario Federation of Labour (OFL) conventions. A number of union leaders openly defied the law, often receiving jail sentences for their trouble (Sangster, 2004), but this was also a major issue behind the formation of an Ontario Royal Commission of Inquiry into Labour Relations (Rand, 1968). In BC, injunctions had become an issue somewhat earlier, but in both cases the labour campaigns were somewhat successful in gaining changes in the law restricting the ease with which employers were able to gain injunctions, although injunctions remained a critical tool for employers, while police continued to enforce the injunctions without hesitation.

Public sector workers also emerged during this period as another new demand on policing resources. Public sector workers had been left out of the immediate postwar settlement, but by the late 1950s they began advocating for the right to strike, which led most notably to a major country-wide national strike by postal workers in 1965 (Palmer, 1992; Parrot, 2005). Most federal, provincial, and municipal workers won the right to bargain and strike over the next several years, which greatly increased the number of unionized workers in Canada and introduced a new public sector dynamic into the industrial relations scene. Although there was relatively little immediate impact in terms of strike volume and confrontations, again with the notable exception of the postal workers, public sector policing would later become a major challenge in the 1980s and 1990s as the frequency of public strikes increased in response to the federal and provincial government shift to neo-liberal policies aimed squarely at reducing the cost and size of the public sector (Panitch and Swartz, 2003; Rapaport, 1999). Public sector unionism also complicated the construction of strikes as private matters, since the state was the employer and public interests such as safety and security were much more entwined with the outcomes of strike activity than in private sector strikes.

As part of this wave of public sector unionism, more militant police unionism also re-emerged during this period, most notably the Montreal wildcat strike in 1969 (Marquis, 1993: 307). Tensions had been building for some time around a number of issues, including wages, police practices, such as one-officer patrols, and overall reorganization. The sixteen-hour 1969 walkout in Montreal featured riots, large-scale vandalism, and arson; in one incident involving another protest group and private security, a provincial police officer was killed. As well as bringing in the provincial police, the provincial government requested assistance from the Canadian military while introducing back-to-work legislation with harsh penalties for the police association and its members if they failed to comply. Threatened strikes in Toronto and Vancouver were narrowly averted when governments met the demands of similarly militant police associations in those cities.

The 1960s also provided challenges of an entirely different and unprecedented order. In Quebec, the Front de Libération du Québec (FLQ) emerged as a formidable threat to the public peace, using assassination, kidnapping, and bombing to achieve the political goal of Quebec separation. This eventually culminated in the federal government's use of the War Measures Act in 1970 after the kidnapping of a British diplomat and the kidnapping and murder of a provincial cabinet minister, Pierre Laporte, leading to an unprecedented peace-time suspension of civil liberties, mass arrests, and the deployment of troops across the province. As noted in the Prévost Commission's preliminary report (Quebec, 1968: 304), the activities of the FLQ encouraged police in Quebec to regard most demonstrators as 'professional agitators' and to view dissent more generally as a serious public order problem.[1]

However, in the late 1960s, with the exception of Quebec where separatism helped to fuel a definite turn to socialist rhetoric among a significant segment of the French labour movement (Heron, 1996), there was no broader resurgence of anti-capitalist radicalism within labour.

Indeed, most of the strike activities during the 1960s were over wages and the inflationary erosion of wages, and most strikes were settled through better wage offers (Panitch and Swartz, 2003). Moreover, many of the strikes, including the wildcats, were well planned, suggesting that this was not just a question of rebellion by young, inexperienced workers. For example, when 15,000 miners and surface workers went on an illegal strike in Sudbury in 1966, police had to deal with well-organized, determined strikers who had barricaded roads, blocked all gates into the mines and plants with cars and boulders, and cut telephone lines and hydro, illustrating their willingness to press their demands outside the legal arena (Jamieson, 1968: 431). Still, as the threat of separatism intensified, and as much of organized labour declared its support, unions in Quebec continued to attract the attention of police intelligence as a potential national security threat (Guntzel, 2000). For example, in the wake of the Quebec October Crisis in 1970, the federal government pushed the RCMP to enhance its intelligence gathering on radical groups including socialist unions, while also establishing an advisory committee called the Police and Security Planning and Analysis Group (Marquis, 1993).

In the early 1970s, the Canadian economy slipped into what many analysts characterize as the beginning of a broader international crisis in Fordism and liberal welfarism (Haiven, McBride, and Shields, 1991; Harvey, 1989), with runaway inflation, major increases in unemployment and government debt, and falling rates of profit. Initially, the federal government continued to show its Keynesian side – for example, by introducing improvements in unemployment insurance in 1973. As well, both provincial and federal governments generally indicated an apparent commitment to the postwar industrial compromise by implementing improvements in labour relations law as had been recommended in the federal 1969 Royal Commission Report on Industrial Relations (Woods, 1969). However, when the federal government introduced wage and price controls in 1975–8, and then again in 1982, these actions were widely seen by organized labour as significant attacks on collective bargaining rights. Indeed, almost as soon as bargaining rights had been extended to the public sector, both provincial and federal governments began to make more frequent use of back-to-work legislation and other measures to contain the efforts of public sector unions to use their recently acquired right to strike (Panitch and Swartz, 2003; Price, 1995). Further evidence of a more 'coercive' turn in government policy was evidenced in increasingly draconian penalties for unions and union leaders failing to comply with wage control and back-to-work legislation. In 1975, for example, the president of the Canadian Union of Postal Workers (CUPW) was jailed for failing to instruct his members to obey the law (Parrot, 2005), with Prime Minister Trudeau arrogantly claiming that he would 'put union leaders in jail for three years if they oppose the wage control regulations' (Panitch, 1976: 1). While the early focus was on stemming inflation through controls on all unions, considerable emphasis was placed on the public deficit, which meant an increasing concern with restricting public sector union demands as well as reducing the size of government through cuts, contracting-out, and privatization.

The unions responded to inflation and increasing employer demands for concessions with a major wave of strikes (see table 4.1). In 1974, the number of strikes skyrocketed to 1218, almost double the peak high during the 1960s (Labour Canada, 1965–75). The Canadian labour movement as a whole also responded to the wage controls of 1975–8 with a national campaign that led to a one-day general strike in October 1976, which it pulled off without significant incidents despite the participation of over a million workers. While the CLC leadership quickly retreated from confrontation and embraced a government offer of a corporatist strategy seeking tripartite arrangements (Palmer, 1992), many unions continued to demonstrate their unwillingness to accept concessions by persisting with a high level of strike activity right through to 1982, when a deep recession took the wind out of their sails. During this period, Canadian unions also demonstrated resilience in terms of union organizing and membership (Kumar, 1995; Russell, 1990; Yates, 1993). This was much less evident in the United States, where the decline in union density and membership happened earlier and more quickly. Although historically quit docile, public sector unions became increasingly militant (Panitch and Swartz, 2003).

However, the 1960s and 1970s were also marked by much wider developments in social movements and protest, particularly in the United States. In the early to late 1960s, the most serious confrontations took place in the United States, especially in the urban black ghettos, where riots resulted in 147 deaths and thousands injured and arrested (Marquis 1993: 302). The civil rights and peace movements were also having large demonstrations across the states, and some of those, such as the Kent State shootings in 1970, had ended badly. For Canadians, the debate over the deployment of nuclear weapons on Canadian soil, the U.S. involvement in Vietnam, and the evolution of a vigorous peace movement also carried potential for public order violence. Canada had relatively few incidents of such violence, and even as the student anti-war movement spread to Canada in the late 1960s with almost weekly street protests and campus sit-down strikes, it never reached the levels of public protest or violence common in the United States and Europe at this time. Still, as Marquis (1993) shows, Canadian police were concerned about the 'communist subversion' of Canada's university students and were still heavily involved in infiltrating labour and other groups in order to counter incipient political movements (Hewitt, 2000). Toronto's Red Squad, developed during the 1950s, was one such force, which, among other things, cultivated high-placed sources within the Catholic Church and many other organizations such as universities, high schools, and women's auxiliaries (Maurutto, 2000).

American Experience and Influence

The end of the 1960s is often viewed as a major watershed in American policing which ultimately had a profound influence on its Canadian counterpart (e.g., Task Force Report, 1972). Here can be seen the failures of Fordism and welfarism to address wide disparities in the material and political conditions separating unionized, blue-collar, white males and impoverished, unemployed, and non-union African Americans, as well as the successes of liberal education in creating an entire generation of youth unwilling to accept American imperialism. Out of this breakdown of consent came the peace and the civil rights movements and, in particular, the political disenfranchisement of black minorities and the lack of representation in government policy of a large group of draft-age, middle-class young persons. The movements coalesced with several other strands of political mobilization to produce a cauldron of simmering discontent in urban and campus settings. Large cities including Detroit, Los Angeles, Philadelphia, and Chicago saw major riots and large-scale violence.[2]

Within the wider context of the insurgency (unemployment, housing conditions, the Vietnam war, civil rights), the 1960s American riots were widely seen by several official government commissions as precipitated in no small part by improper police practices. The initial confrontation was followed in many cases by overwhelming force (Kerner, Commission, 1968), so much so that such actions were often characterized as 'police riots.' It is noteworthy that police actions in Britain were similarly to account for riots in the 1980s (Scarman, 1981), while many of our police informants were quick to use these same arguments in explaining more recent Canadian incidents of significant violence (e.g., Ipperwash). Given the U.S. context of popular reaction to an unpopular war largely by middle-class youth and given a more proactive judicial branch in the curbing of police power under the Warren Court in the United States (and similarly via the Bill of Rights in Canada), conditions were set for new demands on police practice.[3]

According to Lea and Young (1984), when acute political marginality is combined with a greater sense of relative deprivation, there exists the makings for more tumultuous conditions of crime and violence. Such situations were unlikely to be easily managed by police practices of the day, which relied almost exclusively on force. The coming of age of urban black America as a social movement produced a sense of acute political marginality and highlighted the relative deprivation of the young unemployed in a context – to add extra volatility – in which sympathetic college students were hostile to unrepresentative political authority. This was a condition ripe for conflict and, from a regulation perspective (Elam, 1990; Jessop, 1995), constitutes another indication of legitimacy crisis in which police reform was part of a package of responses set to allay deeper political trouble or, to use Edelman's (1967) phrase, a package of 'symbolic reassurances.' Images of riot police chasing and striking university students put police in the eye of the storm, and various U.S. inquiries found it more expedient to blame the messenger than to change the message. Police could easily be constructed as a poor messenger, and commissions into policing stood in as remedies for the malaise of political disenfranchisement, real or perceived. More than this, police could be understood with the deeper problem of how authority ought to be represented. Gone were the early postwar days when the image of the police as indifferent law enforcers was a sufficient palliative. In any case, the manner of addressing urban disturbances was, like the manner of putting down industrial disturbance previously, easily visible as incompetent or ineffective. So visible was it that it was police practices, not unemployment and housing, which ranked first in the grievance categories of blacks (Kerner Commission, 1968), while the others ranked second and third.

Consequently, the conditions of social disorder in the 1960s stimulated lasting changes to American police organization and approach. Following the Newark and Detroit riots of 1967, President Lyndon Johnson established the National Advisory Commission on Civil

Disorders – the so-called Kerner Commission – to review the racial disorders and to make recommendations for reform. The Kerner Commission found that 'some 40 percent of the prior incidents involved allegedly abusive or discriminatory police actions. Most incidents began routinely and involved a response to, at most, a few persons rather than a large group' (69). The commission argued that the riot process included four aspects: an accumulated reservoir of grievances in the black community; precipitating incidents and their relationship to the reservoir of grievances; the development of violence after its initial outbreak; and the control effort, including official force, negotiation, and persuasion (67). It noted that of the 150 cities experiencing some form of civil disorder only some cities had serious disorder, and the testimony they heard pointed as the reason the 'pre-eminent role of police reaction to the initial incident' (172). The commission recommended the creation of crowd control units with special training, while encouraging officials to eliminate 'abrasive policing practices' and create mechanisms for addressing grievances against police (McPhail, Schweingruber, and McCarthy, 1998). Two additional national commissions established by U.S. presidents to look into civil disorder also placed significant blame for the violence on the police (Eisenhower, 1969; Scranton, 1970). The Eisenhower Commission went even further to criticize the excessive use of force as 'magnifying' the rioting rather than controlling it, while recommending not only a respect for the first-amendment right to protest but also a negotiated, self-policing approach to organizing protests so that policing is not needed.

Public Order Policies: The Thread of Militarism

As Canadian police began to expand their intelligence operations in the 1960s to include the broader range of social action groups, they also showed an increasing interest in riot and crowd control policies, technologies, and techniques. As Sergeant William Kerr of the Toronto Emergency Task Force stated in his testimony at the Vannini Inquiry, struck after the visit of Soviet Premier Alexei Kosygin instigated a riot:

The advent of the mass racial riots in the United States and the wide spread civil disobedience throughout the rest of the world, has shown serious limitations within the various police forces to cope with them.

Joint studies by police supervisors has gained unanimous agreement that the police were not properly equipped and the personnel were not properly trained. (Vannini, 1971: 72)

According to Marquis (1993), many senior Canadian police administrators were alarmed about the student protests and urban riots in the United States, in part because the media coverage had encouraged Canadians and public officials to see public order and police violence as a potential Canadian problem as well. For instance, a Calgary police chief suggested to Canadian Association of Chiefs of Police (CACP) delegates in 1965 that in light of recent disorders in the United States, the CACP should examine the problem of crowd control (304). In support, Jean-Paul Gilbert, Montreal police director, visited Los Angeles in 1969 to study crowd control methods (304–5). Subsequently, the Montreal and other police services formed special mobile riot squads (*la force de frappe*) in the late 1960s and early 1970s (304).

Other large services such as Toronto had moved even earlier to develop more elaborate crowd control policies as early as 1966. Between the mid-1960s and mid-1970s, most urban police services developed formal crowd control policies and also emergency task force units with specialized crowd control training; Toronto, for instance, formed its Emergency Task Force in 1967. While the Canadian police chiefs and the Ontario attorney general rejected some of the technologies being promoted in the United States – for instance the use of mace – it was not long before specialized riot squads, special weapons teams, and task forces were being formed and trained with an increasing arsenal of less-than-lethal and defensive tools (King, 1997).

In 1970, the OPP distributed a crowd control manual as the first move toward standardization in Ontario. As King (1997: 59) notes, the manuals had the stated aim of serving as an invitation to closer cooperation and coordination between the various Ontario law enforcement agencies and the promotion of uniformity in crowd control methods (59). Reflecting the major concern over how and when to use force, the OPP and RCMP manuals in the early 1970s emphasized the proper techniques to control and disperse a crowd using specially trained police and specialist public order units equipped with the latest riot gear (King, 1997). Municipal forces also moved to develop crowd control techniques. For example, the Windsor police were trained in the use of wedges in the early 1950s and first used these tactics in a Dominion Forge strike in the early 1960s. While it appears the use of a platoon formation only occurred once in Windsor around 1970 and not again in a strike afterward, public order dress and the use of wedges for snatching agitators and for moving people or equipment through pickets into or out of plants, was used frequently both in Windsor and elsewhere throughout the 1960s and 1970s.

However, it is noteworthy that the early manuals make frequent reference to the psychology of crowds and the typologizing of such crowds as an aid to differential intervention. Here, in contrast to current policies, there is less concern with the 'plotters of evil' and a greater focus on the uncontrolled crowd. As Schweingruber (2000) argues, the police view of protesters at this time emerged from 'mob sociology' stemming originally from the crowd psychology of Gustav Lebon, which was disseminated throughout North America in the late 1960s and early 1970s through civil disorder training programs and a variety of police manuals and magazines. This included the OPP crowd control manual of 1970 and the RCMP's *Manual of Tactical Training* (1971). These handbooks indicate different kinds of crowds from the perspective of generalized psychopathology. The OPP manual describes crowds as 'aggressive,' 'escape seeking,' 'acquisitive,' and 'expressive.' It also suggests that there are 'psychological crowds' and 'physical crowds.' In an undated document, 'crowd and control of mobs and riots,' and in the OPP *Crowd Control Training* lesson plan, this is amended to 'casual crowd,' 'cohesive crowd,' 'expressive crowd,' and 'aggressive crowd.' Those within the crowds are also typified, namely, as 'impulsive and lawless persons,' 'suggestible persons,' 'cautious individuals,' 'yielders,' 'supportive persons,' 'resistors,' and 'psychopathic individuals.'

The *Toronto Crowd Control Policy* describes a process of crowd psychology in which the crowd must 'gather, grow, tire, and disperse.' However, the *Toronto Policy* also advised officers to penetrate the anonymity of the crowd – it states, 'crowds like to remain anonymous' – by 'recognizing individuals,' speaking to them, requesting assistance from specific people, pointing them out, and 'giving them something to do.' The *Policy* divided public order groups into 'orderly crowds,' 'disorderly crowds,' and 'riots.' Its précis stated that 'the police should assist the crowd to obtain its objective legally, rather than restrain it.' It held that the purpose of crowd control is 'to prevent any breach of the peace; to safeguard life and property; to control traffic and to facilitate the normal flow of trade and commerce.' It urges commanders to consider whether they are dealing with a crowd they wish to 'contain or control' or 'disperse' and to consider the educational and cultural 'level of the crowd (e.g., professional people or labourers).' At the same time, this précis or policy included a comprehensive approach to the problem of controlling public order. It recommends taking steps to 'eliminate the cause (if possible),' to utilize civic groups to assist in control (including Boy Scouts), 'having reserves in drill formation' for the appearance of strength and confidence, and, while having plain-clothesmen mixed in with the crowd, also placing 'extra men ... hidden in reserve.' Finally, it advocates that police officers acquaint themselves with 'all available data' on an 'impending event' in order to anticipate all that may happen in advance, and it notes the successful control of the Shriner's Convention of 1962 as a leading illustration (Vannini, 1971: 70–6).

While all crowd control polices developed at this time tended to emphasize very basic procedural principles such as using loudspeakers and photographers, dispersing crowd into smaller groups, targeting and arresting ringleaders, and maintaining constant pressure, they also began to explicitly recognize the public right to protest and the value of using communication and persuasion as methods of control. For example the 1966 *Toronto Crowd Control Policy* stated that 'protest groups should be contained not opposed' and advised that 'the police should meet with the leaders and work through the recognized authority structure of the group, telling them their rights and what they cannot do.'

In these early crowd control policies, we are beginning to see institutional recognition of the idea that it is not just a matter of what kind of force to use, but also whether it is sometimes better to use information, persuasion, and other tactics of 'manipulation' to control without the need for force. Still, 'control' through authority is still the pre-eminent concern, and a full-blown emphasis on service-based public order liaison did not develop until much later. For example, King's (1997) comparison of 1971 and 1995 RCMP manuals reveals that it is only in the 1990s that the preventive steps are presented and accepted as the standard or best practices, including the need for communication. Indeed, a comprehensive national RCMP liaison policy on protest was not introduced until 2001, after a number of politically controversial events and damning inquiries (Bronskill, 2001). Our survey of police services also confirms that the use of persuasion and communication in strikes or other public order situations did not become common practice across the system until the 1990s. Crowd control continued to be responded to in terms of coordination and delivery on an ad hoc basis, and remained uncoordinated across forces.

As noted, these latter developments in Canadian crowd control policy mirror and were informed by developments in the United States, where police had come under attack from a wide range of media, political, and academic sources, as much for their role in fuelling the violence as for their failure to control the riots (Marquis, 1993). In the United States, a number of court challenges, many of which were brought by the American Civil Liberties Union (ACLU), were also instrumental in pressuring police to alter their tactics by creating a body of public forum law which made it very clear that the government had a duty to protect the right of protesters to express their views. In Canada, this emphasis on the right to protest was also emerging as an important public concern following the 1960 passage of the Bill of Rights. Although it did not have sufficient influence to characterize the 1960s as a civil rights period in Canada, Canada's police chiefs did become increasingly sensitized to rights as a social issue and to the question of public welfare.

This is not to say that there were no competing objectives within police executive discussions. Police continued to seek to maintain and extend their arrest and investigatory powers to deter crime through strong measures limiting individual rights. In a brief to the Ouimet Committee in 1967, the CACP urged retention of the lash, stiffer parole administrations, and authority to impose preventative detention. Among other things, the brief called for the detention of suspects for up to 24 hours without charges being laid and 'preventative detention of rabble rousers and troublemakers' when threats were made against visiting dignitaries and heads of state' (Marquis, 1993: 290–1). The CACP also involved itself in a public affray with the Ouimet Commission and Bill C-115 regarding the possible erasure of criminal records in cases of minor crime after a period of non-criminal activity. It was against any 'expunging of criminal records.' It argued that this knowledge is powerful against crime and its forces. 'The collection and exchange of information among police agencies had been [one] of the founding principles of the association since 1905' (Marquis, 1993: 293). On the other hand, they were also receptive to British influence. John Honsberger in the Ouimet Commission's report, cites Lord Denning's address to the Congress in Delhi in January 1959: 'When I came to this Congress I thought of the rule of law as being essentially concerned with the protection of the individual from arbitrary power ... the rule of law is wider than I thought: not limited to a preventative negative function, but laying upon governments a positive duty – admittedly unenforceable in a court of law – to act for the welfare of the people.' While the effect of the Bill of Rights was perhaps limited initially, it focused increasing attention on the responsibilities of police to respect the right to associate and to express protest.

And while there were relatively few major incidents involving police in Canada during the 1960s and early 1970s, there were some notable events which produced negative public scrutiny. For example, as noted, there was violence and serious injuries at both the Toronto and Edmonton protests during the 1966 visit of Soviet Premier Kosygin, leading to considerable public criticism and a formal government inquiry (Vannini, 1971). While this inquiry made a number of findings and recommendations concerning the lack of proper equipment and adequate numbers of personnel, the central conclusion was that police had failed to cooperate with the groups involved despite their overtures seeking such cooperation. As stated in the final report, 'this failure to cooperate and the breakdown in liaison on the part of the police contributed in some measure, albeit indirectly, to the dangerous situation and the resulting confrontation which developed' (Vannini, 1971: 131). Police were also criticized for the inappropriate use of the mounted unit that had led directly to thirteen injured protesters. Significantly, the report also stressed the responsibility of police to respect and protect the 'fundamental right of speech and expression' (see Pue, 2005).[4]

As recounted in Pue (2005), the Kosygin visit to Edmonton resulted in a legal challenge to police authority in the context of rights of speech. In *R. v. Knowlton* (1974), the provincial court found that the Edmonton police did not have the right to prevent a protester from access to a blocked portion of the sidewalk. Police had created a security zone around a downtown hotel that was to be visited by the Soviet premier to which only individuals authorized by police were allowed entry; police also obstructed a small portion of the sidewalk on an adjacent public street. The court took the view that this was an unlawful interference with the plaintiff's right to move freely on a public street. The Supreme Court, on the contrary, found that the public's freedom of movement had been restricted in a marginal and limited fashion in circumstances that gave clear duty on the part of police to take precautions against attacks on the visiting statesman. For the Court, Mr Justice Fauteaux stressed the specific duty to Kosygin, the limited 'strategic point' of the public street that was barricaded, and the necessity of the action taken (Pue, 2005: 7–9). While this decision highlights for the police the importance placed on protecting state dignitaries, police read the case as providing a requirement of due diligence to ensure rights were restrained only where there was clear evidence that persons or property were in jeopardy. Critically, the courts were now sensitized to the question of access to political and civil rights while beginning to set the terms and conditions where those rights could be limited by police.

In the meantime, concerns about police tactics and human rights also drew strength through the embarrassing revelations of 'dirty tricks' by the RCMP in Quebec. A number of commissions, one chaired by Justice Mackenzie in 1969, the other by Justice McDonald in 1977, recommended changes to the mandate of the RCMP, specifically that Canada's security intelligence function be separated from the RCMP and that a civilian service be formed to carry this out. Both commissions recognized that the problem of balancing the need for accurate and effective security intelligence with the need to respect democratic rights and freedoms could not be adequately resolved as long as security intelligence responsibilities remained part of the federal police force (Rutan, 2000).

These controversies and the splitting of intelligence functions away from the RCMP may well have been instrumental in weakening any early movements towards intelligence-based policing in the 1980s. The broader significance of this, although it was a change that took a number of years to be effectuated, was that public policy was viewing political policing as a distinct entity from what Jean-Paul Brodeur calls 'low policing.' Police power, as it was developed early on, and has been recurrently re-established in liberal democracies, excludes the self-conscious and visible promotion of political ideology. Various strains of expertise, militarism, and bureaucratic professionalism within police reform cobbled together a more or less consistent view that maintained the problem of public order as a dosage of regulation which could be applied (through training, legal interpretation, techniques, and tools) without political prejudice.

Policing Strikes: The Early 'Liaison' Innovators

The major initial steps in the 1970s to develop a more coherent approach to public order policing in Canada were focused, following the American experience, mainly on the procedures and rules for using force rather than on methods of force de-escalation. At the same time, and as described above, some municipal services had developed crowd control policies as early as the mid- to late 1960s which at least recognized the importance of communication and negotiation. However, the most significant early steps towards a comprehensive, communication-based, *liaison* approach emerged in a small number of forces in the specific area of policing labour strikes, an approach that was increasingly taking hold across the country first in the area of strikes and then later more broadly in protest situations.

Vancouver and the Burnaby RCMP

Perhaps somewhat surprisingly, considering their overall history as the 'tough guys' in strike policing (King, 1997), one of the first initiatives came from the RCMP in British Columbia. Writing in the *Police Gazette* in 1970, a retired RCMP staff sergeant, Paul Starek, reported on a 'new approach' trialed by the Burnaby detachment of the RCMP in a 1969 strike at an oil refinery (Starek, 1970). According to one of our police informants, this new approach was in response to a 1966 strike at a fish plant in Burnaby which had turned violent, with resulting political controversy including criticisms from city councillors (Burnaby Council Tells RCMP, 1966; see Northorp, 1975). As described by Starek, prior to the 1969 oil refinery strike, two senior police officers met with the union to explain the police position on strikes, stressing that police were impartial and would only intervene if there was a breach of peace. The union was encouraged to direct all complaints to a two-member 'liaison team' that had been established for the strike. Complaints to police had to be cleared first by the liaison team before they were acted upon. The liaison team met with union or company officials to fulfill its communication and information functions and would not be involved in any way with enforcement, court proceedings, or investigations of crimes. The liaison team members visited all the picket lines, 'stopping to chat with individual pickets, thus becoming acquainted on a first name basis.' Uniformed police were kept to a minimum, and when a tense situation developed, a single patrol car was dispatched with one plainclothes and one uniformed officer. Heavy emphasis was placed on the injunction as the main tool for controlling picket behaviour. According to Starek, this approach was also being used quite effectively in Seattle, Washington (Seattle Police *Training*

Bulletin, December 1971), and the thrust of the article was an appeal to consider a broader application of the model across the province, presumably by the RCMP. Interestingly enough, this was presented entirely as an approach to strike policing; there was no reference to the broader area of public order policing, and when the RCMP later adopted this model in BC, it was presented and organized entirely as a method of policing industrial relations.

While the Burnaby police continued to work with this new 'liaison model' through the early 1970s, most RCMP detachments in BC and elsewhere in Canada had not yet adopted the approach. This meant that, like most municipal and provincial services in Canada at the time, there were no specialized personnel dealing with strikes, regular officers were being posted to monitor strikes around the clock, and police were still routinely responding to management requests to use significant force and even tactical squads to open picket lines. However, in 1975, RCMP Inspector B.L. Northorp wrote another limited publication for police audiences entitled *Policing a Labour Dispute*, which was intended to alert police agencies to the importance of this issue, particularly as a public relations problem (see chapter 3), and to articulate guiding principles that should inform the police role. Unlike Sgt Starek, Inspector Northorp was more explicit about his reasons for recommending changes in the police approach:

> The policing of labour disputes in Canada has been recognized as a problem by police departments for many years. There is no reason to believe this problem will ease. In fact, the opposite is probable. During this century, Canada is a country which has had a record of labour unrest and industrial conflict, with illegal and violent overtones, second only to the United States, and far greater than most Western European countries. The courts have also recognized the problem as one Canadian jurist said in 1966 that it was only until comparatively recently that the courts have found it necessary to impose jail sentences in matters arising out of labour management disputes. (2)

As well as being concerned about the levels of strike activity and violence, the inspector goes on to recognize the dilemma facing police in the context of several competing political views about the policing of strikes. In particular, he contrasts the statements of one judge, who stated unequivocally that police must protect the rights of employers to continue their operations and their property, with the statements of the prime minister of the day, Pierre Trudeau, who contended that 'labour should be able to say, unless I enjoy acceptable working conditions I will withdraw my labour and the operations will cease.' Finally, Northorp accepts to some extent the argument that police appear to be operating on the side of management when using force and that this use of force can lead to violent confrontation, with police ultimately being left to shoulder the blame.

Northorp suggests then that the status quo was inadequate and that police should be guided by peacekeeping, prevention, impartiality, and 'carefully planned steps' towards the use of force when peacekeeping attempts fail (5). He firmly rejects the idea that police should only be involved when there is unlawful activity and instead advocates a 'preventive role' (3). More specifically, a labour dispute policy should maintain a close relationship and rapport with management and union officials and gather information to assist in the advancement of their impartial role and to coordinate the reduction of unlawful incidents 'and reduce the need for uniformed personnel' (4–5).

Northorp envisioned an 'Industrial Relations Section' depending on the available resources and the striking of a 'police labour relations programme' on a more ad hoc basis where appropriate. He stipulates that the cultivation of trust relationships is necessary through communications prior to the heat of picket actions (5). Finally, he states that there is a police role even where there is no criminal activity and specifically argues against the view that police ought to be confined to enforcement. Explicitly tying the need for change in this area to police public relations and image, he notes, 'It must be understood that the preventive role in the handling of labour disputes [is] a normal part of a Police Community Relations programme' (5). Indeed, he notes later that 'a factor that everyone is conscious of these days is their public image and in labour disputes as in other situations, "incidents" are capitalized upon. Police must be alert to themselves being used or "set up" to accommodate an objective of either side' (6). Again: 'If the police enforcement is not handled carefully these citizens on strike could soon become anti-police' (7). This point is underlined with the argument that strikers are not criminals but 'neighbours and ordinary citizens' (6).

Northorp also rejuvenated the Burnaby strategy of preventive communications through information gathering and dissemination by the liaison officers. These officers were to meet with parties prior to a strike and provide them with contact information, parameters as to their role, and concrete photocopies of relevant law. The law having

been communicated beforehand, it was then a simple matter of rein-
forcement. 'The benefit of this procedure will be realized when serious
trouble erupts as the responsible citizen will sever himself from activity which is clearly illegal. The strategy in this procedure is to minimize the number of persons who will resist police direction or control
when it becomes necessary' (7). Northorp also advocated a more considered approach to the removal of barriers or blockages interfering
with rights to property and so forth. He argued that police should
themselves determine just how long an '"obstruction" could really exist before it really hampers the operation of the company. It is not surprising to hear companies mention times of 16 to 18 hours. With this
factor known, there is time for the pickets to conform by compliance'
(8). This strategy had the benefit, argued Northorp, of possibly removing the obstruction as quickly as may have been accomplished with
force and of doing so without violence and while retaining or winning
the respect of union, if not management, leaders.

Northorp considered the view that labour disputes are a civil matter
and that police should play no part in them. What he argued instead,
again following the example of the Seattle police force, is that labour
should be encouraged to police themselves, with the benefit of this policy being that police will be on record as having communicated appropriate regulations but limiting their exposure to damaging visibility.
As he reported, the relevant Seattle policy stated that the union representative should 'be encouraged to handle' incidents that arise 'if at all
possible.' Depending on union response, police may intervene with the
implicit if not explicit sanction of the union because the union must either say they can or cannot handle it.

From 1976 to 1982, the entire E Division of the RCMP, responsible for
policing much of British Columbia, began to institute aspects of the liaison approach, as did the City of Vancouver police department. Although RCMP police accounts make little reference to pressures from
the labour movement during this period, there were certainly prompts.
For example, in 1974, the United Steelworkers of America (USWA) director of public relations wrote an appeal to police departments calling
for a better understanding and better training for police officers in
labour dispute situations (Robinson, 1974). And it was soon after this
article that the RCMP began meeting with union leaders through the
BC Federation of Labour, the Canadian Labour Congress, and local labour councils. It was out of that series of meetings – which stretched
through to 1982 – that the RCMP finally established a full-time position

within the Crime Prevention and Community Policing Unit specifically for labour–management liaison for the entire province, along with a network of local detachment liaison officers available for assignment as the need arose (Lyall, 1984). The RCMP also instituted a program of workshops for police officers using labour lawyers and union and management representatives to educate the service on the area of labour relations and the 'peace officers' role (Lyall, 1984: 3). Again, police detachments and officers were encouraged to adopt an approach grounded in communication and negotiation with an intentional emphasis on restraining the use of force.

The timing of the RCMP's formal implementation of this approach in BC is particularly interesting in that it was around the same time, 1983, that the neo-conservative Social Credit government of W.A.C. Bennett proposed major regressive changes in labour legislation which prompted a massive province-wide labour campaign called the 'Solidarity Coalition' (Palmer, 1987; Panitch and Swartz, 2003). This included numerous large protests and strikes across the province, but police and union informant accounts of those events suggest that police use of the liaison approach may well have helped to cement the commitment of the RCMP and eventually the Vancouver Police to this approach. According to Sgt Lyall of the RCMP, the first RCMP Labour Communications NCO, the approach 'worked wonders.' As he wrote in another police report on the approach, despite 'the anger and frustration of many workers, cooperation between the police and labour in 1983 ended with tremendous credibility on all sides ... liaison defused potential problem areas when the dispute threatened to breach criminal law ... both parties always seeking to ensure public safety' (RCMP, 1983: 5). Indeed, this was quite remarkable in that there had been numerous protests of 20,000–60,000 people without incidents or arrests. Whether this period was instrumental in selling this approach to union leaders and activists is hard to say, but many of our labour informants recall that policing was not a concern during that period despite the large size of many protests.

The Vancouver police also developed a Labour Management Dispute Policy in the early 1980s that advised 'communication with representatives from each side' and 'arrest only if all other available remedies have failed' (Vancouver Police Department, Labour Management Disputes, Amended 83-05-10). Informants involved recalled some significant political controversies surrounding particular strikes during the mid- to late 1970s that they saw as prompting the change, including a postal strike and a construction strike. The Vancouver policy was developed and expanded over the 1980s and 1990s, emphasizing police neutrality, peacekeeping, and non-interference. Mirroring the RCMP documents, the Vancouver policy document states that 'police must take the position that a labour dispute is a civil matter which should be dealt with as a difference between individual parties ... the general policy is that every effort will be made to resolve labour disputes without involving the criminal courts or justice systems' (Campbell, 1985).

Although similar to the Vancouver policy in their principles, the RCMP structured their new approach without reference to public order more generally and explicitly on the policing of strikes. They established a full-time HQ position and several part-time detachment positions in industrial relations to carry out the labour relations policy. The Vancouver city police initially located the liaison function in the community policing section but then later integrated their policy and organization under one rubric, public order and event policing. As such, strikes, protests, and parades were all addressed by the same personnel and through the same basic liaison procedures.

Hamilton

In the more industrialized province of Ontario, and from all accounts quite independently of events in BC, the City of Hamilton Police (later the Hamilton-Wentworth Regional Police) also established a labour liaison position very early on – according to informants, the mid- to late 1960s. Hamilton is a heavily industrialized city with a long history of strong unions and considerable strike activity with a record of violence (Heron and Storey, 1986). While we were unable to locate written police records of this early period, retired police informants stated that a special liaison position called the 'labour relations officer' was established as a full-time position devoted specifically to communicate with unions and coordinate police responses during strikes. There was no link to other kinds of public order or crowd control situations. As described by our police informants, there were also no formal written policies outlining the procedures or principles for liaison, and relatively few changes in actual policing practices when this position was first created. Some of our informants also suggested that this was a low-status position often given to people 'who were unfit for anything else,' yet they also acknowledged that the liaison person began introducing some informal new rules of engagement which began to shape policing practices on the ground in important ways.

> R:[5] Back in the seventies, they did have one sergeant ... He was known as our labour relations officer. He was a liaison with the various unions in town and it was kind of a loose-net arrangement but it was an attempt to have one person accountable with what's happening with these strikes, rather than somebody being assigned. But again, he had no training whatsoever, he invented some of these things, like the ten-minute rule. I don't know where he got it from.
> I: You mean demanding ten minutes per vehicle for all strikes?
> R: Yes all strikes. He allowed them to hold up a vehicle to enter or exit for ten minutes. And then of course he would move in and they would exit or enter, whatever the case would be. (R37)

This notion of allowing picket lines to stop vehicles for a prearranged amount of time was also an important aspect of evolving practice in BC, and eventually this did become a standard practice among many police services across Canada, part of the negotiation of a picket line protocol explicitly designed to reduce picket line violence. Consistent with the liaison approach, the liaison officer in Hamilton maintained contact with the unions prior to and during strikes and sought to develop a rapport that could be used when encouraging picket lines to behave.

Right through to the 1970s, the Hamilton police did not formalize many of these evolving rules nor did they establish any clear written policy beyond the appointment of a labour relations officer. A number of key elements in the more current liaison approach were also apparently missing through the 1970s and 1980s, including the fact that the police still routinely used force to open picket lines on demand by management.

Informants' accounts also point to considerable inconsistency in the way in which different command officers approached strikes through the 1970s and 1980s.

> R: In 1972, '71, somewhere in around there, there was a big strike at, I think it was Massey-Ferguson, down Burlington and Wentworth, and I was a brand-new, green police officer. And they brought down the old deputy chief then, his name was R.W., brought down a hundred or so police officers, and our job was to break the picket lines. And we, there was you know, three or four hundred strikers, and we formed a wedge

and ran through the strikers, and with physical force, forced our way in. For no purpose that was ... obvious [to me].
I: You weren't opening up the line for anything or anybody?
R: No, we were just being ... You have to understand that I was not part of the decision-making process; I was cannon fodder if you will, and our only role was to break the picket lines so that people could go in and out. I don't recall. My memory is that we weren't trying to get anybody in; we were just trying to prove that we could break the picket line. And we did a lot of pushing and shoving. Nobody got seriously hurt, but in an incident like that everybody gets strained backs. And for years afterwards, there was this police officer and that police officer that was permanently injured ... there was no charges laid. Everybody was just power and control and we were showing them that we could do it and everybody shook hands and went away. (R3)

The Hamilton service began to formalize policy on strike policing in the early 1980s with the introduction of a new 'Position and Procedure [P and P] Policy for Strikes':

I: When did you first recall a formal protocol for how you were supposed to deal with these situations?
R2:[6] Oh yeah, yeah. We had, there was a P and P in place from earlier on, early 1980.
R1: A 'P and P' is a Position and Procedure.
I: RIGHT. So what was that at that point?
R2: Labour relations officer would be (laughs) ...
R1: Basically contacted and he'd handle it ...
I: ... and he would do anything in particular?
R2: Oh no, there was a big platform. I can't remember it, but basically it was a, you know, like for instance, don't have a loaded firearm at a strike, don't do this. You know, I can't remember all, well a lot of common-sense things. But, never, never said you can't arrest, but you know it was like, and we could, you know we would see the odd time guy, you imagine, grab people. And then you grab them, you're going to arrest them, then they go, ok, don't worry, we'll take it, we'll do the paperwork.
R1: Yep, it would cover a lot administrative things too, like communication, utilization of uniformed personnel and stuff like that. It was a fairly well documented thing. (R40)

However, as described by these and other informants, the 1980s P and P was much more consistent with the crowd control policies of other services, formalizing the manner and conditions in which police use of force would take place rather than outlining an elaboration of the liaison approach. But unlike many early crowd control policies, the Hamilton P and P on strikes outlined specific procedures for communication during the strike. Still, the policy as a whole was still largely reactive and situational with reference to the use of force – that is, the policy specified the need to communicate but communication was mainly in the form of warnings to the union rather than elements of negotiation and exchange with little about the need for preventive communication or negotiations prior to the strike.

According to several police informants, these final pieces in their liaison policy were developed later in the context of a looming strike at Hamilton's largest unionized employer, the Stelco steel plant. In the 1980s, Stelco was a large steel company with 13,000 unionized workers and a long history of sometimes bitter strikes including the well-known 1946 strike, a wildcat in 1966, and the longest Stelco strike ever in 1981 (Livingstone and Mangan, 1996; Palmer, 1992). Just before this, the reputation of the Hamilton police had also come under fire for its handling of a newspaper strike (*Hamilton Spectator*) in 1987. This had led to complaints from the Hamilton Labour Council and discussions with the mayor. However, it was not until 1989, with the prospect of another much larger strike in which the potential for violence seemed high, that the police made some major changes in their approach. As was common practice in Hamilton leading up to a Stelco strike, given its size, the labour relations officer was given responsibility to prepare and plan in advance of the strike. In this case, however, he decided to request a senior officer to whom he could report on a regular basis so that he could negotiate with the certain power of command behind him:

> R1: I ... said look, we need a senior officer that we can report to so that we're not trying to get to the chief or getting deputy chiefs or whatever under him. We wanted a specific person that ... be our contact and would be the person that would represent the chief and give us whatever instruction. (R40)

The superintendent responsible for the geographic area in which the strike was taking place was appointed to the job. Interestingly, this was a superintendent who had raised questions in the past within the service about the legal basis of police intervention in strikes. It was his view at the time that the police did not have a legal basis for opening picket lines since these were civil matters.

So strikes are exactly in that whole realm because I, as a young officer, and over the years I use to puzzle at the fact that, why are we at strikes, like what are we doing here? And the amount officers that were hurt, and what is that authority? And we used to debate these things at the police college. We used to do little workshops and we used to pose various scenarios. And I used to find to my horror, that nobody knows anything about this. And Hamilton being an industrial town has been plagued with strikes for many years, including the large one being Stelco and the steel companies. And yet, we knew less than many other police forces. (R37)

Rather than preparing for large-scale policing interventions, as was the common practice until then, the superintendent proposed a new policy which advocated non-intervention in the strike, with very limited monitoring, and one critical innovation, a requirement for injunctions *before any* action would be taken by the police. The policy also stressed that the enforcement of injunctions was the responsibility of the sheriff's office and any assistance by the police would be contingent on the situation and resource availability.

The new policy also involved more active pre-emptive communications with the union. Accordingly, police labour liaison went to both the union and the company to explain the new policy. They met with the president and members of the executive, and the response was positive. They were invited to speak to a larger body of stewards, who expressed a greater amount of suspicion, but in the final analysis, the police felt that they had made a good impression.

The main thing in that particular meeting which sort of came out of it, all the guys that came, not all the guys, but a majority of the guys that came down to the mikes were rabble rousers more or less. And they, they basically lambasted us as the old police department, 'Yeah, you're come down, you're going to beat us up and get your billies out and lock us all up and break our lines' and this and that. And I kept trying to tell them, we're not going to do that. And we gave them our policy and they wouldn't believe it. But they had to continually shout and yell and try and make their point. When it was over, and as we were leaving, one of the stewards came over to me and said, hey that wasn't us up at the microphones, we know what you're here for and thanks for coming. But, you know, and that sort of told us the story, you know, it was worth it doing it. (R40)

The company, however, responded forcefully, ultimately taking the police to court in an effort to compel them to provide the same level of service offered in the past – that is, the opening of picket lines.

> Stelco has so much power and so much money ... they entered us all including me, the chief, deputy chief, the entire board of the Hamilton police force, it was called the Hamilton Regional Police then, and that's exactly what happened. We ended up in Supreme Court before the various justices there, and of course the argument was, why you're not assisting and ignoring the various requests for assistance, by then there had been injunctions of course, from the local judges here, naming us. And our, my argument was, you can't name a police force in an injunction. It's a civil proceeding, it's under the ... act, it's section 156, it was then, and you can't name the police force. You can name the sheriff. (R37)

The police 'stuck to their guns,' won their case, and refused to intervene. This is not to say that there was no resistance within the police even at the senior levels (see below), and indeed the innovators themselves also understood their role as involving the need to challenge accepted truths as well as being able to weather criticism. However, as in BC, according to a number of Hamilton police informants, the value of the policy became apparent fairly quickly:

> R: That was the last strike I had dealings with. And I don't really remember any, well there might have been little strikes somewhere but. I do remember out in the west end there, there was quite a lot of violence broke out. Bikers were hired to drive Bruce Smith's trucks from Simcoe.
> I: When did you say this was?
> R: Oh, just shortly after the Stelco strike.
> I: So early 1990s.
> R: Yah, maybe early 91. And there was some press pictures on that one. But they drove up over lawns to get into and get around the strikers, and of course the strikers went absolutely nuts and they got on the cell-phone. Anyway, they broke windows, they didn't actually hurt anybody, but they did a lot of things. A lot of damage. Even damage to some of the houses. However the particular union involved at that time quickly got with the people, there was some of them charged. There was three uniformed officers arrived, one of them being female, and when they arrived, hundreds of people all dissipated. There wasn't one [assault on a] police

officer, or in any way. They were so impressed, the uniformed guys, they were completely sold in that, 'Hey, this does work. Because we're not the bad guys here.' (R37)

By 2000, when the main interviews were done with senior command officers in the force, there was very little controversy if any about a policy of non-intervention, whether in strikes or protests. And in one other innovative move, the Hamilton police civilianized the position of labour liaison. Although divisional liaison officers were maintained, the central coordinator is now a civilian. The Hamilton administration describes this move as 'largely a financial move,' but this also reinforces the overall impression that police see many of the preventive functions of liaison as not requiring police powers.

Windsor

Although also widely known as a heavily industrialized and unionized city, the Windsor Police Department did not formally adopt any elements of a liaison approach until 1987. Prior to this, the department had no formal positions or personnel assigned to strike duties, there was no written policy or procedure, and no specific training had been given beyond crowd control and riot policing tactics. Police also commonly intervened directly in picket lines whenever management requested assistance in gaining access to their property.

However, unlike Hamilton, both police and unions in Windsor report that picket line violence was infrequent even before the change in policy. According to various current and retired union informants, this was largely due to the fact that Windsor's major employers, both the Big Three auto firms and the large number of smaller but high-skill tool and die firms, did not use replacement workers, nor did they tend to continue production using management and supervisory staff. As they recall the strikes of the 1960s and 1970s, the police were rarely a problem. As one retired picket captain recalled:

The talk on the picket line was always about whether the fuzz would come by and break heads but they [the police] never really did much. The picket lines were pretty quiet 'cause management was not trying to keep the plant going. They [the police] stayed off to the side and only came in when things were getting out of hand. There were always hotheads and when some guys were drunk and we couldn't control them, then the police were there. (R45)

However, as in Hamilton, when replacement workers were used in Windsor strikes, and the local labour movement responded in organized force to block access to the plant, the police routinely responded to management requests for assistance. For example, when the food processing giant ADM used replacement workers in a strike early in 1987, the local union movement led by the CAW responded en masse by setting up large picket lines which refused to allow buses or other vehicles to pass. There were significant confrontations, property damage, and arrests as the Windsor police force used riot police and arrests to open the picket line.

As in Hamilton and Burnaby, the confrontations and resulting bad press in the ADM strike may well have been an important factor in shaping the shift in police policy soon after, following another politically charged incident in 1987 involving strikers, this time a wildcat strike at a small auto parts plant run by a company called Sheller-Globe. Sheller-Globe was a Toledo, Ohio–based manufacturer of steering wheels with plants in Indiana, Michigan, and Ontario which employed 200 people in its Windsor operation. After a lead-up period of stepped-up production (12–16-hour shifts, 7 days per week), CAW workers of the Windsor plant were told that it would be closed because of declining demand, throwing all 200 out of work. In the midst of a growing debate over free trade and evidence of continuing manufacturing losses on both sides of the border, the newly formed CAW, which had broken away from the UAW, had announced a firm activist strategy to challenge plant closures, endorsing plant occupations as one possible tactic (Gindin, 1989; 1995). On 9 May, three days after the company's announcement to the workers, eighteen employees (later joined by Local 195 President Bruce Boyd) barricaded themselves in the plant in a wildcat strike, with some sixty or so keeping a vigil outside the gates. The protesters were also joined by NDP MPPs Howard McCurdy and Dave Cooke and by city council member Donna Champagne.

Just after midnight on 11 May, twenty-five police officers with long batons, helmets, and visors entered the plant and arrested all the strikers on charges of trespassing. After loading the strikers into a van, they formed two police lines, and holding their batons in front of them in a quick march, they escorted the van through pickets at the gate. As in the ADM strike, there had been no significant attempt to negotiate a settlement, with the only communication being a terse ultimatum to vacate the premises under the threat of a forceful removal. As one senior police respondent who was involved recalled:

> Management wanted them the hell out of the building – so what do we do? We talked a little bit [with the union] first to say you're not going to be able to occupy this building. If you don't come out we are going to come in and get you ... [but] we didn't communicate properly with them. Management [of Sheller Globe] had given us direction and so now we moved and, [laughter] God, they went in there with those big long wooden sticks, they were horribly threatening and we had just acquired new helmets, new blue shiny like you were going to climb into a space ship and they went in with these helmets and these clubs and the media just picked that up and the women were screaming and tying themselves to water coolers. There was a hearing called. The labour community was up in arms like you wouldn't believe ... there were, it seems to me, head-lines for a week [in the *Windsor Star*] ... And clearly I think that that was really the beginning of what we knew we had to do in terms of develop-ing a policy. (R46)

The *Windsor Star* carried articles along with critical editorials and let-ters, while organized labour called for an inquiry and major changes in policing practices, announcing as well their withdrawal of support for the mayor, David Burr, when he failed to reassure them that the police would be taken to task. Councillor Ted Bounsall was reported in the *Windsor Star* as 'blasting' the police for taking tactics that were 'a departure from the norm' of those used in other Ontario cities (12 May 1987).

Two weeks after the event, on 25 May, a motion was passed in city council in which the municipality asked the police chief for a full report on Sheller-Globe. The chief was asked to respond to four questions: whether charges against Sheller-Globe pickets would be pursued; what were the conditions under which the decision to take action at Sheller-Globe was made; what special training was given to police officers in negotiations and in the 'special labour history' of Windsor; and whether that history was 'taken into account when mak-ing important and sensitive decisions' (Windsor City Council Minutes, 705/87). In effect, the police were explicitly asked by the municipality to account for their actions with reference to their (political) labour sensitivity. In addition, the chief was asked about the practices of other police forces in the province in similar circumstances, whose input or consultation was gathered in the decision, and what the financial cost of the action was.

The Windsor Police Board also held a hearing to take testimony from police and labour officials involved. Out of this review came a recommendation to establish a labour liaison position. A deputy chief and a sergeant were required to investigate policies elsewhere in the province and wrote a lengthy report recommending a number of major policy changes. As one of the appointees recalls:

> I was ordered to go around Ontario and various departments and interview them on how their tactics work, what their policies were. So I started, I guess, with the London Police. I went there, I went to the Metropolitan Toronto, I went to the Regional Peel, a few other departments. I was impressed with Toronto and also with Peel Regional [both of which were earlier adopters of the approach]. They took a different strategy and policy than I'd ever seen ... Now what they did is they developed a liaison, and first of all he got to know the unions and the union leaders and the executive. Toronto, they had a group of officers, low-key, now they were more or less responsible to interact with unions and management and try to explain the role of the police although they had no power over the ranking officer in the district who could still handle it however he wanted. We changed that in our model so that the liaison person was the ranking officer. (R47)

The Windsor service adopted a strike liaison model based on this report, appointing a sergeant as well as a constable assistant to the liaison positions. The policy had all the core elements of the liaison policies developed in BC with an emphasis on prior communications, negotiations prior to any use of force, self-policing, and minimal police presence and non-involvement in opening picket lines. The new policy's first major test was a national postal strike. For the first time, the police went to see the union executive before a strike to explain their new policy:

> I approached the union executive ... we went and talked to them and brought out the appropriate laws, assaulting a police officer, obstructing a person's use of property ... we also explained to them that they did have

a right to stop people but only for the purpose of informing them of the reason for a strike and not for threats or anything like that ... So we made it clear we were going to be here, that we are going to take a low-key approach ... very minimal amount of officers and that we expect the union executive to police themselves and if they can't we will. We told them that this is a new policy that we were trying to work out and if it didn't work out the night sticks, helmets, and everything would come out and physical force would be used where necessary and they would feel the full effect of the law. (R48)

According to the police, they developed a good relationship with the union when the strike was called a few days later:

We came to a very good relationship – we did have a minimal of people and they would ask us questions like can we do this, can we do that. We developed a very good rapport. One time we had the CAW, came around noon [support picket] – had over 2000 people; again we had spoken with likes of Gary Parent [Windsor-Essex Labour Council president] and other union leaders who were there and with just six officers you could hear the postal people going through the crowds telling people not to touch the cops. We never had one officer touched, no violence, no assaults on officers the whole strike. (R48)

As part of their new protocol, the police also had a pre-strike meeting with post office management, but again, as in Hamilton, the management reaction was not positive. Management complained about the lack of police and direct assistance in opening the lines and called to the chief demanding more support, which the chief refused.

They wanted the numbers of officers like they had at the postal pickets in Toronto, Quebec, New Brunswick, Halifax. You would see maybe 100 officers at their picket lines. We never had more than me, Sgt Mcknight maybe two or three others. We had no violence and only one arrest for someone throwing a projectile through a window. (R48)

Although there was again resistance within police, both higher up and at the front line, our informants suggest that a Police Services Board member and a handful of officers from the middle ranks were instrumental 'insiders' in pushing for reform. One of these, a police officer credited by others within the service as having been an important contributor to the success of the new policy's adoption, argued that the failings of the 'traditional' approach were apparent to him as early as the late 1960s. He said that during one of his first assignments to a strike (at Plasticast), he had questioned an inspector's decision to speak to the management and not to the union (to which the inspector then replied, 'Get this radical out of here' [P6]). Subsequently, in strikes throughout the 1970s he recalled a conversation with the CAW president of local 195 in which they talked about a particularly nasty strike at Dominion Forge in which they 'both agreed there had to be a better way.' The Police Board member also recalls a similar discussion where it was agreed that 'this wasn't doing the reputation of the city any good and wasn't really doing anybody any good' (P5). It was his opinion that the policy, therefore, was 'a natural evolution' of craft development that had taken some time to fulfill:

I don't know whether I mentioned the need for a fresh approach, a new take, but it was certainly quite obvious to me to take this fresh approach and that approach should be based on this philosophy I expressed to you ... I felt that members of the board should function in much the same way as directors of business corporations. With the same objectives in mind, namely efficiency, cost-effectiveness, and sensitivity to the needs of employees, the consumer, and the persons effected, the now-called stakeholders. So I was very concerned about organization. I was very much concerned about the relationship of the police to the several constituencies, and that simply came down to the police treating everybody in an even-handed fashion, being sensitive to need and being proactive in achieving those results without [violence?]. We [the board] simply said this is the way it's going to be. (R49)

As in Hamilton, the police were criticized for their action at Sheller-Globe in that they had shown little concern for the labour history of Windsor. In presenting Windsor as 'a labour town with a labour history,' the municipal politicians were recognizing the significance of labour's power and legitimacy within the local political context. This partly reflected the substantial and frequently visible political and social roles that labour played in the community as advocates and social activists in various areas of government policy, including housing, the environment, immigration, health, and welfare. Throughout the postwar period, employers set up shop in Windsor, recognizing it as a place in which there would be a concerted effort to certify. As one labour respondent put it: 'I think the relationship we've built up with the [Chrysler] corporation obviously filters through to the rest of the community, and I think the police understand that' (L8). Smaller employers attempting to challenge this relationship have found that the CAW has effectively used its large numbers of Big Three members to challenge them:

> I think smaller workplaces have a little more difficult time, it would all depend but if we had to put massive numbers [of people] out there [on the picket line], it would be an advantage for us. It's always a power play. If there's more of us then who's going to win here. But I guess that relationship has been built up regardless how small or how big the workplace, the CAW has been able to build up a good relationship with city hall and city police.[I: Is city hall pretty important?] Absolutely, that door is always open to us; regardless of the circumstances we know we can call the mayor, we can get his support on certain things. (R50)

In addition to the defence of unionism in industry, the union movement in Windsor puts substantial resources into the local municipal and provincial elections. Consequently, it is perhaps less than surprising that municipal politicians responded to labour demands and that there was a strong community response to the images of police in full gear arresting women workers. The subtext was almost tangible: for whom did the police think they were working?

Along with its local political importance, Sheller-Globe was situated in a national and even continental context. Here we are beginning to see, more explicitly, aspects of neo-liberalism and globalization playing a direct role in emerging labour conflict and changes in labour tactics. We found evidence that the Sheller-Globe incident was played up by the provincial union leadership to show up the deficiencies of the Canada–U.S. Free Trade Agreement. The women barricaded in a doomed plant were a convenient symbol of the threat to job security which free trade was seen to pose for workers throughout Canada. They were offered up in a politically charged context in which unemployment, welfare rolls, abandoned plants, bankruptcies, and job losses were all on the rise, with free trade as the most obvious cause. This politicization of Sheller-Globe was not entirely lost on police management. As one senior police officer argued:

The whole thing was engineered. We learned later that [CAW President] Bob White was there. Which clearly indicated that it was a set-up. The persons who were sitting in had access to a telephone line and they arranged in advance for photographers to be present. (R51)

Liaison Policing Catches On across the Country

Liaison policies in strikes became increasingly common across the country over the course of the 1980s, with some of the earliest innovators being the Peel Regional, York Regional, and Toronto Services in Ontario; St John's in Newfoundland; and Calgary in Alberta. The bulk of the remaining services made the move in the early 1990s so that by the mid-1990s virtually every service in Canada had formally adopted some version of a liaison approach. In 1996, the Ontario government adopted policing standards for strikes which reflected the liaison philosophy, effectively forcing the few remaining services without such policies to adopt them. The BC Attorney General's office implemented a similar advisory to its police services shortly before this (Civil Disorder Policy, 26 July 1990, revised 1 October 1999), although according to our informants from the A-G's office, this was prompted mainly by environmental and Native protests than by strikes in particular. Although many of the provincial divisions of the RCMP had moved much earlier to a liaison approach, most notably in British Columbia, the service adopted a new Canada-wide policy on protest policing in 1999 which followed the liaison model after a number of controversial events in BC (APEC demonstration, Stanley Cup riot) and New Brunswick (Burnt Church).

As reflected in the common accounts of strikes and protests across Canada from labour, management, and police informants, some clarity and consistency in the application of the liaison approach appeared over time, likely in part as more and more services codified emerging practices in formal policies. The first step in most services was the development of a new policy document. Although the policy documents in some services were far more detailed on procedures and principles than others, nearly all of the major police services in Canada now have some form of written policies related to strike and protest policing. To be more specific, in our survey of thirty-eight services (100,000+ population) in Canada conducted in 2000–1, thirty-three of the services reported written policies pertaining to strikes (see table 4.2). Twenty-one of these services reported separate strike policies that were usually

Table 4.2
Variations in liaison structure – Distribution of police services

	Yes	No	Other	N
Formal written labour liaison policies	86%	14%	–	38
Formal written protest policies	58%	42%	–	38
Separate strike/protest policies	64%	36%	–	33
Integrated strike/protest policies	36%	64%	–	33
Separate distinct labour liaison office	13%	87%		38
	FT	PT	No LRO	
Full time (No=PT) labour liaison officer	39%	47%	13%	38

developed first, while twelve had integrated or combined public order and strike procedures in a single policy. Twenty-two of the services reported distinct protest policies. Among the three municipal services and two provincial services reporting no policy, three reported standard practices and procedures that were consistent with a liaison approach.

The second major development in most services was the creation of specific positions, often titled labour relations officers, or LROs, and/or departments for dealing with strikes and/or protests. In most municipal services (55 per cent), this specialized function of labour liaison was performed part-time, with time allocated, depending on the number of strikes and the demands of the strikes, for liaison intervention. Provincial police such as the provincial RCMP detachments, the Sûreté du Québec, and the OPP had full-time liaison officers at provincial headquarters who provided advice and assistance to a number of field officers who performed liaison work on the ground on an 'as-needed' basis. In the OPP, for example, the front-line labour and protest liaison functions are performed by a community liaison officer who has a range of community policing duties. In many services, such as the Vancouver police, the liaison officer or unit is responsible for all types of public order situations, including parades, protests, and strikes. In other services, a stronger distinction is consistently maintained between labour liaison functions and positions and other public order situations. As noted, in Hamilton, a separate civilian liaison position specifically for labour and reporting directly to the deputy chief was established, although again with a supportive network of part-time police liaison at the division levels. Public order had a different unit and personnel entirely. In Toronto, the full-time central labour liaison positions were initially housed in community relations and then moved into the public order unit under a central command, while part-time liaison personnel, often community relations officers, were housed in each division. Although the central Toronto liaison office was formally defined as strike liaison, it was often involved in protest events and staff generally moved back and forth from strike to protest liaison and public order roles. In Windsor, the part-time liaison officer was located in the traffic division. The ranks were also quite different in different services, with sergeants playing the role in Windsor and Vancouver, and constables in Toronto. The command powers of the liaison also varied on the ground in that some services required that their liaison officers work through a regular command hierarchy rather than being able to direct other officers in the field. About half of the respondents (54 per cent) reported that they were usually in command on site as labour liaison officers, while the other half acted only in an advisory capacity.

All services presented these specialized liaison positions as critical to their approach and as requiring a high level of communication and conflict resolution skills. Still, very few services provided any extra training; nor did the selection procedures for the positions require specialized education or experience. In some services, recruiting seemed to be related to activism in the police association, but, more commonly, recruiting was based on recognized communication and negotiation skills.

Most policies lay out broadly similar procedures along the lines specified originally by RCMP Sgt Starek and Inspector Northorp in their 1970s articles, but there are some notable differences between services. For example, the majority of services make contact with both the union and the employer just prior to or just after a strike begins, but some services are much more proactive than others in monitoring negotiations and labour board reports and in initiating the contacts. In BC, the RCMP liaison officer routinely visits union offices to 'chat' with union leaders about upcoming negotiations as well as meeting directly with them just before any strikes. The Hamilton labour liaison coordinator is similarly proactive in maintaining contacts and monitoring the progress of all contract negotiations. However, the majority of the services – and this is strongly related to whether there are full-time or part-time liaison personnel – report that they rely almost entirely on either management or the union to contact them initially when there is a strike. They are not involved in any ongoing way with the development of community relations with union leaders or in monitoring contract negotiations in order to anticipate upcoming strikes. In other words, they rely entirely on the unions and employers to take responsibility for notifying the police.

This suggests that some services are less committed to the 'primary' preventive aspects of the liaison model, operating more as troubleshooters who negotiate or mediate conflicts should they arise.

Whether the police or the union makes the initial contact, the liaison officer, who is almost always in civilian attire, may set up a face-to-face meeting with both parties in the dispute. Again, this varies as some services appear to rely more on phone calls as sufficient, although services often assess the need for face-to-face meetings on whether the two parties are considered knowledgeable about 'proper' strike protocol and the nature of the police role and on whether there is any perceived prospect of 'trouble' surrounding such issues as size of strike, location, safety considerations, and past strike history. The knowledge and experience of union leaders and managers are especially seen to influence the extent of needed communication, but it appears that in practice many services are not as attentive to these differences as others, again suggesting that services vary in their level of sophistication and attention to intelligence and proactivity.

There were also some differences in the ongoing monitoring of the strike. While a good number of forces (N=17) kept in daily contact with the parties in every dispute, many forces (N=13) were only in contact when there were perceived problems or risks of trouble, notice of which would often be relied upon to come from the parties. In many cases, uniforms were told to stay away from the pickets, and the labour liaison people were typically on call if anything developed to advise or direct any interventions. Other services actively encouraged patrol officers and sergeants to visit the site regularly and strike up a relationship with picket captains and the union executive. In talking about an OPSEU strike, a Toronto labour liaison recalls:

> One of the things we encouraged supervisors and front-line officers to do was strike up relations; the ones who were going to be called to respond to the sites, we encouraged that because they're going to be there on a regular basis then, don't wait until a problem arises. Start early and develop relationships with these people so that when you roll up to a scene, you can okay bob. c'mon you stepped over the line a little here ... and because the relationship is developed more, they're more apt to influence them ... So we stress the development of relationships. (R32)

There were also variations in terms of surveillance. About one-third of the services (38 per cent) were sometimes active in video surveillance to ensure that they had sufficient evidence if needed to file charges, but very few (N=3) reported that they often or very often engaged in surveillance. About half of the services (51 per cent) avoided video surveillance entirely on the grounds that this was interpreted negatively by labour since it presumed a high potential for criminal behaviour, undermining the trust between police labour liaison and the union. However, almost all services routinely advised employers to do their own videotaping for use in any injunction proceedings, which is one of the common services offered by security firms. As one respondent described his approach:

> I convince picketers, security companies, and management to get cameras. [Not us.] I am unbiased. Why would I be filming one side? (R25)

The majority of the services stated that they could usually or always count on the labour leadership to exercise control over the union membership in a strike situation, although some respondents stressed that there were always exceptions. Nevertheless, close to half of the services (46 per cent) still felt that it was very important to have 'unofficial sources' of information to assess the potential for trouble, and very few (12 per cent) thought such information was not important at all. Again, this often depends on the stakes involved. For example, in talking about a truckers' blockade of the Windsor-Detroit bridge, one senior officer recalls the importance of a particular informant:

> No, the informant that we had was, how do I put this, he had an inside track, knew what the next moves were going to be by the fellow here that was organizing and would call us and say 'Willy is considering next Wednesday doing this and if you guys want to maintain good order out there then I thought you should know that.' Well, it was absolutely essential to good operations and very helpful to us. (R25)

However, it appears from the descriptions of procedures that in most contexts the collection of such intelligence was not normally conducted in an active fashion unless there was some other indication of potential for trouble or if a union was seen as associating with wrong 'types.'

> Our intelligence units were gathering information on the main core of people that would go out there and cause severe disruptions. [But] the intelligence services they weren't interested so much in the labour unions,

they were more interested, they seemed like they were more interested in something like the Ontario Coalition Against Poverty where they would come out and they would practice at beating police lines and you know. And it just turned out that at that time OPSEU was sponsoring, not so much sponsoring but they were contributing to OCAP, contributing funds. So and they were contributing ... as well because when OCAP showed up, OPSEU were there or some of the other groups were there and they had their flags and they had their banners so you could identify different groups. So our industrial liaison became more and more involved [with OCAP demonstrations]. (R55)

At the same time, it is important to note that for the police an important sign of potential trouble is the way the unions or protest groups respond to liaison efforts:

I. How important is intelligence?
R. We get a sense from day one. We have a number of [possible] sources but the primary one is our industrial relation guys. If the IR guy comes to us and says, 'You know the union won't talk to us. We know they're pissed off and we have a sense that certain things are going to happen.' Then you know that's a source of intelligence we have to give a lot of credibility to. (R60)

As such, liaison officers are themselves important sources of intelligence, intelligence that in turn can form the basis of a more aggressive strategy of monitoring and information gathering.

Another key feature of the liaison approach is the negotiation of strike protocols between the employer and the union, setting out how the picket lines will be conducted and where and how the picket line can be crossed and by whom. Here again there is a fairly significant split between services with respect to the level of involvement in discussions or negotiations of picket line protocols. While 40 per cent of forces were actively involved in the process (often or very often), 49 per cent simply advised the parties to work it out among themselves, in which case the police stayed completely out of the protocol negotiation process (rarely or never negotiated protocols) (see table 4.3). Those who had withdrawn from the protocol process tended to look to recent court cases, with particular reference to the decision on picketing at the Corel Centre in the Ottawa area (*Ogden Entertainment Services v. Retail/ Wholesale Canada, Canadian Service Sector Division of the U.S.WA, Local 440,*

April 2, 1998), as the basis for their reluctance (TP3 and HP2; Observations, Industrial Liaison Policing Workshop, Hamilton, Ontario, 2001). In that decision, the court ruled that a police-negotiated protocol to allow pickets to delay cars entering the property had no standing in law. The police came under some significant criticism from both the court and the public for allowing the protocol to endanger public safety and cause excessive traffic delays.

Those who persisted with protocols argued that it was essential to have some understanding about the practical implications of the pickets' rights to communicate and the employers' rights to access and use their property. Although most police services report that they do not suggest any specific terms for the protocol, some unions report and liaison officers acknowledge that police do try to influence its content, if not initially, then later if certain 'problems' develop. Police report that their major concerns are safety and traffic problems, and on that basis they seek to reshape or influence picket line protocols and behaviour in substantial ways.

Education is another core component of liaison practice, and again the services varied in the effort they put into their educational materials. The Hamilton police, for example, had a series of pamphlets and booklets outlining the liaison policy and the key laws pertaining to picketing, while other services only had a single pamphlet listing the various offences that could lead to charges or arrest. Still others had nothing at all. This relative commitment to information was closely tied to the overall level of communicative activism demonstrated by the liaison officers, which was in turn a good predictor of incidents of violence or arrests – that is, the more proactive services reported fewer problems of this nature.

As suggested already, some important operational principles continued to evolve through the 1990s. Perhaps the last vestige of the old policing regime to fall was the idea that it was the police role to escort management or replacement workers or trucks with product through the line. As one senior officer recalls, this was quite a paradigm shift in that police came to realize that there was no law compelling or even justifying police intervention in this manner.

> I used to believe that a person or employer had a right to enter and exit their property. But where is that written? It isn't anywhere ... I have 218 police officers that I can deploy on this strike, but ... I had no authority to open a picket line at a strike. It's merely a civil dispute. There is a

criminal law about watching and besetting a residence but what about a place of business? I was amazed, flabbergasted, that we, as police, over the years, over the generations, had sort of filled the gap with unofficial duties that suited our purpose at the time, favouring, of course, business with these decisions. (R37)

Although less legalistic and critical in their analysis, liaison officers for half of the services (50 per cent) were adamant that they never or rarely escort management or product through picket lines (see table 4.3), while even fewer said they have anything to do with escorting replacement workers (20 per cent). Services, including the early innovators, claimed that they had made the final hurdle in their policy shift in the early to mid-1990s as the critical step in cementing the foundation of the liaison approach as a substantive change in policing practice, since it provided substance to the claim of neutrality and allowed the liaison police to build trust with labour. Still, it is also the one area where there was considerable variation in policy in that there were still seven services (20 per cent), five of which were in Quebec,[7] reporting that they often or very often escorted management and product through the line. Significantly, these services also reported more strike incidents where they used force and made arrests (r=.372 p<.05). Again these were also the services that tended to exhibit less emphasis on communication, but, more generally, the services that reported less emphasis on preventive communication and maintenance of police/labour relations reported higher levels of arrests.

Most police services rely heavily on the courts as a basis for deferring action – advising the parties to seek civil injunctions if they object to the actions of strikers or protesters (de Lint, Gostlow, and Hall, 2005). Many services have a policy of insisting that the offended party also return to the courts (or in BC, the Labour Relations Board) to seek court penalties and/or an enforcement order for the sheriff and insist that it is the responsibility of the sheriff to enforce an injunction order. While there are some legal judgments in which judges are critical of the police refusal to act more forcefully, the general judiciary tendency has been to accept the approach as an important element of keeping the peace (*S.R. McKay v. Attorney General of Nova Scotia, Nova Scotia Court of Appeal, July 15, 1994; Canada Post v. CUPW, British Columbia Supreme Court, November 18, 1991*). In our case study interviews, police reported that they seek to maintain this position of non-intervention as long as possible, and this includes refusing to use force even if the initial

Table 4.3
Police actions on the line

	Percentage of services				
	Never	Rarely	Sometimes	Often	Very often
Services that escort management	34.3%	20%	25.7%	8.6%	11.4%
Services that escort trucks with products/machinery	31.4%	31.4%	22.9%	5.7%	8.6%
Services that escort replacement workers	40%	40%	11.4%	5.7%	2.9%
Services that negotiate protocols	34.3%	14.3%	11.4%	17.1%	22.9%

injunction is not obeyed by the strikers (e.g., H2, H7, T3, T5, V1, V2, W1, W2.). If an injunction is broken, the police will attempt to mediate and gain compliance through persuasion, again often playing for time in the hope that the union will accept that they have made their point.

If this fails, the complainant is advised to go back to the courts or the labour board for a resolution, which often means seeking a court enforcement order to comply. Critically for the police, the court may allocate specific penalties such as hefty fines for non-compliance, and that, ultimately, is the principle threat which the police look for as a means of forcing union compliance. The sheriff's office is usually charged with enforcing this order, but the police can be called in by the sheriff for assistance, although even here some police services argue that they are reluctant to intervene quickly. At this point, they again seek to convince the union to comply, making it clear that the police will have to reluctantly intervene soon given the court order. For the most part, they claim that this is rarely necessary since the threat of substantial fines is usually sufficient.

Why the Change? The Police View

Although a small number of police services in Ontario were forced to adopt the liaison approach through central provincial government policy in 1995, most municipal services had already adopted the liaison approach on their own, and to this day most provinces have still not implemented provincial requirements. When asked why they thought their service had shifted to a liaison approach, most police informants from both the case studies and the survey interviews gave multiple reasons. Many in the survey (36 per cent) thought that local political controversies or pressures along with negative media coverage surrounding specific incidents had been instrumental in pushing their police administration to act, while all the cases studies seemed to point to local political or public objections to police use of force as playing significant if not critical watershed roles in leading to the adoption of the liaison police.

Some also believed that there was a broader cultural shift in public tolerance for the police use of force which they connected in part to the increased legal recognition of labour and human rights from the 1960s to the 1980s:

> Violence begets violence. If you push them, they're going to push back. If you drive a car fast through the picket line, they're gonna, some of them are gonna get hurt and they'll throw rocks and perhaps injure the driver. You start clubbing them and they gonna hit you back. Violence begets violence, and I think our culture, in my lifetime, or our lifetime, has certainly come around to a point where we all sort of vaguely understand that. The Ipperwash incident is fairly symptomatic of what I'm talking about. It may or may not have been a peaceful demonstration. It certainly was a peaceful occupation and for whatever reason the OPP decided to break that line and there we have it. (R38)

While the 1982 Charter of Rights and Freedoms was seen by some as an important impetus for change in policy, others tended to downplay the Charter and legal changes more generally. As one officer put, 'It wasn't a legal change, it was a change in philosophy' (H10). On the other hand, many liaison officers pointed to changes in labour law as shaping police thinking. For example, in Ontario, a number of officers pointed to the 1992 NDP government's Bill C-40, with its ban on replacement workers, as sending a signal to police:

> The 1992 Bill C-40 section 11.1 where there was, dealt with picket lines, definitely influenced our current approach. The legislation changed with the new [neo-conservative] government [in 1995] but the benefits that police services found in dealing with pickets because of Bill 40 outweighed any new changes that came about with the later legislation. Once we saw the benefits of dealing with picket lines in a non-confrontational manner, we decided to continue to handle it this way. (R64)

While acknowledging broader cultural changes, others argued that there had been very little external political pressure and that the impetus for change came entirely from within the police service. The importance of internal reformers at various levels in the police hierarchy was particularly evident in both the Hamilton and Windsor cases, but our informants also pointed to significant dissatisfaction among the rank and file over picket line duties as playing a role. As one put it, 'As I see it there was already a shift [early on] by individual officers saying "We're going to handle labour relations a little differently," and then you end up with the whole service making actual changes like "No, we're not going to break open picket lines"' (H6). While informants often noted that there were always some constables and sergeants who retained the view that liaison policing 'coddles criminals,' they asserted that most police officers really welcomed and even encouraged the shift because they disliked the task so much, in part because they saw it as dangerous work that often resulted in injuries, but also because they were often uncomfortable with using force against workers on strike, people who in their eyes were law-abiding citizens:

> I'll tell you, initially when I came on the job in the 1970s, and Art [pseudonym] is probably the same way, you'll find any uniformed officer out there didn't like going to strikes, cause you knew strikes could develop into confrontation. And it just wasn't something policemen liked doing ... you have police on one side and picketers on the other lining up and grabbing each other, half the time you have a father and son lining up with each other. (R40)

> I think police officers today are more happy with the idea of consulting type of way or peaceful way. They feel more comfortable doing that role than the conflictual thing. Because either way if you take the conflict and it ends up in violence, the appearance is you are on one side or the other. (R34)

Increased union militancy and consciousness among the police themselves were also cited as important by some police liaison in creating this dissatisfaction among the police over existing practices:

> Part of my culture, my experience in Hamilton is the 1946 Stelco strike, and my father did not work in Stelco at that time, but many people that he

worked with knew he started there in '47 or '48, and the Canadian government nationalized Stelco, and I'm not sure if you know all this. They
nationalized Stelco and tried to break the line with the RCMP and the
army and failed miserably, and there was a huge uproar in Hamilton that
exists to this day about trying to break the Stelco union. You're not going
to do it, not ever. And that's part of their [the police] understanding, their
experience. (R40)

Increasing professionalization and levels of education within the police were also seen as making the use of force more and more unpalatable among the rank and file, as well as shifting emphasis to other
skills such as communication and negotiation capacities:

In my opinion, the number one reason for the change is it reflects the
change in the policing approach more generally – we are generally much
less likely to use violence than we were in the past, to respond with physical force. The other thing is that the police profession or occupation, has
generally become better educated. I think that the old position ethically is
not tenable with many more officers and as those officers have worked
their way up into positions where they are decision-makers, their personal views are reflected in policy. (R6)

I don't think they're coming in now with less than university. You've got a
different calibre of cop operating out there in the policemen where there's
a little more flexibility, a little bit more diversity. (R34)

Even with respect to these latter internal dynamics, informants often
pointed to broader changes in policing with particular reference to
community- and prevention-oriented policing which some linked to
changes in society, again mainly the shifting expectations regarding the
right to strike and protest, and the unsuitability of force. A number of
informants also argued that changes in strike and public order thinking were instrumental in encouraging the broader expansion of these
ideas to the realm of crime prevention. As one put it, 'community policing has the same philosophy but liaison policing predated many of
those changes' (R33).

Perhaps not surprisingly, the police did not couch their explanations
in terms of privatization but they did often suggest that resource issues
within a context of force cuts in the 1980s and early 1990s had played a
critical role in gaining administration support:

What drove it was the police resources. That's where we were coming from. C.P. and I both had that experience of breaking the picket lines in the past and we clearly understood in 1990 that we didn't have the resources to break the Stelco picket line, the union picket line. (R34)

Hamilton has suffered through this economically with plant change. We don't have the tax base we had thirty, forty years ago, so if this police department is undermanned, understaffed and I think part of thing was also Miller was looking at the facts, it was the chief at the time that, we were basically were saying we can get through this strike with less staff tied up and it's gonna cost you less in overtime and that had to be entertaining to him cause previously, you could, I can remember, you know, I first came on the job and it was Dominion Glass, and it got to the point, I can remember they must have had twenty, thirty guys every day doing nothing but the strike, all the big guys or whatever. (R40)

Here many acknowledged a period of rationalization when efforts were made to define the core business of the police while seeking efficiencies through increased specialization and use of technologies. While public order remained an important police function – and, indeed, by some accounts may have been deemed more significant within the creation of specialized crowd control policies and squads – a number of police reformers recalled making specific arguments to administrators about using liaison practices to reduce overtime savings and to keep limited police officer resources on the street responding to crime.

While very few of our informants cited specific research on public order violence as a basis for the change, many felt that it was increasingly common knowledge among the police that police intervention often contributed to the violence rather than controlling it. Some of the advocates of the liaison approach expressed this view somewhat differently by suggesting when the police intervened in strikes using force, the focus shifted away from the labour dispute and onto the police, ultimately prolonging the dispute. As put by one informant,

We have all seen instances such as the Gainers situation in Edmonton (1985?), where police in riot gear are involved in extended confrontations with the disputants. The actual issue in the dispute seems to become lost amidst images of riot helmets, batons, shields and confrontations. (R2)

Interestingly enough, with one or two exceptions, the police did not understand the reduced potential for strike violence and the greater viability of the liaison approach within any awareness of changes in industrial relations, union power, or union tactics. From their perspective, the reduced potential for violence was entirely a function of the police changes in strategy and tactics. Yet some of the earliest reformers (e.g., Superintendent Northrop) seemed to view the need for a new approach precisely because they were observing or anticipating intensified labour conflict, a view that is understandable given the high level of strike activity that had developed over the course of the 1970s when these innovators were first proposing these changes. With respect to BC in particular, it is again interesting to note that the main expansion of the liaison approach across this province occurred when a neo-conservative Social Credit government had introduced major regressive changes to labour laws prompting large-scale protests and strikes (Palmer, 1987; Shields, 1991). Perhaps just as interesting, it was also a neo-conservative government in Ontario which had implemented the province-wide policy requiring a liaison approach, again right around the same time that the labour movement began a rotation of large general strikes in targeted cities.

On the other hand, when most police services made their shift to liaison, that is in the late 1980s and 1990s, overall strike activity had dropped quite dramatically. Moreover, even at the peak of labour militancy during the 1970s in Canada as a whole, or the 1980s in BC and the 1990s in Ontario, there was very little violence and virtually no resurgence of radical factions within labour. It is likely for this reason that the police increasingly did not see labour or strikes as significant threats to *public order*. Indeed, in explaining the shift to liaison, many police informants pointed to changes in the behaviour of the strikers themselves:

The social context and the strikers themselves have pushed the police to change their philosophy. The strikers have changed a lot, they are not as violent as before. (R65)

I think there's a better understanding by people on both sides of the strike situation that suggests there's not the attitude that existed back then. When police were brought on to a strike scene back then the thought that I conjectured was that these people felt that we were out there to beat them. That regardless of what was going to happen the police were going to use such force ... The sight of the uniform suggests force. I think that people are more tolerant to the police officer on the strike line. I believe this is accomplished as a result of education by the unions. (R47)

Police Resistance to Liaison

Of course, as the case studies showed, the transformation to liaison policing did not occur without resistance within the police community, nor did the liaison approach appear full blown from the outset. Many informants involved in the transformation emphasized the resistance among the 'old school' sergeants, patrol officers, and more senior administrators while also recalling that there was a period of transition before policies were clearly established in which orders varied from officer to officer and situation to situation, with little consistency:

> I can recall sitting at the Dominion Glass strike in the back of a truck in the seventies [with six or eight others], and one of the lieutenants at the time comes up and says, 'Look we're gonna break this line open, you just bop them and grab as many as you can.' You know the war cry is on ... No sooner had that happened, another lieutenant who really did a lot for labour came in and he says, 'Now look folks, these people are your neighbours, they're the people who shop in the stores, they're the people who sit in the football games beside you, these are the ones whose kids go to the same schools as your kids ... they're not bad people. I want you there if they start throwing things, take it. They're not going to throw anything to hurt you. And we'll look after it. We'll sort it out after.' Now we're all sitting there really confused. What the hell do we do? Do we go and kick the hell out of them or do we hold their hands? That's really the first step of the new version of labour relations. (R34)

Police accounts of strikes from the 1970s through to the 1990s suggest that many senior and front-line officers continued to see force and the demonstration of force as being integral to picket line control.

However, as the case studies show, along with those police officers who were resisting change, we also see clear evidence from police accounts that there were pockets of more idealistic and reform-minded police officers who were instrumental in leading to change by seizing opportunities to problem-solve and forge new policy direction. What is particularly interesting here is the questioning of the use of public police to intervene in a private civil matter. A superintendent recalls his early thoughts and efforts to challenge the existing approach:

And I must say that a lot of people were very critical of why I was asking. 'Just get on with it,' I was told. Like what are you asking all these questions for? Basically, I kept saying, 'It does matter how we do things because we have to have authorities to be doing what they're doing so that we can protect our members and also, constitutionally, we're protected.' And the thing is, I kept saying that a lot of what we are doing is for convenience and a lot of it, we don't go and repossess cars, why are we intervening in strikes? Because the average strike is a dispute between one group of people and another. Why are we spending this amount of manpower and stripping beats of their lawful protection to concentrate on one area, particularly this business? (R37)

There was also considerable uncertainty even in the senior ranks about whether this approach would work and whether it would test the legal challenges:

I: So that policy was accepted fairly readily, there was not much resistance? Because you had said that the chief and the deputy chief were from the old school.
R: Yah. Only when we were proving that we were on the perfectly right track with the higher courts did some of these people do a complete switch around. The chief, I remember himself said, 'If you had told me six months ago that I would be endorsing this sort of thing, and I'd been a copper out in Burlington and Peel region before that, I would have absolutely just scoffed and laughed in your face.' He said, 'I can't believe that we're doing it.' He said, 'I can see now, where you were coming from, finally but, I had grave misgivings.' (R37)

While claiming considerable success in this and subsequent strikes, our informants also acknowledged a period of transition even after the formal adoption of the new policies where police and sergeants were either confused or quite hostile to the new approach:

R: A lot of sergeants grew up in an atmosphere where they saw the strikers as criminals or certainly people who had to be subdued.
I: How long did it take for the sergeants to come on side?
R: Some never did; they're long gone now but a year or two it took us that long to put in service training and some people never accepted it. They thought we were just coddling them and that we were wimps. (R34)

There were also subsequent incidents in some strikes where the policy was circumvented:

> A lot of these old fashioned sergeants wanted action, particularly I'm thinking about the Windsor Bumper [strike]. They had set up a scenario where they told a sergeant that they had to get into the plant because they had vats of dangerous chemicals. They had this one sergeant convinced of the dire necessity so he ended up arresting the [union] president, all the executive and thirty strikers. (R24)

But as the more activist liaison officers recall, more consistency developed over time as the older officers retired and trust began to develop between the unions and the police liaison. Still, it is clear that these reforms often took hard work and persuasion within the services on the part of the police reformers.

The Continuing Commitment to Liaison Policing

By 2000–1, when most of our interviews were conducted, support for liaison policing among the police hierarchy and front line was extremely high. Although, as we show in chapter 6, many police services began to realize the limits of the liaison approach in some situations, in particular the large multi-group anti-globalization protests of the late 1990s, most services demonstrate continued commitment to this approach, especially when dealing with labour unions, which are viewed almost universally by police liaison and administrators as legitimate, peaceful organizations which can be trusted to self-police within the general parameters of the law. What is particularly interesting here is the extent to which the police liaison and administration were willing to defend their approach even in the face of considerable pressure from individual employers, local politicians, the general public, and even the occasional judge, for failing to act more forcefully and/or more quickly against union pickets or plant occupations. Our police survey and case study interviews yielded many examples indicating these tensions:

> Casino was another case where strikers blocked the entrance; and the number of phone calls we got from that from all over the province, the Lottery Corporation and everything, it was amazing. I have to give them [the strikers] some latitude, but I get a lot of pressure. (R24)

The *Star* had [a] very, very, very conservative and almost demanding view that we arrest everybody and no obstruction take place. The editorials about me and 'how dare I do this' and 'how dare I do that' and holding up trucks and they were very much against this policy, very much against it. (R37)

As discussed in the Windsor case, and as we shall see in the next chapter, sometimes this pressure pushed police to act more aggressively against unions in some situations, but most liaison officers reported that they could routinely rely on their superiors to back them up as long as they were following the basic liaison protocol. For their part, senior police administrators consistently claimed complete confidence that the liaison approach was the correct one for dealing with strikes and most protests and were sensitive to the need to resist employer and other business or political pressure to act precipitously. For example, a senior Toronto officer recalls what happened during a public sector OPSEU strike:

We actually got no pressure specifically from anybody high in the government, but certainly, managers from their command posts ... managers at the sites. Their attitudes were that, by us having a neutral position, not favouring either side, that we were in effect favouring the labour side. And they put a lot of pressure on us to intervene. And we had to kind of resist, and say, 'You know what? You guys are going to have to negotiate, whether you like it or not, you're going to have to negotiate with the guys on the picket line.' (R60)

Indeed, the strength of the liaison strategy can be measured by the persistence of communication and negotiation in the face of these pressures and challenges. This does not mean there were no incidents even among the most committed services where individual field officers or commanders failed to follow the normal protocol, but the rarity of such transgressions, even in relatively charged circumstances like plant occupations, was quite striking.

When we asked police administrators, liaison officers, and other front-line officers to explain more fully the basis of their commitment to this approach, the most consistent response was that the approach was highly effective in maintaining the peace and minimizing confrontation. Service after service and officer after officer emphasized that violence was now much less frequent if not almost absent from strikes and most protests, that arrests were much less common, and that force was rarely being used, all without jeopardizing public safety (see table 4.4). As noted earlier, the police were now soundly convinced that their previous approaches had been a major cause of violence which simply lengthened the dispute, while the liaison approach effectively prevented violence in large part by staying out of it:

> As a matter of fact, I have to say, sometimes when we did come in with larger groups, we incense people, we cause more trouble. Everything was peaceful until we showed up, many times. (R37)

In the phone survey interview, close to one-quarter of the police services (21 per cent) claimed that force had not been used in a single strike in the last five years, while close to three-quarters (71 per cent) claimed that force had not been used in more than 10 per cent of the strikes in the last five years. While none of the services were able or willing to provide statistical data to support their claims, the strike/incident reports that we reviewed in one large police service (N=93 strikes, 1999–2001) seemed to confirm the claim that police arrests or use of force were extremely rare (2–3 arrest/violence incidents per year).

As reported by both front-line liaison officers and senior police officials, the approach has also paid a number of crucial dividends in terms of increased cost savings, reduced injuries, and improved police morale. First, since the services no longer post police officers at strikes on an ongoing basis, some of which last months at a time, the liaison approach minimizes the impact on patrol resources. The minimal police presence during protest situations and the limited use of the public order or riot units also figure heavily in the police view that liaison policing is highly cost-effective with far fewer incidents of overtime. This was also often framed in reference to the limited police resources that were available in the budget restraints of the 1990s as well as the consequences for the rest of the community when those resources were directed to strike duties.

> Let's say you have five sites at Stelco in Hamilton. With their [union] numbers, they could easily throw 300 people on that picket line everyday. So if you want to bring trucks in and out everyday and they've got 300 pickets, it's going to take us at least 200 officers. Where are we going

Table 4.4
Proportion of strikes where police used force or arrest over last five years

	Proportion of strikes/percentage of services								
	None	1–5%	6–10%	11–15%	16–20%	21–30%	31–40%	41–50%	50%+
Use of physical force	22.6%	45%	13%	–	6.4%	3.2%	–	6.5%	3.2%
Arrests	26.7%	36.7%	10%	–	13.3%	13.3%	–	–	–

Change over last five years

	Percentage of services				
	Major decrease	Some decrease	No change	Some increase	Major increase
Change in use of force	29.4%	32.4%	29.4*	8.8%	–
Change in # arrests	31.3%	28.1%	32%*	2.7%	–

* The services reporting no change were all long-time users of the liaison approach. Respondents insisted that the decline occurred soon after they adopted the approach, which, in these cases, was more than ten years before the interview.

to get 200 officers when there's 55 working the street? You can get the chief to call people in but you have to take into account the safety of the [rest of] the community; there's family disputes, assaults, robberies, but all the officers are in one location. (R40)

The emphasis on self-policing and private security also translated into a reduced need for police patrol visits. For example, according to the Windsor Police Service Annual Reports, the average number of annual police visits to a strike prior to the policy change in 1987 was 27.5, while this was reduced to 11 visits per strike after liaison was introduced (Windsor Police Service Annual Reports, 1984–91). The considerable time associated with processing arrests also reduced a main source of cost. Most informants saw the policy on refusing to open picket lines as a crucial step in reducing costs since there was rarely a need to draw patrol officers from elsewhere:

Well the costs involved when you were bringing in, what the unions call, the helmets and sticks, because you are bringing in people on overtime, specifically trained people to deal with large crowds. The costs were much leaner [with liaison], when I got involved, and we got the injunctive process. My costs, the public costs, were minimal compared to years previously. (R7)

I'm not into politics, never have been, but we are required by law to facilitate protesters and that's what we must do. So we try to help them. The Gay Pride Day parade. I went to them and said, we can get you to the front of Queen Street and we did that and they were amazed. Before doing Gay Pride day was brutal, hated doing it. Now no problem at all, and we never have to deploy public order anymore. (R53)

The other major advantage noted consistently by front-line officers and senior police was reduced injuries to the police arising from the fewer confrontations:

It's a big change. I look back over the years when I first came on the job to strike scenes that were marked by violence, injuries, and bloodshed on both sides. Management were hurt, picketers were hurt, and police officers were hurt in a lot of cases. In the recent past, this just isn't the case anymore. (R25)

I mean we've gone over the last twenty years. I remember the last time the police got in a pitched battle with strikers, I think it was Artistic Woodworking. I wasn't part of it but that was a battle. We ended up with injured police, injured workers, and injured family members. (R55)

Front-line morale was also often cited by police administrators and liaison as an important factor underlining their commitment to the approach. As noted above, informants at all levels insisted that most of their officers did not like strike policing duties, which they saw in part as a function of their own identities as union members but again also as a reflection of the growing view of unions as legitimate economic actors and union members as law-abiding neighbours simply exercising their right to protect their family's standard of living (see also Latornell, 1993: 29).

Finally, some of the police administrators acknowledged that the reductions in confrontations also meant less media and public attention for police as a service organization. While conscious of the political risks associated with losing control of a situation (e.g., the charge levied against the Seattle police in the 1999 anti-globalization protest) or with being seen as not acting forcefully to arrest protesters or strikers (e.g., see discussion of Caledonia in chapter 6), police saw the overall effect of the liaison approach as reducing their exposure to criticism from the community and ultimately from their political masters in city hall and the legislature. However, as we show in subsequent chapters, the limits of the liaison approach are increasingly realized as protest tactics and political pressures within a post-9/11 environment begin to alter the risk calculations of failing to act more forcefully.

Conclusion

The case studies and surveys indicate that many police agencies view the liaison policy as the result of the initiative of their agency in isolation or as the result of reformers within the agency redressing personal and professional discontent with the status quo. Governments are seen as having played a minor role in these early innovations. However, many of the accounts, both in the case studies and from interviews with other services, also point to significant political, media, and public pressures as precipitating or opening opportunities for the internal reform efforts. As the case studies also suggest, police were keenly aware of the dangers associated with 'ordering' labour, particularly as the frequency of labour conflict intensified and as union sensitivities within police organizations periodically spilled over and always underscored the necessity of solidarity. Underwriting much of the narrative – as illustrated by the participants – is a theme not of provision or redistribution, but boundary affirmation: although the development of policing provision as we have seen is intimately tied to the lubrication of economy and labour, the articulation of the policy represents a gradual retreat from the visible excesses that saw public police as the primary guardians of commerce and industry. Sloppy public order spectacles came to be seen as unnecessary and costly, a strain on welfare provision where a solution was the ready discourse of at-a-distance policing delivery.

The early moves toward labour liaison were emerging well before neo-liberalism or neo-conservatism began to take hold at the federal and provincial levels. However, the breakdown of Fordist postwar arrangements was instrumental in fuelling the labour confrontations of the 1970s and the widening scope of social protest. A broadening liberal human rights discourse was also crucial in challenging police impulses toward 'business as usual' in responding to these developments. As governments and corporations began to construct their neo-liberal and post-Fordist solutions to the economic crises of the 1970s, the growing emphasis on deficit reduction, privatization, managerialism, autonomy, and responsibility all pointed in the direction of liaison in shaping the contours and features of a new peace. It became dominant because it was effective in meeting the legitimacy requirements of police, unions, politicians, and the public at large. At the most basic level, it offered the hope that strikes would no longer be major sources of political or economic cost. Liaison was grounded in the fact that unions (like most demand or protest groups) bought in, sold in part, by the opportunity it gave union leaders to keep the solvency of the strike and yet restrict the ambiguity of its course. Union leadership could structure and craft their strikes and protests within the parameters of police expectations. Under attack and otherwise with a weak weapon that always ran very close to the margins of the law, unions saw liaison as a major coup for labour. Police professionalism and the decline of labour radicalism allowed both labour and police to retreat from sloppy confrontations that were increasingly antithetical to the careful maintenance of a base of support and legitimacy.

In the next chapter we review some of the finer points of the approach to further the argument that the visibility of liaison was a disciplinary mechanism, a method of insisting on ritualistic observances that eventually pushed labour from its position as the sole or most pivotal actor in the array of mass demonstration grievances.

5 The Refinement of Labour Liaison and the Seeds of Decline

Introduction

In this chapter, we look at the finer points of the liaison approach in order to parse its constituent elements and consider it as a mechanism of control. The liaison approach roughly matches what della Porta and Reiter (1998) and McPhail, Schweingruber, and McCarthy (1998) have called 'negotiated management.' Displacing the prior 'escalated force' control model in which police adapted their use of force protocol to demonstrations, under negotiated management police under-enforce the law and increase the predictability of the event by ceding space and control to picketers or demonstrators (Noakes, Klocke, and Gillham, 2005). As in negotiated management, the emphasis in liaison policing is on a trade-off of predicable disruptions for accommodations in control of the event.

As indicated in the previous chapter, most Canadian police services formally adopted liaison approaches first in the labour area and later applied the approach to the broader spectrum of protest. Although policy documents in some services that we reviewed were far more detailed on strike procedures and principles than others, the common accounts gained from labour, management, and police informants across Canada suggest that clarity and consistency in the application of the liaison approach in labour relations emerged over time as more and more services codified emerging practices in formal policies. In later chapters we will further distinguish developments in the protest areas, but here our main focus is on understanding the common elements that distinguish the liaison approach when applied to strikes. What we seek to do is show how the elements of liaison policing reproduced institutionalized consent to the rule of law, reflected neo-liberal and post-Fordist or post-industrial rationalities and technologies, and reaffirmed the boundaries of public interest and involvement.

The Principles of Liaison Policing

While we have already documented some clear variations in procedures and levels of activity between the forces, our analysis of policy documents and interviews with police liaison officers points to six interrelated operational principles as the common discursive core of the strike liaison approach:

1 Strikes are civil matters.
2 Police are impartial in both appearance and practice.
  Police practices stress:
3 self-policing and trust;
4 flexible enforcement and restraint;
5 preventative information brokering;
6 deference to court injunctions and orders.

These elements underscore the 'service' public order orientation of the liaison approach in which the focus is clearly on integrative policing through consensus tactics and practices.

Strikes Are Civil Matters

The first guiding principle behind liaison policing is the view that labour issues, including picketing and the regulation of strikes, are fundamentally civil and not criminal matters. When asked to describe the key ideas or principles underlying the approach, by far the most consistent comments across all police respondents was the statement that 'strikes are civil matters.' Strikes are not presumptively public order problems but rather economic conflicts between private parties. In defining strikes as civil matters, the picket line becomes a space of 'private dispute' between opposing parties, rather than a public arena. It is therefore outside the jurisdiction of public police unless criminal acts or threats to public safety and peace arise. As one police officer stated:

> A strike as we consider it, as far as the Department goes, it's a civil dispute between two parties. Well obviously it involves contracts coming

due and negotiations of contracts but basically it is a civil dispute. And we handle it like we would any other kind of civil dispute out of the community. As we are obviously neutral, we try to keep the peace as much as possible so we're not looking at having to investigate or laying charges under the Criminal Code, Highway Traffic Act or By-laws. (R24)

Although protests are also seen as civil matters, increasingly with reference to Native and environmental protests in particular, they are understood more broadly as expressions of civil rights, in particular the freedom of expression by one private party to express their views against another. Of course, many protests, including labour protests, are directed at the state and centre on rights claims, which are two factors that complicate the police approach to protests.

Public order issues and strikes have some cross-over because strikers will attend public order events but they are two separate functions with very distinct characteristics of each. Strikes themselves have evolved from a police perspective, it's very much a civil dispute, and a civil dispute – we go there to keep the peace. I mean we don't get involved on either side. We're right down the middle and we work very hard to stay there. Protests are a little bit different in that protests are an expression of somebody's rights in this country and we have to go out of our way as police officers to facilitate that protest. I mean we do all kinds of things as police officers in this country, in this city particularly to facilitate lawful protest. I mean we go as far as providing sound stages, places to demonstrate from ... We actually work very closely with protesters. (R53)

Of course, it is also within this context that we see an increasing corporate reliance on private police to perform these functions, which then simply confirms and reinforces the police claim that the strike is a private matter. Indeed, the police themselves advise companies to use private security:

Yes, they [management] want us to help them. But we can't, we can't ... If we start assisting them and getting their people through to work then unions right away [are] saying here's a bunch of police officers assisting in getting management through to work. Okay? That's what they would hire private security in the event that they feel uncomfortable with the managers going through to work. And if there's an assault, the private security can assist them until the police arrive. (R55)

It is within this context of 'privatization' that police scale down their service activities and withdraw from surveillance and escort and property protection functions. Since the escort operations made the space in which police and labour did battle, the change of policy saved police resources and greatly reduced the points of conflict. In the meantime, the site of industrial disputes is reoccupied by those who offer, as Hobbs et al. (2002: 366) put it, 'private violence as commercial resource.' The primary visible role of private security is video surveillance, but they also provide escorting. Although they have no legal right to use force to achieve that goal, security firms attempt to make up the deficit of authority with intimidation and heft, deploying bulky security guards and large SUVs in the breaking of the lines.

This framing of strikes as private matters with limited purchase on public resources of enforcement is an instance of wider changes to the role of labour in the articulation of government policy. As this also implies, the police appear to be ceding ground in this 'interstitial area' (Hobbs et al. 2002), although still bringing their own violence monopoly (cf. Bittner, 1970) back into play at times if only to curb some of the excesses of private security (as in a Windsor hospital strike incident where police arrested security staff as they were trying to force their way through a picket line).

As noted, spot interviews with picketers on picket lines and interviews with labour leaders suggest that union people on the line often view the police as serving the union by 'helping' to control the behaviour of the security services (see below for more on this). It is also interesting to note that although the use of private security is mainly a management practice, we also came across examples where unions were beginning to hire their own surveillance and security experts to counter private security tactics. This further speaks to the union recognition that the public police are not sufficient to counter private security tactics.

Police Are Neutral

While some union members and leaders see police as protective and sympathetic, the claim of neutrality permeates the discourse of all police services and liaison officers when discussing their approach. Here a broader discourse on rights is more evident as they express a respect for the right to strike along with the employer's right to carry on business. 'Balancing these rights' through both the substance and appearance of neutrality is seen as critical to the approach:

> The main element is to keep it peaceful and I try to do that by fostering a
> good relationship between picketers, management, and the police depart-
> ment ... both sides have a message; management has the right to keep the
> business running and the union has the right to be outside picketing. (R24)

At the same time, this is not to say that on the line many police liaison
officers are not a little less sanguine on this point, noting that while liaison requires an acknowledgment of opposing interests and rights,
the challenge of reconciling and balancing them while maintaining the
peace is often more easily said than done. Indeed, one way in which
the police discursively achieve this balancing act is to de-emphasize
the issue of rights and focus instead on safety:

> We're not looking at any one particular interest, we're looking at the safety
> of everyone involved. We're not much concerned with the rights of the
> company, or the rights of the picketers, because that process is separate and
> apart from what we do. I'm not really concerned with whether the com-
> pany can continue to operate, any more than I'm concerned about whether
> the union are able to picket and shut the company down. Not our concern.
> We don't really want to go there. We focus on the safety. (R25)

Yet, as many strike liaison officers also insisted, they often go to great
lengths to facilitate strike activities and to protect the rights of strikers:

> Well it took a while to build the relationship [with the unions], going to
> the scene of these strikes and letting these people see that we were neu-
> tral, impartial, and that I am going to give them a fair shake, especially
> the union, as far as them getting their message out. I think they are look-
> ing to get their message out, they want some exposure in the media, and
> they want some disruption to the business or obviously it wouldn't do
> any good to be there. So they know that, you know I let them do that ...
> I mean they have a *right* to be out there, they have a *right* to get their
> message across, they have a *right* to stop vehicles or persons to get their
> message across. (R24)

By helping strikers to 'get their message' across, police are both enabling and reinforcing the construction of strikes as mere forms of
communication rather than substantial challenges or threats to capital
or authority. Of course, whether anyone is listening to the strikers is
not the concern of the police since 'they are neutral,' but at minimum,

their neutrality reassures strikers, whether constructed as economic or political actors, that their basic rights to communicate within the picket line context are intact.

This is not to say that the concrete changes in police practices associated with neutrality have no political consequences potentially favourable to labour. The definition of strikes as civil matters forms not only the legal foundation of the police emphasis on neutrality but also a key aspect of the rationale underlying the refusal to open picket lines to escort management, replacement workers, equipment, or production through the line, which, as we show later in this chapter, can be very frustrating to employers:

> They [the employers] used to call us on a frequent basis prior to any strike and they'd dictate to us that we're gonna bring people in here and we want access and that's the way it is going to be. We don't do that [now]. We will meet with both sides, advise them of our neutrality, and that if they have difficulty with obstructed entrances, if they have difficulty with the number of pickets, then there's a civil process in place and that's the Labour Relations Board. They can seek injunctions there [or in the courts]. (R2)

> I think the current philosophy and approach is that the policing services take up a very impartial stand on the issues and trying to resolve through negotiation any issues that management might have or that union might have, to come to an amicable resolve. That way it's peaceful. I mean, the whole objective I believe for a labour relations office is to make sure or hope to ensure that no one is criminally charged through whether it's a mischief or damage to the buildings or somebody's assaulted. (R30)

As these quotes suggest, the affirmation of police neutrality is presented by police as a simple realization that since the strike is a civil matter, police should not be involved in crossing or challenging a picket line because, as one officer put it, 'when we took an active role before, we were taking sides.' At the same time, however, in refusing to open picket lines, the police often see themselves as righting a previous wrong that privileged the power of certain private interests over others (e.g., employers over labour). As pointed out already, the police acknowledge that the past willingness to open picket lines was itself provocative and indicative of employer bias, but it is also widely accepted among both police administration and liaison personnel that prior to the introduction of the liaison approach, the police were clearly working *for* employers. Indeed, one retired superintendent recalled in some detail the close relationship that existed between local businesses and his service right through to the 1970s, which included money and expensive gifts.

For police, then, the strike liaison approach, and in particular police refusal to open picket lines, was a vital indication that police were finally making good on their claims of professionalism and independence. If they could maintain true neutrality over the vociferous objections of local business interests and no longer take their marching orders from employers, then they could regain a great deal of legitimacy as peace brokers representing the greater good or common interest. In the meantime, neutrality, or at least its appearance, is long understood via the rule of law as a prerequisite for gaining the cooperation and trust underlying self-policing (see below). If the state and state authority are off the table as an element of the dispute, then what is left is the maintenance of police effectiveness through (as it were) referee stripes. The cloth of neutrality is literately pointed to resist entreaties for partial resolution. Neutrality comes to be seen not only as a moral or legal position, but essential to the effectiveness of police communications and capacity to mediate and negotiate an end to dispute without violence and the need for force.

However, while police, labour, and protesters often interpret the practical application of neutrality as protecting striker and protest rights, what we also see here is an affirmation of the long-standing tenet of classic liberalism: the principle of non-interference into the private and commercial sphere. As one liaison officer put it, 'it's up to them [the parties to the dispute] to resolve their issues.' While affirming that police have no business protecting business, the unfortunate irony, the relative paucity of resistance from corporate leaders to the liaison approach (see below for more on this), is likely a consequence of the lack of negotiating or bargaining powers of labour in the global and flexible post-Fordist marketplace today (Jackson, 2006).

> We found there was a lot of gamesmanship being played by both sides. And that's part of the reason that we also found that we had to try and keep a neutral position, because we knew both sides would end up trying to play us to further their ends. (R60)

As police informants acknowledge, and as we show more fully in the next chapter, things are a little more fraught when government is more or less explicitly represented as a disputant in the conflict, which is the case in policy protests, and public sector strikes. Police insist that their position does not change but that the threshold of the public interest is met, if only because the threats to property are threats to public or state property interests. For example, a duty officer involved in policing the Vancouver OPEC meetings in 1999 explains that most of the protests were handled without any problems prior to the infamous pepper spray incident:

> There were a number of earlier demonstrations around the Chinese presence and [in] all of those we facilitated the protest. It was only once it became a risk to a VIP, and then we responded the way we did. You just can't get your VIPs cracked on a peninsula with no way out, you can't allow that because of the risks, as long as you have viable options and some way out, then you can continue with the soft approach. But at some point you have to make a decision, then you got to foreclose. (R10)

Similar thinking was evident during a 1996 OPSEU strike that involved picketing outside the Ontario legislature. When MPP access and safety were seen as being at risk, police, in particular the OPP, used significant force through the crowd management unit (CMU), using shields, batons, and pepper spray to break the picket lines. A subsequent inquiry found considerable fault with the OPP's failure to follow a liaison protocol as well as evidence that the speaker of the legislature had undue influence over the policing decisions (Estey, 1996). However, Commissioner Estey has also maintained that there was a clear public interest obligation on the part of the police to ensure MPPs' safe access to the legislature.

As noted earlier, while public sector unions are much more likely to complain about picket line policing than private sector unions, this may have more to do with the setting and size of many public sector strikes, which often tend to be province- or nation-wide strikes in locations which have more impact on public access or safety (government buildings, courthouses, hospitals, schools, and so forth). Some police informants also suggested that the private sector unions are more experienced and exercise more control over their members, allowing the police to keep their distance:

> The policy worked well with Stelco and the Steelworkers union. But when we had CUPW, it didn't work all that well. They were really an

incompetent union. You'd go down to the picket line and when something started to happen, the stewards or picket captains would disappear. Their picket lines were always out of control. (R40)

In sum, the position of neutrality is consistent with the caveat that police will be proactive where the circumstances involving the use or threat of force in strike situations tend to involve public safety or threats to state integrity:

If they're blocking access to, like say a truck, access in and out, well maybe that's something between the parties, But if that then spills out into the public thoroughfares so that you are blocking everybody then that changes the calculus, it is no longer a dispute between the parties; it affects everybody. That changes things. (R10)

Self-Policing and Trust

While opening new possibilities for union actions, the liaison approach also adopts the neo-liberal emphasis on responsibility, autonomy, and choice (Rose, 1996; Rose and Miller, 1992) within its theme of self-policing. As noted in chapter 3, past policing practice was to post uniformed officers either on foot or in patrol cars to monitor the strikes continuously. Within the liaison approach, the presence of uniformed police is minimized, with some services using just their liaison people to visit the line, often in civilian clothes. Other services still have patrol cars or bike patrols visit the line routinely a couple of times in their shift, and they actively encourage the uniformed officers to become familiar with the picketers, especially the picket captain, while minimizing any actual intervention. Sometimes, police rely on phone calls to the picket line (management and union contacts) as their principal source of information. But for the most part, the emphasis on self-policing is largely expressed by the minimal police presence or surveillance during most strikes, along with little or no intelligence commitment. As one of the police service brochures puts it:

It is the policy of this Service to refrain, whenever possible, from stationing uniformed officers at strike scenes. The executive members and picket captains of the union local involved in the strike are given the opportunity of managing their picket lines and the responsibility of maintaining peaceful picketing. (*Hamilton-Wentworth Regional Police Labour Disputes: Information for Labour and Management*, 2001)

Picket captains are expected to play a critical self-policing role in strikes, while protest groups are encouraged to have their own parade or protest marshals. In pre-protest or strike communications, police stress that union leaders and protest group leaders are responsible for the actions of their members, often lecturing them on the political and legal consequences of criminal behaviour as well as making it clear that police cooperation and assistance are contingent on compliance with the law and any negotiated protocols. Picket captains and marshals are expected to intervene directly and persuasively in controlling strikers and protesters, and as we observed numerous times, the police defer to them as much as possible whenever individual members or small groups are diverging from agreed-upon protocols.

One particularly striking example of self-policing was observed in one of the Ontario labour movement's Days of Action in Windsor, Ontario, in 1996. Leading up to the main march were local protests at worksites. One of those protests was at the University of Windsor, adjacent to the main bridge crossing to Michigan. The local labour union movement had negotiated an agreement with the mayor and police to block the access road to the bridge for a short period of time during the main afternoon march but at no other time. However, during the morning protest, a small group of about fifty protesters broke away from the university and began to walk onto the bridge access road. A single police car was on the scene in minutes but rather than attempting to intervene they immediately summoned senior union officials who were patrolling in cars for precisely this contingency. They arrived soon after the police and within a very short period of time, had turned the protesters back to the university after chastening them for failing to follow the marshalling instructions. Blockading the bridge would certainly have gotten both corporate and government attention, as have previous blockades, and as the police acknowledged in later interviews, they would have been unable to repel such an action had the effort been made, but the unions were clearly unwilling to take this step.

As we have been indicating, unions cooperate with police in these situations because they are concerned about investment and economic effects and about the political costs of disruption, including the loss of public support (see below for more on this). While police point to enhanced control, reduced confrontations, and cost savings as underlying their commitment to self-policing, the police are also very conscious of these union rationales, and indeed they often state that their commitment to self-policing is grounded in their perception of union interests in controlling their members and in minimizing violence.

In the meantime, such trust pays dividends. Self-policing reinforces 'good citizenship' and a relation of trust between unions and most police services. While there are differences, broadly distributed police confidence in unions cuts across most police services. Police liaison and administration generally agree that this confidence is grounded in experience: when given the responsibility to self-police, most unions (and indeed most protest groups) have been entirely reliable. For many police, as noted already, this reliability can be explained by an observation they often repeat that most union leaders and members are law-abiding citizens. As many police like to phrase it, they are 'our neighbours.' For others, there is the affirmation that there will be limited public tolerance for violence, and while this has restrained police (particularly in the framing of the strike as a civil matter), it will also restrain unions:

> I think they [the unions] need the police in a lot of ways to keep them out of trouble. They are often going to do something that may end up badly, and I can tell them, warn them about what could happen. They don't want things to go out of control. It's like anything if your group is out of control, you're only gonna get negative feedback and that's not what they want. They want the public on their side, that's why they're on strike, to draw public attention to their problems. (R59)

It is worth emphasizing that although the police expect employers to police themselves in the same way when crossing picket lines or engaging in any other actions that might endanger public or worker safety or rights, the police more frequently express concerns about being able to trust employers and, more specifically, the private security hired by employers. As such, closer monitoring when it happens is less a function of concerns about labour and more about whether managers or private security will 'do something stupid.'

> I remember when we stationed an LR officer at Don Jail [picket line] and he was on the [phone] line with the unit commander when the commander got a call on the other line from a manager and the manager was saying 'It's bedlam on the line, they're drinking, they're smoking up, there's bottles all over the place and they're damaging things.' And so the unit commander says 'Hang on' and gets on the line and says to the LR, 'What can you tell me about this,' and the LR says it's a crock, everything is fine here.' (R60)

The police also see trust relations as critical to the resolution of conflicts when they do occur. Yet as many liaison officers noted, their trust was constantly being tested, suggesting both the work that the police put into these relationships as well as their fragile nature:

> Although you don't always know what's happening, I think you are being tested. Your trust is tested from time to time because they'll say we are planning to do this or that, and then you go and offer some assistance by getting their group of a thousand from A to B and facilitate them as much as possible with the uniform presence. I think you gain their trust as long as you haven't abused it and carelessly mentioned something to the other side, to management … If it's not something that jeopardizes public safely or something, I can keep that confidential and it goes both ways. It'll be years before OPSEU goes on strike again but we've built a lot of relationships, a lot of trust on both sides. (R54)

Consequently, liaison officers place a high value on the development of a reciprocal trust relationship with the picket coordinators, captains, and, to some extent, with managers. As one liaison officer put it, 'if you lie to them, you are dead – they won't have anything to do with you from then on.' Liaison officers argue that it is crucial to keep all confidences throughout the strike, again as long as these do not involve questions of criminal conduct or safety:

> If a union official comes and tells me that they are going to have a rally tomorrow or they are planning to bring in a flying squad to slow up things a little, and some do give me this kind of 'heads up,' I cannot pass that along to the employer or that's it for me; they won't listen to a thing I say after that. And the same thing if an employer tells me a truck is going through the line at such and such as time, I'm not going to go and tell the union that unless I get the permission of the employer. (R54)

Many liaison officers also spoke specifically of strategies by which confidences were established, including expressions of sympathy for the justice of pickets' claims.[1] Establishing themselves as a putative buffer between the union and the employer and even sometimes non-liaison or 'regular' police is an important element of establishing confidence. As one liaison officer recounted, 'I often say to them listen, the police are going to have to come in if you don't move, I think I can get them to back off if you agree to …' (T7). Practical assistance, 'which can

sometimes mean providing traffic support for a march or even con-
vincing a Sgt or another officer to back away from threats of charges,'
is another element of the effort to develop a close relationship of trust.
In exercising themselves as trustworthy confidantes, police liaison officers distance themselves from the role of 'law enforcement' and present themselves as a dispute resolution resource. Of course, this is also
part of the reason why liaison officers do not wear uniforms:

> If you look at the way I'm dressed right now, I'm not in a uniform. I'm
> sure you see what most of the other ones, how they're dressed. Cause I've
> found that if officers who do respond to a picket or to a strike location, if
> they're in uniform, they're viewed as in a position of authority and you
> don't get that same rapport with the union, with the union members. You
> may with the local presidents through meetings if you get to know them
> well. But in most cases as soon as you show up in a uniform you end up
> being in a position of authority and you can't always negotiate. (R55)[2]

Moreover, if conflicts or problems emerge on the picket line, the liaison
does the initial investigation, but if there are concerns or complaints of
a criminal nature, the liaison in most services attempt to stay out of it –
'keeping their hands clean' as one liaison officer put it (T7) – one of
many nods in liaison procedures to the issue of neutrality.

Finally, it is again worth emphasizing that the trust between police
and labour is not simply reflected in the development of personal relationships between liaison officers and labour representatives. The police willingness to minimize their involvement in monitoring and
managing the picket line implies that police services accept that unions
can be trusted to 'play by the rules' in strike situations. This reflects the
police administration's and police officer's emerging perception of
strikers as law-abiding citizens and unions as legitimate organizations
asserting their legal rights to establish fair working conditions. Unlike
in the 1930s and 1940s, unions are no longer perceived as presenting an
existential threat to the state. Moreover, they are a very limited situational risk, to public order or safety, and the low risk they represent is
in part a consequence of the many petty iterations of trust building.

Flexible Enforcement and Restraint

Police seek to minimize interventions in strike events through the use
of information and self-control. However, when called to intervene,
either by management, labour, or a third party, or when they observe

unlawful actions directly, they also use restraint through deferral or ne-gotiations. Arrests or use of force will be deferred through applications to the court for injunctions (see below). For most liaison officers, this also means taking a flexible and tolerant approach to law enforcement, one that weighs the need for legal action against the potential for en-hanced violence, injuries, and reduced trust between police and strik-ers or protesters. Arrests that are made are often deferred until after the event, in order to avoid confrontation. Indeed, agreements are of-ten reached after unions deliver individuals to the police station for formal charges at a later point:

> We had an incident over at Grace hospital where CUPE was on strike and a bunch of security guards got beaten up by CAW who were there for a rally. There was property damage to their vehicle and what have you, but there are 500 to 600 people over there. There's no way we are going to identify all the people involved. I think we had identified two people who definitely obstructed traffic and I said to (the CAW leader), we may have to arrest someone here and I want your cooperation, and he would have done that if I had, cause he'd want my cooperation in some other situa-tion. But no way we are going to risk wading in through the public to arrest these guys. So it's a kind of a little give and take; you have to over-look some things depending on the situation. Is it worth it for a policeman to be hurt, other people to get hurt, to inflame the situation … you got to weigh these things. (R24)

Another officer explained why police prevented management from bussing replacement workers from one city to another following the set-up of pickets in the city of origin:

> For the policing perspective we look first of all at the likelihood of vio-lence or property damage. Then we ask ourselves, what's the likelihood of us successfully containing or managing the situation? And do we want to get ourselves in a situation we're bringing in all kinds of officers, are all we really doing is creating an environment for bad things to hap-pen? It's a tough call, it really is. We certainly don't want to stand in the way of a company's right to conduct business, but we know the likeli-hood of people getting hurt, officers getting hurt, and things going south on us. (R25)

Most police officers readily acknowledged that the liaison approach was premised on a certain level of tolerance and flexibility in the enforcement of the law, and that the line regarding legal and illegal picketing needed to be somewhat opaque. As one liaison officer put it:

> We have to show a lot of restraint and ... we have to understand that a picket line is set up in a fashion to prevent managers from getting through the line. (R55)

Officers point to the importance of providing themselves manoeuvrability as a strike proceeds so that neither they nor others are backed into a corner from which there is no dignified exit (T3). Especially with union representatives, whom liaison officers see as critical to their capacity to act as mediators, flexibility and tolerance regarding the enforcement of the law are seen as important elements underlying their capacity to maintain neutrality. Consequently, the liaison approach represents not only a shift in police framing of 'legal' picket line conduct, but also a change in how they respond when illegal conduct is observed. As we found several times, pickets use force to impose restrictions often well beyond any claim of simple verbal communication, sometimes refusing trucks permission to pass or blocking access for hours or days. Although police acknowledge that pickets do not have the right to delay or obstruct, instead of forcing the line they actively discourage management or public efforts to cross the picket line in an effort to avoid trouble:

> We would only intervene if a *serious* criminal offence was involved. I don't consider blocking vehicle access to be a serious criminal offence so we would look for the employer to get a civil injunction. (R2)

While this officer readily agreed that persistent denial of access is illegal and warrants action, he was in no hurry to intervene, negotiating resolutions, if possible, and waiting for court resolutions if imposed. Another officer subordinated the law violation to the labour–management dispute:

> I: At what point do you use force or your powers of arrest?
> R: When a law is broken?
> I: But if someone walked up to people on the sidewalk and said, sorry, you have to stop and listen to me tell you about my issues with my employer, are they not breaking the law?
> R: Well yes in any other situation that would be obstruction and we would charge them. But [all] laws are circumstantial. A city could enact a by-law

that people can't drive a car in a park but if an elderly couple is walking in the park and the man trips and breaks his leg and then she runs back and drives through the park to pick him up, she's breaking the law but we are not going to charge her. A violation of the law has to be taken in the context of the violation. We enforce the law in the context of a labour–management dispute. Does that mean we wait until someone gets in a serious punch or does substantial property damage? No, but when there's pushing and shoving, and there's some intimidation, those kinds of offences are not going to be enforced unless they are really compelling. (R25)

While such discretionary enforcement is nothing new in public order policing, or in policing more generally (de Lint, 1998, 2000), here a strategic emphasis is placed on enforcement restraint as the leading approach to policing strikes and protests, a position that contrasts with the previously dominant viewpoint that demonstrations of force were necessary features of public order control. Avoiding any direct large-scale use of force is also actively discouraged whenever a liaison approach is dominant. As the RMCP policy on labour disputes and disobedience notes, 'experience has shown that direct police intervention of the confrontational type in these kinds of cases will ignite and turn violent what was otherwise a peaceful demonstration' (RMCP Nova Scotia, Operational Manual, Prevention Chapter, 1999). It is within this context that public order units are rarely put on stand-by or called out for strikes except for larger strike demonstrations, at which they are kept well out of sight.

This is not to say that under the liaison doctrine police do not view the arrest mechanism as a valuable means of disciplining the parties, including management:

It's situation dependent. I mean if people commit violations of the criminal law, the police officer is duty bound to act as a police officer, whether it be by arrest or a criminal summons. I mean there are different ways to proceed for violations. You have to be careful your actions don't precipitate violence. (R53)

In explaining the hospital strike cited earlier, the liaison officer acknowledged that the arrest of security personnel rather than picketers was for their own protection, but this action was also dictated by the police view that 'management had pulled a fast one' in trying to cross the picket line in advance of an agreed time. Although unstated, the message to management from police was that the provocation was too great and would not be tolerated on grounds of public safety. Citing public safety to avoid potentially violent interventions also maintains police in their neutrality and stoic indifference to the passage of time, a stance that makes it less likely that they will be 'played.'

> We had a situation at a correctional center where we had a jail guard. They wanted him out. And they wanted the police to take him out. Now the problem was, now we're inside a locked facility with panic buttons, during a strike. And at the same time all the other jail guards are watching to see how we react. If a panic button is hit, they're going to have every jail guard down there, four police officers and every jail guard down there, nose to nose, on their territory. We're talking about correctional officers okay. Management didn't care what occurred there. It appeared that they would like to see their people arrested and taken out of there. But we wouldn't bite on that. (T4)

Certainly police services and police and liaison officers will vary in where they draw 'the lines in the sand.' Some police we interviewed went out of their way to suggest that they rigorously enforce the criminal law. Most services also emphasize that they will arrest strikers if there is criminal behaviour, a point outlined in their initial meetings and communications.[3] To this end, brochures are routinely distributed which provide the legal definitions of various criminal offences such as causing a disturbance, assault, uttering threats, intimidation, mischief, dangerous driving, and so on. Services reported, and union and company informants tend to confirm, a strict policy of responding quickly and consistently to any accusations or complaints of individual criminal behaviour:

> Now of course, if you want London, I was impressed. They had a policy of strict adherence to the law, charge everybody that obstructed. I'm not saying that's wrong that's just the way they did it and they had the manpower. Toronto, they had a group of officers, low-key, now they were more or less responsible for trying to interact with the unions and management and try to explain the role and try and intercede between the police and the unions. Although they had no power over a ranking officer from the district, however how he wanted to handle it was his choice, whereas our Windsor model, which turned out to be our model was that I would not only liaise with them I would also [liaise] between management

and labour, but I would liaise with the officers and actually be on the line with them. So I wasn't just a paper pusher; I was actually on the line, on the picket line. (R66)

It is clear from many liaison officer accounts that 'flexible enforcement' is an important aspect of the approach. It is important to stress the difference between what police want of the parties and how they view their own approach as a matter of strategy. By calling in investigators and by reacting immediately to incidents and complaints, police seek to make the lines of 'criminality' *appear* as clear as possible so that union leaders are properly signalled on where to draw the line for their members. Yet, especially with union representatives, which liaison officers see as critical to their capacity to act as mediators, flexibility and tolerance regarding the enforcement of the law are seen as important elements underlying their capacity to maintain neutrality. While arrests are influenced by institutional and situational factors, including resources and workload, the fact remains that the maintenance of neutrality works in the direction of avoiding arrest and uniformed intervention. As an indication, our survey (see table 4.4) found that very few charges are laid by the police, with over one-quarter of the services reporting no arrests of strikers over the last five years, and most services (80 per cent) citing arrests at no more than 10 per cent of the strikes.

While there are differences between services, the evidence suggests that in most cases there has been a significant shift in the lines that police draw regarding legal and criminal actions. This shift forms part of the redefinition of strikes as civil matters and of the kinds of situations where the public interest is threatened and where police intervention is then mobilized or not. While this is not to say that considerable enforcement discretion was not used prior to the introduction of this approach (Geary, 1985; de Lint and Hall, 2002), the difference is that there is now an organized and strategic approach which more clearly shifts the lines of involvement and which consciously and consistently looks for and seeks alternative avenues to the use of uniformed personnel, arrests, and force.

Preventive Information Brokering

In off-loading the policing function consistent with 'policing at a distance' (cf. Rose and Miller, 1992), liaison police are by no means inactive or reactive. They meet with both parties before or just after a strike begins, the point of the meeting to instruct or remind leaders of both sides on, somewhat ironically, the limits of the police role. In this meeting they go over the ground rules, stressing that they will not themselves intervene to break open picket lines or monitor the strike unless there are criminal offences. They encourage self-regulation or self-control through instructional communication, taking on coordinating and mediating roles. Information brokering, accordingly, is key to this approach:

> We went from reacting to labour disputes to being proactive – providing information to both unions and employers in the hopes that labour would be encouraged to know their rights and responsibilities and communicate those to their respective management and picket captains. (R57)

> I think [the role of the liaison] is essentially to maintain the avenues of communication and to ensure that, and those avenues are both between the police and the union as well as within the police community. (R10)

Police selectively tutor on the law, emphasizing to each party the rights and powers of the other, as well as the powers of the police:

> If we are doing our jobs right, we're being proactive. Once we have a heads-up that a labour dispute is upcoming, you'll go and talk to the union and management and you'll explain where the police will get involved – you know, you can't do this and you can't do that. You can *educate* them. (R54)

Liaisons are also actively involved in both mediating and managing 'trouble' on picket lines – using various dispute resolution principles and tactics to achieve solutions without the need for uniformed police presence or court intervention. Tactics include playing to the union or employer interests, pointing to pitfalls or negative consequences, providing alternative, less problematic, actions, allowing the leadership to introduce the modifications to save face, and helping to gain concessions from one side to use as a carrot for the other side:

> Well, we call the other side, maybe someone a little more senior, and say you know, you are letting this go too far, and if you let it go too far, the company is going to have the evidence for an injunction. You are going to shoot yourself in the foot. So maybe the president is going

to call back to the picket captain and say you know what, instead of confrontation, let's do this. (R54)

I say 'Hey, I can't settle your strike but I can help you though, I'll make things easier for you' ... Helping them by keeping the area safe, if you want to hold a rally in the middle of the road, I'll arrange it to close off the road for 10–20 minutes. It gets them on my side. (R24)

The strike protocol referred to earlier is one aspect of this approach. Although police report that they do not suggest any specific terms, unions report and police acknowledge that they often try to influence it, especially where problems are seen to be incipient. Police report that their major concerns are for safety and traffic, and on that basis they seek to reshape or influence picket line behaviour. One union strike co-ordinator recalls that police came back to her almost daily for the first two weeks because of traffic concerns and 'ask[ed] us to modify and re-modify our delay times and procedures.' This union respondent reported that they did alter their protocol, although often not precisely in the way requested:

They came to me several times to say that our protocol was not working – that it was tying up traffic and causing safety problems. Each time I would try to find a workable balance – we tried to accommodate their concerns because I felt it was reasonable from a safety standpoint. (R31)

Other unions also report that they changed their picket behaviour whenever they thought police requests were reasonable, for instance where safety and traffic were validly raised as requiring modification to the plan. Critically, most of our union informants regarded such adjustments as 'negotiated outcomes,' not products of police or legal coercion. In turn, police claim that they do not generally move in with fixed bottom lines but seek to find a middle ground:

I try to get either side to see the other's viewpoints and try to stress that both sides have a message to get out. Most of the time I get them to come to some common ground as far as delay of vehicles, delay of people coming and going, most of the time we can come to some arrangement. (R24)

While some union informants express awareness that police are responding to union concerns or interests, they also frequently comply because they are convinced by the arguments. At the same time, the response to conflict and even law-breaking is further communication rather than precipitous force. This may be viewed as another deferral or delay tactic, but it is also about involving the parties directly in the resolution in an effort to get the most 'buy-in,' thus preventing further breakdowns of control.

> Our general inclination is always to negotiate – if it's a question of blocked access, we seek to negotiate access for specific individuals, matter of trespass; our initial response is mediation – try and work it out between management [and union]. (R32)

As we noted in previous chapters, this notion of union responsibility in controlling its members is not a new development (Fudge and Tucker, 2001), but the advent of liaison indicates a clearer and consistent acceptance by police that unions can be trusted to be responsible. This construction of unions as self-regulating and lawful helps to explain why, within the so-called age of information- or intelligence-based policing, police engage in very few efforts to gather significant intelligence on unions or upcoming strikes other than an initial phone call or meeting with the union. Indeed, most services rely on the union or the employer to notify them of upcoming strikes. More careful monitoring and diligence are seen not only as unnecessary but as too risky to the relationship of trust between the unions and the liaison.

> I: Do you use informants to keep informed about upcoming or current strikes?
> R: I don't like to do it. And I've only actually done it once where I had intelligence gathering set up, and where I had some reliable information that something was going to happen. In that kind of situation where I have some information and I don't do anything, I'm really at risk of being criticized … But I don't like to use informants – it could be tainted, all sorts of possibilities. (R26)

The significance of trust for police is not only with reference to self-policing but also in negotiations over points of conflict. As a liaison officer states:

> Trust. When it comes to any two humans interacting, trust is an immense factor and crucial. Realizing when I was dealing with the [company name]

strike and trying to remain impartial, we were developing a rapport and trust between the labour side and then the management side. At times neither side were happy ... but that's where you relate on a human level, you have to have the credibility and the trust. That's why it's in our orders; if there are any meetings we will insist that both parties always be there; we make no separate side deals. We must remain in the middle. (R67)

With relatively few exceptions, police do not feel compelled to place public order resources on alert or to develop contingency plans for potential public order or emergency situations during specific strikes. Similarly, the intelligence gathering is not proactive. This is because the risk of any major confrontation is deemed as too low to warrant the effort and use of resources. If there is an exception to this rule, again it seems to be police preparation for large public sector strikes at the municipal or provincial level.

In a recent public sector strike in Ontario, for example, a number of municipal police services and the provincial police established special task forces to coordinate the policing of the strike in its various locations. Large-scale union-organized marches and protests such as the Ontario Days of Action in the mid-1990s attract more efforts to gather intelligence and mobilize public order resources and contingency planning, especially in protest situations where police worry about possible infiltration by political demand or radical groups. Unions can attract more intelligence attention if they are seen as supporting such groups, as one senior public order officer reports on the case of a local public sector union in Toronto:

Our intelligence units were gathering information on the main core of people that were having the [protest], whether it be one of these groups that would go out there and cause severe disruptions. The intelligence services they weren't interested so much in the labour unions, they were more interested, they seemed like they were more interested in something like the Ontario Coalition Against Poverty (OCAP) where they would come out and they would practise at beating police lines and you know. And it just turned out that at that time OPSEU was sponsoring, not so much sponsoring but they were contributing to OCAP, contributing funds. So and they were contributing as well because when OCAP showed up, OPSEU were there or some of the other groups were there and they had their flags and they had their banners so you could identify different groups. (R55)

But these kinds of cases are notable by their rarity and serve if anything to prove the general point that labour is not seen as a public order threat.

Deferral to the Courts

As we have seen, unions, pickets, and protesters are coached and encouraged to regulate themselves, while police advise employers and corporate interests to undertake policing functions that were common up until the 1960s and 1970s. While this shift in policing responsibility to the subjects of policing is a commonly noted feature of neo-liberalism, the displacement of responsibility to the courts is somewhat less frequently recognized as a feature of neo-liberalism, although it too can be seen as an effort to off-load political responsibility as well as avoiding use of costly public resources. Yet from a policing perspective, the deferral to the courts is not just an effort to rationalize or minimize resource costs but also an attempt to reduce the political risks.

It is nothing new for the police to cite public safety and criminal behaviour as the key rationales behind their actions on picket lines (Marquis, 1993), and as Fudge and Tucker (2001: 19) demonstrate, Canadian employers had been making effective use of injunctions since the early 1900s. However, what is relatively new is police insistence that intervention into collective assembly should be a decision made not by the police, but rather by court order. As one retired police superintendent recalled, line officers used to routinely make decisions to open lines and make mass arrests often with little or no provocation and no reference to the courts (H11). Another senior officer recalled how one of his early staff sergeants responded to a question he had about the legal justification for police opening a picket line by saying, 'I've been in labour relations for years. There's no problem with authority; you just declare the strike a crime scene and therefore you have all the authority [you need]' (H9). Many of our retired police informants suggest that they never understood or felt comfortable with this kind of 'trumped up' legal justification provided by their superiors for police use of force in escorting trucks or vehicles through picket lines, but it was accepted nonetheless. As these officers from the pre-liaison era acknowledge, their superiors were largely at peace with the claim that it was criminal for picketers to prevent the free movement of goods and people onto and off private property, thus justifying the full force of law.

Although police still clearly have these powers, and blocking property access is still illegal, these same actions are rarely defined under liaison policies of the majority of the police services as justification for a *police* decision to use force. Almost all the services interviewed reported that they would at minimum require an injunction before acting in a situation where pickets have blocked access and that even injunctions ordering the police to intervene using force to open lines will be frequently resisted by police through delays to allow more negotiations. Similar practices are common in protest situations, although, as will be seen in chapter 6, the rules of engagement are somewhat different. In either case, this requirement for an injunction before acting is a radical change from the pre-liaison era and follows not from case law but police preference. This deferral to the courts constitutes perhaps the defining character of the liaison approach as a radically different take on strike policing.

> They [the employers] used to call us on a frequent basis prior to any strike and they'd dictate to us that we're gonna bring people in here and we want access and that's the way it is going to be. We don't do that [now]. We will meet with both sides, advise them of our neutrality, and that if they have difficulty with obstructed entrances, if they have difficulty with the number of pickets, then there's a civil process in place and that's the Labour Relations Board. They can seek injunctions there [or outside BC in the courts]. (R2)

Liaison police refer back to the civil courts and labour boards as the proper site for legal orders; that is, if the employer or the union is disturbed by the actions of the other it is advised to seek resolution through civil process rather than relying on the police to intervene. For police it is hoped that the threat of fines and/or imprisonment will be sufficient to bring the strikers or protesters to their senses. If they resist, action by police can be presented as an order of the court. In the meantime, police discretion in the form of delay in acting on the order is less politically visible. In many jurisdictions, as noted, even in situations involving illegal occupations, there is a two-step process that must be followed before police will act. First, the police will require the employer or other interested party to apply for an injunction. If that injunction is ordered, and there is no effect on the picket line, the police will not intervene *until* an enforcement order is provided by the court. The employer must take an additional proactive step and police only act under clear warrant of law.

As one informant from the BC Solicitor General's office also pointed out, there are also negotiations even after a court order has been issued:

> R: I'm not sure what's happening in the rest of the country but in BC, the moment you have the court order you used to immediately walk in and execute that order – this seems to have gone away. The tactic [now] is clearly, we have a court order – let's see if we can negotiate something that accommodates you. If you want a profile, if you want to be seen to be resisting, then let's set the limit of people, everybody else move out and we'll move in and arrest those people.
> I: So it's all scripted?
> R: Yeah it's basically scripted and that satisfies the demonstrators; it preserves public peace and order, and avoids the negative impact of a major violent confrontation. (R9)

There is push-back. Strikers and protesters recognize police strategy and trust is broken. This appears to be the case particularly in public sector strikes, likely as a consequence of the particular challenges, locations, and interests involved in such strikes. Police also reported that managers and private police also often break their strike protocol agreements by moving equipment over a line without notice or using force to break through a line. The courts, in their turn, criticize police inaction explicitly, undertaking to force police action prior to the court order and more forthright police action once the enforcement order is provided. That said, the ripe dynamism of public order is such as to disallow overreach from the bench. The judiciary and legislature can impose order once removed from real-time machinations, but such order is often rightly viewed as inoperable.

One of the conditions that must be met before a judge will grant an injunction is a prior effort by the complainant to seek police assistance (*Ogden Entertainment v. Retail/Wholesale Division, USWA, Local 440, Court of Appeal for Ontario, April 17, 1998*). Police in Ontario are directly tied to the injunction process through the Courts of Justice Act, according to which police intervention becomes a threshold test, adding to the tests for injunctive relief outlined above. Section 102(3) of the act[4] states:

> In a motion or proceeding for an injunction to restrain a person from an act in connection with a labour dispute, the court must be satisfied that reasonable efforts to obtain police assistance, protection and action to prevent or remove any alleged danger of damage to property, injury to

persons, obstruction of or interference with lawful entry or exit from the premises in question or breach of the peace have been unsuccessful.

If the court finds that 'reasonable' efforts have been made on the part of the plaintiff for police assistance and police either were unable to control the situation or were unwilling to do so, then the stipulation made by section 102(3) is said to have been met and an injunction will be issued. Conversely, it has been held that should the court find that not enough effort was made to obtain police assistance or that police were able to adequately control the situation, an injunction will not be issued. It has further been held that not only does section 102(3) authorize the police to intervene in picketing situations, but that it is their duty to intervene where criminal or tortious activity occurs. In *Attorney General v. Gillehan,*[5] Judge Montgomery commented on picketers interfering in the ingress and egress of vehicles from premises:

The police seemed to think they should not help. They were wrong. They not only should have helped, they had a statutory duty to help and a duty to ensure free and uninterrupted ingress and egress to the premises.

Similarly, in *Canada Post Corp. v. C.U.P.W.,*[6] Montgomery further stated:

[The police] cannot sit idly by and watch simply because a labour dispute is in progress. Breaches of the law must be remedied just as assiduously in a labour dispute as in any other situation. I am impelled to introduce this caveat because of the many sworn complaints of police inactivity in some areas.

Despite the court's interpretation of this legislative provision of the Courts of Justice Act and its denunciations of police failure to uphold the criminal law, police policy of non-interference in picketing persists in Ontario. In *Aramark Canada Ltd. v. Keating*[7] affidavit evidence showed that when police requested assistance in clearing passage of vehicles, they held to the position that the blockade was 'a civil matter.' Similarly, in *Toronto (city) v. Canadian Union of Public Employees, Local 416,*[8] police refused to interfere when picketers were hindering waste removal. In *Industrial Hardwood Products (1996) Ltd. v. Hanlon,*[9] after police had unsuccessfully attempted to negotiate an agreement with picketers to ensure better access to a facility, they stated they would do no more. Again in *Toronto (city) v. Canadian Union of Public Employees, Local 416,*[10] when a request was made by the city for the police to prevent picketers from interfering with a cleanup, the police 'responded by stating that they would not remove any picketers from anywhere.'

In practice, 'assistance' tends to mean an effort to mediate a solution and convince the two parties to come to an agreement to resolve the dispute. If this fails the parties are advised to go to civil court or the labour board to place severe restrictions on picket lines including complete picket bans. Some employers, particular smaller 'mom and pop' businesses, will, according to police, attempt to pull them into aggressive action prior to any effort to seek injunctions, sometimes by going over the head of the labour liaison officers to senior ranks or municipal politicians.

This is not to suggest a rigid demarcation between police and court action. Just as police are not all of a single mind on the question of liaison, so too are some courts reticent on the proactive insistence on the inviolability of property rights (de Lint, Gostlow, and Hall, 2005). Some lawyers, however, would prefer a change in attitude:

> I think [police behaviour] changed in the 1980s quite dramatically, not the law, but police, although the court attitude has [also] changed, in the sense that the court is now in [its] recent decisions saying to police authorities: 'This is utter nonsense that you require that an injunction containing specific enforcement provision is needed if this courts' orders are being disobeyed. We expect you to enforce the [original] order whether there's such a thing contained in it or not.' (R11 – management IR lawyer)

From the police perspective, however, the two-step process is a critical aspect of their deferral of responsibility and action. As such, while strike and many protest situations are seen as requiring active preventive intervention in terms of communication, education, and negotiations, the police seek to avoid immediate or direct reactive intervention on picket lines, limited at most to *isolated* breaches of the peace, safety concerns, and *individual* criminal acts. Larger-scale actions against the collectivity as a whole – that is, a picket line, an occupied building, or an entire protest group – are seen as requiring legal judgment. This both defers action, and thereby plays for time so that a peaceful resolution may be negotiated, and transfers further responsibility from the police, this time to the courts. The effectiveness of this deferral of responsibility is demonstrated in part by the comments of one union leader, cited in chapter 4, that the lack of neutrality was not in the police but in the law that they were required to enforce.

The View from Inside the Line

As demonstrated in the previous chapter, police view the liaison approach as a cost-effective strategy for managing strikes, minimizing strike violence, and negotiating peaceful resolutions without the use of force. Indeed, while the changing tactics of protest groups and the heightened security concerns of the post-9/11 period are beginning to shape further changes in public order thinking and practices (see next chapter), the liaison approach not only remains a significant component of broader public order philosophy, it continues to be the normative approach to strike policing across the country. This persistent police commitment to a liaison philosophy reveals the continuing 'special status' of unions as organizations that can be trusted to operate safely within the law without presenting a threat to national security or public order. As the police acknowledge, this status is grounded in the union adherence to the imposed and negotiated rules of the game – that is, although unions may skirt the margins of the law at times, by and large the unions predictably follow the script, in large part by exercising relatively tight control over their members. This then begs the question: Why are unions content to play by these rules, especially given the evidence on the union losses and the declining effectiveness of strike activity in the 1990s (Jackson, 2006; O'Grady, 1995; Piazza, 2005)?

In chapters 3 and 4, we made the argument that postwar unions were pacified in part through the development of a legal industrial relations system that effectively bureaucratized and institutionalized labour organizations and conflict resolution (Fudge and Tucker, 2001). Although the compromise pay-off for unions has been seriously weakened within the context of neo-liberalism, globalization, and labour market flexibility, the evidence points to the labour movement's continued adherence to the principles of rule of law with few if any signs of a return to the radicalism of the 1930s and 1940s. This adherence is reflected in the continuing police view of the unions as law-abiding organizations with narrow economic interests that are predictable in their actions and do not threaten broader political or economic interests (even in the context of anti-globalization protests).

Again, it is here that we see that the politics of enforcement are critical to the politics of the law. By reducing the level of confrontation at the picket line, by conveying a greater sense of neutrality and trust along with responsibility, the liaison approach plays a significant role in sustaining the labour movement's commitment to the law, which, in turn, gives the police little reason or incentive to move away from the approach, further reinforcing the union adherence to the rules of the game. This underscores the importance of the liaison principles as outlined above. For example, both the emphasis on strikes as civil disputes and police neutrality form the key rationales for the police refusal to open picket lines. This gave unions, especially smaller unions that had difficulty mounting significant numbers of pickets, a greater capacity to block property access without the fear of force or arrest, while at the same time binding unions to protocol agreements which ultimately guaranteed and recognized ownership access. The police emphasis on negotiations and flexible enforcement offered enough elasticity within these constraints so that even the occasional law-breaking (e.g., plant occupations), what one liaison officer called 'putting the occasional toe over the line,' could be handled without significant confrontation while paradoxically still renewing the over-all union commitment to the law. By both enabling and scripting the unions' protest actions as mere forms of communication between two private actors, the police helped to pacify and depoliticize strike and protest actions. Whether these new understandings offered any gains to labour with respect to their capacity to negotiate with their employers is another matter, but as we seek to demonstrate here, the police and, by association, the state were rendered far less visible as the source of labour's troubles.

We argue this not only because of police perceptions of labour as trustworthy, and our observed labour cooperation with the police, but also because of positive support expressed by labour towards the police liaison approach. Data from both our survey of local unions, and more detailed interviews with union leaders and strikers within our case studies, demonstrate that a clear majority view the liaison approach in a very positive light with real benefits for the unions (see table 5.1). Over three-quarters of the locals recently involved in a strike (77 per cent) reported they had no complaints about the way the police handled their strike, and almost 90 per cent reported that the police usually or always acted in ways that respected the workers' rights to strike and picket. Seventy per cent said that the police always acted in a neutral fashion, while more than half (64 per cent) reported that the police were usually or always helpful to the union. Sixty-four per cent

Table 5.1
Union perceptions of the police during recent strikes

	Percentage of union responses				
	Never	Rarely	Sometimes	Usually	Always
Police acted in a neutral way	–	5.4%	5.4%	18.9%	70.3%
Police respected strikers' rights	–	5.4%	5.4%	24.3%	64.9%
Police were professional*	3.0%	–	6.1%	42.4%	48.5%
Police were helpful*	3.0%	–	30.3%	24.2%	42.4%
Police were sympathetic to the strikers' cause	–	6.3%	28.1%	43.8%	21.9%
Were police upfront and honest?	3.4%	3.4%	6.9%	24.1%	62.1%
Could you trust the police to keep certain information on picket plans confidential?	21.4%	3.6%	10.7%	21.4%	42.9%

N=39 (*6 missing)

of the unions were willing to give information about strike plans to the police in confidence, trusting that the police would not pass the information on to management. Open-ended comments often included 'very helpful,' 'professional,' 'fair,' 'there when you needed them,' with very few strong negative comments. When asked about any previous experiences with the police, again a clear majority (66 per cent) were very positive, only speaking negatively in reference to the 'way they were before' the shift to the liaison approach.

More detailed face-to-face qualitative interviews with these and other more senior union officials also yielded considerable enthusiasm for the police approach. As one union representative who is actively involved in organizing protests for the labour movement in BC stated about the RCMP liaison person, 'He is a significant resource for us; he's just been incredible, very, very helpful.' He went on to describe numerous incidents where the labour liaison person intervened on their behalf with private security and other police services to enhance their ability to exercise their rights to protest. He recalled one mall incident:

We were at a mall handing out leaflets on child labour – it's a parenthood issue right, and the mall security were on us instantly. But [name of liaison person] came with us and he just sort of held up the court decision [the Supreme Court decision recognizing the right to leaflet in malls], and

said, 'you know they're here for the afternoon they're not here forever.'
He stayed until just before we left but he always leaves his cell number
with us. (R18)

Another senior union official referring to the Vancouver police was
also highly positive in his assessment:

R: There have been no problems with the police since the 1970s – they
understand that they don't have the support of the public by taking a
heavy-handed position in respect to picket lines. So the Vancouver police
in my experience have been pretty well tolerant to picket lines to the
extent that they are fair, if not a wee bit on the side of the picketers.
I: So at minimum, you see them as being neutral.
R: Oh yeah. (R2)

Union leaders in Hamilton were also generally very positive about the
police and about the changes after the liaison approach was initiated
more fully in the 1980s:

Like the seventeen and half week strike we had with Bell Canada. Here in
the city we had 1200 people on the picket line. There was 35,000 in
Ontario and Quebec. Now here it was a peaceful strike, we had no issues
[with the police] at all. But part of the reason was we sat down with them
[the police] and had a protocol established and the officers were not
aggressive on the line, which was a major change. We remember the days
of the postal workers (in the 1970s) when the police would pull up, and
they wouldn't have their badges on, and two or three carloads would get
out, and they'd just toss people around to get the trucks through. Well
that was gone; didn't happen after they put in the new policy. (R39)

Picket lines are definitely more peaceful. Any worker who goes on the
line is a bit apprehensive, or was as to what might happen. You know
there was an unpredictable element there; if suddenly the company
needed to make a delivery or something and the police come dashing out,
you know a group of them and they open the line 'cause we won't open it.
There was always the feeling, okay are they going to bring out the clubs?
Well that went away. (R68)

To be certain that this was not just a leadership phenomenon, we
also visited a number of picket lines and interviewed people on the
line. In most cases, and of course it did depend to some extent on

whether there had been any trouble on the line, the pickets and picket captains were very positive about the police, seeing them not only as neutral but often as supportive, sometimes insisting that the police were protecting them against private security tactics. As one put it at a Windsor strike, 'They've been great, they look after us good.' In this particular strike, the private security had been using various tactics to intimidate strikers including lots of very large men in black fatigues and the constant presence of video cameras and black vans with darkened windows. The strikers, most of whom were women, clearly felt in this context that the police were protecting them from an unscrupulous employer who had effectively given the private security firm carte blanche and the only thing between them and serious harm was the protection offered by police.

In the context of the broader history of labour–police relations, this view of the police as a protector of labour rights is a remarkable development. Does it mean that the police are now seen as being on labour's side? Most union leaders would not go that far in their assessment, and indeed many were unwilling to even describe the police as neutral. The president of a large international union summed it up this way:

R: No. Not neutral. No, no they're clearly on one side here ... I mean if you break the law they are going to come and say, 'Look, you can't do that anymore.' If there's an order and you're defying it and somebody says enforce this order, they enforce it. I mean the law is not neutral [so] ... they're not neutral. Are they reasonably well-behaved, patient? Yes, and I mean I equate it kind of like a hostage negotiation kind of thing, right? 'Well, let's talk him out of it before we storm the building.' It doesn't mean they're neutral.
I: From your point of view, does this work to your advantage as a union?
R: I don't know if it works to our advantage or not. I think it's an advantage to society. Certainly it works to ... at the end of the day there's certainly a lot less violence as a result of whatever dispute. (R69)

Although also expressing general satisfaction with the police actions during their strike, a picket captain on the line from a different union also saw through the claim of neutrality:

They [the police] are not a problem; they largely stay away, and [are] pretty tolerant. But they are biased to management really. The law is on management's side so ... (R70)

However, as the previous and following quotes suggest, the target of union dissatisfaction is not the police but the law that the police uphold:

> Again, the relationship that I think we built up with the police in this community anyway kind of says a lot of the way we do business but I really believe that if it came down and if they needed to move somebody they would do it. They would find the way to do it because property comes before people and they would do it. We don't have no doubt about that. The laws are not on our side. (R68)

Here, we can also see how the politics of enforcement can strengthen the legitimacy of the police without necessarily sustaining the legitimacy of the law and the state more generally. In the period before the Second World War, police repression clearly and consistently reinforced the view that both the law and its enforcement were biased against workers. The lie of the liberal claim of equality under the law was most clearly visible when workers were having their heads clubbed by police batons, making it far easier to see violence and lawbreaking as the only way. By removing this, workers are no longer certain whom to blame nor how to respond except in the institutionally prescribed routines, which the police mirror and advocate in both their words and actions. As unionized after unionized shop fails, unions and workers throw up their hands, but they have not come close to the thought of insurrection.

And since none of these leaders and few of the workers are willing to contemplate direct or sustained contravention of the law, what remains for union leadership and membership is the need to sustain at least the appearance of resistance. Again and again, the liaison officers emphasized the importance of helping strikers and protesters to get out their message in a controlled, in effect, scripted way. This is what we mean when we say that strikes and protests begin to take on the features of a dramatic performance where the key thing is not to win, since unions leaders are often well aware within the context of increased capital mobility that they cannot win through conventional strike or even plant occupation strategies; but rather to present the appearance of a good fight. This may even involve a certain level of violence, such as the smashing of a security truck, but even this is often stage-managed with the cooperation of the police inasmuch as no one is arrested, or if arrests are desired they are prearranged, while the strike captains quickly reassert control to stem any extension of the violence.

This level of cooperation also extends to coordinated police union efforts to control troublemakers and undesirable groups at labour-sponsored or -organized protests. For example, in describing police planning for one of the Days of Action in Hamilton, an officer recalls:

> You know they [the union] didn't want to see riot squads and the riot police all in gear. They worked with us through the whole planning process. We got every step of their plans and we were able to address public safety with their cooperation. Even the anticipation of troublemakers, as did happen a few times, we were able to quickly subdue them, but we subdued them with the assistance of the union; it wasn't a one-sided effort. (R34)

Of course, this does not always work this way, and sometimes it is because the police themselves do not follow the script. But when they do follow the script as per the liaison model, the acting out of the drama does much to reassure the workers and the union leaders that 'the system' works – they are allowed to express their grievances and are treated with a level of respect

As we observed earlier in this chapter, the liaison police often see themselves as consciously playing to the leadership or membership. By giving the union time to delay traffic into a workplace, by helping the union to get its message to the media through an orderly rally or march, and by allowing the union members to express themselves in what may sometimes be almost staged picket line rituals (or even more extreme plant occupations), without the nasty consequences of violence and angry confrontations, unions have been able to sustain the trappings or rituals of resistance and protest. Granted some of these activities may actually help to create or sustain strike solidarity – certainly we observed situations where the lack of police intervention or the police intervention on the part of strikers appeared to have a heartening effect on the pickets in the sense that they saw these as victories. But more importantly in our view, the liaison approach offers little pretext to construct the state as a protector of capital, and in that sense, there is no build-up of angry and emotional confrontations and little grounds for advocating more radical forms of action or sustained union militancy. It is here that we can also apply the argument of Turner (1968: 826) that this privatization of dispute policing is yet another aspect of the withdrawal from public politics. In so doing, the approach helps to avoid more vivid demonstrations of futility and communicates to the general public that labour issues are matters of private dispute rather than public interest.

The View from Employers

While liaison policing may be playing a crucial role in sustaining labour and citizenry consent to neo-liberal policies and corporate restructuring, this does not mean that all or even most business owners and corporate leaders are happy with the police approach. As we have already suggested, the police liaison approach came under considerable fire from many business owners and corporate managers, especially when it was first introduced. Recall in particular the Hamilton case study where Stelco took the police force to court in an effort to force them to reverse their policy of non-interference in picket line blockades. The Windsor police had a similarly negative experience dealing with the local post office management in a strike in the late 1980s:

> R: We tried to develop a rapport with management but they in turn wanted nothing to do with it. If they didn't have the control of the police force themselves, the management, then they didn't want to have anything to do with it, and they gave us little or no assistance.
> I: So you had a meeting with management as well?
> R: Oh yes.
> I: How did that go?
> R: Not well. They wanted a minimal amount of officers at the scene. They didn't want any strikers to hold the mail back or to do it. They wanted control over the police, which in the past they have had. They'd had the full, unfettered cooperation of the police.
> I: So they weren't happy with this new approach?
> R: No. (R28)

In an effort to expand on this line of analysis, we interviewed employers or managers recently involved in strikes (N=21) along with a number of industry representatives and corporate lawyers in our case study cities. Among the managers recently involved in strikes, 30–40 per cent expressed significant dissatisfaction with the police. In stark contrast to the unions, only about 29 per cent of the employer representatives were satisfied with the control exercised by the police during the strike:

Table 5.2
Management assessment of policing

	Very dissatisfied	Dissatisfied	Somewhat dissatisfied	Satisfied	Very satisfied
Satisfaction with police control of strike	17.6%	23.5%	29.4%	17.6%	11.8%
Police protected company rights	–	29.4%	35.3%	11.8%	23.5%
Satisfaction with the protocol	6.3%	31.3%	25.0%	18.8%	18.8%

	Always	Usually	Sometimes	Rarely	Never
Police acted in a professional manner	50%	22.2%	27.8%	–	–

	Several times	Once or twice	Never
Times where force should have been used	9.5%	14.3%	76.2%
Times where arrests should have been made	–	28.5%	71.4%

	Positive	Negative	No
Impact on strike outcome/ length	5.3%	–	94.7%

N=21

> The police should have more discretion to open lines, more power to control illegal activities allowing business to proceed as intended under the law. (R71)

Although most of the firms negotiated picket line protocols with the union (76 per cent) as advised by the police, only a minority (37 per cent) of those firms were satisfied that the protocol worked well for the company. Managers also felt that the police needed to make changes in their approach (67 per cent), with an emphasis on exerting more authority as peacekeepers by being present more often (see table 5.2).

In our more detailed face-to-face interviews, most employer representatives were similarly negative in their assessments, although like the union leaders, they often noted significant differences between forces:

I've had people dragged out of vehicles, I've had vehicles smashed with the police standing by and refusing to do anything. And when the vehicles were trying to gain access and obstructed the oncoming traffic, the Vancouver city police at least, threatened to have us arrested. So I have a very unsatisfactory series of experiences with the Vancouver city police and their attitude towards picketing ... The RCMP tend not to tolerate any kind of significant unlawful activity ... In Toronto, when they tell you to step aside, once they say that's enough now step aside, if they don't get out of the way, they'll arrest you. They don't do that here. (R15)

Employer-side industrial relations lawyers were particularly critical of the way that the police dealt with injunctions and criminal offences:

The police say they will not enforce the law without an injunction. Even if you get an injunction we will still not enforce until there is an enforcement order. And what I say to them is this may well be a civil dispute but you see that videotape I just sent you, that's a crime. Get in there and do your job. They seem to think that because it's a crime committed in a civil dispute that somehow the rules are different. (R22)

On the other hand, fewer than 30 per cent of the managers described the police as doing a 'poor job' of protecting the employer's rights during the strike, which would seem to indicate that most companies did not view the police approach as a major threat to their interests. A clear majority also saw the police as usually or always acting in a professional manner. Indeed, the majority of the managers also stated that there were no situations during the strike where the police failed to use proper force (76 per cent) or failed to arrest a striker (71 per cent) when they should have. And despite the fact that 57 per cent of the employers reported that the union had often or very often impeded their ability to move people and production through the line, only 25 per cent of the firms felt it was necessary to seek an injunction against the union. At the same time, employers and labour lawyers interviewed reported that it was more difficult to get injunctions, and for that reason, they often decided not to attempt one because they did not think they could 'pass the litmus test' (M104).

It is also worth noting that while only a small number of these firms were using replacement workers (19 per cent), the majority were seeking to continue production (62 per cent) and ship product through the line (57 per cent). Not surprisingly, there was a strong negative relationship (r=–.41) between employer satisfaction with the police and production activity during the strike. Still, only two of these employers emphasized the need to be able to rely on the police to open the line, and many expressed the view that private security was sufficient along with the protocol agreement to ensure access, albeit with 'annoying delays.' Most employers also report good cooperation between the police and their private security 'at all times.' Where employers had worked out other strategies for weathering the strike, either through stockpiling or moving production elsewhere, or where the size of the operation precluded meaningful production efforts, the police were also seen as less relevant since there was no significant pressure to cross the line.

> We had flexibility, so when the strike came from the union we could do what we wanted to do, and didn't need to use the police. (R72)

Achieving this kind of 'flexibility' was often not possible, but for some employers, some of the larger ones in particular, the long-term labour relations cost of trying to use replacement workers was judged as too high to warrant an effort to shift or continue production.

The vast majority of the firms had contracted private security to police and monitor the property and the picket line. Regardless, these managers strongly objected to the police efforts to off-load the day-to-day policing of the picket line to private police and felt strongly that an ongoing police presence was required.

However, in the final analysis, only five of the respondents had complained to the police directly, while even fewer (N=2) had made complaints to the local, provincial, or federal government or representatives. This latter finding may well help to explain the fact that while the police report particular situations where local or provincial politicians have pressured them to act, there has been no sustained political pressure from business or government to move the police more generally away from the liaison approach. When asked if employers had made any significant effort to lobby government or police to reverse the liaison policies, an executive director of a major employer association responded by saying:

> I don't think so, and the reason for that may be is that the majority of employers, of the large employers who would have the wherewithal to engage in some kind of lobbying activity, typically don't run during a

strike. The logging industry doesn't; you can't run a pulp mill with non-union employees, you can't run most of the sawmill operations. So it's sort of big industries that are typical of BC are not industries that would be engaged in continuing to run the business during a strike. Now talk to the Canadian Federation of Independent Business or their BC branch; they represent all the small employers and so does Phil Hockstein, Construction associations, they've had more illegal activity ... But this hasn't been a big issue because there's not enough momentum behind the desire to change the police position. (R15)

Other employer representatives were of the view that even though there was considerable dissatisfaction with the liaison approach, policing had not become a major political issue because most unions and pickets were law abiding. As one corporate lawyer put it:

R. Don't get me wrong. Ninety nine per cent of the picket lines are perfectly legitimate and peaceful exercise of a right granted by statute and people's freedom of expression. You know I've been practising twenty-something years and I can only point to three or four incidents in that whole time where I thought the police actions were a factor. Picketers as a group are not lawbreakers.
I. But you don't see the overall lack of violence and illegal activity as a product of the way the police deal with strikes now?
R. Oh not at all, not at all. I think the incidents I can point to in my practice, I believe wholeheartedly that if the police had acted sooner, there wouldn't have been any violence. (R11)

And while managers and employers confirm that they often feel that they have lost some control over the picket line situation, it also evident that some managers/employers recognize the public and employee relations advantages that go with this new approach. As another manager noted, 'at the end of it all, we have to get back to work.'

Although we found no evidence to suggest any major lobbying campaign by business to change policing policy, and no provincial or federal government moved in any formal way to change policies or laws to require more police intervention in strikes, it is interesting to note that in the late 1990s, several police informants reported that there were rumours that the neo-conservative government in Ontario was thinking about imposing new rules in 1999 which would require the police to open picket lines and escort personnel and equipment. While the Office of the Ontario Auditor General denied any such policy considerations, according to our police informants Ontario police services sent clear messages to the government that they were strongly opposed to such a change. Perhaps because of this resistance, this idea never saw the light of day.

In our view, the absence of a strong corporate consensus that the liaison approach empowers labour in any significant way, or threatens business interests in some other major fashion, helps to explain why the liaison approach has not generated sustained contestation by business. While a source of frustration to particular managers or employers, mainly smaller businesses, few of the managers saw policing as having any major impact on the strike outcome. It may be that the weaknesses of the strike weapon itself within a free trade and restructuring environment have undermined the significance of policing (Panitch and Swartz, 2003). Indeed, none of the managers interviewed saw policing as having a major impact on strike outcomes. Just as important, the managers reported that private security had satisfied most of their day-to-day policing needs because there were generally few problems on the picket lines. In other words, either the companies are not particularly threatened by strikes regardless of what the union does because they are not dependent on the plants in question, or the lack of aggressive public policing is simply not experienced as a problem because the unions are generally unwilling or unable to prevent company operations during the strike.

Seeing through the Veil

While there is significant union support for the police approach, it is important to recognize that there were some union leaders and protest organizers who reported negative experiences in particular situations or who were critical of particular police services. In the latter cases, these experiences appeared to reflect substantial differences and even more recent changes in the police approach, a reminder of the findings in the previous chapter that some services were less committed or consistent in their application of certain liaison principles, in particular the refusal to open picket lines. In other cases, union leaders saw through liaison actions of the police as manipulative or unreliable, even in jurisdictions where there was generally a high level of satisfaction. As we discovered, some of this difference is situational, some seems to relate to the individual liaison officers in charge, and some relates to the way in which the police viewed the unions or organizations involved. More generally, these variations in experience and perception reveal that the tensions and dilemmas surrounding public order policing are not fully or consistently resolved within the liaison model even in strike situations.

For example, although most unions were quite positive in their assessment of the Vancouver police service, the service came under increasing criticism from 1999 to 2001. In interviews, a number of protest groups and a few unions were quite scathing in their assessment of the Vancouver police, reflecting certain protest events in the previous year where there had been significant confrontations, violence, and arrests. At the same time, these organizations were universally complimentary of the RCMP liaison office:

> Yeah, it's more of a strain with VPD and I think it's because they deal with so many things. I think they overreact more and I think they have a little different mentality. The RCMP have a full-time liaison and the VPD don't. When we went up to meet the police in Penticton (for a demonstration at a Liberal government convention), the RCMP liaison came with us and met with the local police, and said to them, you don't have to worry about us, we're fine and they can relax. (R18)

In Ontario – and again although many local unions reported positive experiences – respondents tended to be more critical of the provincial police (OPP) and more positive towards their local municipal police:

> R. Yeah, there's still occasionally some pushing and shoving on the line, like the police officers sometimes will say to a group, you're not following the protocol, you said ten minutes, now its fifteen, you got three minutes more or we'll open you, and once in a while they open them. The only times that we've had a real push and shove since then has been, a couple times when Premier Harris came to town and so we were picketing outside of the locations where he was speaking. So it's not a strike situation, but it has the same volatility. They put, I presume, OPP officers in plain clothes in our midst and so all of a sudden they started grabbing people. We're on the outside of a fence, they started grabbing people, well we don't know who's grabbing who and why. So a bit of a scuffle ensued ...
> I: When was that. That was OPP not the Hamilton police, no?
> R: That was OPP. The Hamilton police were great in that situation. They were on the inside of the fence. There was a couple, like once the OPP

officers started to do some things, one or two, like we were carrying flags and a guy had a flag like this and the OPP grabbed it in the middle and pulled. And what it did, it went over and whacked a Hamilton officer in the head. And his response was to, he took the guy inside, we, there was three people taken inside of the fence, held for a bit of time and then they were released back out to us with no charges laid. And people understood it was one of those things where you got a crowd of people just trying to move around and carrying something and someone can get whacked in it. They were really good about it. The OPP on the other hand, they were furious and they wanted people charged. (R39)

However, one union account in Hamilton was markedly different from all the other union assessments of the Hamilton police:

The labour liaison JS [pseudonym], yes, that's right. I really felt she was trying to bullshit me. I was aware of the fact and I was also talking with a pair of officers who were seconded to the labour relations branch for the strike, who were trying to lead me astray, citing things like the trespassing property act and what we were doing. Not quite coercive but close to the line. They would say things like, this is what we can make you do, we can charge you with obstruction ... but it was disinformation, and I knew it. (R33)

As noted, safety was often accepted by union leaders as a legitimate concern, but we did encounter union leaders, especially in the public sector, who saw through the police claims of safety concerns as unjustified efforts to limit their strikes. As they began to question police rationales and interference, this also then tended to undermine their view of the role the police were playing:

They always claimed to be hands off. They always claimed, you know, that they were neutral. You could ask them to do a specific task for you and they would do it, like a facilitation task that would help us, but they ... were always interfering with our picket line, going beyond what they said they would do. (R33)

In some cases, these experiences spilled into subsequent strikes, where police were not trusted to fulfill the union's expectations regarding a hands-off and neutral approach. Another public sector union leader expressed concerns:

We did not develop a protocol in 2002, did not meet with the police before the strike; one of the reasons is that we had experience in [the] 1996 [strike]; we met with them in '96 before the strike, we did sign a protocol with the employer and we found that for various reasons the police were more interested in keeping the peace and quiet rather than maintaining our particular rights. Management abused the protocol and cheated, and when we tried to stop them the police would show up and wave the protocol. And so this time around we absolutely refused to sign a protocol. (R61)

Here the union leader also felt that police used injunction threats directly to pressure them to either comply with the protocol or make accommodations for safety or other reasons:

The threat was always there; if we did anything we would lose the picket line [in an injunction]. (R61)

Still another public sector union in Toronto reported a very negative experience when asked if he would describe police actions as neutral during their strike:

Oh no not at all. I felt they were really working at the behest of the employer, whatever the owner wanted, they were going to enforce their wishes. If you talk to the people who were on the picket line about the police who came to the picket line at different times, I think they will tell you that they felt very much like they weren't being treated as citizens anymore but treated as picketers. (R52)

And like the Hamilton informant above, some of the union informants from other cities defined the police tactics as manipulative and insincere:

R: From my point of view the police were constantly trying to persuade us, not necessarily on the law but just on whether we wanted to really be causing this much disruption. You know you're already withdrawing your labour, if someone waits a half hour that seems quite enough. – the regular phone calls and visits from the police were really kind of reinforcing this ... and telling us too, you know once there is an injunction, we'll have to enforce the injunction ...
I: Were they overtly saying these things?
R: Overt and informal, like in the tactic they used, it was quite apparent to us they were trying to befriend the strike coordinators by presenting

themselves as neutral parties and trying to earn our confidence, and we knew that was happening. The person who was doing this, it was quite obvious – he was playing the nice cop. But when charges came up, they would turn up the bad cop thing. (T1)

Our evidence also indicates that where unions expressed less trust of police, it is also more likely that police themselves viewed these unions as less reliable and responsible. In the case of the union cited just above, the police viewed the local involved as exhibiting 'radical' leadership because it was providing financial support to certain poverty groups that police had classified as high risk for violence or illegal activity.

Other union representatives also reported quite tough negotiations when trying to work out larger-scale events or protests, with lots of posturing and threats on both sides. One recalled his efforts to organize a march during the 1999 APEC meetings in Vancouver:

We were dealing with the Vancouver police, a women superintendent who was quite high up and I remember the RCMP guy from the prime minister's office writing down everything but not saying anything. Right at the last minute she tried to get me to rearrange the route and I says, look we're taking off in three quarter of an hour and I'm not going to change horses in midstream. We're going, we're going, and let the dice fall where they're going to. She says, for Christ sake, it's pouring rain. I says no fucking way there are gonna be changes. That's the route we're taking. I says it's our rights here. So she says, Don't give me that shit about your rights. With all your rights, you are going to end up in jail. I said, so be it. I knew she was trying to lean on me. She said you're not going to cross that street and I said we were, and we did. We did what we did and there were no problems. (R2)

However, the now-infamous police pepper spraying and arrest of APEC protesters later at the University of British Columbia became a major embarrassment to the RCMP, resulting in a public inquiry and ultimately playing a critical role in the formal adoption of a more extensive liaison policy at the national level.

Conclusion: Redefining the Public Interest

Liaison policing may constitute a substantive redrawing of the public–private divide. Under the liaison approach, labour strikes and many minor protests come to attract only qualified interest from public police. In these events, the routine activities of actors are redefined by police as civil matters. As one senior police official put it, 'the job of our labour relations officers is to prevent police involvement' (H4). When the police say they see strikes as civil not criminal matters, they are explaining their refusal to post police at picket lines and respond to management requests for escorts across the lines. While the words in statutes regarding picketing have changed very little, what police and the courts countenance as legitimate actions by picketers has changed substantially. Pickets and protesters still do not have the legal right to delay or block access to private property, and using physical force (i.e., the picket line) to achieve that outcome is still a criminal act, but police now actively avoid becoming parties to the affray by communicating to union and management, by maintaining their distance, by deferring judgment to the courts, by emphasizing self-regulation or self-policing, and by stating baldly that the matter is a civil dispute.

Although not all the parties to these events agree, for police within the new public accountability of neo-liberal governance the public interest is refocused around the need to rationalize and maintain resources, especially expensive coercive applications. The use of significant police resources to resolve private disputes is defined as both wasteful and inappropriate (Murphy, 1998). It is in this sense that police are prepared in this site of conflict to hand over direct front-line mandates to the parties themselves, preferring to broker information about the proper dispensation of force and law. In this way, they externalize or off-load the delivery of services (while preserving some steering capacity): they responsibilized the disputants.[11]

While the police cede ground or at least visible presence, we see other forms of capacity being brought into play: again, communication, particularly trust-building exercises, fills the gap. In any new accord, relationships between parties go through reassurances, a particularly onerous undertaking where parties depend a great deal on institutionalized or routinized and even ritual displays. Police promoted the new accord by proving themselves consistent and reasonably transparent in their dealings with both parties (three parties, if one includes other governing bodies). In Canada, police construct their role as expert advisers to the picket site, a site of civil jurisdiction *unless* criminal acts are observed or public safety and peace are observably at risk.

Two elements that play a role in the police construction of themselves as distanced experts are safety and trust. 'Safety' is a flexible and powerful construction that police and the unions themselves use in exercising self-discipline. Police liaisons report that they always seek to use union sensitivity to public responses or perceptions as a tactical tool in their efforts to persuade. Most liaison police were careful to avoid any threat of using force in these discussions, telling the unions that 'it's up to them,' while pointing out that certain consequences such as accidents could work against their cause. As explained by labour informants, a significant motivation behind their compliance in many cases was concern about the public perception and response to potential accidents and disruption. As we have seen, some union informants express some awareness that the police are consciously playing to the union's concerns or interests, but they acknowledge that they frequently comply because they are 'convinced' by the arguments.

As already noted, trust is a significant factor in the liaison relationship, but the significance of trust extends to how the liaison policy developed: a series of discrete iterations over long and short periods of time in which both parties toggle between suspending monitoring and verifying the fit between actions and promises.

On the whole, our evidence suggests that this strategy has worked not only to reduce police confrontation and involvement, but also to gain labour and protest consent to a set of rules and procedures that further routinize and depoliticize the picket line. Whether this plays a role in weakening the effectiveness of strikes or protests is difficult to say. Certainly, the unions themselves tend to see the police as helping them to get their message across, while not directly undermining their capacity to delay and impose costs on management. And the frustration expressed by some managers, especially those in smaller businesses, suggests some support for the argument that the police withdrawal is advantageous to unions and protestors in some ways. However, as evidenced by some of the union and protester complaints, the police are still drawing some lines in the sand as matters of public interest and political integrity, and where unions or protesters cross those lines, police stand ready to respond with considerable force. More generally, however, the lack of any sustained political effort by business or their political functionaries to push for a general return to command and control policing suggests that liaison policing is not seen as existentially threatening. Arguably, this is part of a broader repositioning of picketing and protests in the terrain of more reflexive and scripted public relations exercises. Whether because of this or other factors, the increasing weakness of the strike as an economic weapon has been noted by various authors (Rifkin, 2000; Krugman, 1994).

As we have tried to show in this chapter, labour liaison is a deliberate, strategic approach that more clearly modifies rules of engagement and implements alternatives to the display of uniformed personnel, arrests, and force in a public order context. Police have restricted the range of situations in which the public interest for police intervention is recognized.[12] Largely as a result of their own dissatisfaction with the status quo ante, they have pushed back a large portion of public order into civil courts and labour boards.

6 Liaison in an Institutional Context

Introduction

In previous chapters we explored the development of strike liaison policing as a consequence of emergent police professionalism, including concern for public relations, streamlining of the mandate, and powerful motivations among reform-minded officers to remedy a long-standing bane. We also attributed liaison to the wider context of post-Fordism, welfare state decline, and neo-liberal thematics, which both angered and weakened organized labour and many other social movements. In addition, we witnessed the emergence of sensitivity on the part of municipal police to the legitimacy of labour that is organized around routine work demands rather than wider political agendas. Attention to the public relations consequences of public order policing events was also a powerful consideration in the context of anti-authoritarianism.

As we have shown, the strike liaison approach gradually asserted itself over a period of two decades between the mid-1970s and mid-1990s. As noted, this was a period of great transition for labour but also for policing more generally. The development of liaison policing was supported by an environment in which both police and labour embraced its benefits. For labour, it was a period of normalization and retrenchment in which postwar gains were consolidated into routine practices that accommodated the strike and the picket line without requisite expectations of violence. The liaison approach acknowledged the right and necessity of picketing according to relatively predictable parameters, even where such activity produced inconveniences or economic and social consequences, and it allowed labour to express its dissatisfaction in a controlled and managed fashion in ways which were widely seen as positive for labour's public profile if not for enhanced negotiating power. This became especially important as other postwar liberal accommodations began to unravel or weaken within neo-liberalism and globalization. At the same time, the increasing weakness of the strike as an economic weapon within the context of automation, outsourcing, and globaliza-tion, as noted by various authors, helped to shape picketing as more scripted public relations and organizational exercises than direct forms of economic sanction or pressure (e.g., Broad, 1995).

For police, liaison was a means of addressing labour strife in a cost-effective manner without unduly politicizing actions, while also spar-ing police a black eye in the court of public opinion. In addition, it reflected labour-union sensitivities now that police agencies had to be keenly responsive to their own labour–management issues and rank and file police. Indeed, police administrators identified with labour grievances (cf. Marquis, 1993). As we also observed, the liaison ap-proach was extended subsequently to other forms of public order po-licing, including protest demonstrations, marches, and rallies, to a significant extent for the same reasons it had been applied to strikes: it was cost-effective, many if not most protest groups could be educated and trusted to self-police, and it usually avoided political fallout. How-ever, in this and the next chapter, we look more closely at how liaison policing was applied to other types of public order situations, while also seeking to document and analyse other continuing developments and adaptations in police thinking and strategies in response to police experiences with specific events and broader changes in the political and protest environment. Paramount among these 'other' developments are the parallel extensions of paramilitary and intelligence-gathering capabilities, which, as we showed in chapter 4, first began to emerge in the form of riot and crowd control policies in the late 1960s and 1970s.

We start this chapter by going back to the riots and protests of the 1960s and 1970s, this time suggesting that they were instrumental in pushing broader developments in community policing that were subse-quently critical to the adoption and extension of the liaison approach from strikes to a range of public order situations. We also recognize other changes in police management and organization under the ban-ner of new public management that also speaks again to the impact of neo-liberal and post-Fordist ideas about management in general and public management in particular. We then go on to consider in greater detail the main changes that happened from the 1960s to 1990s around the creation of paramilitary units and the use of force. In understanding the context of adaptations in the 1990s, we review the circumstances and rationales underlying the use of force, even in the face of a developing commitment to liaison policing. As we shall see, both the practice and the policy outcome of the tumultuous 1960s were more varied for police reform than is often assumed. On the contrary, the roots of a much more nuanced response to public order than liaison affords is also the legacy of post-1960s experience. Two key internal or professional factors were the wider review and articulation of the use of force and the normalization or adoption of community policing. If for policing in Canada the mid-1970s through the mid-1990s was a time of sweeping reform, the main organizing concept around which that reform was sprung was 'community policing.'

Community Policing and the New Public Management

Although they did not threaten Canadian politics and institutions, the youth, urban, anti-war, and race riots of the late 1960s and early 1970s had a profound impact on Canadian policing and policing generally. As observed in chapter 4, a key finding in official inquiries of U.S. riots was that reactive, mechanical (and what we would now call 'disembedded') forms of 'official social control' were counter-productive, 'tending to aggravate the already volatile nature of the urban poor' (Platt et al., 1982: 128). Balkan, Berger, and Schmidt (1980: 104) argued that 'because of criticism in the late 1960s that the technical and managerial approach to policing would alienate large sectors of the population, the need for closer police ties to the community were stressed (Barlow and Barlow, 1999: 664).'

Directly linked to the public disorder context, community relation programs and subsequently community policing as an organizational mandate emerged as a profound reform in public policing. As noted by Barlow and Barlow (1999: 664), through police–community relations programs, which grew to include 'ride-along programs, neighbourhood storefront offices, fear reduction programs, police academies for citizens, cultural diversity training, police–community athletic programs, and the Drug Abuse Resistance Education (DARE) program,' police re-embedded themselves into communities out of which they had previously 'professionalized' themselves.

In the institutional response, Platt et al. (1982) identified the expansion of two distinct types of policing: a gentler, public relations–sensitive approach reminiscent of Robert Peel and his selling of the new police through service and civility; and a harder, preventative countering effort that would step up police capacity particularly to interdict large-scale order crises. As reviewed briefly in chapter 4, there is no doubt that paramilitary policing and intelligence efforts (like COINTELPRO) were anted up to address what might be called hard knowledge shortfalls, but it was the 'velvet glove' approach which was touted by reformers and attracted attention for its promise to deepen police professionalism and remedy the legitimacy shortfall. Again as shown in chapter 4, this did not lead automatically to the liaison approach in public order situations, inasmuch as the initial focus was on crowd control techniques and technologies, but it did create the organizational structures (public relations and community police units) and rationales (e.g., emphasis on prevention) within which the strike liaison approach could emerge and quickly spread to public order more generally.

On the 'gentler' side of the ledger, then, there was indeed an effort to re-traditionalize and revitalize police services through re-embedding them into places from which they had been gradually ex-communicated or with which they were out of touch. This was a gradual process, beginning, it is generally agreed, with projects like that of the foot patrol officers in Flint, Michigan (Trojanowicz and Bucqueroux 1990), and, more commonly, in the community service, diversity training, and public relations efforts mentioned above. However, confronted by the long-standing traditions of the police occupational culture and also by service expectations of residents in serviced communities, community policing was slow to develop on the ground. It did not work its way deeply into police organizational philosophy, let alone reward structure, until well into the 1980s. Although the push to reform may have been hastened by the flashpoint of public disorder, it was the widespread adoption of new business models and philosophies in the early 1980s that boosted support for line officer discretion and decision-making that provided the further encouragement (cf. Deukmedjian and de Lint, 2007; de Lint, 1998).

As such, closely connected to the development of community policing was what some have called 'new managerialism' (du Gay, 1994; Entemann, 1993; de Lint 1998) or 'new public management' (NPM). The aim of the new managerial discourses, according to analysts like David Harvey, was to resocialize the worker within post-industrialism (or post-Fordism) while enhancing better organizational adaptability to emerging global markets and information-age market conditions

(Harvey, 1989; Lash and Urry, 1987). Within this discourse, knowledge society organizations are conceived as active 'learners' that cultivate and exploit their knowledge bases (Senge, 1990; Morgan, 1993). Worker ingenuity and creativity were not to be shunned with insubordination but rather utilized as an asset: workers were to enjoy more decision-making power in exchange for more active or creative involvement. Worker discretion or 'empowerment' was touted as more efficient than cumbersome chains of command. Managerial texts like Peter Senge's *The Fifth Discipline* (1990), Gareth Morgan's *Imaginization* (1993), and Osborne and Gaebler's *Reinventing Government* (1993) celebrated this post-bureaucratic organizational structure, one not pre-occupied with rules and regulations, but with unleashing pro-organizational creative power (du Gay, 1994). According to Giddens, neo-liberal organizational systems are in this way a more reflexive blend of agency and structure (Giddens 1984; 1990). They 'hail' responsible choosers that are then discursively deployed as political currency. New managerial discourse and practice seize upon human agency as an achievement of pro-organizational missions and competencies. The new managerialism, or as some call it when referred to state institutions, new public management (Cope, 1993), influenced many corporate missions and organizational plans in North America, including police services.

Indeed, community policing became strong as a policing reform movement precisely because it dovetailed with these 'experimental' organizational techniques that were launched throughout the 1970s and 1980s, including various 'systems,' 'organic' or 'holistic' approaches to the corporate organization. It had common stock with the view that both worker efficiency and corporate productivity were dependent on and served by more participatory decision-making cultures and the cultivation of teamwork or team competition. It incorporated narratives now regarded as part of the new public management or managerialism that has changed how public agencies are controlled and run, including public accountability, service, public relations, efficiency, and crime prevention. Consequently, with roots in the 1980s, prescriptions for a 'new police' were developed in the public agencies of many English-speaking countries. Under the 'new public management' rubric, state agencies become 'enterprises,' measured for their 'responsiveness,' 'accountability,' 'efficiency,' and cost-benefit analyses.

Community policing proper, particularly problem-oriented policing, or POP, became a reasonably suitable tool in the promotion of reorganizational or structural changes and emerged internationally as the most popular policing 'philosophy' in the early 1980s. According to its protagonists (Goldstein, 1979; Himmelfarb, 1991) it offered a way, potentially, of integrating both occupational and administrative agendas: to the rank and file it offered discretion and a new form of service professionalism and autonomy; to the administration it offered ways of shaping officer decision-making and ensuring information uptake in a way that advanced inter-agency cooperation and fostered good public relations. Problem-oriented policing was a way of providing law enforcement–oriented police with tools to gather information in a way that could be presented as service oriented in its method and sometimes in its intent.

In Canada, this new public management and the development of community policing as a principal organizational mandate can be traced in part to the Hickling-Johnston report of 1982. Commissioned by the Metro Toronto Police, the vision statement of this document stipulated a focus on local community needs and organized crime and placed a greater emphasis on planning and research, public affairs, and the use of civilian administrators. It called on the chief of police to do more external or public relations and on middle management to be more 'professionalized,' 'civilianized,' decentralized, and involved in planning. With regard to the rank and file function, it called for 'generalist' policing: following the earlier recommendations of the Ontario government's 1974 *Report on the Task Force on Policing*, police constables were to be involved as generalists in the delivery of all police services, and specialized resources limited and retained for support of the frontline constable. Finally, the evaluation criterion was to be efficiency, which, as noted already, was one of the key benefits of the liaison approach cited by police administration and reformers.

By the early 1990s, community policing was reaching its zenith of influence on policing policy. It had widespread support from high-ranking reformers and managers, was celebrated and elaborated in the contents of American academic and trade conferences and journals, and was fleshed out in the most powerful policy documents, including an influential discussion paper and RCMP policy document, Andre Normandeau and Barry Leighton's A Vision of the Future of Policing in Canada: *Police Challenge 2000*, published in 1990. Employing the management talk of Peters and Morgan, Normandeau and Leighton (1990: 1) argued that the police organizations will be required to 'pursue excellence' and will be funded according to 'total quality service' in an environment of competition for funding. Followed by other community police scholars, the document recommended a shift in outreach strategy from public relations to partnerships (and this can be read in retrospect as an effort to create stronger strategic links for the RCMP). With regard to the debate about reactive, legalistic service delivery, the paper saw the police mission as preventative and brought into play the popular issue of police responsiveness to fear and disorder. According to this model, rank and file police were to get more autonomy to solve local problems in the manner articulated in Goldstein's POP. Thus in the *Police Challenge 2000* report, community policing became more than mere public relations and involved community consultation, inter-agency cooperation, proactive crime and disorder prevention/resolution, and problem-solving. The document also suggested that police organizations should 'take actions and risks' much like innovative private corporations and have effectiveness 'measured by consumer satisfaction.' Police agencies should 'be flexible and dynamic' and 'use core values to cohere actions.' Breaking from Hickling-Johnston, it de-emphasized technology, worrying that technology would assist greater intrusiveness and dehumanize police services. Finally, it shifted jurisdiction for policing needs over to non-police-accredited persons and agencies such as private security, volunteers, civilians, other agencies.

As noted, the *Police Challenge 2000* report reflected on organizational practices and principles that had already been adopted in places in the United States and had been gaining momentum in Great Britain, influenced by the new public management under Margaret Thatcher. One of these was, as O'Malley (2005) suggests, a new use of the audit as a means of disciplining public sector agencies. A second was changing the police organizational culture from one that was paramilitary, autocratic, and hierarchical, a change implemented through corporatism, especially the idea of flattening, responsibilization, and the substitution of bureaucratic rules for creativity and innovation (O'Malley and Palmer, 1996: 42). Third, the adaptation was predicated on the notion that police agencies needed to justify themselves in terms of costs and services to consumers and clients. In Great Britain's Audit Report (1993), police were told they had to 'make do with less,' and partnering and outsourcing (including civilianization) were part of a new austerity regime.[1]

In many of the ways reformers had envisioned, the major police agencies in Canada were significantly different organizations at the end of this period (between the 1970s and 1990s): they had fewer layers, had adopted radical changes to training and selection, had embarked on aggressive outreach campaigns, and had at least re-established the viability of a holistic approach to service delivery. They had also made changes to how police were situated in the arena of policing and security – the latter involving partnerships, civilianization, and a longer view of the relationship between police agencies and policed communities, customers, clients, and so forth. On the other hand, as we have argued, Canadian governments generally did not fully embrace the neo-conservative revolution of Reagan and Thatcher, perhaps with the notable exceptions of two provincial governments (BC in the 1980s and Ontario in the 1990s). Canada's welfare and union provisions were still relatively strong (Fudge and Tucker, 2001). The ambition of NPM police reformers was in excess of actual changes to police agencies, including the major services like the RCMP, OPP, Metro Toronto, and Peel Regional. Fundamentally, police in Canada were still blue-collar workers on shift work. As is especially evident in RCMP documents and practices, the new corporatism treaded carefully around craft sensibilities (see, for example, Deukmedjian and de Lint, 2007). So while the RCMP envisioned the constable as the primary node of the organization – it was to that position/office that all the necessary resources to fulfill the mandate were to flow – at a time of great sensitivity to declining union power rank and file resistance with much more powerful police association politicization and lobbying was also formidable. The traditional authoritarian style of management and police delivery suited police unions, and cultural resistance to reforms tended to reassert the clear lines of the authoritarian style which saw strong, 'real cop' union 'bosses' confront 'wise cop' managers (cf. Shearing, 1981).

In sum, liaison policing was caught between the emergence of the new public management and community policing and continuing resistance to those changes. It gelled with the notion of the specialist officer brokering peaces in the interstices. The liaison officer was a vehicle for the transmission of policing and security responsibilities to other partners: trade unions, private companies, civil courts. Not only did this reduce the public relations costs of visible coercion, but it also allowed the transfer of resources to preventative initiatives. In this respect, the liaison officer was in style and substance part of the larger movement toward community policing (more specifically, problem-oriented policing) and NPM. These developments influenced the way police approached their mandate, including keeping public order.

Militarism and Intelligence

Also coming out of the American confrontations of the 1960s was technological militarization in the delivery of public policing. As noted, law enforcement that deploys the training, equipment, rhetoric, and tactics of warfare has been on the rise in the United States and Canada since the late 1960s. Cultivated in particular via the professional associations and unions, the military lineage of policing was coddled by the tight relationship between weapons manufacturers, the police occupational culture, and in particular its *sine qua non* of 'officer safety.' Emergency task forces or police paramilitary units (PPUs) were first established in Los Angeles in 1966 and inspired by a specialized force in Delano, California, made up of riot police, crowd control officers, and snipers that had been assembled to counter farm worker protests. First intended for barricaded persons or hostage situations, PPUs quickly multiplied and morphed from this original mandate, so that currently in the United States there are, by one estimate, 40,000 raids per year.

PPUs were first established in Canada in the mid-1970s to handle hostage or terrorist incidents to meet security assessments for the Montreal Olympics. In 1975, the OPP created five tactical and rescue units. Following that, the RCMP was allowed to create its first emergency response team. By 1998, there were sixty-five PPUs, with the RCMP having twenty-six of them. Almost every Canadian force with more than 100 officers now has a PPU. In Ontario in 2007, the OPP had three TRU teams of twelve members apiece, each costing close to $5 million to establish and millions more each year to maintain. Although their use has perhaps been less aggressive than in the U.S. experience, according to a report led by Ontario Police Commissioner Douglas Drinkwalter, between 1984 and 1989, the OPP received over 2700 calls (Drinkwalter, 1990). Only 75 involved hostage-taking, the rest being mostly barricaded persons or high-risk arrests such as the capture of suspects who might be armed. This extensive OPP review of TRU operations found that there was reluctance on the part of regular police commanders to call for TRU assistance because they had come to be widely perceived within the regular force 'as commando types and not police officers.' Nonetheless, their use followed the pattern, noted by Kraska and Kappeler (1997), of incorporating regular policing call-outs. For example, the London TRU team went out on 80 calls in 1986, whereas it did only a handful in 1982.

This vein of police professionalism, while occasionally trumped by the public relations concerns of community policing, did not expire but rather regrouped. Indeed, Kraska and Cubellis (1997) found that this rise in PPUs coincided with the developments in community policing, and that the styles operate harmoniously when paramilitary units are deployed in situations where community officers cannot manage expected or manifest violence. We observed this kind of synergy in a number of police services but most notably in those organizations such as the Toronto police where integrated liaison and public order units are deployed almost seamlessly as part of a checklist and risk assessment process: liaison makes contact to protest group A; if A refuses to communicate or negotiate, a risk assessment is made using any and all existing intelligence including input from the liaison. If the risk is high or unclear, intelligence and public order units are mobilized.

In the area of public order specifically, militarism has not been absent. In Canada its roots, as we have seen, are connected to the import of British colonial policing via the Royal Irish Constabulary model (cf. Weitzer, 1995). More recently, not only is there a direct connection to the development of the PPUs, but there is also much cross-connection with the traditional role and the aggressive countering strategies of the military itself. Consequently, we see the encroachment of military terminology into policing and phenomena described through military jargon (cf. Haggerty and Ericson, 1999). This includes the tendency to use acronyms. Operations other than war (OOTW), military operations in urban terrain (MOUT) and low-intensity conflict (LIC) are some illustrations. Thus, low-intensity conflict is described as a doctrine whereby social control over a civilian population is maintained through the implementation of a broad range of sophisticated measures involving the coordination of police, paramilitary, and military forces.

This reflects efforts to reclaim grey-area, or domestic, sites for military-style combat; these are subjected to developing technologies specifically aimed at countering crowds or civilian 'uprisings' through non-lethal force. In the United States, the firms Darpa and American Technology, and in Britain, the defence firm Qinetiq are among those driving the proliferation of less-than-lethal or non-lethal technologies. In Britain the initiative sprang from attempts to replace baton rounds (or plastic bullets) after they were heavily criticized in the Patten Report into policing in Northern Ireland in the late 1990s. Emergent technologies include: low-frequency (sound) emissions that can potentially incapacitate an entire crowd, microwaves that knock out equipment, crowd control foams that immobilize people caught in it, lasers to temporarily blind, an ID sniper rifle that can implant a GPS microchip under the skin of a protester so that he or she can be tracked and apprehended at the convenience of law enforcement, and 'sensor management architecture' consisting of an array of sensors, surveillance cameras, and monitoring and detecting equipment that can be programmed to alert responders to subtle changes in chemistry in a targeted zone.

The other 'hard' side of professionalization is intelligencification. But, as noted earlier, it can be said that particularly in the period from the mid-1970s to the mid-1980s, intelligence was receiving a great deal of bad press. In the United States, in the mid-1970s, three inquiries relating to intelligence malpractice were held (one for each branch of government), of which the 1975 Senate Select Committee to Study Government Operations with Respect to Intelligence Activities was perhaps the most robust, exposing illegal activity and recommending new FBI guidelines. Senator Frank Church, chairman of the committee, described the FBI activities as 'a secret war' against those citizens it considered a threat to the established order (United States Senate, 1976). It was revealed that the FBI's counter-intelligence operation, COINTELPRO, operated with good cover between 1956 to 1971 in the surveillance, infiltration, and countering of mostly lawful civil rights and anti-war demonstrators who appeared connected only by their opposition to government policies.

At the end of the 1970s and in the early 1980s, the McDonald Commission provided Canada with its own sensational findings on illegal activities (Canada, 1981). Here, it was the security service of the RCMP that was fingered as the main culprit, with its practices of illegal searches and seizures, property destruction, evidence planting, and other 'dirty tricks.' Consequently, a new agency, the Canadian Security Intelligence Service (CSIS) was established by legislative authority. However, the intelligence hiatus in the late 1970s through the early 1980s was, as we now know, followed by a similar up-tick of activity, culminating in 2006 with the release of the O'Connor Commission Report on Maher Arar (O'Connor, 2007). As with PPUs, criminal intelligence has gradually proliferated in Canadian police agencies, and it has likewise been fostered by the same jargon of prevention and deterrence that had promoted community policing. Also like militarism, it has pushed and pulled' inter-operabilities' that have gone a long way to breaking down traditional walls between police and military, domestic and foreign, warfighting and crime fighting.

In sum, the rise of 'gentler' policing as a consequence of both urban discord and public order and intelligence scandals is not the whole picture despite how it has informed the narrative of liaison policing. In the United States, most of the federal government policy was centred on increasing the effectiveness of local police by coordinating their activities, enhancing organization and planning, and investing in new technology. According to Platt et al. (1982: 36), 'the primary focus was on technology and administrative problems, and the overall thrust was toward reorganizing the police as an effective *combat* organization' rather than enhanced communication and negotiation skills. As police agencies, successively, embraced the discourses of community relations, problem-oriented policing, partnership building, and capacity building, it was Los Angeles, with its widespread introduction of new technologies and strategies, such as computers, electronic surveillance, undercover infiltration into militant organizations, new weaponry, advanced training, and the special weapons and tactics teams (SWAT), and later the NYPD, with its 'broken windows'–inspired Comstat systems predicated on the notion that crime could be dramatically reduced by attacking major criminals via minor crimes, that were seen as the leading benchmark, or standard-bearing police organizations. Almost in opposition to what the U.S. commissions had called for in the reaction to the failure of the police to control the disorder of the 1960s, what operated within the 'soft glove' visage of community relations and community policing was a revitalized hard countering: an increase in the professionalism, militarization, and the hard technologies behind intelligence. In the United States, attempts were made to mobilize the police, nearly at a national level, into a better-trained, educated, armed, disciplined, specialized, and technologically advanced fighting unit, capable of suppressing any insurrection. These separate reactions only reaffirmed the long-standing schism in police work between service and the welfare benefit and the security and warfare appropriations in the protection or legitimation of extant economic relations.

Use of Force

As militarization proceeded apace, there was pressure on police use of force. This is partly because the military jargon on permissible use (rules of engagement) and police occupational concern with 'officer safety' often go in the same direction in the undervaluing of non-violence. This could be observed when the use of force became a public issue in the late 1980s and early 1990s. Especially following the inquiry into police shootings and a riot in Toronto (Ontario, 1989; 1992), Ontario and other provincial governments began work on rethinking how officers should be trained to think about the use of force.

Ontario seconded officers to a working group and consulted widely within the police community in North America and beyond to discover, if possible, a technical or training solution to the problem of perceived errors to the use of deadly force. This came at the same time that the Ontario government was attempting to incorporate less-than-lethal technologies into the training 'templates' which were being used. Specifically, 'pepper spray' was being added to the ready arsenal but posed a problem for trainers because it had not been configured into the 'stairway model' by which the use of the firearm represented the last stage in increasingly strong response options. The working group of the government came up with the Ontario Use of Force Response Options Model (OUFROM). The relationship of this development to public order policing becomes clear when training on the use of force is understood as a 'cognitive schemata,' a realization which was beginning to take hold as the old training models were being thought about and assessed by police and ministry officials in Ontario.

Instead of a staircase model, often characterized as an 'escalator' with its concomitant imagery of force escalation, the OUFROM depicts three circles surrounding the constable. The first denotes the 'assess, plan, act' of the situation. The second consists of interpretations of the affect or aggression of the 'suspect.' These move up from 'compliant' to 'passive resistant' to 'active resistant' to 'assaultive' and to 'serious bodily harm or death.' The third represents the use of force options, which have no starting point, but which offer options from 'officer presence' to 'disengage,' with deployments building clockwise through 'tactical communication,' 'empty hand techniques,' 'impact weapons (soft),' 'aerosol spray,' 'impact weapons (hard),' and 'firearm.' Neither of the outer two circles are fixed with the other, although they tend toward natural resting places, which would link 'compliance' with 'officer presence,' and 'risk of serious bodily injury or death' with 'firearms' or 'disengage.'

In Canada, this problem of 'getting off the escalator' and disengagement was addressed in the changes to the use of force training models (providing the basis for all use of force decision-making) which derived from the working groups struck in the late 1980s and early 1990s. Key was the Ontario model (based in large part on the BC model), adopted in 1992, which substituted the figurative escalator (in which the subject moved up the levels of lethality in response options to the last stage of lethal force) for a series of concentric circles in which the subject was positioned in the centre and from that position was to constantly assess and adapt responses, including disengage, which was at the time a controversial inclusion to the response repertoire.

The disengage option is perhaps most central in distinguishing the new model. Previously, the reigning convention on the use of force understood the officer as responsive to the level of threat of a suspect, and depicted him as a stand-in, figuratively, for the totality of state intervention. The officer either went up or down the stairs to deadly force, but once he had 'escalated' to it, he could not 'back down' from the suspect, although 'tactical communication' did afford the rationale for pausing and assessing the situation. The working group rejected this powerful belief that disengagement was illegitimate. Instead, they came to the belief that rather than needing to be tacitly rejected, the disengage option had to be positively taught. The disengage option represented, figuratively, a reprieve, but a reprieve, in a fundamental way, from a way of thinking about policing.

This technological achievement was widely perceived as proffering a significant departure from past practice. It concretized themes that had been percolating regarding the relation between control and consent, among other salient issues. For public order policing, it offered technical means for the incorporation of a variety of weapons that were at once consistent with constabulary discretion and professional review. For instance, and adapting Vitale (2005: 285) and King and Waddington (2004: 119–20), extant research on police response to public order situations is more or less categorized into four emphases: past police experience and culture (della Porta and Reiter, 1998), strategic considerations including the size and militancy of the group (Button and John, 2002), political characterizations (de Lint and Hall, 2002), and interactive factors (Waddington and King, 2005). This accords with U.S. and European research (McCarthy and McPhail, 1998; McPhail, Schweingruber, and McCarthy, 1998; Vitale, 2005) which has found a movement from 'escalated force' to 'negotiated management.' Rather than seeking to control protesters through the threat and application of increased levels of force, there is an increased promotion of minimizing force and controlling principally through negotiations and communications. As

Waddington and King (2005: 499) point out, police in Great Britain in the 1990s were strongly influenced by Smelser's theory of collective behaviour. Accordingly, while a crowd may enjoy an initial categorization (political, festival, urban, sport), once 'the wheels come off' police apply a standard 'riot curve,' with the Smelser-influenced stage progression from normality > high tension > sporadic disorder > riot > serious rioting > lethal rioting > immediate post-riot > community unrest > normality (Waddington and King, 2005: 500). These stages, as Waddington and King note, 'conjure up the notion of natural escalation.' They state that while this model provided training via a Central Planning Unit document published in 1992, a reformulation occurred in 2001 with an ACPO manual, *Manual of Guidance in Keeping the Peace*, which widened the categories of protest events, recognized that the causes and escalation 'may be linked to police activity' and 'community issues,' and modified the stages of escalation, stressing a 'flexible framework' and the possibility of exit.

Re-institutionalizing Police Discretion

In policing, the fault lines in the admixture of neo-liberalism and managerialism stand out rather starkly. Police constables are agents of governance who need to be trained, it is argued here, through their discretion or autonomy. Although always a discretionary decision-maker, the constable has only recently become a chooser. It has been the extreme dissonance between the profession's portrayal of a disinterested technocrat, law enforcer, or state agent and the everyday reality of low-visibility decisions which has forced this discovery. Articles by Jerome Goldstein (1960), W. La Fave (1962), G. Abernathy (1962), and H. Goldstein (1963) revealed the discretionary power of the constable as anathema to this image of the technocrat/enforcer/agent. These works demonstrated that constables could choose not to invoke the criminal law, and that this was a large power indeed. Judicial rulings in America like *Escobedo v. Illinois* (378 U.S. 478, 1964) and *Miranda v. Arizona* (384 U.S. 436, 1966) highlighted illicit police practices and brought them into the public eye.

In Canada, the passage of the Bill of Rights in 1960 set the stage for decades of rights consciousness, which was then heavily reinforced by the creation of the constitutional Charter of Rights and Freedoms in 1982. Concurrently, ethnographic studies began to sketch a reality of a police culture in which behaviour and action were promoted according to values and interests which were relatively autonomous from or even oppositional to those which were fostered under the administrative purview (Westley, 1970; Banton, 1964; Neiderhoffer, 1967; Cicourel, 1976; Bittner, 1970; Reiss, 1971; Cain, 1973). Efforts by police administrators to depict front-line police as de-individualized technicians and neutral functionaries began to be revealed as somewhat disingenuous. Studies of police–suspect interactions (Piliavin and Briar, 1964; Black and Reiss, 1970; Sykes and Clark, 1975) confirmed that non-legal factors influenced police decision-making. The myth that liberal freedoms were protected by a highly supervised and neutral agent of governance was exposed. Far from being regulated through formal systems which travelled to the front-line officer in dispensations of consent and forged a transparent rule of law, the revelation of widespread police discretion pointed to the police constable as a rather autonomous agent who had great power to deny freedom, make law, and certify criminals (Ericson 1981).

When police discretion and 'low visibility' police action began to be exposed not as peripheral, but rather as central to police work, the idealization of the law enforcer could no longer serve to justify inattention to police decision-making practices or judgment. Whereas formerly police discretion could be understood as a sort of no-person's-land which was formally ignored but informally utilized (and could be seen as a residual of the administrative structuring of police constable action), subsequent to the public scrutiny of legal rulings and academic analysis, it started to become an explicit object: something that required the attention of proactive top-down intervention. The space of police interpretations was becoming a hotly contested terrain. Thus, it had become clear that if agents of law under liberal governance were to reflect principles of liberal rule, then something beyond the perpetration of more formal rules was going to be necessary. And in part because of developments in management theory, devices other than more rules and standards were needed in order to ensure that the liberal principles would be routinely manifested in the actions of police officers, even in conditions of low visibility. Police officers would need to be shaped not around and in spite of their autonomy, as was the practice that ignored discretion and relied chiefly on the absorption of formal law and procedure, but rather in or through their decision-making.

A number of problems and tensions could be perceived. There was a civil rights rejuvenation calling for more formal and transparent practices in policing. There was at the same time a movement, driven in manufacturing but also in the emergent managerial literature, towards a flattening of hierarchy and, as can now be said, a responsibilization of the worker (Cruickshank, 1993). To this, it may be added that police agencies began to appreciate within a community policing philosophy that their mandate was predicated on their community profile, and this was often clearly hampered by the clumsy, bureaucratic, and legalistic approach such agencies had evolved to take to this mandate. There had been a disembedding of policing from the community which was claimed to result in an absence of goodwill between police and especially the most disenfranchised groups. Police recognized that hiding behind a blue wall of disinterested affect could not guide them safely past the dark moments, as when they were featured in the daily news with truncheons beating down on labourers protesting loss of work or students protesting against war. Lastly, any solution to this police delivery problem had to accommodate the power of police associations, which was not inconsiderable as we have suggested already.

Community (and liaison) policing was a rejuvenation of traditional craft skills which attempted to reconcile legal accountability, craft interest, and market or community demands. In the area of the public order, and particularly labour, this was, as we have seen, perceived by some simply as a withdrawal of services. Not only was it so perceived, but community policing and indeed liaison policing do cede space that was available for occupation by others. Civil courts and private security were two obvious choices.

Extending the Liaison Approach to Protest?

As we noted in chapter 4, written policies for dealing with public order riots and protests of various sorts began to emerge in the 1960s, but these initial policies tended to make little mention of a liaison approach as such, emphasizing instead the conditions and procedures for deploying public order units and the use of force. While these early policies contained some reference to the value of police communications and respect for the right to protest, our police informants uniformly insist that a full-blown 'liaison approach' in the area of protest did not materialize until after one had been formulated and tried first in the area of labour relations, and that it was only over time that the liaison principles were adopted more generally as a useful strategy for dealing with all protest situations. As one BC RCMP informant described it:

I would say the initial move in this direction was in relation to labour, and they discovered that the approach worked in reducing violence, dramatically I think, and then it seemed to work well with the First Nations, and so on. (R9)

Indeed, many labour liaison officers recall that although their liaison service was initially formed strictly to police strikes, the overlap and value of liaison in protest more generally became clear both as liaison officers were increasingly used to help with protest situations involving labour and more and more frequently in protests where labour was not involved at all. Some services such as Vancouver came to this conclusion very early on in the mid- to late 1980s. They formalized the finding by establishing a community liaison section with a broader mandate for dealing with all public order events including strikes. In this context, liaison officers did not specialize in any one area of public order policing and tended to minimize the procedural distinctions between events. Others, including the BC RCMP and the Hamilton Police Service, continued to focus principally on a very distinct strike liaison service quite separate from a public order unit while only gradually adopting the liaison procedures for protest in the mid- to late 1990s. However, other services, including the Toronto police, explicitly integrated strike and public order policing within a common public order unit. As explained by one informant, the Toronto service felt that there was increasing cross-over in functions as labour became more involved in protest actions during the 1980s and 1990s:

What happened was the industrial liaison fell under community policing services unit. But what occurred was that a number of times that the public safety unit was going out to crowd control functions that were labour disputes, not so much labour dispute but ... rallies that were ...happening downtown. Even when the university students were rallying downtown and they decided they were going to close up some of the banks or try to get into some of the banks and disrupt the industry in the downtown core, [the] public order unit, the crowd management side, were being dispatched. But we also found that at the same time industrial liaison, their contacts, the unions, were joining up in the different rallies that were transpiring in the downtown area. (R55)

As a more senior officer from the Toronto force explains, even though the distinct positions of labour liaison officers were retained in this administrative structure, they are frequently involved in protest situations even when labour is not involved:

> Like everybody else in this unit, they are cross-trained and multi-tasked. So for example, BJ and GT, they're also public order officers, crowd control specialists as well. So 99.9 per cent of their work is industrial liaison [...] but a few times a year, if I need them to assist me with a public order call-out, then they're trained to do that. But their skills, their mediation skills are well recognized and I have used their mediation skills at crowd events where I've had two opposing groups. Because two opposing groups are similar in context to labour and management, are they not? And if I can get them out there and liaise with the leaders and speak to both sides and prevent violence, I think we've won. And I used, to good effect, the best example I can give you is the Chinese and the Tibetan demonstration when the Chinese premier was here about [...] two years ago. (R53)

In some cases, it is clear that a formal shift to a liaison approach was prompted by the same kinds of public controversy over the police use of force that were identified as fuelling changes in labour policing – making it evident that rules of engagement are not enough – and that the police also need an alternative strategy for preventing police intervention. For example, the RCMP adoption of a national protest policy in 1999 that explicitly mirrors the labour liaison approach clearly followed the major controversies and resulting public inquiries and complaint commission reports surrounding the APEC protests, the Stanley Cup riot, and New Brunswick (Burnt Church) (RCMP Complaints Commission Report, 2001).

Still, it is interesting to note that many services, especially in Ontario, had still not developed formal liaison policies in the protest area by 2001, other than the traditional public order procedures that addressed use of force issues. Despite the absence of clear written policies among many services, virtually all reported that in practice they employ liaison principles and procedures in both labour disputes and demonstrations – that is, they seek to meet with demonstrators in advance, they communicate their rights, and they negotiate a location and procedure for the strike or demonstration:

> We meet with the activist groups weeks in advance and I make it clear to

them that the dispute is not with the police ... How we treat protests goes back to the same philosophy. We see our job as guaranteeing that they have the freedom to do those things as long as it is lawful and that it does not stop other people from doing what their lawful rights are. (R73)

Arguably, this lack of posted or written liaison protest policies in Ontario reflected the influence of provincial-level jurisdiction, which by 1999 had adopted provincial policing standards for both strikes and public order situations. While the strike standard clearly grounded itself in the liaison approach, effectively forcing the few remaining services without such policies to adopt them, the public order standard made no mention of a liaison approach and followed a practice established in earlier crowd control policies by dealing exclusively with the deployment of the public order unit for crowd control purposes. Provincial standardization also occurred to an extent elsewhere, such as BC, where the Attorney General's office implemented a 'charges advisory' to its police services in 1995. Although this was aimed more clearly at public order procedures with no distinct standard for strikes, this policy was also more focused on setting the conditions for charges and the use of force and arrest powers rather than providing a detailed liaison procedure. As noted previously, reflecting an increasing trend towards the formalization of liaison within public order more generally, the RCMP adopted a Canada-wide policy on protest policing in 1999 that more explicitly follows the liaison model.

Policing Protests: Not Quite the Same

While some liaison officers working in both the strike and protest areas were quick to claim that their approach to protests was essentially the same as with strikes, some acknowledge that there were some important differences realized from the outset which have shaped some important differences in approach.

Certainly some of the fundamentals are the same. As in strikes, the police widely report that they generally rely on the protest groups themselves to alert them about upcoming events, sometimes because a permit or licence is required from the police, and sometimes because the groups themselves are requesting a police escort for traffic safety purposes. Also with the strike liaison approach, protest liaison usually prescribes face-to-face meetings or phone discussions, often involving negotiations on rally locations or the parade route. These discussions emphasize, again as per the liaison standard, the value of transparent, consistent, trust-building communications:

> We meet with the activist groups weeks in advance and I make it clear to them that the dispute is not with the police and tell them not to turn it into a situation with the police because this will only take away from their issue. We emphasize don't let the media wash out the issues by making it a thing with the police. (R73)

Occupations and blocked access to property are largely treated in the same way as well, seeking to defer action and particularly the use of force as long as possible, using all the same tools: persuasion, compromises, and court injunctions.

Notwithstanding this common emphasis on communication and negotiations, it is also clear that many services see protest as different from strikes. First, they require a greater diligence and, significantly, a more robust threat or risk assessment:

> I: Do you approach protests in the same way as strikes?
> R: It all depends on the threat level. If there is a possibility of violence, if we are told there is a guy who is an extremist who is protesting, we will have tactical response teams. In a strike, I do know what is going to happen and the numbers of people are not usually too high.
> I: Is there a different policing philosophy for protests?
> R: You have to be prepared, have people ready to react. At a labour strike, things rarely get crazy. The relationship to a demonstration is very different. In the demonstration, we go there and we tell them if you go over the boundaries you will be arrested. (R74)

As this suggests, it is the levels of routinization, institutionalization, and certainty that figure as the key distinguishers between labour and a variety of other public order events. Under labour law, unions are required to operate within a limited script and range of action which often includes accepting significant restrictions on picket numbers and activities. Police services accordingly see strikes as highly predictable events where union leaders generally exercise tight control over the picket lines and their members while keeping liaison officers well informed about upcoming actions. If there is any problem with predictability in strikes, as we saw already, most liaison officers point to employers as more likely sources of unanticipated actions, such as bringing trucks through the line without warning. Consequently, it is often more difficult for employers to get quick police action when they are dissatisfied with the actions of the union. We have also already recognized that police agencies may categorize labour unions and strikes with reference to threat levels in that some unions are seen as more likely to cause trouble than others. Public sector unions are also more readily seen as introducing issues of public interest. Some picket line events such as the crossing of the line by replacement workers are seen as requiring more caution and preparation, including having public order resources on readiness. The vast majority of unions and strikes are defined as low threat. Indeed, more often than not, no formal threat or risk assessments are made. And where no force is contemplated, there is no need to pay attention to different measures of force.

However, protest groups and some protest actions are typified as more likely than unions and strikers to present significant threats and greater challenges to the police approach. Political or demand group protests are seen as less predictable, with variable dynamics including the size of the crowd, the nature of the issues, the often public location of protests, the less clear or deliberately ambiguous leadership structure, and consequently the lesser amount of control which protest leaders often exercise over their members. This problem of leadership and ambiguity for the most part requires adaptations to the liaison approach, a point we will explore more fully in the next chapter.

While the perceived lack of predictability is an important factor in police approach to protest, the more significant question in terms of police preparations and deployment is whether the protest groups can be trusted to self-regulate and follow the liaison script and the law. But as one protest leader complained, the expectations of the police were often beyond their capacity even if their intentions were good:

> They expected us to control our people. And we explained to them: we can't control our people because we can't control everybody. We can try to talk people out of the line but ... (R75)

For police, this is exactly the kind of response that undermines their confidence in the capacity of protest groups to self-police. But experience is the crucial determinant here, and within the various localities groups develop or fail to develop the trust relations that the police require over time as they organize and field different events. The script or the terms of parade and other protocols are of course more tightly enforced the more an organization has been experienced by police as non-compliant or uncooperative. As in the case of a few unions, some organizations are unambiguously categorized as high-risk lawbreakers and come under considerable scrutiny and forceful intervention at the slightest hint of illegal activity.

A good example is the Toronto police characterization of the Ontario Coalition Against Poverty (OCAP) as a radical group which is unwilling to play the police game of lawful and peaceful protests. Largely active in the city of Toronto, and known to use a variety of tactics including land and building occupations, the group is constantly monitored by Metro Toronto police, who use informants and undercover officers to spy on the organization. Several of their events have resulted in violence. At one of the OCAP protests outside the Ontario legislature on 15 June 2000, there were significant confrontations with police leading to a number of arrests, including their leader, John Clark. Similarly, a protest on 22 and 23 March at a provincial Progressive Conservative convention led to the use of the riot police and emergency response team, with fifty-eight arrests one day and seventy-nine the next, and complaints of police harassment. As a high-risk group, the police are ready to respond to OCAP events with well-briefed riot police, but if the stakes are particularly high, as in meetings of international leaders, they are clearly willing to pull out all the stops. Yet the persistent controversies surrounding the use of force, and the continued recognition of its limitations as the principal tactic of control in liberal democracies, encourage an effort to find other ways of reducing or controlling the use of force or, at minimum, making it less visible. In that sense, the police remain highly conscious of the need to use a measured level of force only where the risk warrants it. This clearly enhances the importance of information in public order policing.

However, it would be wrong to suggest that police services are subjecting all protest events and groups to careful scrutiny, even in the current post-9/11 environment. Most services acknowledge that like the vast majority of strikes, many protest events by known, well-organized, 'legitimate' protest groups are treated as routine matters with the only major issue often being traffic:

How we treat protests goes back to the same philosophy. We see our job as guaranteeing that they have the freedom to do those things as long as it is lawful and that it does not stop other people from doing what their lawful rights are. (R73)

For the most part, unions and most small protest groups are judged from the outset as offering no significant threat warranting public order attention or explicit intelligence-gathering activities and are dealt with entirely within the rubric of a liaison procedure often without any involvement on the part of public order units. As one public order commander stated:

The only protests we attend are the protests where there is a potential for disorder, or the threat assessment is there, the assessment's been made and there's a potential disorder or it's a huge crowd. Because not only are we in the crowd, response team for the crowd, we're the disaster responders. So if you got a huge crowd walking on one of those bridges on Lakeshore, and the bridge collapses, we will respond; we're the ones with the equipment and the training for it to remove people from unusual environments of flat structures and things like that. So, so there's, its not just the disorder end of it, but we'll be there for what [inaudible – sounds like 'for what you face'] that's gonna be a huge crowd and there's always the potential that there could be a structure collapse or you know or lightening strike or something and you would need to have a trained group of police officers respond and that's us. (R53)

As the above quote suggests, large-scale events involving large crowds or multiple groups are seen as exponentially troublesome, as are events at certain sites such as political conventions, legislatures, and international meetings. As we demonstrate in the next chapter, these latter events appear to carry considerable significance for the Canadian police, which provides some support for Waddington's (1993) finding on the British police that the police act more aggressively, or as he puts it, are more 'willing to die in a ditch' in situations which they define as important to their identity as peace officers. This view was expressed quite clearly by a senior officer when describing the reasons behind police show of force at an anti-globalization protest in Windsor in 2000:

The difficulty with OAS was that you had people with that demonstration who were peaceful demonstrators and then you got other people, anarchists, their sole purpose is to damage property and to wreak havoc on our community. So, on every street corner, every rooftop, there are police officers. People are saying, they're just kids, university kids. We recognize this, their role, why they are there but in these groups there are punks, thugs, you know, the anarchists, and that's the dilemma ... it looks high handed, as if the balance of power is definitely on the side of the state 'cause every time they turn around there is a cop staring them in the face with pepper spray in his hand, but the issue of every police commander is gonna be measured at the end of these things in terms of how peaceful it was ... In Seattle the bill is still rolling up. (R25)

Here we recognize again two-track diplomacy in play. There is still an effort to negotiate the terms of the protest and to encourage self-policing among those who are willing to cooperate – and unions clearly and most protest groups also fit into this camp. However, for uncooperative, politically networked groups unwilling to keep to the liaison script, or where the circumstances or stakes heighten the risk, large numbers of police and an array of coercive tools, including public order units, will be deployed both as preventive and reactive measures. While the two tracks of public order policing have been with us for some time (to some extent even back to the early 1900s when the police first began differentiating deserving unions from radical ones), what we saw in the 1970s and 1980s and into the 1990s was a clear adaptation on the gentler end of the spectrum. After Seattle, and in the early part of this century, protest protocols engendered what, in some ways, can be seen as the continuing effort by the police to modify the balance between consent and coercion. More than this, what can be perceived is an effort to fully integrate liaison and forceful intervention within a more seamless intelligence-based approach. This clearly positions targets and situations for measured responses according to risk and threat assessments.[2]

Conclusion

Great changes in policing are often attributed to watershed events of the late 1960s, a period of signal importance to the history of social movements and the development of liberalism generally. Much like the post–Second World War period, it was a time both of great anxiety and of anxious hope. For Canadian policing and in particular for the policing of labour and protest, there was far less urgency. Yes, Canadians could watch in awe from across the river and see Detroit burning during the riots of 1967, but the incendiary event was still a world away. And thus the urgency of changes to policing: the gap in legitimacy could be considered and adaptation to the mode of delivery made without the need to rush matters.

That said, significant reforms did gestate and sprout in this period. The old way of applying ready force (in fire-brigade policing) was a greatly diminished enterprise once the U.S. fires were out and the police role in producing (dis)order was assessed; at the least, police administrators were compelled to provide a fuller account for their actions, not only in court but within an emergent expert dialogue and knowledge base, one in which the function of policing and its relation with the state and governance were pitted against anti-authoritarian cultural sentiment. Policing, once ignored by 'polite society,' began to require a letter of explanation to the body politic.

Yet the anxieties from south of the border produced a new wave of support for technological countering solutions, a subterranean counter-narrative of the hippy generation. The requirement for more 'sensitivity' to diverse policed communities spawned public relations initiatives on the part of police organizations. Police organizations began to understand that the spectacle of force could produce unexpected backlashes against their routine administration of business. Inattention to how police officers in the field exercised discretion could be an opportunity lost for greater disciplinary inroads on the police culture. Public order use of force was not merely a dilemma of lesser or greater evils: use of force training was an opportunity to demonstrate the superiority of liberal governance.

And this was the wider frame in which the new initiatives of policing were being worked out. The Japanese manufacturing miracle forced a rethinking of management practices and the welfare state's moral superiority was battered by the problem of incentives. Police and big labour in the meantime were institutionalized. In the next chapter, we will look at the new season of protest in the 1990s and beyond: one more chapter in the reflexive iteration of mass political expression, only now with the macro-politics of neo-liberal globalization itself the target.

7 A Season of Discontent

Introduction

In the previous chapter we examined the application of the liaison approach to the broader realm of protest policing as well as the continued development of more sophisticated coercive tools that were used in selective ways. In an effort to show how these different developments have played out within the context of other public order situations in the 1990s, we now consider the extension of the liaison approach during the 1990s to the thorny problem of policing Native land claim occupations and large-scale protests. We show that while the liaison approach is adapted to Native protests, there are continuing tensions and resistances among police, courts, political constituencies, and the public at large with regard to its viability. In investigating large-scale public protests, we are not only shifting focus to another type of public order operation, we are also unpacking a progression of police thinking about public order, and indeed policing itself, as police and political leaders confronted, at the turn of the millennium, widespread discontent with public policy. These changes in philosophy or rationality depended greatly on powerful if ideological interpretations of geopolitical circumstances, which more often than not allowed a more authoritarian turn.

As we have described it, the period from the late 1980s to the end of the millennium was one of momentous change for labour, police services, and the assumptions and discourses about governance that shaped what came to be understood as neo-liberalism. Several anti-logging disputes and Native land claims protests, the Days of Action labour campaign, and anti-globalization protests were among the public order highlights of the period. Although strike activity as a source of tension actually declined during the 1980s and early 1990s, social tensions as just listed emerged in other forms, presenting new challenges to police and their emerging public order strategies, including the liaison approach. Here, we consider two major areas of protest in the 1990s: Native protests and land occupations, and anti-globalization protests.

Land Claims Protests

We have argued that public order policing is a question of how the politics of law or the legitimacy of rule-making interacts with the politics of consent (the legitimacy of rule-following or the necessity of choice-making on the part of the policed and policing) and the politics of enforcement (the relative integrationist capacity of the police function). As we theorized in chapter 2, the interactions of these three values will produce public order ideal types, from the service variety of liaison policing that incorporates high demand for consent to the control variety that has incorporated a base assumption of conflict and adversity. And where police themselves do not adequately manage the politics of enforcement and integration is low, disordered or crisis policing results.

There is no doubt that land claims are a special problem for police because the grounding of the rule of law and the politics of law place police in an exquisitely difficult position of having to make up for deficiencies of other authorities. One can trace this deficiency back in classical liberal thinking and the problem of the property and legitimate contracts (Nozick 1975). Accordingly, the heart of liberalism is property rights stemming from the free contract, but the free or non-coerced contract is everywhere hard to find, particularly if one looks deeply enough into history of struggles between peoples. To the familiar adage 'property is nine-tenths of the law' is added the homily 'property is theft.' While the Canadian version of the dismal record of broken or coerced contracts with respect to First Nations peoples goes back to the very establishment of Canada, and includes significant rebellions against incipient constitutional accords (the Louis Riel rebellion of 1885), we can only provide a limited account of the most recent iteration, including four significant land claims protests and police strategies in their containment, countering, or accommodation.

Oka

In March 1990 in Quebec just west of Montreal on the Ottawa River, a dispute between the Mohawks of the Kanasetake reserve erupted when the municipality of Oka voted to proceed with a golf course expansion and construction of a private housing project. The area to be used for this development was part of an outstanding land claim and, according to the Mohawks, sacred lands. To oppose the proposed land use, Mohawks began a protest on a road leading to the golf course. The municipality responded by obtaining an injunction that affirmed the illegality of the demonstration and provided for the protesters' forcible removal. The Mohawks ignored the injunction and erected barricades to bar access to their reserve and the disputed lands. However, by July, the matter had not been resolved and more than a thousand police officers from the Royal Canadian Mounted Police (RCMP) were deployed to assist the Sûreté du Québec (SQ) in the crisis. On 11 July about one hundred SQ officers attempted to remove the blockade using assault rifles, concussion grenades, and tear gas. SQ Col. Marc Lemay was fatally shot in the clash, widening the crisis and putting it on the international stage. Mohawks of the Kahnawake reserve demonstrated support for the Kanasetake reserve by blocking vehicular access between the South Shore and Montreal on the Mercier Bridge. On 17 August the militarization of the crisis was ramped up considerably when Quebec Premier Robert Bourassa authorized Canadian armed forces troops to replace the SQ and RCMP units at the barricades. When the armed forces set up intensive surveillance and cut off critical infrastructure, the Mohawk warriors eventually relented and took down the barricades in late August, ending the seventy-eight-day standoff. The final cost of this public order crisis was $112 million, discounting the military.

A number of features of this event made it significant for subsequent police and public reaction to First Nations land claims. First, it was a public relations disaster for the SQ in particular but also for both political and police leaders. It highlighted the extremely thorny problem of historical grievances that were deemed by short-term political incumbents as too big and too difficult to solve. There were many possible sites for grievances to explode into public order crises, but political expediency was the fire-brigade response. Second, it highlighted the fact that police were ill equipped to make up the legal vacuum: they had guns and bullhorns but they did not have the authority to correct deep-seated problems of law. This point was made most explicit when police sought an injunction in the attempt to defer the decision to the court, a gambit consistent with liaison that only placed the necessity of action back on police when the courts ruled in favour of an enforcement of an injunction, lessening room for a negotiated settlement. Third – and this was where police had clear responsibility – there was as yet insufficient tactical and strategic planning to accommodate the lack of proper political and legal cover. While it was true that police were between a rock and a hard place, it was also true that police resources were sufficient, if properly used, to avoid or defuse or defer such public affrays, but this required much prior planning and ready implementation of resources.

Ipperwash

After decades of frustration concerning 'homelands' seized in 1942 for a military base and not returned at the end of the Second World War in 1945, a couple of dozen Stoney Point, Ontario, Natives moved on to the Camp Ipperwash military base in April 1993. Following a two-year occupation, they moved into the adjacent Ipperwash Provincial Park in September 1995, taking the park on the claim that it contained a burial site. The evening before an injunction was to be filed, there was a minor altercation between police and protesters, resulting in a pre-emptory call-out of the crowd management unit (CMU) and the tactical rescue unit (TRU) (in the absence of the incident commander, Inspector John Carson) to meet this resistance. The altercation resulted in the death of Native protester Dudley George by sniper rifle fire.

Following closely, and perhaps fatefully, the pattern at Oka, the Ontario Ministry of Natural Resources (MNR) straightaway prepared a submission to the court that an *ex parte* injunction was needed to enable the police to remove the protesters. The OPP believed that the court would rule with the MNR and order them to forcibly remove the protesters from the park. The OPP had taken criticism from the military officials regarding their non-interventionist approach to the occupation of the camp, but with respect to the occupation of park, they took the view that the Natives were trespassing and that minor law violations needed to be met with arrests and with the enforcement of the Trespass Property Act (TPA).

At that time the OPP had a policy that specifically guided land claims blockades. It stated:

When dealing with anti-social or alleged criminal behaviour involving protesters, hostage takers, and armed persons, the initial response of the OPP has traditionally been one (1) of negotiation, in an effort to avoid the use of physical force if at all possible ... The only exception to this approach has been in situations where death or serious injury was imme-diately probable if force was not used to control events ... This philoso-phy remains the OPP's approach to demonstrations of social unrest including blockades. (Ipperwash transcripts, 27 June 2005: 178)

The policy held that 'regardless of the validity of the claim, it is pru-dent on the part of the police to ensure that the ownership issue is resolved prior to taking action.' However, the policy proceeds to say that the courts can be relied upon as the mechanism for establishing rightful ownership:

In most cases, the question of ownership or rightful occupation can be addressed from a police point of view if the complainant is successful in obtaining an injunction, which specifies what action, if any, the police must take. It must be remembered that an injunction, being a Court order, leaves the OPP no option but to follow its directions. (Ipperwash tran-scripts, 7 June 2005: 156)

John Carson, the incident commander, specifically, and the OPP, gener-ally, had already been involved in communications with the MNR re-garding their approach to the park based on a perception/opinion on the 'colour of right' and appropriate enforcement. A meeting with MPP Marcel Beaubien a month before the standoff yielded the follow-ing, according to him:

As the Ipperwash campground is provincially owned, we should be in a position to legally uphold this property. 2. Enforcement is only a short-term solution. 3. Ministries involved have to give the OPP clear guide-lines for law enforcement. 4. A long-term solution is negotiated settle-ment. (Ipperwash transcripts, 9 June 2005: 245)

With the encouragement of the Conservative provincial government and local politicians, the OPP supported the MNR's pursuit of a court injunction, specifically an *ex parte* injunction, which they believed would give them clear authority to remove the Natives from the park and provide them with adequate political cover should this result in the use of force and unfavourable publicity. Just before the incidents of 6 September that led to the death of Dudley George, the OPP was preparing to contribute to the legal case for the prosecution of this outcome. Prior to going in front of the judge, Inspector Carson was asked if he would be prepared to state that there were exigent circumstances that would support the need for the court to find on the matter without submission from the Natives. When the injunction was applied for to evict the Native occupiers,[1] the MNR did not mention that Ipperwash Provincial Park was indeed being claimed as a burial ground, according to notes taken by a provincial lawyer on the day Dudley George was killed.

Thus, in leading up to their use of force that resulted in the shooting of Dudley George, the OPP had superseded the correct order of events as stipulated by the OPP liaison policy. That is to say, instead of being neutral observers to the court process in which the claim was adjudicated, police contributed to an injunction process that centred on 'the exigent circumstances' or the escalation of threats to public safety that the status quo standoff was deemed insufficient to repel. The injunction process did not establish the frame in which the police were to proceed but rather became part of the overall plan already conceived. The court would have little opportunity in an interlocutory *ex parte* context to adequately consider the claim; rather, it would be considering the claim that action was needed whatever the status of the land claim.

As in Oka, pre-emptory recourse to the court proved problematic. Protester action was interpreted as an illegal infringement without 'colour of right.'[2] This was also a position buttressed by the political context in which the land claim was also viewed as a non-starter by the Mike Harris government. Given this apparently unambiguous legal position, Carson admitted to putting a very low priority on working to establish communications with Native leaders via other go-betweens. In the meantime, Carson also stated that a court order calling for the removal of the Natives 'was the only context I would accept' as the basis for the coercive action that attended removal of the occupiers. Thus police provided support but were also sufficiently removed from making the lawful determination to authorize the action that police had already deemed appropriate. The lack of disinterest in this court process came out under cross-examination:

I: You keep saying you were going for an injunction. That's not correct, is it? I mean, the OPP was never going for an injunction –

R: Well, that's maybe the wrong terminology, but I'm sure you understand. The Ministry of Natural Resources was going to make an application and there would be a hearing the next morning. (Ipperwash
transcripts, 27 June 2005: 176)

In addition to the death of Dudley George and the conviction of OPP
constable Kenneth Deane, charged for the shooting, Ipperwash resulted in a public commission of inquiry headed by Sidney Linden,
with a total cost of over $20 million. The eventual disbanding of the
TRU team (Barrie TRU) in 2004 was also (although the immediate fallout of an alleged cover-up of the effacement of a Mohawk symbol in a
private residence at the Chippewa of the Thames reserve by TRU
member Heinemann) not unrelated to the George killing and the con-
tinuous heat the Ipperwash Inquiry hearings (extending from July
2004 and to late 2006) brought to First Nations policing.

Before subsequent Native land claims standoffs in New Brunswick
and Ontario, police had already been assessing the mistakes of Oka
and Ipperwash. The liaison policy that stipulated deferral to the courts
was not transferable to the land claims arena and, indeed, was effectively not a form of deferral to macro- (or micro-) politics that served
police interests. Police interests, consistent with other parts of the liaison doctrine, included maintaining neutrality, using fulsome negotiations and communications, and understanding the event as much as
possible as a civil dispute between property claimants. But in cases involving government authority, this last piece of liaison in particular
was observably untenable. That left communications and neutrality,
two distinctive features of the strategy at Burnt Church.

Burnt Church

In 1999, a ruling of the Supreme Court of Canada in R. v. Marshall found
that treaties from the 1760s gave Donald Marshall, Jr, the right to catch
fish for sale and excused him from fisheries regulations. The court
stated that the 1760 Peace and Friendship Treaty signed between the
Mi'kmaq band and the British crown gave Mi'kmaqs the right to earn a
'moderate livelihood.' The Native community in Burnt Church, north-
eastern New Brunswick, was one of thirty-four Native bands in the
eastern provinces who responded to the ruling by fishing lobster out of
season. Non-Native fishermen demanded that the government put a
ban on the catch. In the waters and on the shores of Miramichi Bay, the

two sides clashed as non-Native fishermen destroyed hundreds of Native lobster traps and Natives retaliated by trashing three fishing plants. In the summer of 2000, the dispute worsened and Natives at Burnt Church put a barricade of fire on the only access road. Local police had already arrested eighteen Native men before the RCMP was called in. There was much pressure on the RCMP to act quickly, but the incident commander took a different approach altogether.

The RCMP institutes inspector-level liaison with various other agencies, such as the federal Department of Fisheries and Oceans and First Nations in BC's lower mainland. This affords high-level conduits between parties. Under the leadership of Inspector Kevin Vickers, the RCMP did a thorough assessment of the crisis, using CAPRA strategy (clients, acquiring and analysing information, partnership, response, assessment), under what the RCMP called a 'measured response.' The 'measured response' approach may be considered an adaptation of the liaison strategy in that it involves extensive preventive communication and conciliation. The RCMP spent time with both sets of fishermen throughout the standoff. Facilitators were selected, based on their community credentials (status and respectability), cross-cultural training, and grasp of the underlying issues. These liaison officers were instructed to allow frustrations to be vented at them rather than the opposing disputant. They also provided information on the record of mutual aid and tolerance between Natives and the early French settlers. Unlike at Oka and Ipperwash, lines of liaison were established, in particular with the 'clan mothers,' chosen because of their status in the Native community and because they could provide a trusted conduit for the outcomes the RCMP wanted. The 'clan mothers' were in this way 'responsibilized' to the problem of order and resolution but also provided a vehicle for 'face-saving,' where withdrawal from disputed ground could be presented as an uncoerced initiative of the warriors. Trust was further enhanced through the provision of services to the fishermen and youth population. As with the 'clan mothers,' appeals to the youth broadened common ground: the RCMP provided food and coffee at its command post, participated in school programs, and helped build skateboard ramps. As for intelligence, facilitators, in addition to other sources, provided data for the real-time status of the dispute for daily roundtables. These were held to check on what required immediate action in the effort to avoid violence (Vickers, 2004).

Reflecting a more complete liaison philosophy, their approach stressed that violence was to be studiously avoided, both because it was an option delimiter and because it carried unpredictable management and cost risks. In addition to communications, this objective was also achieved through the avoidance of strict enforcement of the law. For instance, warrior nation members who were carrying prohibited automatic weapons were not arrested for this violation, under the argument that there was no provision that required immediate arrest for such violations. In the end, the RCMP mediated an end to the standoff without recourse to the use of force and in the process likely gained considerable capital in its future relations with Native communities. Still, it was not cheap: one hundred police officers were involved in this operation at a total cost of $3.7 million. The Department of Fisheries and Oceans also spent $13.8 million on fisheries enforcement officers during this period, bringing the total to $17 million.

Here we see two significant developments of the liaison approach as it is adapted to land claims public order crises. First, there is a much more proactive involvement of police in communications and negotiations. Second, there is a suspension of the strategy to involve courts and to ante up the conflict by imposing, as it were, the law of the victor. RCMP officers knew that the minor violations of the law were also a claim of self-governance by Mi'kmaqs and that RCMP neutrality would be jeopardized if they were to rely on law enforcement. Perhaps the most important adaptation is intelligence- and information-gathering. Inspector Vickers under the 'measured response' approach took the view that there could not be too much information, and that it could be gathered simultaneously through covert and overt means. This was deemed necessary because the RCMP could not afford to be acting blindly in committing resources to a peaceful resolution and face the possibility of being played. In the event, the fact of covert intelligence gathering did not undermine trust because the RCMP openly admitted to gathering information. And, inasmuch as we see this harder edge of information uptake sutured to community service (e.g., youth program assistance), we see the seeds of the sophistication of intelligent control.

Caledonia

Finally, in Caledonia, Ontario, another standoff over land claims with Aboriginals erupted in late February 2006 when a small group of Six Nations protesters from the Grand River Territory reserve moved onto disputed lands that Henco Industries was developing into estate housing. The protesters erected tents, a teepee, and a wooden building.

The developer immediately obtained an injunction ordering protesters off the site, and Superior Court judge David Marshall gave protesters to mid-March to vacate. They continued the occupation past the deadline while some community residents staged counter-protests to demand action to restore the construction of houses. The judge then ordered the province to charge the protesters with contempt of court for not complying with an earlier court injunction and ordered negotiations between the Six Nations reserve and the government suspended until the land claims activists vacated the construction site. However, a three-judge panel of the Ontario Court of Appeal ruled that Aboriginal protesters were permitted to remain on the occupied lands for at least another month.

This apparent concession notwithstanding, on 20 April before daybreak, OPP officers conducted a raid on the protesters occupying the housing project, arresting sixteen people. OPP denied that excessive force was used, but protesters claimed that police, armed with M16 rifles, tear gas, pepper spray, and tasers, aggressively subdued them. A spokeswoman for the protesters said one female protester was 'beaten by five OPP officers.' The immediate consequence was that additional Six Nations protesters numbering in the hundreds arrived at the site, set fire to piles of tires, commandeered a dump truck to block the road into the development, and climbed on vehicle perches to wave Mohawk flags as police helicopters squatted overhead.

The following month, Ontario Premier Dalton McGuinty announced that the standoff would be resolved peacefully. However, at the time of writing, there have been several skirmishes, a handful of arrests, and thousands of hours of paid duty to police, needed to keep agitated counter-demonstrators and Six Nations protesters apart. In the meantime, the province had racked up a large bill of between $25 and $55 million for the total cost of the operation by early spring of 2007, including $12.3 million to Henco Industries to buy out their investment and additional compensation for loss of future profits as well as $1.7 million in compensation to area businesses hurt by the blockades. OPP Commissioner Julian Fantino also stated that by April 2007 forty officers had been injured in the standoff. Some residents of the disputed community have initiated civil suits against the OPP and the government for failing to resolve the situation.

At Caledonia two observations are prominent. The first was the relative invisibility of the event, initially at least, to the wider public. The second was cause of that relative obscurity. In the shadow of the

Ipperwash inquiry hearings being held less than 200 kilometres away in Forest, Ontario, the Ontario government and the OPP were both acutely sensitive to potential fallout from another public order faux pas. As the Aboriginal Affairs Minister Michael Bryant put it, the lessons of Ipperwash and the legacy of Dudley George demanded that 'Ontario resolve the ongoing aboriginal occupation in Caledonia with diplomacy not force' (Puxley, 2007). The OPP and the Liberal government wanted no repeat of the public relations disaster of Ipperwash and affirmatively adopted a bystander role in the conflict. OPP Commissioner Fantino stated publicly: 'It has to be a federal response here. These are federal issues that go back to treaties' ('Native Conflicts a Federal Matter,' 2007).

The court, police, and government would appear to be looking for a common playbook with respect to the role of each in the resolution of land claims disputes. In Oka and Ipperwash, the use of the injunction was a common thread and appeared in each case to exacerbate rather than clarify the conflict. By the time of Caledonia, the OPP had a framework policy that 'recognizes the need for flexibility' in regard to supporting applications for injunctive relief. In addition, it backed government policy that 'articulates factors that would inform the [framework's] approach to applying for, or supporting, injunctive relief, and the timing of such applications.' 'Where the provincial government asserts a direct interest in the subject matter of an Aboriginal occupation or protest (e.g. as a landowner), it may be advisable that the OPP, at its initiative, be separately represented in Court. This enhances the appearance and reality of the OPP's neutrality in any claims dispute, and its ability to negotiate on public safety issues' (OPP, 2006: 25).

Still, the heat in the year-long standoff boiled over for the OPP and its commissioner, who has long advocated for a federal solution to an increasing number of backlogged land claims. Fantino told reporters outside a meeting of the Radio-Television News Directors Association in Toronto in late April 2007 that 'enough is enough now and we're just not going to take it any more ... Police are neither the cause of the problem, nor are they the solution' ('Native Conflicts a Federal Matter,' 2007). Fantino expressed concern because a group of Mohawks had blocked a passenger rail line between Toronto and Montreal in early April in recognition of the anniversary of the initial OPP raid at Caledonia. Since Oka Mohawks had been using the land claims equivalent of 'flying pickets' to up the ante in standoffs with authorities. From the police perspective, this introduced a particularly unruly cohort into the mix of resolution politics, an unruliness not as easily stymied by preventative intelligence (see below), perhaps due in part to the special status, particularly mobility rights, of Natives.

Transnational Activism: APEC, OAS, and the G8

Along with the increasing challenge of Aboriginal occupations and protests, the period between the mid-1990s and the early 2000s was a dynamic time for public order events, which were increasing in size, scale, and complexity. While this section deals mainly with the development of so-called anti-globalization protests that dogged the free trade and other international summits of the late 1990s and early twenty-first century, there were also heightened challenges from labour in some areas of the country.

For example, from late 1995 to 1998, Ontario unions, in coordination with community organizations, held a series of political strikes against the provincial neo-conservative government of Mike Harris. After Harris threatened major changes in labour legislation, there were eleven one-day 'shut-downs' of targeted cities and towns involving workers, activists, and community organizations. In many of these events, called 'Days of Action,' hundreds of thousands of people filled the streets in mass rallies throughout the province. The first, in London, involved 20,000 protesters and shut down non-essential services. The largest, in Toronto, saw an estimated 250,000 people gathered at Queen's Park and unprecedented shut-downs of non-essential services and businesses. In Windsor, the Days of Action protest marked one of the few times that the Ambassador Bridge, Canada's busiest border crossing, was shut down to traffic, albeit for only a short, pre-negotiated period of time. While there were some instances of minor violence and property damage, the labour protests were remarkably peaceful. Negotiations with police, even though they involved unprecedented economic as well as social and political disruptions, were also for the most part amicable and reciprocal. Police agreed that marshals would act as the first line of defence and that the labour organizers would be given first dibs on discipline.

At the turn of the century, anti-globalization protests emerged at a scale and intensity not seen in North America in previous times. In Canada, the largest of these were in Windsor for the OAS in 2000, and then Ottawa and Quebec City in 2001, Montreal in 2001, and Calgary in 2002, where several thousand police officers were assembled from all over the country. Although protester numbers were relatively small, it was the 1997 APEC conference in Vancouver that signalled a new wave of mass demonstration grievances and involved the largest police operation in Canada's history. This demonstration ultimately yielded a major controversy that included a long and messy public inquiry into police excessive use of force as well as accusations of political interference in police operations by the prime minister's office (PMO).

APEC

In November 1997 the Asia-Pacific Economic Cooperation (APEC) conference was held in Vancouver. Security was the overall responsibility of the RCMP, which had sole command of the policing arrangements for the final day. Three thousand officers participated in what RCMP Commissioner Giuliano Zaccardelli called 'the largest and most complex security assignment that the RCMP had ever undertaken.' These security arrangements were informed, as the commissioner put it, by the fact that 'amongst the attending dignitaries were 75 Internationally Protected Persons [IPPs], 12 of whom were at the maximum level of security' (Zaccardelli, 2001).

It was the question of access and counter-staging by protesters that dominated much of the planning and negotiations for this event. Many protesters wanted to register their objection to the human rights record of Indonesian President Suharto. The prime minister's office, in particular through the zeal of one of its officials, sought to shield the dignitaries. The contingency plan to deal with protest problems at the University of British Columbia campus was drawn up two weeks before the event, and a quick response team of RCMP and Vancouver police and bike squads was formed only a week before the event. Members received a few hours of instruction on crowd control and did not train together (King, 2004: 16). A demonstrator area and a 'noise-free' zone were demarcated. The police and most protest groups were in frequent communication, and protocol involving structured, peaceful demonstrations was negotiated. However, six protesters were arrested on 22 and 23 November 'and released on undertakings that placed restrictions on the protesters' activities for the duration of the APEC conference.' Another protester, Jaggi Singh, was arrested on 25 November. In addition, several incidents attracted national and legal attention. The RCMP removed several protest signs and flags, arrested two protesters for using walkie-talkies, and evicted protesters on the grounds of the Museum of Anthropology. Mark Brooks was arrested and pepper-sprayed at Gate 6 'as he was asking for calm.'

The political fallout generated from suggestions of improper political interference by the PMO and Canada-wide coverage of youths being pepper-sprayed contributed to the striking of a public inquiry. In his report for the Commission for Public Complaints against the RCMP, E.N. Hughes found that there was indeed political interference with Charter rights (CPC, 2001b). He emphasized that it was the RCMP and not political authorities who were responsible for weighing security requirements against the Charter rights of citizens, and that they violate this responsibility to the Charter if they do not give adequate weight to rights. At APEC and afterwards, an RCMP strategy of preventative arrest was also challenged. Placing the conditions on the protesters was found to be inconsistent with the Charter. Although the timing of Singh's arrest was not found to be inappropriate, the 'conduct of S/Sgt. Plante in recommending charges, a warrant and release conditions for Mr. Jaggi Singh was not appropriate to the circumstances although not inconsistent with the Charter.' In addition to arrests on undertakings, the commission found that the action against Mr Brooks was a 'precipitous arrest' 'made in an atmosphere of crisis.' It was 'directly attributable to the chaos that resulted from inadequate police planning to ensure the orderly and safe exit of the world leaders' (CPC, 2001b). Hughes also found that arrest powers were not always properly used, that there were inadequacies in communications and command in addition to a lack of training and preparedness, and that there were shortcomings related to the RCMP's use of force. While he found that the establishment of a security perimeter as well as a demonstrator area and a noise-free zone was not in principle inconsistent with the Charter nor inappropriate in the circumstances, several instances of the muting of free speech by the RCMP were not consistent with the Charter or appropriate. These included the removal of the Tibetan flag and of signs from protesters in front of Green College, the arrest of two protesters using walkie-talkies, and the removal of protesters on the grounds of the Museum of Anthropology. Hughes recommended that the RCMP ensure that 'a generous opportunity will be afforded for peaceful protesters to see and be seen in their protest activities by guests to the event' (CPC, 2001b).

Like the Seattle anti-globalization protest in 1999, APEC was instructive to police because shortcomings of police response were not the result of constitutional impediments. While the Commission for Public Complaints against the RCMP found that there was political interference with Charter rights and that arrest powers were not always properly used or that there shortcomings related to the RCMP's use of force, it was inadequacies in communications and command in addition to a lack of training and preparedness which provided most grist for the mill of reform. Despite the two-year pre-planning process for this event, several shortcomings in the delivery of security were attributable to a lack of proper information flows. First, there was too much separation between those planning the event and those executing the plan. The commission found 'poor liaison between the RCMP's APEC planning process and the UBC (University of British Columbia) detachment' (CPC, 2002). And Hughes criticized 'the ill-advised decision to separate the planning and operational responsibilities which left the senior officers who had planned the operation out of the chain of command' (CPC, 2001b). Consequently, there was no one 'in command who was aware of the protesters plans.' Second, contingency plans, drills, or instructions were too last-minute to generate confidence. The members received only a few hours of instruction on crowd control and 'never trained together' (King, 2004: 16). The commission determined that 'inadequate briefings' and 'last-minute assignments' contributed to the chaos at some of the sites. The advice of the threat assessment group that a set of protesters known as APEC Alert were likely to engage in civil disobedience and vigorous non-violent protest action was felt by the CPC inquiry not to have been matched by adequate pre-planning. To address these shortcomings in coordination and communication, the report recommended that the RCMP 'adopt an integrated or similar command structure of planning and operations for public order events. When one position reports to another, the same officer should not fill both positions' (CPC, 2001b).

With APEC, many different police practices along with liaison communications were brought together that previously had been tried on a more ad hoc basis. This included preventative arrest, the construction of free-speech zones, and the integration of multiple intelligence sources. For the police the lesson was not that some of these practices stretched too far, but rather that the plan was clumsily or inconsistently implemented. They also believed that they were dealing with a very organized foe in the anti-globalization protesters:

The significance of APEC was the realization that responsibilities for protection of international protected people was suddenly the reality of that's not a guarantee unless you're prepared. And probably in this case, I don't think the proper risk assessment was done and suddenly there was a situation which created some chaos which I think the police saw as a potential, serious threat to their ability to protect these people. And certain officers .reacted ... but when they sat back and looked at that, I think it was probably the first realization in Canada that they were dealing with the issue of globalization, and ... the backwash from that issue. And it really was ... the first time that Canadian police had to deal with that kind of an issue. And it had happened in Seattle, and in Canada I think we kind of took the view that that happens in the U.S., it doesn't happen in Canada. Suddenly there was the threat that that sort of thing could happen in Canada and as a result the police have realized they have to be far better prepared, far better informed and far better at putting together an effective plan. (R12)

This assessment was backed up by another officer, who stated that police had to respond aggressively against a possible pincering of the VIP escape route in what he called orchestrated criminal actions:

R: Yeah, and you just can't get your VIPs cracked on a peninsula with no way out, I mean you can't allow that because of your risks, your VIP's escort. And I guess that comes back to your risk analysis point, that that's an ongoing process and as long as you have viable options and some ways out as it were, then you can continue with the soft approach. But at some point you have to make decision where it's...?
I: Where the risk is getting too high?
R: Too high, yeah. Then you got to foreclose, so. (R2)

The same officer implies that the line from APEC to the 2002 G8 summit was based on the adaptations of practices rather than the application of legal precedent. APEC was perceived as broaching a new militancy on the part of a significant subset of the activist community that required a change of tactics on the part of police:

R: APEC is near and dear to my heart cause I was a duty officer through all the shenanigans. And in fact while, you know a lot of what APEC focused on was a ten minute window. What we had actually done throughout was ... provide forums ... And we've adopted a prototype tier, the response in some of the protest issues of actually using trained negotiators to deal with protest and to interface. And a lot of those things were reused then at G8 and that's what's kind of come through ...

We were the first of that prior to Seattle, and that would be one of the lessons learned was that while past behaviour is a good indication of future behaviour, it does change and you have to be cognisant of that, I mean we certainly had never seen in Canada, organized sort of, I'm trying to think of the proper way to characterize it. But there was very clearly, directed criminal actions and we simply hadn't run into that previously.

I: In protests?

R: In protest situations like that. And then we've seen that develop in Seattle, Washington, Quebec City, and it continues to escalate, so.

I: But in the APEC did you think there were orchestrated …

R: Undoubtedly, undoubtedly. We watched downstairs here and the reason for a lot of our decision making was watching the very clearly directed and controlled crowd movements in order to block the leaving of the VIPs.

I: And those were counter to, you had understandings, right?

R: Oh, certainly.

I: In terms of how this was all going to play out?

R: Yeah, and based on how things had been umpteen times before. But the willingness to take very clear, purposive criminal action was quite new and that's certainly followed through ever since. (R2)

But one labour respondent stated:

R: It was absolutely incredible that anyone who was just sitting on the side of the motorcade route was arrested. I mean that's unheard of, I mean I don't know of anywhere.

I: You had negotiated …

R: We had been meeting with them all the way through. I mean, they said there's gonna be a fence around this place, and we said, we'll be up protesting at the fence. But I mean literally along the motorcade route, where Suharto was being brought, there was someone sitting there holding up the sign and was plucked off the lawn. And there were other people arrested the day ahead, and kept in jail overnight so that they couldn't be on the protest route. It was absolutely incredible. And all of us were on this thing, this threat assessment that they do, and we all found our names on this threat assessment (laughs) list. (R76)

After Seattle and APEC, strategies concerning large-scale political protests (especially anti-globalization) changed. As argued by Gilham

(2008), Seattle in particular was an eye-opening experience for police. Rightly or wrongly, they understood themselves no longer confronted with groups that could be counted on to observe the protocols or ground rules established during pre-event negotiations. They also perceived the maturing of a much more savvy generation of activists. Like police, these were students of public order in their own right who had studied police responses to previous activist gambits and were eager to develop the next counter-move. Already observable at APEC, one result of Seattle, was more emphasis on pre-emptive intelligence. Another was the use of barricades and the development of so-called free-speech zones or the cordoning off of activists. Intelligence also assisted in the identification and classification of demonstrator cohorts and the measurement of visible and coercive response.

Windsor and the OAS

At the Organization of American States (OAS) summit in Windsor in June 2000, 3700 officers from the RCMP, OPP, Peel Regional, Toronto, Chatham, and Windsor police services provided security. The RCMP provided 1400 officers, while 2300 non-RCMP officers were in Windsor to police the event (other reports estimate 2000 to 5000 police on site.) Although the total cost was $3.34 million, and there was some conflict after the fact between the federal, provincial, and municipal governments over who was going to pay, the price tag for this effort was apparently not a major concern. That this appeared as overkill is an understatement inasmuch as estimates for the total number of demonstrators range from 2000 to 3000. However, from the perspective of the government and ultimately the police, the meeting was a high-stakes political event of symbolic significance. The OAS Shutdown Coalition, which involved both local and national organizations including the Windsor Peace Committee, the Council of Canadians, the Windsor OAS Action Network, People's Global Action, the CAW, and other labour organizations, was planning a large-scale action aimed at delaying or shutting down the meeting, while other groups were reportedly planning direct action, possibly including property damage. After the Seattle event, in which the Seattle police had been roundly criticized for failing to protect the integrity of WTO meetings leading to their dissolution, the Canadian police were clearly determined to avoid a similar outcome.

During the OAS event, and considering the small numbers and the lack of serious property or physical violence by protesters, an astonishing seventy-eight persons were arrested, sixty-three for breach of the peace. As we directly observed, many of these arrests were carried out by snatch squads, both undercover and uniformed, often for no apparent breach of the peace. There were some violent altercations throughout, but most of these were police actions against protesters who were at most engaging in civil disobedience. The most visible police use of force occurred on 4 June just outside the security fence, when police used pepper spray on demonstrators who sat in the path of a bus carrying delegates into the cordoned-off meeting compound and the RCMP then dragged away thirty-five protesters for blocking a bus trying to get into the meeting (Laidlaw, 2000). According to journalists Dimmock and Baxter (and as observed by one of the authors), 'about seventy-five commando-trained police, wearing riot helmets and tapping batons on their shields, emerged from the chainlink security fence and surged towards the crowd. Behind them, two tactical officers stood with their assault rifles drawn. They pepper-sprayed around a dozen demonstrators and a news photographer, then dragged away some twenty-five protesters, most of them kicking and screaming obscenities' (Dimmock and Baxter, 2000).

Novel countering strategies at Windsor included the construction of eight-foot chainlink fencing mounted on interlinked concrete highway dividers which surrounded the site of OAS meetings and two city blocks. There was also a two-tiered police representation. Windsor police had extensive discussions with protest organizers regarding the plan for the placement of the security fence. Windsor police and liaison officers negotiated with activists but also made them believe that the final authority rested with senior officers and the RCMP. Protesters were told that the RCMP was 'responsible' for physical security of IPPs 'from the fence in' and that the OPP and the Windsor police were responsible beyond the fence.

Police also engaged in extensive pre-planning, liaison, intelligence gathering, joint training, development of standardized communications, and clear command and control. They took a number of preventative measures, many of which were not in the liaison handbook. For instance, the RCMP, the Windsor police, and the OPP gathered intelligence on the groups involved, including the numbers in the groups, leadership, and their relationships with other groups. There also appeared to be involvement from other municipal and regional intelligence units, such as Toronto. On-site surveillance of residences associated with the OAS action was also conducted. One method of intervention was to gather up names of leaders, interview these persons as to the plans of their group, including intentions for violence and where equipment was stored, and broker separate assurances with each participating organization with regard to actions that would be countered or countenanced. RCMP and Windsor police officers visited or telephoned union and activist leaders, attended protest organizers' meetings, and monitored websites in order to gather information and also to cultivate protocols and develop strategies.

For some of the activists involved, these efforts were viewed as forms of intimidation. One activist recalled:

> At our next meeting two [municipal] police officers showed up in plainclothes but introduced themselves. But later one of the officers called me and I met with him. He identified himself as an intelligence officer with the [municipal] police … It was clear that he was here to try to squeeze information out of me … The RCMP had no interest in meeting with us as a group but [then] they [the RCMP] started showing up in people's homes … they came to my office; it was very unreal – for one it was really terrifying for [name of person] who was from Central America, El Salvador, police show up at the door asking questions, really terrified – she left town. She just said I'm leaving town; she was really terrified. (R77)

Another said:

> They had our house bugged, and they'd come up and be like, 'Hey, so I heard your girlfriend is sick' … cars circling the house all the time; you see it go down the street and back down the alleyway, and again twenty minutes later. Always being tailed, looking over your shoulder. (Wood, 2007: 385)

As well, over 500 Americans deemed by Canada Customs to be connected to unwanted OAS demonstrator groups were denied entry to Canada (Rennie, 2001; also interview, senior police official). Protesters or persons fitting a protester profile were stopped at the border, interrogated, and searched. Other visitors to Windsor were subject to preventative detention under an Immigration Act provision allowing such measures where reasonable grounds were believed to exist that an indictable offence would be committed (WPC, 2001: 10). Bus traffic into Windsor from the rest of Canada was also monitored. Police made extensive preparations to prevent those fitting a protester profile from taking up accommodations at campsites in the Windsor area and received licence plates of those camping at Holiday Beach from the Essex Region Conservation Authority and an agreement from a local KOA not to allow 'non-family campers' to make reservations (WPC, 2001). Visiting OPP and RCMP took all available University of Windsor residence spots, and, unlike the Université de Laval in the 2001 Quebec City protest, the university did not open its massive gymnasium to protesters.

At the event, police allowed protesters exposure to the protest site, albeit behind the barricades. In particular, a rally location was negotiated principally with the labour unions just outside the east end of the fence on the waterfront. Police stayed on the other side of the fence or away from the rally for its duration. Whenever anyone approached the fence during the rally or threw anything over the fence, the protest marshals, mainly labour union people, intervened to push them back. This appeared to incorporate the recommendation of the APEC inquiry – and police experience in Seattle and Washington – that protests could be diffused with such accommodations. One of our police respondents claimed that police accommodations to the staging requirements of protesters were pivotal to the success of the event:

R: That's why the OAS here in Windsor went off very well because of the pre-planning in which they negotiated a pre-set up, an area where they were going to be satisfied so they didn't need to push down the fences 'cause they're twenty blocks away and knew they'd never be seen but they wanted to be seen. And they were allowed that exposure and that's what they were after. So again through that, by their leaders coming forward and agreeing to meet and with the police leaders they were able set a limit; here's where we're looking at containing this area because we'll be technical and they realized that as well. So does this meet your needs for doing your protest action, and where they'd had problems is where the police lines had been set so far back that people feel totally frustrated in not being able to get their message across and that's when they decide we got to push forward here and get closer, and that's when the confrontations start and so on. So that negotiation process of pre-planning is, we're finding again from the ones in Seattle in Washington, we've studied all of those states, that those seemed to be the key. And when they did the latest ones when we went to help out west, that last year, that, our police leaders in this area, that experience with Windsor and the OAS used much the same strategy and it …

I: Allowed visibility?

R: Allowed the process to take place ...

I: For them it's the media, it has to ...?

R: Yep, they've got to get the message out and this is their chance plus they want to be seen by the people that are meeting; they want to get the message across. And that seems to be key that the people want to be heard, and they have their right to be heard, that's our society, that's the way we are. So if you meet both ways, both then safety and security has to take place too, we're not going to allow them to shut down a meeting or shut down a government legislature, or shut down a plant. That is the delicate balance where that still has to carry on, but then they want to do their thing. (R25)

Despite the view of police and municipal officials in most news articles and by many area residents that the OAS event was handled with professionalism, an overwhelming impression of demonstrators, local residents, and participant-observers is that a large section of downtown Windsor became a militarized zone. Certainly as we observed, when one moved away from the negotiated rally zone and closer to the Cleary conference centre (where the dignitaries were located) the intensification of security was matched by a suspension of 'regular' Charter rights. Low-flying helicopters, temporary 'secret' jails (Rhodes Drive detention centre), saturation police presence, concrete barricades, phalanxes of paramilitary police, large contingents of plain-clothes intelligence officers, snatch squads in special vans and trucks, and police non-observance of property and Charter rights (right to counsel, encroachment on property-owners, etc.) contributed to this impression. Some arrested persons and resident witnesses reported that on at least two occasions police used intimidation, abusive language, and unnecessary force, and violated property rights.

As Wood (2007) reports, in one instance a protest organizer recounted witnessing an activist being knocked off his bicycle after a white panel truck pulled up beside him, an officer leaping out and bundling him into the back of the unmarked vehicle. The organizer caught up with the activist later, who reported that he was taken by police and spent eight hours in interrogation with the RCMP. As noted, one of the authors also observed two similar snatch squad incidents and was amazed at the speed with which this took place.

In a letter addressed to the OPP commissioner and to local and federal legislative representatives, Joan and Meghan Dimmick and Lewis

MacLeod recounted the arrest of teens on their front lawn that involved unnecessary and 'dangerous' force. They reported that when they objected to police at the time, they were told in effect to mind their own business, that the street was 'now owned by the police.' An OAS organizer commented on police intimidation as follows:

> Well, I think the police actions during the day were against a lot of the younger demonstrators, particularly later on down Riverside Drive, west. Frightening. I actually saw the ... this was very upsetting to me. At one point where the police were, the RCMP I guess were banging their shields and marching, clearing the way for no apparent reason. They marched out about ten to fifteen yards. People would scramble out of their way and then they'd march back. Tear-gassing people, for what? Pepper-spray people, for what? And I saw in plainclothes, the cop who was from Intelligence Unit, who I had met with. And I went over to him and I said, 'Why are they doing that?' He said, 'Why you know, the boys get restless every once in a while' (laughing).
>
> I mean, earlier that morning on my way down I saw some police open the trunks of cars actually that were parked and I went over and asked them 'What was going on?' And in some they were opening and checking trunks of cars that were parked around there. There didn't seem to be the owner of the car around ... And I went over and asked them, 'It seems to me you're not allowed to do that?' (Laughing)' Just go and start prying open people's trunks in parked cars' and they kind of said menacingly 'If you know what's good for you, you won't ask that again. Get out!' (R78)

These tactics also had a lasting effect on the activist groups. As noted by one organizer, the organizing body of the anti-OAS demonstrations did not meet again as a body following the events of that day, having been 'ripped apart' by 'internal tensions' fostered in part by the repressive countering of police: 'People had been really taken for a ride by the whole mindfuck of the CSIS/RCMP/OPP action, in terms of the all the psychological things that they pulled ... A lot of people left totally burnt out and bitter' (Wood, 2007: 386).

From our discussions with police and protesters, the mix of extreme coercion and liaison was not accidental or ad hoc. It was part of post-Seattle planning that signalled that police were rejuvenated on the agenda of the proactive countering of large-scale protests. It also indicated that the strategies and tactics against large-scale protests would not follow the pattern of land claims. Whereas in the land claims

environment public spectacles of coercive authority led to a modification from reference to force and intelligence in the first instance, in
these mass political public order events, the embarrassment of APEC
was not sufficient to daunt the resolve of police in protecting, as it
were, the plans of government vis-à-vis the interests of capital. Quite
the contrary, Windsor suggested that police could experiment with
deeper countering measures, measures sifting right down into the
body politic. These measures involved the coordination of a large number of police and security agencies in a common purpose, a kind of
coordination that made OAS Windsor a transnational and intelligence-
led public order countering event. The Windsor approach would be
further modified and improvised.

Quebec City and G8

The third Summit of the Americas – a meeting of the heads of state
from thirty-four nations – was held on 20–1 April 2001 in Quebec City.
The subjects of the meeting included hemispheric integration and mi-
gration, security and terrorism, democracy and human rights, in addition to the Free Trade Area of the Americas (FTAA) agreement. As in
OAS and APEC, the police priority was the protection of visiting dignitaries and the non-disruption of the summit (King, 2004: 6). The event
surpassed previous 'high-stakes' policing operations to become the
most expensive in Canadian history, topping $100 million in resources
used. In addition to personnel of over 6000 riot police, costs included
the construction of a 3.9 kilometre chainlink and concrete fence
around the convention area, and the use of water cannons, stun guns,
and 5192 canisters of tear gas, 903 rounds of rubber bullets (Mackay,
2002), and a lead-shot ball (King, 2004: 8). Four police forces participated: the RCMP, the Sûreté du Québec, and the municipal services of
Quebec City and Sainte-Foy. As in Windsor, each was given explicitly
demarcated roles, with the RCMP taking on site security, dignitary
protection, national investigation and threat assessment, military liaison, public relations, and overall coordination (King, 2004: 6). On the
basis of civil emergency regulations, the Sûreté du Québec requested
and was granted control over criminal investigation and arrest and
court processing from the Ville de Québec (VQ) municipal police.
Meanwhile, the Ville de Québec police had authority for protecting the
external perimeter and ensuring access and escort for conference participants and for dealing with spontaneous demonstrations (King,

2004: 7) Ville de Sainte-Foy police secured the airport. Some 60,000 persons participated in demonstrations and 463 arrests were made (Killam, 2001: 31). Overall security also involved other agencies including CSIS.

In preparation for the summit, police practised much of the extensive ground preparations witnessed at Windsor. Police cancelled reservations made by unions in certain hotels at the containment site (Le Soleil, January 20, 2001). The RCMP rented all the available apartments inside the area both to prevent 'terrorists' from staying inside the security area before and during the summit and also to house officers (Le Soleil, 9 November 2000). The authorities also required that the 7500 residents of the area register themselves in order to get a pass allowing them to enter the security area during the summit (Le Soleil, 10 January 2001). A thousand workers also required a pass (Le Soleil, January 27, 2001). Residents were not allowed to have visitors during that period. Much like OAS Windsor, there was a distribution of authority on the ground that was differentially intensified for delegate protection and protester penetration. Communication was also extensive, involving the VQ and the RCMP, with police stressing the inviolability of the security fence.

Negotiations with Quebec labour unions led to a controversial agreement that labour would march and rally in the lower part of Quebec City, well away from the fence. Most other protest groups began their march at the Université de Laval, some three kilometres from the downtown area. Organizers divided these protest groups and protesters into three groups – those who wanted to stay away from the fence entirely, those who wanted to approach the fence and then depart without taking any action, and those who wanted to approach the fence in an effort to disrupt the meetings. The bulk of the labour movement followed a negotiated agreement to stay well away from the fence with their own march in the lower part of the city (Mackay, 2002).

Despite the plethora of preventative measures, there was significant violence and injury in Quebec, as indicated by the spent munitions and volunteer street medic accounts (King, 2004: 8). Unlike Windsor, there were explicit assaults by small numbers of 'direct action' protesters against the fence, rocks were thrown, and Molotov cocktails were lobbed at police by at least one demonstrator. (King, 2004: 14). The perimeter fence was breached at one place and police riot units used batons and tear gas among other tactical devices to beat back the demonstrators (participant observation). Protesters who climbed over the fence were also promptly arrested, while undercover police and snatch squads also operated outside the fence, as at Windsor. Police strategy during much of the remainder of the weekend was to prevent any further breaches. Huge amounts of tear gas and munitions were used whenever anyone approached the fence, while periodic charges into the crowd by riot police were used to keep the protesters from regrouping. However, there were points later in the protest when police dispatched riot squads to disperse crowds and arrest individuals, as in the evening of the 20th, even when protesters were no longer near the fence. As noted, most of the labour unions had opted to stay away from the fray, but some unions such as CAW had dispatched a small number of 'flying squad' members who marched right up to the fence in the morning of the first day waving their union flags. They were attacked brutally and quickly overcome by tear gas (participant observation). The tear gas was so thick by the evening of 20 April that residents had to be evacuated.

After it was all over, a number of protesters filed formal complaints. TV stations and newspapers in Canada and around the world covered the event intensively, sometimes with graphic pictures of police beating protesters (e.g., Sallot, Sequin, and Freeze, 2001, 1). While commentators were not uniformly critical of the police, many were unwilling to pin the extraordinary level of violence on the protesters alone, and so the police came under considerable public scrutiny, far more than had happened in Windsor. Chief Commissioner of the RCMP Public Complaints Commission, Shirley Heafey, found in her report on RCMP conduct at Quebec City that the RCMP had abused its power while using 'oppressive' and 'excessive and unjustified force' against protesters in some instances, resulting in a violation of the Criminal Code and the Charter of Rights. Her report said the RCMP's tactical squad violated its own procedures by giving inadequate warning and then using tear gas, rubber bullets, a 'flash bang' grenade, and a taser gun to scatter crowds during a day of protest. She recommended that the two senior RCMP inspectors responsible for crowd control be 'dealt with accordingly' and that individual officers who 'abused their power and authority' be subjected to 'appropriate sanctions' (O'Neil, 2003).[3]

While the police were not otherwise scolded for their performance in Quebec by any of their political masters, the scale and cost of the violence in Quebec also encouraged further refinements in police tactics and strategies. And although police considered their main goal had been accomplished (that is, the OAS meetings were concluded on schedule), they came out of the event keen to avoid spectacles of violence the next time around (Allen, 2003: 52). Protesters, on the other hand, felt that they were 'shut out' of Quebec and disallowed from expressing democratic rights. The general public, in the meantime, was treated to another round of news reports and an inquiry that painted police actions as unnecessarily aggressive. Consequently, police held meetings, contracted consultations, and refined their 'high-stakes' public order policing strategy. That refinement was in evidence at the next major high-stakes policing event, the 2002 G8 summit.

By the time of the G8, police had developed a further iteration of space manipulation in line with international precedent: this time, the sequestering of the target or hot zone to a remote location. Originally scheduled for Calgary, the RCMP pushed for the relocation of the G8 to a rural area with all access routes closed to protesters. Protesters were forced to demonstrate in the closest city, Calgary, or in another satellite location in Ottawa. Police had largely neutralized the principal threat of protests by isolating the meeting well away from the protests, thus circumventing any need to exert more coercive control over protest movements.

The 2002 G8 meeting in Kananaskis entailed the largest Canadian security operation that had ever been mobilized. The event had a price tag of $500 million. In the context of post-9/11, the police were concerned not just with anti-globalization protesters but also the possibility of terrorism. Kananaskis was chosen for its remote location, 90 kilometres from Calgary, facilitating the authorization – and 'lockdown' – of an exclusionary or security zone of 6.5 kilometres in radius. It also encompassed a 150 kilometre no-fly zone monitored by fighter jets and helicopters, 5000 soldiers, and 1500 RCMP officers to maintain the integrity of the perimeter. Checkpoints and search zones were also set up at access routes throughout the region. Concurrent with protests against the G8 at Kananaskis and Calgary were protests in Ottawa, and countering these was also part of the operational plan (Allen, 2003: 51). Satellite security zones were created in Calgary itself, where public park space was prohibited for protest rallies, although this idea was quashed in a court decision which found in favour of a legal challenge.

This event featured a number of innovations. A joint intelligence group (JIG) was struck about four months prior to the event to provide an infrastructure for information sharing. It was mandated to provide 'accurate and timely' intelligence to incident leaders from the participating security and police agencies. Its first function was to establish source information operations to collect historical and current information on 'persons, tactics, and protester planning' (Allen, 2003: 50). This source information pool was much broader than in Quebec and Windsor, and included the Internet, commercial information databases such as Dialog and Newscan, the Foreign Broadcast Information Service (FBIS), Interpol, and regular police databases, including ACIIS and NEICH RMS. Informants provided additional information on tactics and plans.[4]

The JIG information was used to track all buses travelling to Ottawa that carried persons to the protest site. Protesters were tracked en route, and a major events liaison team (MELT), consisting of 'soft hat' community/communications police, was struck and met the buses on arrival. Again, this was far more sophisticated than the monitoring of bus stations that happened in Windsor. In addition, protesters known to have criminal records for violent offences, protest leaders, persons in violation of parole or arrest conditions, and unspecified others were identified ahead of time and tracked throughout, no matter their mode of travel. Mug shots and other information of such persons was copied into a booklet and provided to street-level personnel.

> Tactical police were kept close to the scene and ready at all times throughout the protest period of June 26–27. Real-time surveillance footage from several tracking cameras mounted on buildings was sent back to the command center. Video downlinks from the RCMP helicopter camera and the Ottawa Police Service fixed-wing aircraft were also sent in real time to the command center and were used to track the protests, demonstrators, and buses. (Allen 2003: 53)

The information gathered by the JIG allowed police and security to target key meetings and persons. The JIG identified all protestor busses before they left for Ottawa and tracked them en route. All protestors with violent criminal records were identified ahead of time and a book of photos and information on targeted persons was provided to street-level personnel. Plainclothes police attended the protest march in Ottawa, and transmitted real-time tactical data to a command centre. Surveillance footage from video cameras mounted on buildings as well as an RCMP helicopter and Ottawa Police Service fixed-wing aircraft was sent to the command centre to track protestors and buses (Allen, 2003: 51–3).

In the meantime, non-police political authorities were also proactive. As in Quebec City and previously in Seattle and Davos, Switzerland, political authorities beyond the police made efforts to 'institutionalize' anti-globalization activists. As Michel Chossudovsky (2001) reports, before the meeting of the WTO in Seattle, leaders of selected civil rights organizations were invited to 'dialogue' on the issues.[5] Leading up to the summit in Quebec, the Ministry of Foreign Affairs and International Trade sent, according to its own statement, invitations to the summit to 'approximately 60 representatives' of interest and lobby groups (Chossudovsky, 2001: 1).

High-Stakes Protest Policing: Moving beyond Liaison

Policy, standing orders and regulations, commission reports, and 'best practices' for protests, marches, rallies, and demonstrations were now apparently best articulated in the G8 Ottawa and Kananaskis model. Liaison policing as applied to large-scale protests was now transparently inadequate. It was no longer sufficient to rely solely, as liaison policing does, on the civil nature of the conflict, the neutrality of police, protester self-regulation, or communications. This does not mean that liaison is dead. In the second half of the 1990s 'specialty programs' such as ART, MELT, and crisis mediation were developed to operate within a 'framework' that emphasized 'flexibility, relationship building, dialogue,' 'cultural knowledge,' and 'use of force' only 'as necessary' and 'carefully measured' according to the risks and circumstances. However, in this new formulation, measurement and risk assessment became increasingly important dimensions underlying public order practices on the ground.

To understand this point better, let us consider more closely how public order policing was readapted following the events just outlined. Although APEC and, more importantly, Seattle were shots across the bow, this was in the main a gradual adaptation. And although the liaison approach was only just gaining its own institutionalization within police agencies, police did not need public commissions to tell them that something more than the liaison steps was required in certain protest situations.

Intelligence over Liaison?

The turn of the millennium was a gyration of public disorder, disrupting the largely sub-political machinations of neo-liberal globalization power brokers. Seattle, Genoa, Montreal, Vancouver, and many other major sites witnessed the next generation of mass demonstrations, sending shock waves through the policing and security communities. For protesters, Seattle was a great strategic success, resulting in the tangible prize of the WTO's failure, so acknowledged from the highest office (the American president), and affirming the public's discontent with the status quo that the protesters registered. On the other hand, among police officials in Canada whom we interviewed, Seattle was seen as a watershed that signalled the need for much more aggressive intelligence collection and analysis, more preparation and control of perimeters and IPPs, and better management of significant public order force. Arguably this sealed the fate not only of liaison policing but also of the community policing model and its replacement with intelligence as the base of the dominant paradigm. The aftermath of 9/11 pushed the intelligence-based paradigm over the top.

As Warwyk (2004) suggests, the Seattle anti-globalization protest in 1999 was instrumental in prompting this latest rethinking of public order strategies, one that now invited close cooperation of police and security agencies in what would come to be called 'fusion':

> Post Seattle, the police had to revise their readiness and rely ever more on intelligence to avoid a repeat. More importantly, the police must interpret the available intelligence correctly in the transition to police actions on the streets. It is now understood that what seems an agreement from one group does not always apply to all participants. In this more intense environment, police forces have become networked and are studying protest by sending officers to act as observers. In Canada, what was done by a singular police force can no longer be done, as the size and complexity mounts. We are now seeing multi-police force participation with joint command entities as the normal approach to large events. Some smaller events also receive this treatment when jurisdictions coincide or overlap. This is very common in the capital of Ottawa where the RCMP protective role is carried out within the city policed by the Ottawa Police Service.

Police experiences at APEC, Windsor, Quebec, and the G8 meetings in Kananaskis, as well as Native land claim protests, all reveal a process of continuing modifications or adaptations to new circumstances. Consistent with Hughes's recommendations for tactical changes following APEC, one of our police informants notes that the line from APEC to the 2002 G8 was based on the adaptations of practices rather than the application of legal precedent. APEC was perceived as broaching a new militancy on the part of a significant subset of the activist community that required change on the part of police (see also Wood, 2007). The actions of the police in Windsor and Quebec City revealed an enormous capacity for coercion. Police strategy at the G8 Summit in Kananaskis, Alberta, was more solidly intelligence-based, but still multi-dimensional, including key elements of the liaison approach. Police in Calgary made a renewed liaison effort, as did police in Ottawa in 2001. Clearly, the initial wave of anti-globalization protests beginning with APEC and Seattle, strained the toolkit of responses police were ready to use; police adapted to the new environment by relocating liaison in the public order field as a particular rather than universal approach.

Although one can say that much the same thing seems to have happened with Native land claims protests, both Burnt Church and Caledonia indicate that the commitment to liaison and the brake on coercion is more substantial. This may be a reflection of the perceived legitimacy of Native claims relative to those of the anti-globalization movement, but we suspect that police identify more strongly with the protection of international and political meetings than with the property rights of white fishers and white homeowners or developers. This may of course have been part of the dynamics underlying police refusal to open strike picket lines so employers can access their properties. As police like to say, a strike is a private dispute. Ironically, then, one of the unintended consequences of the shrinking boundaries of the public interest is that police are no longer willing to fall on their swords for what have always been essentially private interests – the interests of property owners. Of course, the anti-globalization protesters see governments at these international summits as nothing more than functionaries for corporate capital, but police are compelled to defending the state's business seriously. As this also implies, the police capacity to act in a neutral fashion in these situations is compromised, while their willingness to tolerate a particular level of risk or cost to the state is much lower relative to what they define as acceptable risks or costs to private interests.

Again with respect to the anti-globalization protests, much of the pre-planning for demonstrations or public protests concerns parade routes, no-go or IPP and free-speech zones, barricades, and so forth. Following the bungling of the APEC parade route (through violations of free speech, voluminous pepper-spraying), police at the OAS Windsor developed the first use of steel fence barriers around conference centres and hotels where diplomatic meetings were taking place. While these barricades were interpreted by activists and others as a clear restriction on protest rights, police justified them as necessary to ensure the safety of diplomatic participants and the integrity of the meetings. The court would appear to concur. As Pue (2005: 7) notes, the court ruled in 1974 in *R. v. Knowlton* that Edmonton police were within the law in cordoning off a zone around a hotel in which Soviet Premier Kosygin was staying and disallowing citizens from entering. This justification emanated from, according to Supreme Court of Canada Chief Justice Fauteux, the duties of 'constables' to preserve the peace and to prevent crime.[6] Similarly, the most extreme use of the 'manipulation of space' (Noakes and Gillham, 2005) at the Summit of the Americas in Quebec City in 2001, represented by a fence around downtown Quebec City, also survived a Quebec Superior Court challenge that found that it was a reasonable restriction on freedoms. While the fence was breached as a symbolic gesture, police response was swift and severe: as if the government itself was being toppled. Police innovated further with the Kananaskis model, apparently trying to avoid confrontation by physically isolating the meetings in an inaccessible rural area. The economic cost was enormous, almost five times that of the Quebec City protest.

Perhaps more important, however, is the increasing importance of intelligence. Already at APEC, police engaged in unprecedented intelligence gathering and threat-assessment activities including the use of surveillance, spies, informants, and open interviews with local movement leaders and activists (Pugliese and Bronskill, 2001). Intelligence communications had been enhanced to offer direction to the snatch squads. After APEC, there was also extensive collaboration between police services, locally, provincially, nationally, and even internationally. At the Windsor OAS protest, the flow of criminal intelligence, border security, and national security mandates in the interoperability of police and security agencies was lauded as instrumental in disrupting efforts by U.S. protesters to participate.

In Seattle and APEC and to a lesser extent at the OAS Windsor, police took previous intelligence of groups' demonstration profile (willingness to comply with brokered agreements or to engage in criminal violations) and countered accordingly. This methodology proved too clumsy given the recognition that intelligence and countering strategies could be continuously adapted and since there was no advantage to cutting off communications merely on the basis of a prior assessment of a group's intentions. As Warwyk (2007) notes, protesters also practised their own tactical intelligence, and Seattle was the landmark event where protester intelligence brought results beyond expectations:

The loosely organized coalition used and exploited intelligence, the principles of mass and manoeuvre, good real-time communications, and well-practiced techniques to meet its objectives. Ultimately the police were overrun by this unique combination, demonstrating their failure to discern between lawful demonstrators, anarchists, opportunists, and bystanders. (Warwyk, 2007)

But for labour and for many protesters it was the police deviation from liaison commitments that was a major issue. Their organization and control of their own people relied on the predictability of police response and police commitment to agreements or protocols. The inability of police leadership to provide predictable countering in Seattle and APEC engendered incredulity and ultimately undermined trust.

In an apparent effort to deal with this problem, police developed better real-time distinctions for identifying targets for a range of different countering strategies. In particular, the police recognized that solidarity dress and symbols or demarcations by colour-coding or other branding exercises distinguish protester sub-groups according to a graduation of militancy, so that 'self-selection' of protesters can be matched to countering efforts. In the first iteration of this exploitation of dress, it was the more militant protesters who concealed their faces to counter surveillance and identification (for example, in Seattle). In large demonstrations, various participating groups often wear armbands, bandanas, buttons, t-shirts, or other items in common to allow group identification and enhance solidarity.

Building on this during the planning for the OAS protest in Windsor, police suggested to 'responsible' groups that they wear visible markings such as unique t-shirts to distinguish themselves so that the police would not target them.[7] At the Summit of the Americas in Quebec City, protesters were grouped into colour-coded blocs that matched how close they were willing to get to the fence. In an elaboration of Windsor, police response was colour-coded according to type of activity: green[8] represented a 'festive demonstration,' yellow meant controlled civil unrest or staged sit-ins and non-violent obstructions, and red meant engagement in more disruptive action, and perhaps criminal actions (King, 2004: 7). In anti-globalization protests against the G20 summit in Ottawa on 17 November 2001, police arrested fifty protesters, all but one of whom wore black and many of whom had their faces covered. As reported by Tim Harper in the *Toronto Star* (19 November 2001), this led Pamela Forster of the Halifax Initiative to lament that 'all of a sudden we're seeing fashion profiling. If you dress in black, you're arrested.' Victoria police chief Paul Battershill appeared to confirm such profiling when he told a reporter after a protest in November 2003 that 'if you're masked up during a protest, you're not there to sing nursery rhymes' ('Police Chief,' 2003)

As mentioned, protest tactics and behaviour also did not stand still. Even by the time of the OAS protests in 2000, more militant activists were becoming wary of the practice of solidarity dress and symbols. One recognized problem was that 'Black Bloc' solidarity invited repressive police response and resulted in arrest and remand that was more favourable for white, middle-class protesters, who were more likely than minority, lower-class counterparts, to be quickly released without further incident. In addition, it began to be recognized by activists that coding for militancy (wearing black, wearing masks) reduced the diversity of participants, inviting and facilitating precisely the kind of relatively invisible police repression that already selected the most vulnerable participants and justified such differential coercion. As one protest organizer put it, 'we debated the idea of wearing t-shirts but in the end we thought why should we help them [the police]' (R79). The invitation of repression via solidarity dress and tactics was recognized as furthering the divide between anti-poverty, anarchist, and anti-globalization activists and organized labour (with its financial and tactical backing), as well as assisting police targeting.

Scheduling or measuring coercion according to colour-coding is an almost inescapable consequence of greater nuance in the countering effort. Police match visibilities, 'profile' or categorize protesters, and schedule dosages of countering accordingly. Again, organized labour, in this context, has a 'whitening' impact that is well known on both sides. Like other organizations viewed as compliant, labour representatives receive assurances and cell phone numbers of police contacts should trouble arise, while others deemed non-compliant are subject to arrest, lengthy interrogations, and, in some cases, intimidation. In Windsor, it was reported by many who participated in the event that police were very aggressive against young protesters, including many high school and university students, while leaving older protesters and those with union-identifying banners or jackets alone. Some argued that there would have been greater violence were it not for the participation of labour, and indeed it was only after the bulk of union people left the Windsor rally that the police started arresting pre-targeted people.

The recursivity of demarcation and visibility is also expressed in the relative capacity of identification and counter-identification. In particular, the police have also become more sensitized to their own visible expression, be it through crowd control paramilitary, community police, or plainclothes. In Ontario, the Police Services Act does not make the wearing of name tags mandatory, and police officers countering demonstrators have regularly been accused of failing to provide those being arrested or coerced with their names and ID numbers. At the G8 in Ottawa, the Ottawa Police Service, following feedback from members of the community that public order unit officers were not identifiable during the G20 demonstrations, required all its members to wear name tags. However, as acknowledged by the OPS, some of the Ontario security agencies involved did not provide identification.

At the G8 meeting in Ottawa, in addition to the modulation of the major events liaison team (MELT), also described by Allen (2003) via the familiar metaphor 'iron fist in velvet glove,' there was a further adaptation of spatial manipulation: no event barriers were erected and parkland was not restricted from protester use. While communications collection (obvious surveillance, the ostentatious greeting of the protesters by MELT, saturation coverage by uniformed and plainclothes police officers, uniformed police lining the route, and openly displayed surveillance equipment)[9] was made forcefully obvious, paramilitary force was purposely kept oblique. Tactical and riot police squads were closely stationed, but out of sight. Allen says the idea was to remove the typical elements of police mobilization that are seen as being 'provocative' to protesters. At the same time police opted to use intimidation tactics in an effort to deter some protesters from using direct-action methods. For example, they loudly announced the opening of a large temporary holding facility for use during possible mass arrests, which Allen claims helped to intimidate protest leaders. As he also reports, the intelligence gathered by the joint intelligence group (JIG) was a key factor in implementing intimidation tactics that limited the amount of violence in Ottawa.

By the time of the G8 Ottawa, a cautionary note on tactics was sounded by a community group in Ottawa (Witness Group) that articulated the problem of trust as liaison and intelligence are integrated in intelligence-based public order countering (cf. Tilly, 2004). The group said: 'The liaison mandate should be separate and independent from any intelligence gathering function … intelligence gathering should not undermine the potential for dialogue between police and protester organizers during the planning phase or replace ongoing communica-tion during an event' (Ottawa Police Service, 2002). Some of our police liaison informants concurred, recognizing the inevitable effects on neutrality and trust that arose when they were playing a dual role as conciliator and spy. It is also worth noting that a few claimed that they refused to play that role and intentionally held back information from their superiors precisely because they recognized the conflict. It would appear, however, that the tension between service and control, liaison and intelligence, community and state is unlikely to be lessened by entreaty alone.

Preventative Arrest and Detention

As we have observed, an innovation tied to intelligence-led public or-der policing is the use of preventative detention, in particular where police arrest leaders and activists, sometimes using snatch squads, be-fore the activists or leaders can do anything illegal. One of the best-known examples of this is the arrest of Jaggi Singh in Quebec City, ostensibly for possession of a dangerous weapon, which was a small catapult which Singh's group was planning to use to throw toy teddy bears over the fence. While many of these arrests never resulted in formal charges, they often resulted in citizen complaints and counter-charges which in some cases led to official confirmation of inappropri-ate arrests (RCMP Complaints Commission, 2001). For their part, the police have maintained that they were acting on information that led them to believe, with reasonable cause, that these persons were going to engage in criminal activities. Of course, many of these targeted ar-rests are efforts to undermine protest leadership, exactly the opposite of what liaison officers seek to do with groups identified as benign.

The idea of preventative arrest has existed for quite some time in law and in policing practice. Police arrest powers have long been grounded in the principle that they must have a reasonable basis for suspecting that a person has committed, *or is about to commit*, a criminal act. Con-spiracy provisions in the Criminal Code also allow the police to prose-cute people on evidence that they were planning a criminal act, while public order provisions such as the War Measures Act and the Riot Act give the police wide powers to arrest people for simply being in the street. But, of course, we are less interested in what the police can do within the law and more in what they are actually doing as a matter of common public order practices.

Although we have suggested that early strike policing was very re-active, preventative intervention does have a long history in labour and public order policing. As noted in chapter 3, Canadian police, em-ployers, and private security had an array of legal tools in the nine-teenth and early twentieth centuries that they used to criminalize union, socialist, and communist activists. Spying was quite common, allowing police to identify, arrest, and often deport individuals even before they had done anything in particular. Of course, given many of the laws at the time, these workers were technically breaking the law simply by being at a meeting or a picket line. As legal protections for labour expanded, and radical elements within labour largely disap-peared, especially after the Second World War, the rationale and capac-ity of police to intervene in this manner waned. The criticism of police handling of American riots of the 1960s, the relatively benign demands of new social protest movements, and the increased focus on human rights also dampened any enthusiasm for an extension of pre-emptive action against most protest groups during the 1970s and 1980s.

What happened in the 1990s, and especially after 9/11, was not just a return to the view that such tactics are necessary in some situations, but also a shifting of the boundaries concerning the reasonable basis for such action. This speaks to both the claimed threat posed by the predicted actions of protesters as well as the level of certainty required to justify preventive action. Arguably, the ramping-up of the claimed threat is integrally tied to the discourse on the 'war against terror,' where preventive arrests of suspected terrorists have included the avoidance of legal niceties through so-called 'extraordinary rendition.' New anti-terrorism laws have also made it possible for liberal demo-cratic states such as the United States, Britain, and Canada to arrest and hold people for extended periods of time without charges or ha-beas corpus, a serious challenge to liberal notions of the rule of law. These development have not gone unchallenged by civil rights group, the courts, and legislators, but the projected seriousness of terrorist threats – the fear of another 9/11 or a nuclear conflagration – allows such innovations as U.S. Vice-President Dick Cheney's 'one per cent solution' to appear almost reasonable: that is, whenever there is even a 1 per cent chance of a (terrorist) threat, preventative action may be un-dertaken (Suskind 2005).

It can be argued that these new rules of engagement apply only to 'foreign' Islamic terrorists and do not represent in any way a shift in thinking about domestic social movements and protests more generally, where the stakes are not as high. However, many have suggested that the distinction between war and security, military and law enforcement, domestic and foreign security interests and mandates are being cut away and the outward look of war-fighting is being turned inward on domestic populations. As security is globalized, not only is the line between crimes and acts of war blurred, but the boundary between crimes and minor public order infractions is also being erased (Hornquist, 2004). Here the clear concern is that the technologies and means of foreign countering are being applied to domestic countering, thus displacing or encroaching on legal values, including equality, efficiency, and liberty (cf. Haubrich, 2006; for an alternative position, see Waddington, 2006).

Arguably this is happening to a greater degree in countries other than Canada. A recent American example is illustrative. In the United States, law enforcement officers are restricted from monitoring domestic groups unless there is clear suspicion of criminal activity. However, in a Washington, DC, war protest in 2002, a 'secret' FBI unit dressed in street clothes detained some of the demonstrators and interrogated them on videotape about their political and religious beliefs. The allegation was denied by FBI and DCI police until 2007, when a civil suit unearthed police logs. According to the police records, the protesters were targeted because they were wearing the colour black and were perceived to be anarchists (Leonnig, 2007) According to one of the arrestees, Nat Meyensburg, they were interviewed by plainclothes police who had no identification:

> We exited through the lobby of the building, where, once on the street, we were stopped by the police and lined up along the building, had our bags searched. And we were taken off –several of us were taken off, one by one, to be interviewed on videotape by the FBI ... The two that had no identifications were the ones who took us off and away from the rest of the group and interviewed us on video camera. ('Walmart Accused,' 2007)

In another, perhaps more ominous, example, Vitale (2005: 284, 292) argues that shortly after 9/11 the New York Police Department began to develop an approach based on the 'broken windows' philosophy that emphasized 'command and control' and 'zero tolerance' for disorder. In preparations for anti-war protests planned for 15 and 16 February 2003, this included denying parade permits, deploying a large array of units (mounted, aerial, special weapons, etc.), severely limiting access to demonstration sites, and arresting and remanding participants. This strategy, which is a return to the public order model of command control that was so contentious during the birth of the labour movement in the United States, may also be distinguished from the 'escalating force' approach of the 1950s and 1960s, inasmuch as it is not predicated on the threat level of the demonstrators. Vitale states that in the New York example, demonstrators who were gathered up for arrest and detention may simply have been standing passively in the street and were fair game for coercive countering (291). In addition, command and control public order policing reserves little discretion to the front lines and for negotiations with protesters. It is punitive and inflexible rather than restorative and pliant. Along with zero tolerance it includes, according to Vitale, an aversion to disruption, tight control of access points, a divide-and-conquer orientation, and the visible expression of extreme measures in order to effect 'shock and awe' (292).

There is little indication that Canadian police are about to follow this approach. On the other hand, the security integration of Canada, the United States, and Mexico suggests that there is necessary concern that measures that appear to be acceptable to a large proportion of Americans and certainly to a great number of American politicians and law enforcement officers will, through harmonization and 'fusion,' become routine here.

Conclusion: From Liaison to Intelligent Control

We have been following the argument that police experience is contributory to police response to protests and demonstrations. From Seattle and APEC, police learned that they needed ample scope, particularly in intelligence gathering and pre-planning, but also in the breadth of operations, to counter disorder. The toolkit of strategies and tactics is often considered more or less coercive or inflexible. Communications and liaison itself are a flexible response, while the mobilization of the crowd control unit is not. However, police have a large array of responses, flexible and not, which can be brought to bear in different combinations, producing a dynamic set of variables to make each operation distinct. Add the many other variables, including demonstrator variety and tactics, type of event, legal and constitutional considerations, the wider political and cultural context, and media spin, and countering operations become complex indeed.

As we have also seen, police experience with Native protests is modulated by politics. This is most evident where police are mandated to protect the security of important persons in what we call 'high-stakes' protests. These are different from Native or environmental protests or blockades and also different from labour strikes and demonstrations. The difference is mainly in the relative values of the constituencies and interests at play. It goes without saying that a high-profile event like a meeting of the G-8 will attract the most comprehensive police operations. Not only does this involve various agencies of the federal level of government, but it requires guarantees or assurances to foreign states as well as commitments to bilateral or multilateral or international agreements. Examining such high-stakes events serves a few functions. First, it allows us to see that police movement to liaison in one arena may or not be followed in other arenas. Again, the importance of institutionalization and stakes is placed in sharper relief. Also, the examination allows us to see that the labour question will be modified in the context of those other developments. The importance of labour mobilizations and police response to them is historically located, especially post-NAFTA, when policies determining the transnational fluidity of capital become central. At the same time, by looking at Native policing, we also find that the stakes and interests themselves change, in part because the boundaries of public and private interest are being redrawn.

That being said, police are not *simply* a political weathervane, heading whichever way the politics of the day points them. This is represented by the label 'integration' in figure 2.1. Although politics clearly plays a large role, police experience, skills, professionalism, and long-term institutional interests also motivate their response. They may perceive dangers others may not. Experience may tell them of a pattern of behaviour regarding a particular group. Their organizational philosophy (community policing, intelligence-led policing) may inform their conduct. Altogether there is much that can be said about the character of the police response to public order events, especially as they have changed over the past several years. Accordingly, police action will range from shock absorption to shock troops, choosing more integrative or disaggregating methods depending on their interpretations.

While the liaison approach sought to prevent the need for covert intelligence and paramilitary intervention, we have argued that the process of building relations of trust and responsibility also serves as a preliminary method of risk analysis through which the police identify and assess groups and leaders in terms of their willingness to communicate and negotiate with the police. Groups and leaders who refuse to 'play ball' are identified as 'untrustworthy troublemakers' who present a potential for violence, thus warranting more careful public order scrutiny, often in the form of covert intelligence gathering and a greater readiness and preparedness of riot police and crowd control deployments. As groups, individuals, and situations become defined as representing greater risks of violence or serious disruption, both overwhelming tactical force and more precise forms of surgical force (e.g., snatch squads) can be deployed using the specialized, well-equipped, and trained personnel who constitute the paramilitary component of public order policing. Thus, a key dimension of intelligent control is the quick-change act between absorptive (community or liaison) and retardant (paramilitary) police forms. The ideal expression is chameleon-like: slowly absorptive and invisible on one hand, instantaneously expressive on the other. This transitivity between liaison and repression is necessary to minimize the range of disclosures: one without the other cannot maintain political authority (Giddens, 1985; Turk, 1982). For us, the current policing of labour and protest reveals a dual hybrid purpose of both accommodation and coercion.

It is also important to recognize that while coercion remains a critical aspect of police control within this new context – and indeed the public police retain their virtual monopoly over the legitimate right to use force in these situations (Jones and Newburn, 2003) – what is different about the use of force here is that it is more selective, more strategic, more preventive. It is a coercion that more consciously plays to both protester/striker and larger public and media concerns, leaving the former with more restricted opportunities to capitalize in public relations terms on police violence.

Despite concerns about the limits of the approach (the shortcomings of the reliance on courts and brokered arrangements), police continue using parts of the liaison approach for protest. They largely replicate techniques perfected in strike situations while adapting and modifying the approach for more complex or risky public order crises. As we have seen, the latter adaptations responded to protest tactics that superseded the traditional street protest, thus presenting police with more complex challenges (Button, John, and Brearley, 2002). Frustrated by the ineffectiveness of standard street protests and lobbying, protest groups began to blockade and occupy land. Thus, in addition to Native land claims, another type of public order conflict that required rethinking during the 1980s and 1990s were the environmental protests. In the logging province of BC, where environmental groups fought the major logging companies such as MacMillan Bloedel over their cutting practices, the NDP provincial government adopted a civil law approach to these occupations that explicitly encouraged the police to use liaison methods. Similarly, the RCMP at the national level and OPP at a provincial level also developed specific protocols for dealing with Native land occupations which emphasized communication, negotiations, and protracted use of the courts and injunctions.

However, as we have seen in the Native protests described above, the initial police response in the early 1990s was to deploy significant public order force with limited liaison efforts, leading in virtually every case to significant injuries and public relation disasters for the police. While it is clear in the accounts of these events that part of the reason for this deployment was the perception of the Native groups as 'radicals with guns' who were not trustworthy or self-controlled, even in this context police administrations gradually came to the realization that 'playing with time' through communications and negotiations paid the same dividends as in strike policing despite the greater challenges and risks. As we have also argued, especially with the lesson of Ipperwash, police found that another element of laision, deferral to court and injunctions, was mistaken. In addition, they came to the conclusion, as demonstrated dramatically in Chief Fantino's comments, that Native land occupations were not a ditch in which they were any longer compelled to die in. What the 1990s also demonstrated to police was that labour (certainly big labour) continued to be easily manageable or institutionalized through liaison, even when participating in high-profile events. Large-scale labour events such as the Days of Action in Ontario and the labour contingent in the anti-globalization movement served to confirm the police conviction that labour was not part of the new war.

Liaison was not sufficient for the last type of public order, the 'high-stakes' anti-globalization protest. Like the land claims protest, this involved extra-territorial and extra-national interests, but unlike Native land claims, it could not be resolved at the political level and did not attract the same public sympathy, especially in unprovoked violent actions by activists who were deemed to be defying self-policing protocols. While the integration of excluded groups was to be understood with the reorganization and larger transformation of public policing, and community policing did drive professional reform in the 1980s and early 1990, recasting how public order could best be achieved, that initiative, together with the 'new public management' (and more prosaic changes in use of force and other protocols), occurred along-side the enormous and gathering appeal of a more incipient agency: pre-emptive intelligence.

8 Intelligent Control

As to a proper memorial for the Prime Minister, a man I would dearly love to be praising now, we must look no further than the empty plinth in Trafalgar Square which falls inside the area where spontaneous demonstration of any sort has been banned by Labour. A modest bronze of an ordinary man, gagged and holding a blank placard perhaps? Or a cascade of birds falling from the sky, each one representing a lost right or freedom?

Henry Porter, *The Observer*, 1 April 2007

Introduction

Our account of the history of public order policing in Canada over the course of the twentieth century has sought to recognize both changes and historical continuities in police ideas, tactics, and strategies. While our central analysis has focused on a relatively recent shift to a consensual liaison approach, we have also recognized a long-standing and persistent use of both consensual and coercive tactics on different groups in different situations. The overall direction of police strategy has been towards limiting direct police action (particularly the use of force) in both strikes and protest situations. A the same time, we have also observed that the development of public relations and community policing was attended by a parallel development of paramilitary units with technologies, tactics, and training capacity that are targeted and forceful. On the whole, we have tried to show that police are constantly adapting strategies and tactics to changing political terrains and social movements as well as to changing knowledge and experience bases, and this has coalesced most recently in the development of an emphasis on intelligence. In this chapter, we seek to interpret and account more fully for the development of intelligence-based policing and its implications, to show in particular that the reproduction of consent remains an integral part of this approach.

Exceptional Consent

Taking our cue from writers such as Nikolas Rose (1996) who conceptualize the current state of affairs in late modern liberal democracies, it is evident that some long-standing notions are undergoing modification as governments and politics more generally address or reconcile the information age, globalization, neo-liberalism, and what some have called a post-ideological condition to the everyday problem of public or common order. In particular, liberal democracies like Canada are trying to find a way to match up what to past generations would be typified as practices of a police state to the necessity of preventing public order spectacles from being showcased around the world as a symbol not of healthy participatory resistance but crisis.

One of the key paradoxes in a liberal democracy is the power of the sovereign – often in the actuality of the executive – to make law for exceptions. It is not necessary to trace this too far down (cf. Lazar, 2006; Pederson, 2006), but it can be encapsulated in the thorny problem of how law is made where an existential crisis is perceived (or, as is often the case, invented). This is a great problem because public order policing might be viewed as mere stagecraft in front of this backdrop: one may think in the metaphor of a large hammer hoisted by pulleys above the players. And it brings the issue of the constitutionality of governance always back in play. In the speeded-up juggernaut of high modern liberal democracies, the question of crisis (exemplified in mass protest, in refusals to provide labour) is most easily dramatized by finding the best threat caricature: who is 'the other,' the stranger, the enemy alien, the not 'one of us' who must be identified and neutralized? Put in other terms, what is the nature of the dangerous constituency or cancerous presence that will reveal itself ultimately to officials for definitive identification and elimination? As many theorists have noted, the liberal democratic paradox of openness and necessary (as perceived) exceptions constantly reinvigorates the question of who or what is to be countered and excluded. There is a self-fulfilling prophecy in which the necessary foundations or totems must be re-deified.

This quandary of order endures at the base of modern liberal democracies, but the immediate context and technological possibilities change. The instant availability of what police call actionable information has meant that the foundation notion of checks and balances is being threatened if not overrun. The idea of judicial or legal check is everywhere endangered by the entreaties of a regime of immediate satisfaction. The long-standing notion that the sovereign must have an advantage against the exceptional is parlayed with the technological possibility and the cultural affirmation of instantaneity to work against both the judicial and legislative check. We have seen this in action in the problem of the injunction. In the terminology of high modernity, applying for an injunction is to misapply old solutions to a reconfigured problem: if the parameters for action are not readily available, they are no more available to the judge than to the incident commander. If, on the other hand, good intelligence provides *actionable* knowledge, then deferring to a judge is to diminish the cybernetics in undue and ambiguous replication.

To put the problem another way, in what Deleuze refers to as societies of control, it is the control not of law but of information that becomes the godhead. More prosaically, control involves greater use of categorical suspicion, pre-emption, containment, and expulsion. As Hudson (2003) and Roach (2003) among others argue, the significance here is that a rights discourse is gradually evacuated as schedules of security become more pressing. Indeed, it might be said that police tactics, while evaluated and vetted on constitutional and legal grounds, increasingly find reference to exceptionalism, or politics privileging the right of state. Biopower methods are combined with the power of institutions of the secret state and a state privilege discourse to yield, in larger and larger measure, the breaking up of the polity according to perceived risks and threats of dangerous cohorts. While, as Roach has put it, this process is made 'Charter-proof,' such Charter-proofing is by way of subordinating the rule of law to the so-called priority of the state.

Of course, a key part of the danger that this represents is that in the intelligence-led or intelligence-based preference, information control is accomplished through mastery of persuasion, secrecy, espionage, and evaluation (cf. Wilsnack, 1980). Security management, in the preferred parlance, requires the maintenance of exclusive knowledge and actionable information (in the validation of exclusive action capabilities). Information control policing, consequently, is not conceived with self-government or original authority in the recovery of an already integrative order, but rather in proactive production: police and security agents shape or discover hidden cohorts according to the requirements of control exclusivity. And they fix viral identities (cf. Ericson and Haggerty, 1997) according to a deliberately wider brief than criminal designations. Knowledge, particularly in the limited disclosures of police and security information, is here not liberating, but volatile (cf. O'Malley, 1999): unpredictable from without. But that is the key to the direction of this line of development: increasingly it turns the political ambiguities that define the liberal democracies into little puzzle pieces that are measured, and then anticipated, and then acted on before they take concrete shape.

Talk of intelligence-based public order, let alone rigidity and secretive investigations, would not in the 1980s have been an acceptable public policing discourse. The context was already too much a reaction to rigidity and exclusivity in policing, and in Canada (as in the United States), the countering of political activism had left an ugly mark on police institutions. In the late 1990s and beyond, however, that political culture began to change. And after 2001, it shifted even more dramatically, as is evidenced by legislation such as Bill C-36, which would not have received sufficient parliamentary support even just two decades ago. As we have indicated, the Canadian picture is a kaleidoscope in which a variety of domains (environmental, labour, high-stakes, Native) register diverse responses across police at federal, regional, and even municipal levels. The current rightward movement of federal politics may also afford a more penetrating preventative police posture, although there is no clear shift in Canadian public opinion supporting tighter police controls at the cost of human rights or freedoms, nor is there a clear rightward shift in provincial governments. Nevertheless, it is in this neo-liberal and post-9/11 environment of uncertainty and insecurity that risk and threat assessment has become more salient; and political and police authorities are able to claim the necessity of preventative intervention. These trends may be captured by reference to a few major terms of the current public order domain. These include pre-emptive surveillance, boundary blurring, and reflexive dramatization.

Pre-emptive Surveillance

While we have already observed that Canadian police show little inclination towards the more extreme approach in New York City, the noted increase in pre-emption in police and domestic security work and indeed the re-politicization of the internal security mandate can also be viewed as an incremental process. Conceived in terms of the gradual expansion of external and border technologies and exceptions into the spaces occupied or frequented by domestic subjects or citizens, this pattern of the incremental advance of forward pre-emption and 'border blurring' or 'creep' (Innes, 2001) is most clearly visible in the development of security protections in the European Community. That system, as Statewatch has analysed, was 'first and foremost' an instrument of border control, but has gradually incorporated a variety of 'interoperabilities' so that it is also a system of police investigation and forward deterrence. Under the justification of 'prevention' people can be entered into the SIS (Schengen Information System) for the purpose of 'observation' (under Article SIA), a category that, according to Statewatch, has doubled between 2003 and 2006.[1] The exceptional data collection and retention (including biometrics)[2] that differentiated subjects from others or aliens as part of the biopower logos of modernity is incrementally inching inwards or downstream, first to other actionable cohorts, like travellers (independent of citizenship), who now require biometrics in their passports, then to commuters (who may require them in their licences).

Similarly, the United States after 9/11, following the guidance of the GAO Audit Commission Report of 2004 and the 9/11 Commission Report, also enhanced the flow of intelligence between its various security and policing agencies, a monumental undertaking topped up with a host of exceptional and illegal data collecting and sharing practices. Consistent with the pattern found by Statewatch, it also exploited the more limited protection on non-citizens and moved from there to push inward towards residents and citizens. Under the National Security Entry-Exit Registration System, it began to biometrically register all males between the ages of sixteen and forty-five coming from Muslim countries who were visiting or travelling through the country – 80,000 men were biometrically registered in this way. Under US VISIT (United States Visitor and Immigrant Status Indicator Technology), and with the new requirements of passports and/or biometric driver's licences, the ambit of this collection and verification scheme has been or is being expanded to European and Canadian visitors. As Maureen Webb (2007) has put it, 'I think the aim of this new surveillance regime is first to register populations with biometric identity documents ... The idea is that when you have a biometric identifier for everybody, you have a kind of gold standard for making sure you've got the person that you want. And then you can start to, with greater confidence, link information to that biometric identifier.'[3]

In Canada, following UN conventions and U.S. and law enforcement urgings in the wake of 9/11, similar practices have been developed or expanded. Surveillance initiatives that were introduced through international forums like the G8 (in Europe also the G6), have yielded a common goal which Webb (2007) identifies with 'the disappearance of a Canadian citizen.' In shades of U.S. Vice-President Dick Cheney's famous '1 per cent doctrine,' the RCMP, as indicated in testimony before the O'Connor Commission, understood that they had been given a mandate of prevention that required a zero-tolerance approach to risk. Canadian officials developed more proactive measures to collect data and trigger alerts regarding the communication, travel, visa, and financial transactions of people. In addition, passenger watch lists, financial transactions monitoring (FINTRAC), exceptions to regular court procedures (e.g., the Security Certificate), the drafting of Canada's first national security strategy (Canada, 2004), and the development of a new national security bureaucracy (security committee, a national security adviser, etc.) have significantly altered the intelligence field since 9/11.[4]

The security measures regarding internationally protected persons (IPPs) at public order sites, as in Windsor and Quebec, are clear instances of 'downstream consequences.' The RCMP call for a threat assessment (an independent subset of intelligence activity) if they are conducting duties that involve the protection of IPPs (as defined in section 2 of the Criminal Code) or have assigned obligations to protect Canadian persons, such as the prime minister.

> The significance of APEC was the realization that the responsibilities for protecting international protected people was the reality that you can't guarantee this unless you are fully prepared. I don't think the proper risk assessment was done and then suddenly there was a situation that created some chaos and the police saw the potential serious threat to their ability to protect these people. And certain officers reacted. (R9)

At the same time, the police balancing act weighing the security of the singular person or entities (evaluated via the continuously updated assessment of threats) against various Charter rights, like freedom of assembly and speech, will be watched by the court and the public. And of course, in the case of APEC, there was a public inquiry as well as an RCMP complaints commission investigation, which were highly critical of the police.

The political act of protest will be girded by limits, including proximity to the representative object (the visitor, dignitary, group). To preclude or pre-empt such a sovereignty spectacle, the government of Canada consults with security officials before finalizing where summits take place, a practice much more essential following the fallout of APEC and Ipperwash and when lines of communication are not sufficiently formalized. As we show in the next section, boundary blurring is part and parcel of pre-emption.

Boundary Blurring and Fusion

As noted, another cultural feature of the control society in general and intelligence-based policing in particular is its boundlessness, and in this we also see the undermining of the consent bases of modern liberal democracies. While neo-liberal globalization and the spread of information technologies are supposed to hasten an ideological and teleological harmonization (Fukuyama, 1989), post-Soviet geopolitics concentrating on Islamic terrorism provides a discursive demarcation for militancy loosely along Western/non-Western lines.[5] The notion of asymmetrical warfare captured this problem of integration of economies and nation-states in a context of significant value differences and resource scarcity. The spread of border justice has been the dominant response. If the border is everywhere, border justice adjudicates everyone, with the requisite dropping out of rights. Since the outsider or the monster[6] of terrorism is not alien but deep in the heart of the body politic, the exceptional circumstances of war and information control must also be both deeply embedded and widely dispersed.

The correlate of border spread is a blending or fusion of police and security provision. If the border is the centre, security practices are raised above democratic practices (in 'securing democracy'). The discretionary privileges of border justice may drift across any terrain, occupy every nodal point, and penetrate each identity.[7] Buttressed by the value preferences of dominant realist security discourse, the harmonization of police and security protocols across distinct and differing national and political interests proceeds apace. And the traction of exceptionalism improves with invisible, ubiquitous, and boundless (without boundaries) society-wide (catastrophic, ideological) threats.

In the United States, countering practices against a variety of protesters have been stimulated by the fusion of internal and external security orders. The surveillance, disruption, and detaining of persons deemed to be risky of terrorism or critical infrastructure attacks have brought a wide array of subjects into an expanded net, made wider still by the interoperability requirements of law enforcement and national security. In 2003, FBI director Robert Mueller put it to the Senate Intelligence Committee that in the fight against terrorism, local police have become 'important force multipliers.' The number of Joint Terrorism Task Forces (JTTFs) – which are commanded by the Justice Department and combine federal, state, and local agents – leapt from 35 across the nation before 11 September 2001, to 66 since in 2003, to over 100 in 2007. In Canada, joint teams were set up between agencies formalized as INSETS, or Integrated National Security Enforcement Teams, and IBETs, or Integrated Border Enforcement Teams. These new fusions have exacerbated data protection and privacy concerns where, for instance, a denial of entry into the United States may be registered as an alert for the criminal intelligence unit operating in the denied person's ambit (de Lint, O'Connor, and Cotter, 2007).

In mass demonstrations today, particularly in the anti-globalization events, interoperability is being showcased as demonstrators encounter a remarkable array of police and security officials. As we noted earlier, this is demonstrated in the allocation of dosages of police or security presence spatially and temporally. Thus, the experience for activists begins with a visit by the RCMP or a denial of entry into Canada by the Canadian Border Security Agency and might include a denial of a camping permit or hotel registration. If and when the activist gets on site, a graduated array of security awaits. There will be a smorgasbord of municipal police as well as provincial and federal representation of both police and, as noted, other security service agencies. Increasingly, and particularly where the existential right of the nation-state itself is said to be threatened, military involvement is also in evidence, although the distinction to the activist or protester might not be sharp, given the phalanxes of public order units, the snipers on the roofs, and the helicopters in the sky.

Still, the acceptable parameters of blurring and fusion are dynamic as witnessed by the national controversy in Canada over a September 2005 report that FBI agents were conducting investigations of Canadians on the Canadian side of the border.

Reflexive Dramatization

Giddens (1990; 1991) has argued that late modernity is reflexive. This means that agents responsible for social or public order must be attentive to the representations of their actions.[8] In this book, we have been concentrating on what we call collective or mass demonstration grievances. The 'demonstration' qualifier is, in today's highly reflexive modernity, more and more pivotal. Indeed, part of the often-noted cultural change in the information age is that power is affected more through the management of representations. Consequently, and following up our earlier discussion of the importance of public relations and the management of appearances, that control *must be seen to be done* is a fact that underlies much police and security work. Crime control, accordingly, is decreasingly an action that can be factually measured in the Archimedean sense. It is increasingly recognized in the terms of performance art. Police operations or 'projects' are understood in terms of their public relations – as a vehicle to push popular opinion.

This has been a subtle shift in the way that control agents themselves view the spectacle. So recursive and reflexive are we today that police productions and their intentions are viewed in terms of their public relations effectiveness. This is to say that people are persuaded of the value of the control of crime and of the utility of those who are empowered to carry out the performance only to the extent that the performance is compelling.[9] Since the effectiveness or utility of the action of those 'controlling crime' is already a question of review, and control is accomplished through management of perceptions, actions that are pre-scripted (coded) are likely to maximize such control (simply by being the most compelling).

One illustration of the reflexivity of emergent public order countering practices is provided in the actions of the Ottawa Police Service (OPS) following the major event operations associated with the meeting of the G8. Describing their approach as 'new' and dedicated to ensuring 'public and officer safety,' the OPS publicly posted answers to questions from the public regarding the event. For example, to the question 'Why was the police videotaping so obtrusive and aggressive, even interfering with the march on June 26 and June 27?' the OPS responded:

> Again, in response to community consultations where concerns were expressed about covert video taping and photography, teams of identifiable Police videographers were deployed. The intent was to conduct this

necessary element of the event (see Questions 1 & 4) in an open and transparent manner. The fact that police would be videotaping the two-day event was repeated at each of the public meetings hosted by MELT leading up to the G8.There was criticism of the manner in which the videotaping was accomplished and this feedback will be used in the further development of the Agenda for Excellence. (OPS, 2003)

Another practice that conveys the loose reflexivity and specularity of current mobilizations (cf. Bajc, 2007) is the 'surge.' Some police agencies now stage random dramatizations of force at landmarks, critical infrastructures (banks, hotels, bridges, etc.), or targets of high symbolic value 'to keep terrorists guessing and remind people to be vigilant.' Surges are most developed in New York, where 1000 officers from the 37,000-person force are dedicated full-time to counter-terrorism and 600 comprise a secretive counter-intelligence unit (CBS, 26 March 2006). The entire force is subscribed, rotationally, to daily surges in which heavily armed officers congregate in massive numbers in self-described 'shock and awe' intimidation displays.[10] NYPD uses ex–intelligence officers in mimicking the security practices of a nation–state (CBS, 26 March 2006). Officers 'might, for example, surround a bank building, check the IDs of everyone going in and out and hand out leaflets about terror threats.' 'What we're doing is very similar to what the military does, and to what Israel has been doing for many years ... This is an in-your-face type of strategy' (Lieutenant Simonetti, in Kolbert, 2003).

It is worth noting that control simulation is also visible in a move towards 'reassurance policing' in Great Britain (cf. Fielding and Innes, 2006). Like community-based policing, reassurance policing is not intended by its protagonists to appear as an iteration of public relations or mere mollycoddling (in the same way that fear of crime is not dismissed as a mere epiphenomenon). Rather, it suggests the deepening of the sort of police relationship with 'the real' that we have been describing: police do not 'respond' to 'crime,' they respond to the perception of crime; police do not control persons or create order, they stage the simulation of control and order. This process means that for them organizationally the substance or 'the real' becomes that ground of perception and review: it, not crime rates or the countering of disorder, is what they 'are about' (de Lint, O'Connor, and Cotter, 2007).

As this interpretation implies, intelligence-based policing is not just about gathering information to use in making threat and risk assessments and in fixing the correct form and proportion of tactical responses – it is about *controlling* information both behind and on the stage itself so as to manipulate both the actors' and the audience's view of the spectacle. It is in this sense that intelligent control seeks to combine displays and degrees of communication, compromise, and forceful intervention in the correct measure, simultaneously sending multiple messages to multiple actors and observers. For those who are contemplating unlawful behaviour in high-stakes *public* order situations, the message is definitely 'don't try it,' while for those who pursue *public* interests in a lawful manner in those same situations, the message is 'we'll do what we can to help.' For those who pursue private interests, the message is 'it's your business as long as you don't endanger public safety.' While these messages are not entirely new, and indeed were definitely embedded in the liaison approach, intelligence-based policing invests a new police confidence in the capacity to send the right messages to the right people at the right time in the right space. Here the promise is better management of the central dilemma of liberal policing – to be able to use the right amount of force when consent breaks down in particular contexts, to control the situation without undermining consent to democratic capitalism more generally.

As the NYC 'surges' illustrate particularly well, intelligence-based policing is also about simulation – that is, the disappearance of the gap between the real and imaginary (Baudrillard, 1998). This 'produces a reality effect, while at the same time concealing the absence of the real' (Bogard, 1994: 9). Drawing from the previous points that the power relation is reviewed, the control of government information is relatively exclusive, and the threat is boundless, control is exercised with a longer view on 'the real.' Information control is practised as a departure from positivistic or empiricist adherence to representation. 'Reality' is a production conceived and carried out in demonstration projects.[11] Accordingly, the object of police and security technologies is the harnessing of the uncertain, ambiguous, and indefinite in the production of control simulations.

Hybrid Policing: Intelligent Control

In service-based consent (liaison) policing, we found that policing was a reflexive enterprise feeding and being fed by practices derived from principles of impartiality, limitation, visibility, and representation. Under more recent police reforms, intelligence, secrecy, and knowledge exclusions become the standard-bearing practices. While in our view the legacy of consent still informs policing at its core, we have suggested that three trends already evident prior to 9/11 have been reinforced:

- pre-emption or preventative intervention (on the basis of exceptionalism);
- fusion, or law enforcement and national security integration; and
- reflexive dramatization.

Underpinning each of these is the intelligence process and the deployment of information in the control of spaces of governance and governability. It is particularly the fusion of vertical and horizontal regulatory or security capacities that has redrafted how public order is being managed. In retrospect, we can now understand liberal democracy and consent policing as the application of information control through the available registrations of the time: consent is therefore a discourse of control.[12] Liberal democratic order becomes idealized as the deferred consent of self-government realized only in the necessity of control and containment.

As we have seen, Canadian policing of labour strife and most protests is now largely accomplished within a service model involving a combination of community policing and public relations strategies and tactics or 'liaison policing.' However, within the context of large-scale anti-globalization protests and the post-9/11 war on terror, practices have very recently melded together in a recursive or iterative, specular, and dynamic mobilization that might be called 'intelligent control.' Intelligent control (IC) is a hybrid of liaison strategies (integrative service) and intelligence-based coercion (authoritative control), resulting in an overall approach that is measured, flexible, targeted (precise), and stage-managed. This adaptation takes heed of the specularity of power relations, the pre-emption of social control, and the transitivity and recursivity of action.

The key to understanding intelligent control is preventative action, whether consensual or coercive, that may act prior to the politicization or mobilization of order-destabilizing counter-forces. Police exploit the scarcity of legal permissions, legitimate force, and actionable information. In this designation, then, public order policing becomes, first and foremost, action on information. Specifically, it is action on information drawn as a result of pre-emptive or covert targeting, collection, analysis, and dissemination that then is used to manage conditions of mass public grievance expression. Manipulating special access to authoritative information or intelligence is a means of indirect coercion. It is the strategic plan and template for strategic plans governing the logistics of pickets and mass demonstrations where the emphasis comes to lie.[13] Preference for negotiation over confrontation is also an insistence that the expression of grievance is framed within proper formats.[14]

The application of intelligent control to labour and political protest also manifests as the graduation of action through a variety of liberal democratic intermediaries (responsibilization, self-management, commitment to non-violence, adherence to 'lawful' direction). Through such intermediaries, it is possible to denude the potential dynamism of the labour action or protest as a series of routines played out over an extended period of time. The graduated disclosure of coercion also means that IC is the coordinated application of an outcome through numerous agencies. In the ideal, there is a stepwise process that moves up to violence after exhausting, one by one, lesser intervention.

At the same time, an essential feature of current policing continues to be its specularity. To frame this in the power debates (cf. Digeser, 1992), it is important to see our site of contestation in terms beyond the binary relationship. The power relation is observed. It is then true not only that A possesses power because B does or does not do what A intended her to do or not to do. It is also important to consider that A does to B so that C may watch and change her behaviour. The *framing or staging of the power relation* is vital, and certainly we see that such staging and drama are why authorities and resisters perceive the public grievance as a venue for shifts in power relations. Thus, while much policing if following the turn to control becomes more pre-emptive and information-grounded, the authority of authority, as Raz (1990) informs us, is yet still dependent on visibility. As bodies made of flesh and bone we are never fully 'data doubles' (Haggerty and Ericson, 2000) that may be shunted around in the information flows. Authority continues to depend on the regular *demonstration* of capacity with regard to territoriality and sovereignty. However, it is the enhanced precision of exemplifying capacity or the demonstration of capacity to a selected audience that is important. While it is unnecessary to broadcast capacity in the exponential fashion of the early modern state (as by scheduling special trains to usher citizens to London to witness executions), a limited, managed, targeted display of visible coercion is still consistent with the dramaturgical necessities of authoritative rule (Giddens, 1985). A movement towards limited targeting over indiscriminate broadcasting is consistent with the privatization of violence thesis to the extent that the utility of violence is restricted by class and target. So while there is no reason to over-emphasize capacity (to do so betrays weakness) for general deterrence purposes, there is also no utility to under-emphasize it for specific deterrence of target groups. This also follows E.V. Walter's (1969) argument that terror is used to engineer compliant behaviour not only among victims but among target populations.[15] Hybrid policing or intelligent control is a flexible, recursively sensitive, graduation of applied violence and terror.[16]

This also recognizes labour strike or political protest as dramatic acts performed for an audience. This performance is dependent on the backstop of possible violence (therein lies the drama). The indeterminacy of the outcome, however, does not exclude the preference of participants for predictability. This preference results in the cooperation of participants in the staging of action as a watched performance. The actual demonstration is more or less a deviation from the simulation or dramatic representation of the negotiated protocol. Taking visibility (above) into account, we see that consideration of the dramaturgical dimension of the 'public' or 'political' grievance would appear to require the occasional show of demonstrative or spectacular violence. Here the backstop of violence is necessary to fix the endless play of significations.

All of this is to say that we are sensitive to the co-existence of pre-emptive and informational policing and paramilitary and specular policing. Rather than seeing a simple gradual displacement of the spectacular with the pre-emptive, we see a pre-selection of the venues for expressive policing.[17] As police become more skilled in asserting their utilities, they choose to display coercive capacity only where necessary to maintain the political order or their position within it and use what we call 'liaison policing' to maintain their hold on the goodwill of the polity. In long-standing liberal democracies, police have public relations skills and a wide variety of special units that may be brought into or taken out of the public eye as desired. They can change colour from black to light blue. For their part, union leaders and protest organizers alike have become more media-savvy, preferring the scripting of action over spontaneity while appreciating the necessity of long-term commitments even in the arena of social transformation.

Implications for Democracy

Reduced to its simplest terms, intelligent control seeks to manage the dilemmas of consent and coercion within a neo-liberal context, while at the same time contributing to a widespread withdrawal from public politics. However, there is an important paradox here. At one level, as we show in chapter 5, the liaison aspects of this approach to policing are grounded in trust relations between police and labour/protest leaders, while the restraint on force more generally can be read as a positive shift away from authoritarian control. Yet, as Charles Tilly (2004: 5) argues, this withdrawal from public politics is ultimately a withdrawal from 'trust networks,' by which he means 'ramified inter-personal connections within which people set valued, consequential, long-term resources and enterprises at risk to the malfeasance of others.' Tilly argues that after wartime, states tend to be guilty of such malfeasance of life and liberty and public politics suffers because it is perceived as having failed or dishonoured that trust. Strikes and protests are consequently more prolific. In Canada and in many countries today we see with neo-liberalism a strategy that calls for a relocation of responsibility for governance with private and voluntary trust networks. But if, as Tilly argues, extensive withdrawal of trust networks from democratic public politics 'threatens democracy in principle,' we have to ask then whether neo-liberalism in general and police practices consonant with neo-liberalism in particular, are also anti-democratic. Turner (1968: 826), too, alerted us to this prospect much earlier by theorizing that the privatization of disputes 'may keep third parties disinterested and uninvolved.'

This brings us again to the framing of protests with liberal institutions, defined as acts which express a grievance together with a conviction that exceptional means of communication are needed to send the signal of a perceived injustice to the target and an observer (cf. Turner, 1968). If injustice, following Homans and Blau, is an interpretation 'of inadequate reciprocity in social exchange' (quoted in Turner, 1968: 820), the framing of a grievance and its reception depend on a number of factors strongly demonstrating the situatedness of the power relation. Turner argues, for instance, that to gain credibility as a legitimate protest against injustice, groups must have extensive lead-up advertising of their grievances and must, among other things, not lose 'moral credit' by overreaching in their tactics or rhetoric. Turner notes that dominant groups, when faced with potential conflicts, may try to criminalize the agitating group or to define them as rebels, for which retaliatory repression is legitimate. Conciliatory responses are more likely where the grievances have been interpreted as unjust by the target and the observer. A further detriment to the success of protest reception is the effect of routinized bargaining. According to Turner, such routines detract from the open-ended commitments of the protest meaning, making the injustice at back of the grievance more invisible and impersonal. This is to stress the role of the venue for grievance expression.

In theorizing the development of collective or mass demonstration of grievances, it follows that ambiguity or uncertainty is an elementary constituent of democratic forums. The trajectory towards the routinization, ritualization, and institutionalization of strikes and mass demonstrations of grievances may be anathema to democratization rather than exemplary of it. Legalization and civilization are also movements that reduce the ambiguity of the relationship between police and resisters, protesters, or labour demonstrators. Pre-emptory forms of risk reduction found in current transformations of public order policing also stab at a form of security through exclusion at the cost, following Bernstein (1996), of freedom of our uncertainty. This also seems consistent with Chris Phillips's (2004) contention that civilizations are shown to be in decline when comfort and security become the principal objectives of leaders and when leadership itself with certainty is preferred over process and differences. Ultimately, then, this scholarship seeks to explore whether the removal of uncertainly and ambiguity within service and hybrid policing represents another nail in the coffins of democratic protest and labour strikes.

Conclusion

Intelligence gathering and preventative intervention are only two aspects of what we mean by intelligent control. There is an array of coercive, informational, and legal strictures, prohibitions, or weapons, including liaison techniques, which constitute the current police arsenal, but what is particularly distinctive about intelligent control is that police use these tools in a multidimensional, flexible approach to resolution, problem-solving, or regulation. Each category of these tools may be 'harder' or 'softer': police may deploy criminal law or seek to involve civil remedies; police may take a control approach to information and communications in which there is a deliberate asymmetry of flow; police may take lethal, less-than-lethal, or no hardware at all to sites of conflicts. As we saw with many anti-globalization protests, these approaches may be mixed and matched for different groups in the same event. Police may give a different priority to each category of tool: police may see a disorder first and foremost as a question of legal authority or they may see it primarily as a question of adequate communications or coercion.

It should also be recognized that police are not entirely ordered in their selection, prioritization, and use of their various policing tools. Police services are differentially democratic and autocratic (in particular, public interest–centred) in inclination, and policing tools within any service may be employed differentially to reintegrate or keep integrated troublesome people and problem populations. Selection and deployment of tools is first and foremost grounded in the collection and analysis of information, threat, and risk assessment, but it should be added that this is also dependent on police training and confidence. Where there is a gap in training or a lack of appreciation for the full range of options available, there is a greater chance that an inappropriate response will be taken.

At the same time, as we saw in this and the previous chapters, police are not standing still. They learn and adapt from their experiences. And through interactions with each other common trends emerge in public order policing more generally. This identification of trends is grounded in our observation that, in different combinations, the various policing tools articulate a more prohibitive or regulatory, exclusionary or inclusionary, democratizing or authoritarian public order policing regime. In our framework, a control orientation is repressive and violence is one of the means of that repression, but communications and law are also utilized, albeit not to further integration. As we have seen, traditional conflict conditions were accompanied by public order police delivering comprehensive and multiplied shows of force under permissive rules of engagement. Currently, the craft of public order policing (or its professionalism) is bound up in how the dimensions of temporality, spatiality, and visibility are deployed. This craft is a way of finessing the offer of closure, or the stripping or containing of the ambiguous in contentious affrays; the object of public order policing in its consensual or democratic form is to keep order without sanctioning politics. In its high-stakes variant, the object is to push forward toward an order without appearing to sanction politics. In general, this will mean attempting to intrude the absolute minimum into the political order that a reading of the event will allow.[18] In highly preventative public order mobilizations consistent with law enforcement–enabling legislation after 9/11, police use greater powers (i.e., preventative intervention and/or liaison) to defuse potential public order events and can then drop deployment when the event actually occurs. To the extent that intelligent control involves alternating or combining soft and hard tools selectively targeted to different groups based on risk or threat assessments, it is what we would call a hybrid approach – that is, the utilization of dual control strategies (information and hard countering [paramilitary, intelligence]) grounded in the exploitation of informational or communications resources in particular. While finessing the appearance of service policing, it readies hard countering behind the absorptive layer of accommodation.

9 Conclusion

Liberalization and privatization have been central to our argument. As welfare liberalism took hold over the course of the twentieth century, police increasingly discovered, as Giddens (1985) argues, that flagrant and spectacular disclosures of coercive capacity yield diminishing returns. According to liberalized rule of law, too much discretion, particularly of authorities, is also constructed as problematic. The tightening of police legal and political accountabilities in the new public management was part of the effort to maintain liberal democracies as capable of absorbing a great deal of conflict and dissent without recourse to liberalism's antithesis: authoritarianism. With increased emphasis on the rule of law and the designation of police as entrusted with coercive powers in enforcing the law and protecting rights, police began to see coercion as craft, to be used with restraint and professional care. In stable liberal societies like Canada, police are encouraged to develop skills in choosing from their arsenal, electing to display coercive capacity more efficiently and only where necessary to maintain the political order or their own capacity within it. What we call 'liaison policing' was an instance of this phenomenon, developed to maintain an appropriate relationship of goodwill with the polity. In the context of long-standing liberal democracies, police increasingly developed both public relations skills *and* a wide variety of intelligence and paramilitary special units and personnel that may be brought into or taken out of the public eye as desired. In its ideal hybrid form, consent and coercion are brought together through highly sophisticated information-gathering and assessment technologies and techniques, allowing police to manage the dilemmas of liberal controls by measuring and selecting responses based on threat and risk assessments.

The result is that the appearance, at least, of liberal democratic governance is more or less maintained.

Is Political Economy Back In?

As we have tried to show, the sensibility to violence that marks the trajectory of public order policing has been attenuated to political economy and the shifting character of industrial and class relations. For their part, police made few formal changes through the development of the Fordist and welfarist period, and remained ready to use force routinely to open picket lines on demand from employers into the 1960s and 1970s. In our estimation, it was largely the unions that first committed themselves to peaceful and lawful picketing as part of the postwar bargain. This included a purging of radical elements in the union movement, an initiative that helped to undermine the capacity and willingness of the police to sustain a coercive orientation. The militant unionization of police themselves in the 1960s also played an integral part in the extension of Fordist industrial regimes to the public sector and informed how police viewed unions and strikes.

But these factors were not sufficient in themselves to push widespread change in strike or public order policing. It was not until the Fordist and welfarist bargains begin to unravel in the context of the mid-1960s and 1970s, when a combination of factors produced an initial surge in illegal wildcats and then later a wave of legal strikes, as well as yielding an explosion in new social movements and activism, that we begin to see the police rethinking their approaches to strikes and public order. The simple increase in the scale and scope of strikes and protests was instrumental in precipitating change, in part because of the demands they placed on police resources, but, perhaps even more important, because they greatly increased the potential for politicizing police actions around their dealings with unions and with movements which were increasingly middle class.

While strike numbers began to wane by the early 1980s, police organizations were also undergoing increasing demands to restructure and to rationalize services under a new neo-liberal public management ethos. In this context, community policing, especially as developed under the RCMP, was a means of justifying a more selective delivery through responsibilized 'access brokers' (de Lint, 2003). Hit with the requirement to better account for expenditures, to better profile their own interventions, and to find partners and download delivery where possible, police were forced to develop better discretionary vehicles for inaction and to package choices for service delivery in a meaningful rhetoric (cf. also de Lint, Gostlow, and Hall, 2005). It is not coincidental that the liaison approach is consistent with the proactive, preventive, and communicative aspects of community policing philosophy. Liaison policing was certainly supported by the development of community policing, and its growing acceptance over the 1980s and 1990s was due in part to the same dynamics and pressures reshaping policing more generally. But as we have tried to show, it is a mistake to conclude that community policing gave birth to the liaison approach or was the only critical factor shaping its development.

Even in the context of service rationalizations, the police continued to spend considerable resources on paramilitary technology, training, and special units. And as the expenditures in Quebec City and the G8 Kananaskis meetings demonstrate, at the turn of the millennium the state and the police were quite willing to spend the money and use their public resources to the fullest when the stakes warrant it. Consistent with the observations of P. Waddington (1993) and della Porta and Reiter (1998) in other countries, Canadian police have largely used these coercive resources selectively in some situations and against some groups. While the liaison approach can be seen as setting the ground for this selection process, the police were also responding to certain political conditions. In our view, one of those conditions was that there was little resurgent socialist radicalism among unions or the new social movements from the 1960s through the 1980s. The 1980s decline of the Soviet Union leading ultimately to the fall of the Berlin Wall, and, a little later on, the unbridled Chinese embrace of capitalism only served to reinforce the conclusion that class conflict was no longer a serious threat to the state or to capital.

As such, the police had few grounds over this entire period for viewing labour as a serious threat to the state or capitalism, or for justifying forceful action against labour in existential security concerns. But it was not just the absence of a radical ideology; it was also the level of control that unions began to exercise over its members with its bureaucratic, service-oriented business model (Heron, 1996). Even before the police took on the mantle of self-policing in the liaison approach, many unions had demonstrated repeatedly that they could be 'trusted' to self-police, opening a clear opportunity for the police to redraw the boundaries and terms of their involvement in strikes. This opened a political space for reformers within police organizations to push alternatives such as the liaison approach when local politics intervened against the use of force. Again, it helped tremendously that police administrators were looking for ways to rationalize services within community policing and new public management models, but the coercive capacity was also always there, being developed and refined should things turn the other way.

For its part, labour did not step 'outside the line' in its strategies and tactics even through the 1970s and 1980s, when strike levels reached their peaks, consistently following the path of responsible unionism and industrial legalism (Fudge and Tucker, 2001). This was evident even in the relatively militant BC during the 1980s, where a staunchly anti-labour neo-conservative government was seeking to radically undercut labour rights (Palmer, 1987). The 'solidarity' movement response was never perceived by the police as threatening or insurrectional. Similarly, in Ontario in the 1990s, when a neo-conservative government began promoting significant regressive labour reforms, the labour movement went to great lengths in all its Day of Action protests to co-operate and operate within the law.

Significantly, the newer social protest movements, although reacting initially against the contradictions and limitations of liberal welfare and Fordist capitalism, also did not identify with class struggle or revolution. Like post–Second World War labour, they were committed to achieving reform within capitalism and, consequently, pledged their allegiance to the rule of law and peaceful protest. Even in Quebec, where the separatist movement briefly flirted with both socialism and terrorist tactics in the 1960s, the threat was largely neutralized in the 1970s and 1980s, first by a short-term burst of extraordinary coercion in 1970 (for example, the declaration of the War Measures Act, which suspended civil liberties and brought in the army), and then more long-term when the separatist Parti Québécois began winning political power in provincial elections and declaring that a referendum was the only legitimate means of gaining independence.

This is not to say that the adoption of the liaison approach was a fait accompli. As we saw, there was considerable resistance within police and from some corporate interests, and we should not dismiss the persistence of the more authoritarian threads in police culture. In the final analysis, however, the liaison approach was increasingly adopted in strike situations across Canada because it worked largely as promised – it reduced police involvement and expenditures, police injuries, and political heat, and because it fit neatly into emerging theories and discourses on cost-effective policing (i.e., community and private policing).

The liaison approach and the maturing of that approach were also recognized by police themselves as helping to reproduce continued commitment to the rule of law, even as the Fordist crisis deepened and neo-liberal globalization took hold. The importance of this approach in limiting the potential for radicalization became particularly evident in potentially explosive situations where desperate workers occupied plants slated for closure, Natives blocked bridges and trains, and environmentalists tied themselves to trees. Here we saw the increasing refusal of the police to act aggressively even in the face of business, political, and court pressures, seeking instead a peaceful negotiated settlement, revealing political patience on the part of police as the terms of labour's defeat were being brokered. Part of this exchange was that unions, workers, and protesters were to settle 'for having made their point,' often gaining little more than their dignity, while police were to do nothing to inflame or further mobilize them.

This took a strong institutional commitment, one that should not be underestimated when considering the more recent development of intelligence-based policing. But to police, labour in particular was already becoming yesterday's war, already vanquished. And to labour, police were no longer the object or target of demonstration or grievance and did not stand for those targets. This truce or depoliticization of strikes is now firmly entrenched in the minds and actions of both police *and* labour. As noted, even when organized labour joined other protest groups in large-scale anti-globalization protests, it remained a beacon of moderation and self-control, as in the 1996 Windsor Day of Action, when labour avoided confrontations over the bridge to the United States, as in Quebec City in 2001, when the official labour protest march stayed far away from the battles outside the 'fence.' If nothing else, these protests helped to further entrench the police view of labour as trustworthy allies in the common goal of keeping the peace. The failure of labour to react aggressively to the police show of force during the anti-globalization protests, an apparent tacit approval of police tactics and targeting of particular groups and individuals, also says volumes about the reliability of labour from the standpoint of the police.

In summary, then, we have presented the parallel and shifting developments of coercive and consensual public order policing as reflecting the tensions within liberal and neo-liberal capitalist democracies (Harvey, 2007). Under neo-liberal capitalism, especially the redrawing of the public–private divide, there has been a reworking of liberal rights discourses in the development of liaison policing and public order policing generally. Accordingly, under late liberal capitalism or neo-liberal capitalism, the dynamics and forms of policing, labour, social movements, and protest are increasingly privatized, narrowing the public domain of policing, leading to rationales and practices that limit and alter policing involvement, strategies, and tactics. Yet, core constitutional values, including the rule of law, the right to protest and free speech, and the independence of a professional police service, continue to exert critical influences on police thinking and public politics, and in particular, as constraints on police capacity to use full force. As such, while police retain the exclusive right and responsibility to use force to enforce laws made by putatively democratic political authorities, legal and moral restraints on the use of police power (information, law, force) are still widely seen as separating democracies from authoritarian states.

The persistence of this gentler liberal impulse is especially problematic in the area of public order policing given the greater potential ambiguity of the legitimacy of actors and actions, but it is also clearly a key element underlying the particular development of strike policing. While, as we have seen, the rights discourse among the police is particularly prominent in shaping their responses to public protest, we have also sought to locate many of the changes in both strike and protest policing within a macro structural analysis of changes in labour processes, markets, and power relations between capital and labour, to explain both the particular and continued differentiation of labour as a target for consensual rather than coercive policing, as well as an important contributor to a more generalized, liberal public order discourse. Yet as we have tried to show in the previous chapter, the dynamics of public order policing within a post-9/11 world illustrate the continuing tensions between neo-liberal privatization and neo-conservative demands for security. What happens next depends much on the direction of labour and social movement protest and on whether these continue to play by the police rule book. Despite police efforts, this is clearly not under the complete control of the police. What then are the prospects for future challenges from labour and protest movements?

Prospects for Future Challenges from Labour and Protest Movements

While some analysts point to evidence of union renewal (see various articles in Fairbrother and Yates, 2006), it is generally agreed that most

Canadian unions are in a defensive mode, seeking to negotiate whatever they can as union jobs disappear in the face of capitalist restructuring. Some stronger unions are capable of resisting and a few have done so more aggressively when challenged directly by a company, as in the case of an International Trucking strike in Chatham, Ontario, in 2002, where the company tried to force major concessions on CAW by using replacement workers (Williamson, 2002).[1] Many multinational companies in the primary industries have taken a more gradualist approach to their restructuring (Yates, Lewchuk, and Stewart, 2001), maintaining the privileges of ever-declining numbers of elite unionized workers, while slowly bleeding jobs through lean production, contracting-out, plants closures, and cushioning any layoff blows through early retirements and buyouts.

Consciously or not, union leadership participates in this process, apparently hoping to somehow stem the bleeding without needing to challenge the system that appears to give them no choice. Even the mighty CAW, once praised universally for its more militant and democratic approach, has resorted to extremely controversial 'no strike/no steward representative agreements' with auto parts firms such as Magna in an apparently desperate effort to maintain its membership. We also suspect that most large corporations dealing with the larger unions understand the need to retain enough of the union membership to sustain the union bureaucracy as a cost of business, just as they understand the value of avoiding violent confrontations on the picket line. In the meantime, the weaker unions and workers in the second and third labour market tiers of industries, including auto, get very little when their plants downsize or close. Here the employers may be more likely to prefer aggressive policing, but whether the police are at all responsive, and our evidence suggests they rarely are, unions are often incapable of mounting significant resistance even if the leadership was inclined or capable – beyond the relatively rare short occupation aimed at getting severance or pension guarantees.

Non-union workers, many of whom are temporary or part-time, get nothing. They have no vehicle for organizing, in part because the stronger unions provide no meaningful support, so they fade away when their jobs disappear or become intolerable, disconnected individuals moving elsewhere to different jobs and different towns and responding with individual coping and labour market strategies. Many of these workers are conditioned to this insecurity and accept it because there is no evident alternative. As losses and declines continue to mount, especially in the manufacturing sector, the impact appears gradual enough and buffered by various other factors so that there are few signs of either radicalization or sustained resistance.[2] Those few organizations that do seek to represent the more marginalized workers and that willingly and overtly challenge this hegemony, such as the Ontario Coalition Against Poverty (OCAP), are kept in very close surveillance and are subject to considerable coercion (Palmer, 2003). Isolated and indeed alienated from the larger union movements and its accommodations, these organizations may have little chance of surviving sustained countering. Moreover, as we have seen, those few unions that show any significant support for these organizations may also find that police target them for more aggressive treatment when it is their turn to strike or protest.

Gradualism in the neo-liberal project may also help to explain the lack of aggressive resistance or radicalization on the part of labour and other elements of civil society, in Canada at least. Unlike in Britain, Australia, or especially New Zealand (Dannin, 1995), where neo-liberal restructuring was undertaken through 'shock' and aggression (cf. Klein, 2007), Canadian and most provincial governments have moved methodically – probing for weakness and avoiding overt provocative reforms. Those few provincial neo-conservative governments that tried to follow the British or American 'blitzkrieg' tactics, like BC in the 1980s and Ontario in the 1990s, were unwilling to assert the entire agenda in the face of significant but still peaceful labour protests (Panitch and Swartz, 2003). On the other hand, arguably, it has not mattered: free trade agreements, technological change, privatization, offloading, partnering, contracting-out, and other restructuring have worked in a comprehensive fashion to weaken the political, social, and cultural context of unions, garnering only moderate union response with few indications of emerging radicalization. This is not to say that there is not considerable talk about labour movement renewal (Fairbrother and Yates, 2003; Kumar and Schenk, 2006; Levesque and Murray, 2006) and perhaps even some action in that direction, as in the development of community unionism and worker centres (Bickerton and Stearns, 2006; Cranford et al., 2006). Yet these changes are coming slowly and many union leaders continue to fall back on the same old strategies that appear more like empty gestures than coordinated, consistent strategies. Critically for the police, industrial legalism remains the defining doctrine of union activism and renewal, providing little impetus for change in policing from this direction.

By continuing to treat labour in particular with a velvet glove, even during the few times when labour raises its fist, police are aiding this process of gradual disempowerment. In the short term, police refusal to intervene in response to the employer demand can be viewed as having assisted unions to gain some bargaining power (Hall and de Lint, 2003), but these interim gains are largely offset by long-term defeat and decline. For example, in a plant just outside of Windsor occupied by its union local during a strike in 2000, the OPP response illustrated a classic liaison job by refusing to move in on the occupiers for several days, serving instead as mediators between the employer and the union over terms for ending the occupation. They deferred coercive action even in the face of a judge's injunction, and in the end the strikers left without any violence, damage, or arrests, and with an agreement to meet with management. The strike was settled soon after with modest contract gains, and the unions gave considerable credit to the police, but less than one year later, the employer closed the plant and went elsewhere, leaving the workers without severance. Here, the police provided workers the illusion of bargaining power, a power less and less effective in the context of capital mobility and heightened labour market competition.

Yet recent developments remind us that the absence of domestic radicals is not the only game in town. Behind neo-liberal globalization is a structural problem for labour and civil society: the so-called 'end of ideology' (Fukuyama, 1989). For a good fifteen years, beginning with the 1989 fall of the Berlin Wall and the subsequent collapse of the Soviet Union, the Cold War clarifications of politics in communism versus capitalism were rendered defunct. Into this vacuum came threats of terrorism under a racialized 'fear of barbarism' rubric. Unlike previous political countering campaigns, the current generation is preoccupied with asymmetrical de-spatialized threats. Although war analogies from the First and Second World War era continue (sympathizers and fifth columns), today it is not labour and communists but terrorism and radical Islam that justify exceptional measures of information control and militarism. Identified largely with the vanquished communists and socialists of the last war, labour and many protest groups continue to be profiled as relatively harmless relics.

It is also clear that police and security officials have reassessed the liaison approach within the context of the shifting strategies of anti-globalization groups. The failure of liaison strategies in protests like Seattle pushed intelligence-based and coercive policing tactics back into the centre of policy and practice (Wood, 2007). While there was still a level of confidence that liaison could work quite broadly within limits, especially for certain groups requiring greater political sensitivity (e.g., the Native protest movement), police saw the need to treat certain protests differently than strikes. Identification and classification of threats represented by different groups, pre-emptive arrests, as well as spatial ordering, such as the use of fences and zoning, are illustrations of these changing practices. While this had very little impact on labour, the effects were keenly felt by many protest groups and leaders involved in anti-globalization actions: so much so that it can be argued that the anti-globalization movement has failed to recover its initiative and is increasingly unable to stem efforts of the WTO and other globalization advocates to further liberalize international markets (Wood, 2007).

The spectacle of mass demonstrations is an enduring mode of political, economic, and social mobilization. Whether aimed locally, extra-locally, or at political, economic, or social targets, the mode of mass demonstration in picketing, rallying, parading, or blockading and occupying is a long-standing vehicle of grievance promotion. While there appears to be great resilience in this practice, significant ruptures may also be starting to show. For while it is true that the mass demonstration has long been a mainstay of social expression, changes to the nature of much of the common interaction between peoples within and across various jurisdictions or places are said to be occurring. If so, 'going downtown to join the rally' may be a nostalgic mode of expression, hearkening back to a day when 'the social' was itself a more robust weigh station between government or governance and the social individual (Rose and Miller, 1992). Indeed for some analysts, these changes have moved not only beyond individuals and rights, and population management and biopower, but to registrations by which individuals become 'dividuals' (Deleuze, 2000) and masses are seen as artefacts or derivations of practices that occur at the level of code or information (not property, not access, but control becomes what is sought).

In concentrating on the relation between alternative politics and political authority ordered by police, we can observe this trajectory at least in parts. The first wave of reform occurred in Canada in the 1850s and 1860s in tumultuous times when partisan riots frequently spilled out into the streets, aggravated and sometimes sparked by partisan police response. Police reform was a large part of the unification push, as consolidation (treaties, etc.) of the internal order was perceived as a compulsory precondition for the positive rebuffing of American advances. Yet, given the limitations on formal vehicles of participation, mass demonstrations were integral to the legitimacy of governance and provided a key indicator of popular opinion that governments could not easily or routinely ignore, a point that has often been mentioned. Others have also noted the apposite point that large demonstrations may even siphon political expression so that much of the force of the call for change is left wasted or spent on the cobblestones of the town square. Either way, reliance on this mode of political expression poses acute dangers for governments, as unpredictable and relatively unmanageable referenda on policy can easily become nonconfidence spectacles. However, once again, where police are seen indiscriminately beating down such political expression, most currently as in Pakistan in 2007, the challenge for states claiming membership in liberal democracies becomes acute.

To go back to our typology in chapter 2, the historical response of police tended to fall between that of the control and service typologies or between professional, knowledgeable, representative, and effective order maintenance in a politico-legal context of exclusivity and division on one pole and integrative consent on the other. At the same time in a politico-legal context that toggled between inclusionary and exclusionary orientations, police easily drifted toward under-professionalized, inexpert, under-representative, and ineffective order maintenance.

This being understood, we have seen there were no significant changes to the way police countered or addressed the problem of mass demonstrations of grievances until the 1960s. Despite the tumult of 1919 and 1937, in particular, the scale, frequency, and timing of key events were not such as to place policing or police in the crosshairs of reform. On the contrary, the best explanation for police reform is almost to be found in the opposite direction. Grievances were becoming more structured and routinized. The modality of the spectacle was being neutralized. Police later played a role in this in their recasting or emergent view of labour grievances and picketing in particular as a civil matter. In the 1960s, however, it was also an American problem that compelled police leaders in the United States and Canada to proactively reconsider the tools and tactics of public order countering. Witnessing the legitimacy spectacles of the urban race riots (sometimes called 'police riots'), the executive branch of the government perceived an acute danger to the image of liberal democracy in the violent countering of political expression.

However what did finally emerge by the 1970s was a deeper reform rooted to the diminishment of the welfare state. In the late nineteenth century, variants of liberal rule concentrated on population management understood as the promotion of health, wealth, discipline, and well-being. Delineated through territorial boundaries, there was a systematic attempt to make the care and control of populations thinkable and actionable through new statistical techniques developed in the various emergent professional and academic disciplines (Foucault, 1977). This new knowledge and expertise, buttressed through official and privileged state means, was pushed by ethnic, religious, and other sites in civil society in the service of a variety of subpolitical, popular, or solidaristic movements. It constituted what has been called a particularly 'social' form of rule (Rose and Miller, 1992). By the 1960s and 1970s, the social mode of rule, particularly the care *and* control *object* of whole populations, was re-problematized. Under the guise of scarce resources and self-entrepreneurship the universalistic service provision assumptions of the welfare state gave way to advanced liberalism and the partial relief of this state burden of population care and control. Discursive phrases such as 'societies of control,' the 'exclusive society,' and the 'culture of control' were coined by experts to account for the distinctions between the distributions of scarce government, so that sites were de-problematized as not a matter of state intervention (or, at best, regulated 'at a distance' through civil society) or seen as a reminder of problem populations (not whole populations) that needed to be sequestered or removed, with the machinery of sequestering and removing dedicated to the criminal justice professionals in a play understood in Simon's terminology as 'governing through crime' (Simon, 1997).

This deeper root is obvious not only to police but also to those objects differentially problematized by police under the new rubrics of governance. The movement past territorial populations is also a movement toward neo-liberal globalization and its recasting of individual and collective rights and its diminishment of other bases of solidaristic supports. The anti-globalization activists and labour organizations share common cause in resistance to efforts to bisect the social into criminal and deregulatory regimes, countered by a 'lean mean state' and 'corporate captured' regulatory or civil jurisdictions. Nonetheless, we see the bifurcation quite clearly in the police division of protests and protesters in 'measured response' or intelligent control. Liaison is here indeed a kind of anachronism, because it suggests the bygone welfare days where police were part of the welfare dispensation, cutting populations, but still applying to that cut or processed portion the inclusionary regime (Cohen, 1985) of the welfare subject.

In this respect, we see that the move to service policing in the adaptation of the liaison response to public order was in one sense already dead on arrival, coming as it did when the wider socio-political discourse was already moving into neo-liberalism and leaving behind the classic liberal ideas of the sovereign subject, the notion of consent, and the individual/state dichotomy on which, as well, welfare liberalism was grounded. This means, of course, that our typology is itself a kind of relic, also devoted too fondly to the old categories of liberal governance and the checks, transparency, redundancy, and balance that informed that governmentality or its rationalities and discourses. Hybrid intelligent control policing can in this way be seen as a route out of these old categories into the new field of the security apparatus. What once began in the intent to manage a variety of constituent interests or discourses (depending on the preferred terminology) such as consent and control, private and public, authority and subject, norm and exception, is now a practice, relatively autonomous, that feeds off liberalism as if it were a host, needed once to give life but long since decaying.

One final juncture in the trajectory shows its outlines. In the movement towards fusion and pre-emption, the calculations are not of territorial cohorts or dangerous individuals, but rather the recipe of conditions that prefigure interruptions in the flow of commerce or information itself. Given the pre-eminence of cost, public relations, or the visibility of governance, and the containment and pre-emption value of information control policing, it is not too far a stretch to believe that public policing itself will for the most part consist of delivering the kind of exemplary spectacles that it for so long has been instituted to counter. The difference will be that these spectacles will mostly be farcical and hyper-real or simulations. It would be already too late for those invested in the new countering logic to depict the last gasp of police action through the visuals of real people carrying real sticks.

To recall the point we made about uncertainty and ambiguity at the end of the second chapter, there can be no general solution to the problem of public order. For police in liberal democracies, countering work that makes the outcome of public demonstrations predictable or risk-free is anathema because, as Bernstein (1996) argues, it is uncertainty that makes us free. For labour and also for less institutionalized grievers or political movements, the movement towards the prophylactic ordering countered by set-piece, showcase encounters runs the risk of denuding the very vitality required, substituting a new 'tyranny of averages' (Bernstein, 1996).

We embarked on this research struck by the role of police between labour and capital in a system of law and economy that is predicated on contest. For us, a point of interest has been how public order has challenged the constitution of police and liberal democracy itself. The liberal policing project, as we have been stressing, has always been an attempt to observe lines of demarcation between public/private, domestic/foreign, autonomy/regulation. The application of policing, especially to counter public order, has always needed to be particularly sensitive to preserve these lines not least to preserve the power and vitality of economy itself.

Yet, early liberal policing was also an effort at saturating the polis, and the technological changes to territorial organization and communications (in beat mobilization and deployment and colonial policing, for instance) were predicated on the notion of distributing, relatively widely, dosages of 'law and order.' Consent, or 'discipline,' was key to unlocking pockets of resistances or difference (de Lint, 2000). That police were mandated into what Foucault referred to as the 'internal refinement of "reason of state"' in *polizeiwissenschaft* or 'police' (Foucault, 2004: 29) and subject to external restraint through the operation constitutions, rights, and questions of legitimacy in public law is not, of course, inconsistent with the kind of law-guided domestic pacification that we have seen developed in the countering, ordering, or managing of labour and protest. The duality of inductive and deductive gestures periodically showed strains, as in 'times of troubles' in 1919 and, in the case of American experience, the urban riots in the 1960s. Community policing followed as a deliberate attempt to regain the consent mandate.

In the end, it may be argued that information control policing is the most recent gambit in a long chain of efforts to balance economic, political, and social vitalities and constraints. In this vein, 9/11 brought forward a 'massive redirection of resources toward new patterns of governance and policing that might be called a warfare/security state' (Chappell, 2006: 313). Police adoption of information control is this way in line with the widespread post-liberal practice of placing the control of information at the heart of the business of governance. In this register, the craft of police and security work involves adaptations that finesse the control of information for the maintenance of legitimate commercial or public enterprises. At its most sophisticated, it works at the level of the plan rather than action, interjecting long before feet hit the pavement or pickets find their way to the streets.

Regulating Access to Political Authority

At the outset of this book, we positioned the problem of countering collective labour and political protest at the heart of the processes of democracy. Legalization, civilization, and the institutionalization of responses to the threat posed by precisely that aspect or portion of a mass demonstration that is dynamic and ambiguous is a conundrum for governance. Even the Canadian Charter of Rights and Freedoms entrenches the conflict by providing the weapons of exceptionalism in the so-called override clause in section 1 ('subject only to such reasonable limits prescribed by law as can be demonstrably justified in a free and democratic society') at the same time that it stands as the last guarantor of 'fundamental freedoms' (as, for instance, are outlined in section 2: 'freedom of conscience and religion; freedom of thought, belief, opinion and expression, including freedom of the press and other media of communication; freedom of peaceful assembly; and freedom of association'). To follow Mouffe (2005), Unger (1986), and Ewick and Silbey (1998), the measure of a society's democratic institutions is found in the degree to which common folk are excluded from participation in setting the priorities of governments. Mass public agitation (involving labour, capital, and the distributions of governance generally) has long performed as a vehicle to test the mettle of political authorities. A mass demonstration grievance is the appropriation of public or private property to make a pitch and representations into the public sphere and governing authority.

As such, we want to finish this book by suggesting one further way of interpreting police action, that is, as regulating access to those political authorities. The police perform access brokerage for governing authority; they permit or deny access to the property and means of expression by deploying their informational, legal, and coercive advantages. However, central as this function has been to the institutionalization of domestic public policing, like the democracy conundrum behind it, it is a troublesome and thorny mandate. As we have seen, police will eagerly relinquish the task where the whole political array allows them to do so. They will also gladly defer decisions to the court or to the political authorities themselves, so long as this can be done without relinquishing precisely the institutional functionality they have engendered (de Lint, Gostlow, and Hall, 2005).

Today, the preferred mechanism of deferral within liaison is the stretching of time in and through the regulation itself. The insistence on categorizing and typologizing events and turning them into set-piece rituals with complete dress rehearsals and detailed scripts and roles is a way of taking the ambiguity or dynamism out of what otherwise might also make police response too unpredictable for police comfort. This mechanism of risk management or security assessment is like the older mechanism similarly destructive to the core of participation and the unruly march of democracy. Javeline and Brown (2003) make the social-psychology argument that unexpressed political frustration will encourage social pathologies, including lower labour productivity and voluntary participation rates, and so on. They argue that a robust protest environment (one which is also accommodated) of political activism is good for the public health. A similar line of thought is implicit in Tittle's (1997; 2004) work on 'control-balance.' Tittle argues that where too many people languish under a control deficit (in which people experience an inability to change the conditions of their existence positively), the frustration will lead to periodic outbursts of aggression and violence or clumsy efforts to assert control. This is also in line with Gramsci (1971), who argued that substantive challenges to hegemony emerge precisely when such frustrations become endemic.

It is in that sense that official reaction to mass expression grievances not only is important in the professional and craft development of police, but is a measure of the absorptive capacity of governance to accommodate contrary opinion and alternative or resistant politics. As we have seen, police know this already. Their own experience has taught them that disallowing expression will tend to be counterproductive to their own interest in overseeing an event that does not have the potential of casting their action negatively. Police will try to manage their own visibility and find a balance between a service and control orientation in affording platforms for grievance expression. Oftentimes, this means they will indeed weigh the message and messenger against the context of political trade winds, both locally and beyond.

Important to this discussion then is the extent to which there is further reflexivity as police assert and finesse their relative independence from government directive. Here we should note again that there is often no singular 'police' entity that serves the policing function, but rather several agencies which coordinate responses and assume distinct mandates. And where there is a multi-agency response coordinated by a task force or 'project,' the result can be far different than if there is only a singular agency authorized to address the problem. An analogy is that the many will often do what the one or two will not. Recent research on police use of force indicates that the presence of multiple officers is a significant factor in over-coercion, one reason for which is that officers are then also staging their action for an audience of other officers. Since officer safety is a key craft evaluative criterion in the use of force, and inter-agency reputations are a qualifying factor as well, the result can be violence escalation. The fact that it is a complex organization which distributes roles and assignments to counter or manage a public order problem rather than a single (tight) unit will obviously result in communications and coordination hazards. For instance, the more units, agencies, resources, mandates, and constituencies, the more police may send out the signal, advertently or otherwise, that they intend to use the capacity they possess, despite efforts to sequester it from visibility. Protester-receivers may receive the message as a provocation.[3]

This brings into frame another dimension that needs to be recognized – the professional nomenclature used to inform police practices. Intelligence-based policing has encouraged police agencies to view events as more or less risky based on check-offs, profiles, or out-of-the-box assessments. There has been a shift from the transactional or emergent dynamic (rooted in crowd psychology) in which moves and counter-moves would be attended by on-site interpretation and decision-making. As noted in chapter 2, research has also demonstrated the movement from 'escalated force' to 'public order management' in the distinction between public order policing between the 1960s and the 1990s (Schweingruber, 2000; King and Waddington, 2006). The RCMP, for its part, has developed what it calls 'measured response' (Vickers, 2004). Following the model we presented in that chapter, we prefer to view action on public order as a continuum encompassing the values of rule-making, rule-following, and rule enforcement, with five ideal types of public order policing, including service, control, disordered, hybrid, and crisis. Looking back over our accounts of key public order events, it is clear that some fall into the category of *service* or integrative policing in a context of consent, while others are more *control* based, that is, professional, knowledgeable, effective authoritarian order maintenance in a politico-legal context of exclusivity and division, and more recently, in *hybrid* form, that is, the combined utilization of both information and hard countering (paramilitary, intelligence) moving flexibly between authoritarianism and republicanism while being amenable to integrative efforts.

With regard to legal tools, our argument is that, in the public order context at least, police view the law as a resource for pursuing an end to their involvement and a termination of their discretion in conflict resolution. That end may be suspended indefinitely (police may not be hastening the resolution of their own involvement) or it may be pushed forward. The injunction has become a significant legal tool. Like all such tools, police cannot determine how and when they will be used, but they endeavour to take out as much unpredictability as such a tool may present. The injunction also fits into a narrative or template of conflict management, and police may see that narrative and the tool as falling closer to the consent or coercion and integrative versus disintegrative pattern of intervention.

For example, while we saw the police use injunctions to delay forceful action in many strike and plant occupation situations, at Ipperwash the injunction was seen as a means of expediting a forced resolution. Inspector John Carson saw it as providing the 'paperwork' or the court sanction and a clear watershed between a civil or minor trespassing issue and a criminal matter. Because police understood by their own experience that consent for police action was weak (that is, there was a weak ground on which to act against the Natives), they wanted the cover of an injunction and the perceived mandate for expedited action that it would give them. However, while police in the matter of this particular injunction could appear as servants of a separate authority who were limited by the court in their own discretion to resolve the conflict, they also worked behind the scenes to assist in effectuating this line of action. Police spoke with the Ministry of Natural Resources, in this instance, and assured them that they would provide supporting evidence should the injunction be asked for by the ministry.

With regard to communications tools, we have been stressing that public order policing is a highly mediated and reflexive enterprise and that presentation is much of the craft of what police seek to accomplish: *the presentation of an ordered resolution being effected according to script.* We mentioned earlier that much public order has been interpreted by the police as a 'no-win situation' because it has the potential of casting police in a bad light. Police experience with previous fallout to public relations has inspired a much more careful and choreographed response to public order problems when they arise – whether a straight liaison approach or a hybrid intelligent control approach. This very much includes layering police dosages against immediate or proximate view. The flip side of the communications coin is the countering of untoward, unsightly, or ambiguous expression. At its most forceful, this is repression. But police negotiate the symbolic terrain of the public protest with picketers or demonstrators in order to co-author a production which affords expression that can be absorbed [hopefully] without rebounding on the police themselves.

Bajc (2007) has referred to order-making in what we call high-stakes events as 'security rituals.' This concept captures how the 'security apparatus' – that is, institutions, organizations, technologies, techniques, specially trained individuals, and the logic that accompanies their practices – will order the orchestration of events as sterilizations of territories and interrupted flows of routine activities.[4] We might add here that there are ritual templates for different classifications of public order events, and that once a ritual template is established, a narrative of permissiveness or imposition of order obtains. The initial classification may be that an event is civil or criminal, a matter of public safety or national security, meets the threshold of special authority, and so forth. The extent to which a security ritual will recreate a space as a comprehensively controlled order will depend on the initial classification and further modifications. It is now quite a familiar metaphor that disorder is a contagion from which the social body or places therein may be protected or immunized through public order policing dosages and prescriptions. But it also presumes a certain view of contagion, of what contaminants will look like, and the relation between purity and safety or health. Calls for sterilization are based on a schedule of public order permissions that police read out of local and extra-local pressures and pulls.

This leads us to our final point. When communications between protesters and police become more exclusively symbolic, it may lead to the worst excesses of violence. This is especially the case where the manipulation of dominion becomes challenge and counter-challenge. That is to say, when coercive action has become the mechanism for communicating will and capacity, there will be little room to ensure favourable audience reception or non-violent resolution. Still, police and protester action also depends on a political and cultural context of expectations. In contexts that are those closer to societies of control, police seek to counter expression or manage it sometimes to a point of simulation (Bogard, 1996). In contexts closer to those of liberal democracies, and we want to continue to count Canada as one of those, police seek to afford expression based on an understanding that a public order platform (or stage) is a legitimate vehicle for alternative political messaging. The question for labour and social movements is whether they can use those platforms, stage-managed as they are, to achieve meaningful change.

Notes

1. Policing Labour / Policing Protest

1 In this context, community policing is often seen as a means through which public policing is downloaded onto the community, while public relations functions seek to educate the community about the significance of personal responsibility and the need to redefine and limit expectations of the police.

2 Uglow (1988), for instance, argues that after a constitutional truce disappeared in the early 1970s, violence has since been more commonplace and the ambiguity of legal rights has been replaced by the more restrictive police powers of the Public Order Act 1986. Kahn et al. (1983: 75) argue that the picketing carried out at the Saltley Coke Depot during the 1972 United Union of Mineworkers strike left an indelible mark on police and generally those responsible for maintaining order, with the view that the state itself might be jeopardized when police are seen to be unprepared, especially when overwhelming numbers of pickets and a lack of Home Office support enter into the mix.

3 For research instruments see http://www.utparchives.com/archive/delint_hall_appendix.pdf

4 A bilingual interviewer was hired to conduct interviews in French with the police in Quebec. However, we decided not to pursue a case study in Quebec because neither of the authors is bilingual and we did not have the resources to hire someone to conduct the level of research required. We have sought to include Quebec in our historical analysis that does suggest some differences from English Canada. Moreover, while the survey indicates that Quebec services mirror English Canada in adopting a liaison approach, there were no early innovators in Quebec, and the form that the approach has taken still involves more direct police intervention. In particular, six of the eight services (75 per cent) reported that they often or very

often escort equipment, production, or non-striking personnel through the line whereas only 13 per cent of non-Quebec services reported this. Although we suspect that these differences revolve in part around the particular political history of Quebec and Quebec's labour movement, more research is needed to provide a full explanation for these differences. Still, the general thrust in Quebec is still consistent enough with the rest of Canada to warrant their inclusion here.

2. Interpreting Public Order Policing

1 In BC the 1997 meeting of the Asian Pacific Economic Cooperation Conference in Vancouver and, in Ontario, the Ipperwash standoff between the OPP and a group of Kettle Point and Stony Point Natives and the 2006–7 Caledonia standoff in which OPP officers have been accused by some residents of looking the other way during illegal acts by Native protesters.

2 However, as Turner (1968: 815) has argued, labour strife 'has sometimes been understood as [public] protest and sometimes not.' This begs the question of the interdependence, historically and presently, between public and private ownership, a relationship analysed by Spitzer and Scull (1977) and revitalized in Johnston's (1992) important work on the re-emergence of private policing. As Johnston (1992) argues, the full-time paid professional public police may only be a blip in the history of liberal policing.

3 The Fordist crisis is normally identified as beginning in the early 1970s, when inflation, rising state deficits, and unemployment combined with falling rates of profit.

4 Moreover, when we look at the broader regulation literature on neo-liberalism and hegemony, there are ample bases for arguing that many of the social tensions arising from the downgrading of labour, feminist, racial, and environmental rights within neo-liberalism have been managed or moderated through a host of political, ideological, and cultural mechanisms and discourses. For example, the ramping up of anti-welfare discourses which blame the poor and the welfare system for creating a system of dependency were extremely successful in weakening the political response to increased economic inequality and poverty, while the discursive emphasis placed on individual and family responsibility more generally has intensified the decline of 'the social' as people respond to deteriorating employment and financial security by looking within themselves, by working harder and longer, and by circling the wagons around narrow self and family interests.

5 Although neo-liberalism and globalization are often seen as the main culprits for these declines, analysts of the U.S. labour situation have also

noted that American organized labour was in free fall well before the 1980s.

6 Tracing back to even before Peel, several institutional scholars have also positioned public order policing as crucial to the development of public and governmental conceptions of policing more generally (e.g., Willis, 2001; Reiner, 2000; Jefferson, 1990). This also draws from the liberalism argument in that protest policing is seen as fundamental to police self-definition or philosophy because it is a domain that challenges police personification with the state (Winter, 1998: 207). Winter argues that police philosophy and the philosophy of public order policing are mutually dependent – the development of police philosophy cannot be separated from the development of (public order) or protest policing. However, Fielding (1991) also points out that the policing of public order highlights the police relationship to military and to political authority. This emphasis on knowledge also speaks to the glaring differences in the skills of the law enforcement forces in the field and their ability to assess crowds (Monet, 1990; T'Hart and Pijnenburg, 1989). More generally, there are cases in which the technical mistakes of the commanders turn into one of the causes of disorder on the part of police forces, when their leaders are not sufficiently skilled or trained in the control of such gatherings (Montjardet, 1992; Chatterton, 1976). When several police forces intervene at the same time, execution-related problems are likely to arise, for example when the communications systems are defective and/or are not interrelated (Monet, 1990; T'Hart and Pijnenburg, 1989). It then becomes more difficult to control the gatherings. It is also difficult to keep order when too many leaders at different levels are involved, each with their respective interests and regulations. This leads to interpretation problems and causes misfires in responses (T'Hart and Pijnenburg, 1989).

7 Nonetheless, there is also disenchantment with what many view as the normative non-disclosure underpinning of Foucault and governmentality approaches (Fraser, 1989).

8 In many ways, we go back to the beginning with the problem of rule: if there is a postmodern fragmentation, perhaps it is not unlike a feudal mosaic or a pre-Restoration interregnum. It requires policy informed by local and democratic processes, and the protection of self-government would appear to require the ready availability of diffused legitimacy. It would indeed seem to require resistance to corporate, private, and pre-emptive policing and a re-establishment of the bidirectional ideal which has seen expression in the office of the constable. However, it is arguable, if we include the uses to which client or server states are put, that distant rule and the 'societies of control' (Deleuze, 2000) are attended by or accomplished through at least an equivalent, if not greater, reliance on violence

and monarchical power (expressed as a continuum of coercion from bodily violence through denial of service to deception). The nature of geopolitics and global trade demonstrates the importance of political, coercive, and economic mobilization capacity, but so does the technology-afforded militarization and re-militarization of policing in advanced democracies (Kraska and Kappeler, 1997; Jefferson, 1990). While this does not tell us that the influences of a networked society are trumped, it does compete with the view that the authority of authority (and the subject) is in irrevocable disarray or insuperably fragmented.

9 It may be possible to typologize police service delivery on horizontal and vertical grids. On the horizontal axis is the degree of harmonization for profit and not-for-profit sectors and agencies. What is the cogency of jurisdiction and privacy in restricting such harmonization? On the vertical axis is the degree of harmonization through local and supranational politics. What is the cogency of local versus extralocal orders in restricting the delivery of service? In any event, our view, following Johnston (1992) and Sheptycki (2002), is that it is important to distinguish sectoral, vertical, and horizontal dimensions when assessing the police role. These two views involve the question of harmonization. Harmonization may be helpful to professionalization and civilization and thus lead to more sophistication in the application of policing to industrial disputes, but it may also assist central government agendas in a more rigid, executive-directed response to labour.

10 As we will see in chapter 6, at the Summit of the Americas at Quebec City (April 2001) and at the OAS meeting at Windsor (June 2000), unions acted and were treated differently by police than unaligned youth and demand groups.

11 The 1995 Second International Police Executive Symposium found that democratic policing is characterized by: rule of law; accountability to the public; transparency of decision-making; popular participation in policing; minimal use of force; learning about civil rights and liberties; internal democracy in the organization (Das, 2000).

3. Liberalism and Labour/Police Development

1 In Canada in the early 1800s, the progenitor of the modern policing system consisted of justices of the peace and an amateur constabulary augmented by militia. The constabulary, as in Great Britain, included both capable and mediocre service. In most cases, there was much turnover, with Judge Gowan claiming that in Upper Canada only one-third of the men were

confirmed in office year to year (in Marquis, 1993: 17). For the vast majority of county constables, the office only required part-time, fee-for-service commitments, and, as has also been reported in Britain, more affluent persons were able to deputize others to stand in for them if their name was called to serve. It was not so much in the law-enforcement but the order-maintenance role that this arrangement was successfully criticized.

2 It was also seen as giving the provincial government more power than it was safe to give them. It was denounced in the Toronto municipal council by 19 to 3 votes. The bill died and was one of the legislative casualties of the ministerial crisis of 1856 that culminated in McNab's resignation. The Toronto city council made a counter-bill in which responsibility for the police was to be invested in a board of commissioners that would be responsible for appointments and discipline.

3 The police force he had raised continued to serve the area of the Niagara frontier. The Niagara River Frontier Police was taken over by Magistrate Hill and led by Chief Malcolm MacDougald from 1870.

4. The Crisis in Fordism and Welfare Liberalism?

1 This may partly explain our findings in chapter 5 that many Quebec services had only partially moved to adopt the service liaison model. However, the fact that Quebec also operates under French civil law may also offer important insights into this somewhat different history.

2 Between 1964 and 1968 riots affected every major city and many were characterized by incidents involving police (Piven and Cloward, 1971). The Harlem (1964), San Francisco (1966), and Atlanta (1966) riots were triggered by the shooting of a black youth by a white police officer. In Philadelphia (1964), Watts (1965), and Newark (1967) riots developed from routine traffic incidents. The Detroit (1967) riot developed after a police raid on a bar. At the apex of the civil rights movement 164 civil disorders took place in the first nine months of 1967 in cities across the United States (Harris and Wicker, 1988: 663).

3 Chief Justice Earl Warren was Chief Justice of the United States from 1953 to 1969; his term of office is widely considered a time of progressiveness on matters of civil and minority rights, police arrest procedure, and the separation of church and state.

4 In addition to the more spectacular events just mentioned, this was also a by-product of a handful of riots or near-riots in Vancouver and Toronto, in particular. Various commissions and task forces, including the 1989 and 1992 Ontario Race Relations and Policing Task Force reports (Ontario, 1989;

Ontario 1992), the 1993 Task Force Report (Oziewicz, 1993), the Oppal Commission (1994), and the Quebec Human Rights Commission Report (Bellemare, 1988), were struck, in part, to investigate the problem of police professionalism, use of force, community relations, and public order policies, each emphasizing the multiculturalism of Canadian society (Jain, 1994). The Lewis reports (Ontario 1989, Ontario 1992), particularly 1992, was struck to determine the cause of a Toronto riot vis-à-vis police race relations. There were also inquiries into Stanley Cup riots in Vancouver (1994) and Montreal (1993). In the latter, the Malouf Inquiry, the liaison approach informed the strategy: 'Our officers were trained in a philosophy which was somewhat new to them: to let people participate and have fun, and to intervene only to maintain control and prevent abuses' (Malouf, Arsenault, and Brodeur, 1993: 27).

5 'R' refers to respondent and 'I' refers to interviewer.

6 'R1' and 'R2' refer to the different respondents interviewed at the same time.

7 This somewhat different pattern in Quebec suggests that Quebec services were more inclined to use force and were accordingly more likely to report arrests and violence. The reasons for this likely speak to a host of differences between Quebec and English Canadian law, labour, and police history (Lipsig-Mumme, 2005). Unfortunately, we did not have the resources to do a detailed case study of a Quebec service and are therefore not in a position to theorize or elaborate on these differences more fully.

5. The Refinement of Labour Liaison and the Seeds of Decline

1 This is not to say that the liaison officers are never actually sympathetic to the union cause. As one officer put it, 'it is hard not to identify a little with them when you are yourself negotiating for better wages.'

2 In one service, the liaison position was held by a civilian.

3 Although the police are more likely to use the parameters of 'safety' as the basis for their decisions to intervene rather than criminality.

4 RSO 1990, c.43.

5 [1991] O.J. No. 2617, online: QL(OJ).

6 *Canada Post Corp. v. Canadian Union of Postal Workers et al.* (1991), 84 D.L.R. (4th) 150.

7 [2002] O.J. No. 3505, online: QL(OJ).

8 [2002] O.J. No. 2731, online: QL(OJ).

9 (2001), 52 O.R. (3rd) 694.

10 Supra note 74 at para.5.

11 Another variant of this responsibilization was achieved within the Ontario Occupational Health and Safety Act, 1976, 1978, which established an

internal responsibility system which limited the role of the Ministry of Labour inspectors to mediators and arbitrators of conflicts dealt with principally by the interested workplace parties (Tucker, 2003).

12 This is not to say that considerable enforcement discretion was not used 'in the past' prior to the introduction of this approach (Geary, 1985; de Lint and Hall, 2002).

6. Liaison in an Institutional Context

1 As in the United States, the benefits and costs of reform fell unevenly across the polity as the 'service' of police intervention was still up against police antipathy (and that of many nascent neo-liberal reformers) to 'welfare work' (de Lint, 1997). In addition, the United States under Ronald Reagan's presidency and Great Britain under Margaret Thatcher were radical in their retrenchment of the welfare state, essentially revisioning security not as an augmentation of welfare but as a form of insurance attending commerce's necessity of traversing public spaces.

2 As a final point, it is important to note that the police often use unions as important sources of intelligence and control when conducting threat assessments and planning for large protests, particularly in protests organized by labour where there is often close collaboration in identifying and controlling potential trouble-makers. 'Certainly within the labour movement there's a recognition that their issues and processes get hijacked by others with different agendas, and in those cases we've found them to be exceptionally cooperative' (R34).

7. A Season of Discontent

1 As is clear from the transcripts of the Ipperwash Commission (31 May 2005: 145–55), in a conversation recorded on 7 September 1995, both Inspector Carson and Acting Detective Staff Sgt Mark Wright (second in command) viewed the possibility that because of an earlier shooting incident the OPP could still enter at least parts of the occupied territory under the authority of securing a crime scene. Detective Staff Sgt Wright called Inspector Carson regarding his testimony to the court on the matter of the injunction to inform him that despite 'giving the evidence of my life' (151) there was still a possibility of not deriving from the court the clear authority he and Inspector Carson appeared to want. In the same conversation Wright also mentioned that he was pressed to explain why the notice to appear could not be given to the Native occupiers.

2 John Carson acknowledged in testimony that before the dispute erupted into the occupation he felt that there was no legal claim on the park by the Indians: 'Yeah, there is – there was no land claim, that's a fact.'

3 In one cited instance of improper conduct, an officer shot 50,000 volts of electricity from a taser gun into a protester who was lying face-down on the pavement, waiting to be arrested, with one arm held up for a handcuff and the other over his head flashing the peace sign. In another instance, officers fired rubber bullets at a group of well-dressed men who had simply gathered 10 to 15 metres from an RCMP post and shook hands. The laughing officers aimed their multiple laser range finders at the crotch of one man, who appeared to be hit in the buttocks and was hiding behind a tree. 'One member clearly said: "These guys don't speak a word of English, boys," to the laughter of others. The struck civilian switched to English, pleading to speak with the 'officer in charge.' He was laughed at by unknown members and told to "go home" in English,' Heafey wrote. 'This conduct was inappropriate and oppressive. The four civilians were not aggressive and posed no threat' (O'Neil, 2003).

4 According to Allen (2003), 'the source information operations also received input from the JIG, enabling it to better target key meetings and persons. JIG meetings were held weekly and later biweekly to ensure a constant informal flow of information in addition to the JIG reports that were distributed.'

5 For Davos, leaders of some fifty-nine 'civil society' organizations were invited to attend the conference in a 'collaboration with principal stakeholders' (Chossudovsky, 2001: 2).

6 Pue (2005: 9) summarized the court's ruling: 'The police obstruction of a small stretch of sidewalk was permissible under the general authority of constables to preserve the peace, prevent crime, protect public safety, preserve order, and prevent offences against provincial laws.'

7 In Windsor, police also placed both uniformed and plainclothes police in with the protesters. This, according to the police view, provided a more reliable interpretation of the intentions and mood of the protesters:

> R: In some the techniques are, like they used at the OAS and things like that, is to put groups of police right into the crowds. Because otherwise you can't watch from the outside, both uniformed and plainclothes so that you can know what's going on. You can't just wait for the outside to see the ripple effect …
> I: How many was that, when did that develop, do you know?
> R: Oh, the last five years. (R25)

8 In the United States, National Lawyers' Guild representatives also wear green hats as legal observers to monitor police action and counsel arrested people.

9 Allen (2003) also notes that police sources could smell gasoline on protesters at certain points of the march and that some demonstrators who attempted to break away from the main march were followed and prevented from carrying out planned acts of sabotage against corporate property.

8. Intelligent Control

1 According to Article 99 of the SIA, intelligence services are entitled to issue surveillance alerts. In its development and interoperability with the Customs Informations System (CIS), the Visitor Information System (VIS), and the Europol Computer Systems (TECS), the SIS II integrates domestic policing and border control priorities and provides internal security authorities and police with access to data on the view that efficiency in the countering of crime and terrorism requires such interoperability.

2 Biometrics is the use of biological characteristics that people have, like fingerprints, iris scans, facial dimensions, which the technology records and then stores either in a database or in a microchip, which can be inserted into identity documents.

3 Until 11 September, the surveillance by the police of First Amendment–protected activities had been one of the most controlled and limited of all police powers, not only in New York City, but in big cities around the United States. New York Mayor Michael Bloomberg and N.Y. Commissioner Raymond Kelly both sought to ease those restrictions, claiming the threat of terrorism was so great that they were handcuffed in preventing future terrorists because of these rules. After 11 September, many revisions were made to those controls. They were done in each jurisdiction, but they all essentially moved in the same direction, which was to ease those restrictions. Charles S. Haight, a federal judge in Manhattan, ruled that the dangers of terrorism were 'perils sufficient to outweigh any First Amendment cost'('Police Infiltrate Protests,' 2005).

4 However, in early 2007, some corrections to far-reaching policy adaptations were seen in the implementation of the O'Connor Commission recommendations and in the Supreme Court decision overturning parts of Canada's counter-terrorism measures, including concerning the right to a fair hearing.

5 At the height of the Cold War, and now post–Cold War, asymmetrical power between 'democracies' and 'terror, madmen and missiles' has forced the view, in the American (and the geopolitical) narrative, that the exception must be practised as the norm in support of the timeless, universal, and general. This applies not only abroad, but also domestically, because there is 'no safe harbour.' The events of 9/11 have helped to make this American narrative a 'Western' and 'civilization' narrative (Ignatieff, 2003; Scruton, 2003).

6 The reference to monster in this context follows Pederson (2003).

7 And even as it interjects into domestic security, this discretion rails against rules even of war. For example, John Reid, British defense secretary, called for a review of the Geneva Conventions claiming that 'the laws of the twentieth century placed constraints on us all which enhanced peace and protected liberty. We must ask ourselves whether, as the new century begins, they will do the same ... We now have to cope with a deliberate regression towards barbaric terrorism by our opponents ... The legal constraints upon us have to be set against an enemy that adheres no constraints whatsoever, but an enemy so swift to insist that we do in every particular, and that makes life very difficult for the forces of democracy' (BBC News, 3 April 2006).

8 Recent conceptualizations of power following the radical view of Lukes (1975) and the post-radical view of Foucault (1977) have made the point that the power relation between A and B is witnessed by others and, as such, can be seen as a demonstration project. It is not simply that A wants something from B (the original power relation of Bachrach and Baratz [1965]). Rather, there is a tripartite or spatialized matrix in which the viewer in effect becomes the target or object. Thus, A instrumentalizes B in a controlled dramatization and object lesson for witness C, D, and so on. In a further contribution, Mathiessen (1987) points out that the operation of power relations includes the few viewing (hence informing) the many (panopticism), as well as the many viewing (and being persuaded by) the few (synopticism). However, because Foucault was intent on distinguishing disciplinary from sovereign power, he under-conceptualized formats of persuasion as a means of guiding viewer responses, particularly through the novel spectacle or dramatized conflict. In the international relations field, for example, the power of the dramatization and the influence of public relations firms in manipulating the opinion of a target or witness population is widely understood.

9 This is tied to the importance of optics or persuasion or the review of power and authority. Authority is reviewed, and much of what authority will be depends on that review.

10 In addition, NYPD makes daily checks of landmarks, as by example, with mine sweeps of the Brooklyn Bridge, and posts officers overseas to keep abreast of the latest terrorist activities for first-hand reports to its own command.

11 Under the postmodern reference, the cycles between real-world practice and training simulations shorten with each turn. Given that the gap cannot be closed in any empirical sense, what is left is the 'simulation of surveillance,' by which the evidence of effectuality is the successful demonstration (Bogard, 1996). It is not that such spectacles do not require empirical supports, but rather that they – much like empire-overreach as Giddens (1985) or sovereignty as Foucault (1979) theorized it – are intended for consumption as proof of capacity (Baudrillard, 1983).

12 While governments administer larger segments of redundant populations or 'waste' (Bauman, 2004), the liberal legacy requires support for the claim that there is widespread opportunity. In managing increasing numbers of unnecessary people, governments attempt to demonstrate a narrow ambit of proficiency (Fitzpatrick, 2001; Garland, 1998). In a post-humanist aesthetic and epistemic in which stating bald underlying 'realities' is not a favourable gambit, simulation covers the contradiction.

13 For example, In-Q-tel, a venture-capital arm of the CIA, invests in high-tech start-ups that offer data targeting, collection, and analysis features which are protected from being revealed to government, customers, targets, and citizens. These are used to canvass and profile political opinion and opinion makers.

14 As Giddens (1991), Garland (1996), and Bogard (1996), among others, have shown, in conditions of high modernity control of institutional and social practices may be affected at a distance both spatially and temporally. The deployment of control, in Deleuzian terms and following also the work of Simon and Feeley (1992), represents a shift from the interest in disciplinary normalization. Following Foucault and others, power is embedded in the formats and schedules as a utility or necessity which belongs with governing, no matter who does it. In the information age where action must be taken through the mediation of information technologies and platforms, it is the programming and 'insecurity' capacities of platforms that increasingly become the object. The ideal is to intervene before action or the contemplation of action by potential targets. Intervention is then prior to discourse: smart coercion is applied at the level of the code. It is 'the look before the look' of the information age or telematic societies (Bogard, 1996) that has for many indicated the ascendancy of means of control which are affected without violence or visible force.

15 Walters differentiates between victims and larger targets: the former suffer direct consequences; the latter understand the message. The goal of state terror is to eliminate potential power contenders and to impose silence and political paralysis, thereby consolidating existing power relations.

16 There are levels of terrorism: fear of being watched; fear of being interfered with; fear of permanent harm to opportunities; fear of loss of identity, social, or family life; fear of physical harm.

17 As an example, CSIS agents may use the midnight knock to, in effect, perform a kind of sovereign terror, but it is not indiscriminate, and deliberately not indiscriminate, the intended audience or observer being those whose intentions might be close to the target. Similarly, the snatch squad, if its work is executed perfectly, is only telegraphed to the victim and an immediate target of a like-minded cohort.

18 Baxter (2001: 281) has usefully analysed this in terms of levels below or beyond 'normal policing.' Thus, if the scale of anticipated social turbulence is at the level of an insurrection or breakdown, the requisite level of policing may be justified at somewhere between military aid to the civil power or even martial or military law. Where the difference between an objective assessment of the scale of social turbulence perceived and the level of policing imposed is significant, one has a potential police deployment error. However, given that such events develop over a period of time, levels of policing may be altered, as Baxter suggests, between the 'contemplative stage,' the 'initiating stage,' and the 'intervention stage.'

9. Conclusion

1 CAW mobilized its various locals in the nearby cities of Windsor and London to block company efforts to recruit and transport scabs from their cities and to reinforce plant picket lines.

2 For example, while income inequality has increased and wages have stagnated, family incomes have largely kept pace with inflation, often through increased wage labour by women.

3 At Ipperwash, for instance, police had white cube vans known as 'gun trucks' which carried tactical unit gear which they wanted available for backup but out of sight (Ipperwash, 17-05-05: 150). 'I didn't want to present any appearance that we were raising the anxiety level in regards to the tools we had at our disposal.' They also endeavoured to get light armoured vehicles to the site as another contingency. There were also complex communications as several units mobilized (ERT, TRU, CMU) on the day that Native protester Dudley George was shot dead.

4 One question which animates discussion of police behaviour is whether
police discriminate in using their authority to facilitate or deny access on
the basis of the content of the message and the political nature of the messenger rather than on concerns of public safety and law violation. University of Virginia law professor John Harrison, speaking with reference to the
American constitutional first amendment rights notes that what police cannot do 'is discriminate on the basis of content. The decisions must be content neutral' (quoted in Bailey, 2003). As Bailey also notes, the use in the
American experience of 'free-speech zones' around presidential visits has
not been consistent with the content-neutral criteria. Police are not to
restrict access to political authority on the basis of substantive politics or
viewpoint, but this is what has been done via Secret Service insistence in
the United States.

References

Abella, I. 1975. *On Strike: Six Key Labour Struggles in Canada, 1919–1949*. Toronto: James Lorimer.

Abernathy, M.G. 1962. Police Discretion and Equal Protection. *South Carolina Law Quarterly* 14: 472–86.

Adams, R. 2003. Hard Times for Trade Unions – Nadir or New Era. *Workplace Gazette* 5 (1): 79–85.

Adkin, L. 1992. Counter-Hegemony and Environmental Politics in Canada. In *Organizing Dissent: Contemporary Social Movements in Theory and Practice*, ed. W. Carroll, 135–56. Toronto: Garamond Press.

Agamben, G. 1998. *Homo Sacer: Sovereign Power and Bare Life*. Stanford, CA: Stanford University Press.

Allen, S. 2003. Velvet Gloves and Iron Fist: Taking the Violence Out of Major International Protests. *Police Chief* (February): 50–5.

Althusser, L. 1971. Ideology and Ideological State Apparatuses. In *Lenin and Philosophy and other Essays*, 122–89. London: New Left Books.

Arthurs, H.S. Carter, J. Fudge, and H. Glasbeek. 1993. *Labour Law and Industrial Relations in Canada*. Markham, ON: Butterworths.

Attorney General of BC. 1990. *Policy on Civil Disorder*. 26 July. Policy number 57680-00 CIV 1.

– 1999. *Policy on Civil Disobedience*. 1 October. Crown Counsel Policy Manual. Policy number 56740-00.

Audit Commission. 1993. *Helping with Enquiries: Tackling Crime Effectively*. London: HMSO.

Avery, M. 2004. The 'Demonstration Zone' at the Democratic National Convention: An 'Irretrievably Sad' Affront to the First Amendment. www.truthout.org (accessed 25 July 2004).

Bachrach, M., and P. Baratz. 1962. Two Faces of Power. *American Political Review* 56: 947–52.

Bajc, V. 2007. Surveillance in Public Rituals: Security Meta-ritual and the 2005 U.S. Presidential Inauguration. *American Behavioral Scientist* 50: 1648–73.

Baker, N. 2002. The Law: The Impact of Antiterrorism Policies on the Separation of Powers: Assessing John Ashcroft's Role. *Presidential Studies Quarterly* 32 (4): 765–78.

Balkan, S., R.J. Berger, and J. Schmidt. 1980. *Crime and Deviance in America.* Belmont, CA: Wadsworth.

Banton, M. 1964. *The Policeman in the Community.* London: Tavistock.

Barlow, D., and M. Barlow. 1999. A Political Economy of Community Policing. *Policing: An International Journal of Police Science and Management* 22 (4): 646–74.

Baudrillard, J. 1983. *Simulations.* New York: Semiotext(e) Foreign Agents Series.

Bauman, Z. 2004. *Wasted Lives.* Cambridge: Polity.

Baxter, N. 2001. *Policing the Line: The Development of a Theoretical Model for the Policing of Conflict.* Dartmouth: Ashgate.

Bayley, D. 1985. *Patterns of Policing: A Comparative International Analysis.* New Brunswick: Rutgers University Press.

Bayley, D., and C. Shearing. 1996. The Future of Policing. *Law and Society Review* 30 (3): 585–606.

– 2001. *The New Structure of Policing: Description, Conceptualization and Research Agenda.* Washington: U.S. Department of Justice.

Beattie, J. 1984. Violence in Society in Early Modern England. In *Perspectives in Criminal Law*, ed. A. Doob and E. Greenspan, 36–60. Toronto: Aurora Press.

Beck, U. 1992. *Risk Society: Towards a New Modernity.* London: Sage.

Bellemare, J. (Chair). 1988. *Investigation into Relations between Police Forces, Visible and Other Ethnic Minorities.* Montreal: Quebec Human Rights Commission.

Bercuson, D. 1974. *Confrontation at Winnipeg; Labour, Industrial Relations and the General Strike.* Montreal/Kingston: McGill-Queen's University Press.

Bernstein, P. 1996. *Against the Gods: The Remarkable Story of Risk.* New York: John Wiley and Sons.

Bickerton G., and C. Stearns. 2006. The Workers' Organizing and Resource Centre in Winnipeg. In *Paths to Union Renewal: Canadian Experiences*, ed. P. Kumar and C.Schenk, 251–60. Toronto: Broadview and Garamond Press.

Bittner, E. 1970. *The Functions of the Police in Modern Society.* Chevy Chase, MD: National Institute of Mental Health.

Black, D., and A. Reiss. 1970. Police Control of Juveniles. *American Sociological Review* 35 (1): 62–77.

Black, Donald, and M.P. Baumgartner. 1980. On Self-Help in Modern Society. In *The Manners and Customs of the Police*, ed. Donald Black, 193–208. New York: Academic Press.

Bogard, W. 1996. *The Simulation of Surveillance: Hyper Control in Telematic Societies*. Cambridge: Cambridge University Press.

Bovard, J. 2003. Free-Speech Zone: The Administration Quarantines Dissent. *The American Conservative* (15 December). www.amconmag.com/issue/2003/dec/15.

Bowden, T. 1978. *Beyond the Limits of the Law*. Harmondsworth: Penguin.

Braiden, C. 1994. Policing from the Belly of the Whale. In *Police Powers in Canada: The Evolution and Practice of Authority*, ed. R.C. MacLeod and D. Schniederman. Toronto: University of Toronto Press.

Brearley, N., and M. King. 1996. Policing Social Protest: Some Indicators of Change. In *Policing Public Order: Theoretical and Practical Issues*, ed. C. Critcher and D. Waddington, 101–16. Aldershot: Avebury.

Brewer, J., A. Guelke, I. Hume, E. Moxon-Browne, and R. Wilford. 1988. *The Police, Public Order and the State*. London: MacMillan.

Broad, D. 1995. Globalization, Free Trade, and Canadian Labor. *Critical Sociology* 21 (2): 19–41.

Brogden, M. 1982. *The Police: Autonomy and Consent*. London and New York: Academic Press.

Brogden, M., and C. Shearing. 1994. *Policing for a New South Africa*. New York: Routledge.

Bronskill, J. 2001. Mounties Soften Protest Policy. *Windsor Star*, 7 February.

Brooks, D. 2004. Faction in Movement: The Impact of Inclusivity on the Anti-Globalization Movement. *Social Science Quarterly* 85 (3): 559–77.

Brown, L., and C. Brown 1973. *An Unauthorized History of the RCMP*. Toronto: Lewis and Samuel.

Burawoy, M. 1985: *The Politics of Production*. London: Verso.

Burnaby Council Tells RCMP to Stay out of Labour Disputes. 1966. *Vancouver Sun*, 17 May.

Button, M., and T. John. 2002. Plural Policing in Action: A Review of the Policing of Environmental Protests in England and Wales. *Policing and Society* 12 (2): 111–21.

Button, M., T. John, and N. Brearley. 2002. New Challenges in Public Order Policing: The Professionalisation of Environmental Protest and the Emergence of the Militant Environmental Activist. *International Journal of the Sociology of the Law* 30: 17–32.

Cain, M. 1973. *Society and the Policeman's Role*. London: Routledge and Kegan Paul.

Cain, M. 1996. Policing There and Here: Reflections on International Comparison. *International Journal of the Sociology of Law* 24: 399–425.

Campbell, P. 1985. *Police and Labour*. Policy and Procedure Guidelines, Vancouver Police Department.

Canada. 1981. *Royal Commission of Inquiry Concerning Canadian Mounted Police* (McDonald Commission). Ottawa: Supply and Services Canada.

Canada. 2004. *Securing an Open Society: Canada's National Security Policy.* Ottawa: Privy Council Office.

Canadian Police College (CPC). 1981. The Management of the Police Response to Crisis Situations: The Proceedings of the Tactical Unit Workshop, Canadian Police College, June.

Cantarow, E. 2003. The Day of the Barricades. *Counterpunch* (27 February). www.counterpunch.org/cantarow02272003.html.

Carroll, W. 1992. Introduction: Social Movements and Counter Hegemony. In *Organizing Dissent: Contemporary Social Movements in Theory and Practice,* ed. W. Carroll, 1–21, Toronto: Garamond Press.

Castells, M. 1998. *End of Millennium, The Information Age: Economy, Society and Culture.* Vol. 3. Cambridge, MA. Blackwell.

CBS. 2006. 'Inside the NYPD's Anti-Terror Fight.' *60 Minutes*. 26 March

Chappell, B. 2006. Rehearsals of the Sovereign: States of Exception and Threat Governmentality. *Cultural Dynamics* 18 (3): 313–34.

Chatterton, M. 1976. Police in Social Control. In *Control Without Custody,* ed. J. King, 104–22. Cropwood Papers no. 7. Cambridge: Institute of Criminology.

Chossudovsky, M. 2001. The Quebec Wall. http://emperorsclothes.com/articles/choss/quebec.htm www.tenc.net (accessed 18 June 2007).

Cicourel, A. 1968. *The Social Organization of Juvenile Justice.* London: Heinemann.

Citizens Panel on Policing and the Community (CPPC). 2002. *Overview Report and Recommendations.* Ottawa: CPPC.

Cohen, J., and M. Centeno. 2006. Neoliberalism and Patterns of Economic Performance, 1980–2000. *ANNALS, AAPSS* 606: 32–67.

Cohen, S. 1985. *Visions of Social Control: Crime, Punishment and Classification.* Cambridge: Polity Press.

Commission on Public Complaints against the RCMP (CPC). 2000. *Chair's Interim Report with Respect to the Events of May 2 to May 4, 1997, in the Communities of Saint-Sauveur and Saint-Simon, New Brunswick.* Ottawa: CPC.

– 2001a. *Chair's Final Report with Respect to the Events of May 2 to May 4, 1997, in the Communities of Saint-Sauveur and Saint-Simon, New Brunswick.* Ottawa: CPC.

- 2001b. *Chair's Interim Report Following a Public Hearing into the Complaints Regarding the Events that Took Place in Connection with Demonstrations during the Asia Pacific Economic Co-operation Conference in Vancouver B.C. in November 1997 at the UBC Campus and Richmond Detachments of the RCMP.* Ottawa: CPC.
- 2002. *Chair's Final Report Following a Public Hearing into the Complaints Regarding the Events that Took Place in Connection with Demonstrations during the Asia Pacific Economic Co-operation Conference in Vancouver B.C. in November 1997 at the UBC Campus and Richmond Detachments of the RCMP.* Ottawa: CPC.

Committee on the Administration of Justice. 1996. *The Misrule of Law: A Report on the Policing of Events during the Summer of 1996 in Northern Ireland.* Belfast: CAJ.

Cooley, D. 2005. *Re-Imagining Policing in Canada.* Toronto: University of Toronto Press.

Cranford, C., M. Gellatly, D. Ladd, and L. Vosko. 2006. Community Unionism and Labour Movement Renewal: Organizing for Fair Employment. In *Paths to Union Renewal: Canadian Experiences*, ed. P. Kumar and C.Schenk, 237–50. Toronto: Broadview and Garamond Press.

Cruickshank, B. 1993. Self-Government and Self-Esteem. *Economy and Society* 22 (3): 329–44.

Cruikshank, D., and G. Kealey 1987. Canadian Strike Statistics, 1891–1950. *Labour/Le Travail* 20: 85–145.

Cumming, E., I. Cumming, and L. Edell. 1964–5. The Policeman as Philosopher, Guide, and Friend. *Social Problems* 12 (3): 276–86.

Dandeker, C. 1990. *Surveillance, Power and Modernity: Bureaucracy and Discipline from the 1700 to the Present Day.* New York: St Martin's Press.

Dannin, E. 1995. Brother Can You Spare a No Wage Job: Labour and Law Reform in New Zealand. In *Labour Gains, Labour Pains: 50 Years of PC1003*, ed. C. Gonick, P. Phillips, and J. Vorst, 405–34. Winnipeg: Society for Socialist Studies/Fernwood.

Dean, M. 2002. Liberal Government and Authoritarianism. *Economy and Society* 31 (1): 37–61.

Deleuze, G. 1992. Postscript on the Societies of Control. *October* 59: 3–7.

de Lint, W. 1997. The Constable Generalist as Exemplary Citizen, Networker, and Problem Solver: Some Implications. *Policing and Society* 6: 247–64.

- 1998. New Managerialism in Canadian Police Training Reform. *Social and Legal Studies* 7 (2): 261–85.
- 1999. 19th Century Disciplinary Reform and the Prohibition against Talking Policemen. *Policing and Society* 9 (1): 33–58.
- 2000. 'Regulation and Autonomy in the Police Beat.' *Social and Legal Studies: An International Journal* 9 (1): 55–83.

– 2003. Keeping Open Windows: Police as Access Brokers. *British Journal of Criminology* 43 (2): 379–97.

– 2005. Public Order Policing: A Tough Act to Follow? *International Journal of the Sociology of Law* 33(4): 179–99.

de Lint, W., R. Gostlow, and A. Hall. 2005. Judgement by Deferral: The Interlocutory Injunction in Labour Disputes Involving Picketing. *Canadian Journal of Law and Society* 20 (2): 67–93.

de Lint, W., and A. Hall. 2002. Making the Pickets Responsible: Policing Labour at a Distance in Windsor, Ontario. *Canadian Review of Sociology and Anthropology* 39 (1): 1–27.

de Lint, W., D. O'Connor, and R. Cotter. 2007. Controlling the Flow: Security, Exclusivity, and Criminal Intelligence in Ontario. *International Journal of the Sociology of Law* 35: 41–58.

de Lint, W., and S. Virta. 2004. Security in Ambiguity: Towards a Radical Security Politics. *Theoretical Criminology* 8 (4): 495–519.

de Lint, W., S. Virta, and J. Deukmedjian. 2007. The Simulation of Crime Control: A Shift in Policing? *American Behaviorial Scientist* 50: 1631–47.

della Porta, D. 1998. Police Knowledge and Protest Policing: Some Reflections on the Italian Case. In *Policing Protest: The Control of Mass Demonstrations in Western Democracies*, ed. D. della Porta and H. Reiter, 228–52 Minneapolis: University of Minnesota Press.

della Porta, D., and R. de Biasi, 1998. The Policing of Hooliganism in Italy. In *Policing Protest: The Control of Mass Demonstrations in Liberal Democracies*, ed. D. della Porta and H. Reiter, 213–27. Minneapolis: University of Minnesota Press.

della Porta, D., and H. Reiter. 1998. Introduction. In *Policing Protest: The Control of Mass Demonstrations in Western Democracies*, ed. D. della Porta and H. Reiter, 1–34. Minneapolis: University of Minnesota Press.

de Schutter, J. 2003. *Montreal Report*. Centre for Media Alternatives, Quebec, 2 August.

Deukmedjian, J., and W. de Lint. 2007. ' Community into Intelligence: Resolving Information Uptake in the RCMP.' *Policing and Society* 17 (4): 239–56.

Digeser, P. 1992. The Fourth Face of Power. *Journal of Politics* 54(4): 977–1007.

Dillon, M. 2005. Global Security in the 21st Century: Circulation, Complexity and Contingency. *Chatham House ISP/NSC Briefing Paper* 05 (02): 2–3. London: Chatham House.

– 2007. Governing through Contingency: The Security of Biopolitical Governance. *Political Geography* 26(1): 41–7.

Dimmock, G., and J. Baxter. 2000. Huge Police Presence Stifles OAS Protesters: The 3000 Demonstrators Who Came Seemed to Be Protesting All Possible Causes. *Ottawa Citizen*, 5 June 2000, A3.

Donzelot, J. 1991. The Mobilization of Society. In *The Foucault Effect*, ed. G. Burchell, C. Gordon, and P. Miller, 169–80. Chicago: University of Chicago Press.

Drinkwalter, D. 1990. *Inquiry into Ontario Police Tactical Units*. Vols 1, 2, and 3. Ontario: Queen's Printer.

du Gay, P. 1994. Making Up Managers: Bureaucracy, Enterprise and the Liberal Art of Separation. *British Journal of Sociology* 45 (4): 655–75.

Earl, J., S. Soule, and John D. McCarthy. 2003. Protests under Fire: Explaining Police Presence and Action at Protests in New York State from 1968–1973. *American Sociological Review* 68: 581–606.

Edelman, M. 1967. *The Symbolic Uses of Politics*. University of Illinois: Illini Books.

Eisenhower, M. 1969. *Report of the National Commission on the Causes and Prevention of Violence*. Washington, DC: U.S. Government Printing Office.

Elam, M. 1994. Puzzling Out the Post-Fordist Debate: Technology, Markets and Institutions. In *Post-Fordism; A Reader*, ed. Ash Amin, 43–70. Oxford: Blackwell.

Elias, N. 1978. *The Civilizing Process*, vol. 1, *The History of Manners*. Oxford: Basil Blackwood.

Enteman, W. 1993. *Managerialism: The Emergence of a New Ideology*. Madison: University of Wisconsin Press.

Ericson, R. 1981a. *Making Crime: A Study of Detective Work*. Toronto: Butterworths.

Ericson, R. 1981b. *Reproducing Order: A Study of Police Patrol Work*. Toronto: University of Toronto Press.

Ericson, R., and A. Doyle. 1999. Globalization and the Policing of Protest: The Case of APEC 1997. *British Journal of Sociology* 50 (4): 589–608.

Ericson, R., and K. Haggerty. 1997. *Policing the Risk Society*. Toronto: University of Toronto Press.

Estey, W. 1996. *Report of the Commission of Inquiry into Events of March 18, 1996 at Queen's Park*. Toronto: Publications Ontario.

Ewick, P., and S. Silbey. 1998. *The Common Place of Law: Stories From Everyday Life*. Chicago: University of Chicago Press.

Fairbrother, P., and C. Yates, eds. 2003. *Trade Unions in Renewal: A Comparative Study*. London: Continuum.

Farrow, T. 2003. Negotiation, Mediation, Globalization Protests and Police: Right Processes, Wrong System, Issues, Parties, and Time. *Queen's Law Journal* 28: 668–703

Feeley, M., and J. Simon. 1992. The New Penology: Notes on the Emerging Strategy of Corrections and Its Implications. *Criminology* 30(4): 449–74.

Fielding, N. 1991. *The Police and Social Conflict*. London: Athlone Press.

Fielding, N., and M. Innes. 2006. Reassurance and the 'New'Community Policing. *Policing and Society* 16 (2): 127–45.

Fillieule, O., and E. Jobard. 1998. The Policing of Protest in France: Toward a Model of Protest Policing. In *Policing Protest: The Control of Mass Demonstrations in Western Democracies*, ed. D. della Porta and H. Reiter, 70–90. Minneapolis: University of Minnesota Press.

Fitzpatrick, T. 2001. New Agendas for Social Policy and Criminology: Globalization, Urbanization, and the Emerging Post–Social Security State. *Social Policy and Administration* 35 (2): 212–29.

Forrest, A. 1995. Securing the Male Breadwinner: A Feminist Interpretation of PC1003. In *Labour Gains, Labour Pains, 50 Years of PC 1003*, ed. C. Gonick, P. Phillips, and J. Vorst. Winnipeg: Society for Socialist Studies and Fernwood.

Forsey, E. 1982. *Trade Unionism in Canada, 1812–1902*. Toronto: University of Toronto Press.

Foucault, M. 1977. *Discipline and Punish*. New York: Vintage.

– 2004. *Naissance de la biopolitique*. Paris: Hautes Études, Seuil Gallimard.

Frank, D. 1987. Contested Terrain: Workers' Control in the Cape Breton Mines in the 1920s. In *On the Job : Confronting the Labour Process in Canada*, ed. C. Heron and R. Storey, 75–110. Montreal/Kingston: McGill-Queen's University Press.

Fraser, N. 1989. *Unruly Practices: Power, Discourse and Gender in Contemporary Social Theory*. Minneapolis: University of Minnesota Press.

Freeman, J. 1997. The Strike Weapon: Can It Still Work? *Dissent* 44 (2): 60–5.

Fudge, J., and E. Tucker. 2001. *Labour before the Law: The Regulation of Workers' Collective Action in Canada, 1900–1918*. Toronto: University of Toronto Press.

Fukuyama, F. 1989. The End of History? *National Interest* 16: 3–18.

– 2006. *The End of History and the Last Man*. New York: Simon Schuster.

Garland, D. 1996. The Limits of the Sovereign State: Strategies of Crime Control in Contemporary Society. *The British Journal of Criminology* 36 (4): 445–71.

– 1998. The Limits of the Sovereign State: Strategies of Crime Control in Contemporary Society. *British Journal of Criminology* 36 (4): 455–71.

– 2001. *The Culture of Control: Crime and Social Order in Contemporary Society*. Chicago: University of Chicago Press.

Geary, R. 1985. *Policing Industrial Disputes: 1893–1985*. Cambridge: Cambridge University Press.

Giddens, A. 1984. *The Constitution of Society: Outline of the Theory of Structuration*. Berkeley: University of California Press.

– 1985. *The Nation-State and Violence*. Berkeley: University of California Press.

– 1990. *The Consequences of Modernity*. Cambridge: Polity.

– 1991. *Modernity and Self-identity*. Cambridge: Polity.

Gill, P. 1994. *Political Policing*. London: Cass.

– 1998. Making Sense of Police Intelligence: A Cybernetic Model in Analysing Information and Power in Police Intelligence Processes. *Policing and Society* 8 (3): 289–314

Gillham, P., and G. Marx. 2000. Complexity and Irony in Policing and Protesting: The World Trade Organization in Seattle. *Social Justice* 27 (2): 212–36.

Gindin, S. 1989. Breaking Away: The Formation of the Canadian Auto Workers. *Studies in Political Economy* 29 (Summer): 63–85.

– 1995. *The Canadian Auto Workers. The Birth and Transformation of a Union*. Toronto: Lorimer.

Glasbeek, H. 1987. Labour Relations Law as a Mechanism of Adjustment. *Osgoode Hall Law Journal* 25: 179–237.

Goldberg-Hillier, J. 1996. The Boycott of the Law and the Law of the Boycott: Law, Labour and Politics in British Columbia. *Law and Social Inquiry* 21 (2): 313–51.

Goldstein, H. 1963. Police Discretion: The Ideal versus the Real. *Public Administration Review* 23: 140–8.

– 1979. Improving Policing: A Problem-Oriented Approach. *Crime and Delinquency* 25: 236–58.

Goldstein, J. 1960. Police Discretion Not to Invoke the Criminal Process: Low-Visibility Decisions in the Administration of Justice. *Yale Law Journal* 69: 542–94.

Gordon, C. 1991. Governmental Rationality: An Introduction. In *The Foucault Effect*, ed. G. Burchell, C. Gordon, and P. Miller, 1–52. Chicago: University of Chicago Press.

Gordon, T. 2005. The Political Economy of Law and Order Policies: Policing, Class Struggle and Neoliberal Restructuring. *Studies in Political Economy* 75 (Spring): 53–78.

– 2006. The Canadian State and the War on Drugs. *Social Justice* 33 (1): 59–78.

Gramsci, A. 1971. *Selections from the Prison Notebooks*. London: Lawrence and Wishart.

Grant, D., and M. Wallace. 1991. Why Do Strikes Turn Violent? *American Journal of Sociology* 96 (March): 1117–50.

Greer, A. 1992. The Birth of Police in Canada. In *Colonial Leviathan: State Formation in Mid-19th Century Canada*, ed. A. Greer and I. Radforth, 17–49. Toronto: University of Toronto Press.

Grimshaw, R., and T. Jefferson. 1987. *Interpreting Policework: Policy and Practice in Forms of Beat Policing*. London: Unwin and Allen.

Gunderson, D. 1978. Police Uniform: Study of Change. *FBI Law Enforcement Bulletin* 47(4): 13–15.

Guntzel, R. 2000. Rapprocher les lieux du pouvoir: The Quebec Labour Movement and Quebec Sovereigntism 1960–2000. *Labour/Le Travail* 46 (Fall): 369–95.

Haggerty, K., and R. Ericson, 1999. The Militarization of Policing in the Information Age. *Journal of Political and Military Sociology* 27: 205–15.

– 2000. The Surveillant Assemblage. *British Journal of Sociology* 51 (4): 605–22.

Haiven, L. 1995. PC1003 and the (Non) Right to Strike: A Sorry Legacy. In
Labour Gains, Labour Pains, 50 Years of PC 1003, ed. C. Gonick, P. Phillips, and
J. Vorst. Winnipeg: Society for Socialist Studies and Fernwood.

Haiven, L., S. McBride, and J. Shields. 1990. The State, Neo-Conservatism and
Industrial Relations. In *Regulating Labour: The State, Neo-Conservatism and
Industrial Relations*, ed. L. Haiven, S. McBride, and J. Shields, 1–13. Toronto:
Society for Socialist Studies and Garamond Press.

Hall, A. 1999. Understanding the Impact of Mine Health and Safety Programs.
Labour Studies Journal 23 (4): 51–76.

– 1993. The Corporate Construction of Occupational Health and Safety. *Canadian Journal of Sociology* 18 (1): 1–20.

Hall, Alan, and W. de Lint 2003. Policing Labour in Canada. *Policing and Society*
13 (3): 219–34.

Hall, S., S. Critcher, T. Jefferson, T. Clarke, and B. Roberts. 1978. *Policing the
Crisis: 'Mugging,' Law and Order, and the State*. London: MacMillan.

Hänninen, Sakari, 2000. The Ghost of Politics in the Soft Machine. In *Displacement of Politics*, ed. S. Hänninen and J. Vähämäki, 27–46. SoPhi: University of
Jyväskylä.

Harring, S., and L. McMullin. 1975. The Buffalo Police 1872–1900: Labor
Unrest, Political Power and the Creation of the Police Institution. *Criminal
and Social Justice* 4: 5–14.

Harris, F., and T. Wicker, eds. 1988. *The Kerner Report: The 1968 Report of the
National Advisory Commission on Civil Disorders*. New York: Pantheon.

Harvey, D. 1989. *The Condition of Post-Modernity*. Cambridge, MA: Blackwell.

– 2007. Neoliberalism as Creative Destruction. *ANNALS, AAPSS* 610: 22–44.

Haubrich, D. 2006. Modern Politics in an Age of Global Terrorism: New Challenges for Domestic Public Policy. *Political Studies* 54: 399–423.

Haywood, L. 1992. *Replacements of Striking Workers during Work Stoppages in
1991*. Toronto: Ontario Ministry of Labour.

Heron, C. 1996. *The Canadian Labor Movement: A Short History*. 2nd ed. Toronto:
Lorimer.

– 1998. Introduction. In *The Workers' Revolt in Canada 1917–25*, ed. C. Heron,
3–10. Toronto: University of Toronto Press.

Heron, C., and B. Palmer 1977. Through the Prism of the Strike: Industrial Conflict in Southern Ontario, 1901–1914. *Canadian Historical Review* 58(4): 423–58.

Heron, C., and R. Storey. 1986a. On the Job in Canada. In *On the Job : Confronting the Labour Process in Canada*, ed. C. Heron and R. Storey, 3–46. Montreal/Kingston: McGill-Queen's University Press.

– 1986b. Work and Struggle in the Canadian Steel Industry. In *On the Job: Confronting the Labour Process in Canada*, ed. C. Heron and R. Storey, 210–44. Montreal/Kingston: McGill-Queen's University Press.

Hewitt, S. 1997. September 1931: A Re-Interpretation of the Royal Canadian Mounted Police Handling of the 1931 Estevan Strike and Riot. *Labour/Le Travail* 39 (20): 159–78.

Hewitt, S. 2000a. Watching the Watchers: Why Isn't Anyone Following the R.C.M.P.'s 'Dirty Tricks' Trail? *This Magazine*, July, 25.

Hewitt, S. 2000b. 'Information Believed True': RCMP Security Intelligence Activities on Canadian University Campuses and the Controversy Surrounding Them, 1961–71. *Canadian Historical Review* 81(2): 191–229.

– 2002. Spying 101: The RCMP's Secret Activities at Canadian Universities, 1917–1997. In *Whose National Security? Canadian State Surveillance and the Creation of Enemies*, ed. G. Kinsman, D. Buse, and M. Steedman, 91–109. Toronto: Between the Lines.

Higley, D. 1984. *OPP: The History of the Ontario Provincial Police Force 1984*. Toronto: Queen's Printer.

Hills, A. 1995. Militant Tendencies: Paramilitarism in British Police. *British Journal of Criminology* 35 (3): 450–6.

Himmelfarb, F. 1991. A Training Strategy for Policing a Multicultural Society. *The Police Chief* (November): 53–5.

– 1992. *Training and Executive Development in the RCMP*. Ottawa: RCMP.

Hobbs, D., P. Hadfield, S. Lister, and S. Winlow. 2002. Door Lore: The Art and Economics of Intimidation. *British Journal of Criminology* 42: 352–70.

Hodgson, J. 2001. Police Violence in Canada and the USA: Analysis and Management. *Policing: An International Journal of Police Strategies and Management* 24 (4): 520–49.

Holdaway, S. 1983. *Inside the British Police*. Oxford: Basil Blackwell.

Holquist, P. 1997. 'Information is the alpha and omega of our work': Bolshevik Surveillance in Its Pan-European Context. *Journal of Modern History* 69 (3): 415–50.

Hornquist, M. 2004. The Birth of Public Order Policy. *Race and Class* 46 (1): 30–52.

Horrall, S.W., ed. 1975. *A Chronicle of the Canadian West: Northwest Mounted Police Report for 1875*. Calgary: Historical Society of Alberta.

Hudson, B. 2003. *Justice in the Risk Society*. London: Sage.

Huggins, M. 1998. *Political Policing: The United States and Latin America*. Durham: Duke University Press.

Huxley, C. 1979. The State, Collective Bargaining and the Shape of Strikes in Canada. *Canadian Journal of Sociology* 4: 223–39.

Ignatieff, M. 2003. *The Lesser Evil: Political Ethics in an Age of Terror*. Princeton, NJ: Princeton University Press.

Innes, M. 2001. Control Creep. *Sociological Research Online* 6 (3).

Isbester, F. 1975. Asbestos 1949. In *On Strike: Six Key Labour Struggles in Canada, 1919–1949*, ed. I. Abella, 163–98. Toronto: James Lorimer.

Jackson, A. 2006. Rowing against the Tide: The Struggle to Raise Union Density in a Hostile Environment. In *Paths to Union Renewal: Canadian Experiences*, ed. P. Kumar and C. Schenk, 61–78. Peterborough, ON: Broadview and Garamond Press.

Jacobs, D., and J. Carmichael. 2002. Subordination and Violence against State Control Agents: Testing Political Explanations for Lethal Assaults against the State. *Social Forces* 80 (4): 1223–41.

Jaime-Jimenez, O., and F. Reinares. 1998. The Policing of Mass Demonstrations in Spain: From Dictatorship to Democracy. In *Policing Protest: The Control of Mass Demonstrations in Western Democracies*, ed. D. della Porta and H. Reiter, 166–87. Minneapolis: University of Minnesota Press.

Jameson, F. 1991. *Postmodernism or the Cultural Logic of Late Capitalism*. Durham: Duke University Press.

Jamieson, S. 1968. *Times of Trouble: Labour Unrest in Canada: 1900–1967*. Ottawa: Queen's Printer.

– 1971. *Times of Trouble: Labour Unrest in Canada: 1900–1967*. Ottawa: Queen's Printer.

– 1973. *Industrial Relations in Canada*. 2nd ed. Toronto: Macmillan.

Jaynes, A. 2002. Insurgency and Policy Outcomes: The Impact of Protests/Riots on Urban Spending. *Journal of Political and Military Sociology* 30 (1): 90–112.

Jefferson, T. 1990. *The Case against Paramilitary Policing*. Buckingham: Open University Press.

Jessop, B. 1994. Post-Fordism and the State. In *Post-Fordism: A Reader*, ed. A. Amin, 251–79. Oxford: Blackwell.

– 1995. The Regulation Approach, Governance and Post-Fordism: Alternative Perspectives on Economic and Political Change. *Economy and Society* 24 (3): 307–33.

– 2002. *The Future of the Capitalist State*. Oxford: Polity.

Johnson, M. 1976. Taking Care of Labor: The Police in American Politics. *Theory and Society* 3 (1): 89–117.

Johnston, L. 1992. *The Rebirth of Private Policing*. London: Routledge and Kegan Paul.

– 2000. *Policing Britain: Risk, Security and Governance*. London: Longman.

Johnston, L., and C. Shearing. 2003. *Governing Security: Explorations in Policing and Justice*. New York: Routledge.

Jones, T., and T. Newburn. 2002. Understanding Current Trends in Policing Systems. *The British Journal of Criminology* 42 (1): 129–46.

Kahn, P., et al. 1983. *Picketing*. London: Routledge and Kegan Paul.

Kealey, G. 1984a. Orangemen and the Corporation. In *Forging a Consensus: Historical Essays on Toronto*, 116–40. Toronto: University of Toronto Press.

– 1984b. 1919: The Canadian Labor Revolt. *Labour/Le Travail* 13: 11–44.

– 1986. 1919: The Canadian Labor Revolt. In *The Character of Class Struggle*, ed. B. Palmer, 90–114. Toronto: McClelland and Stewart.

– 1992a. The RCMP, the Special Branch, and the Early Days of the Communist Party of Canada. *Labour/Le Travail* 30: 169–204.

– 1992b. State Repression of Labour and the Left in Canada, 1914–1920. The Impact of the First World War. *Canadian Historical Review* 73 (3): 281–314.

– 2000. Chauvinism and Masculinism in the RCMP Security Service: The Early Years. In *Whose National Security? Canadian State Surveillance and the Creation of Enemies*, ed. G. Kinsman, D. Buse, and M. Steedman, 18–36. Toronto: Between the Lines.

Kebede, A. 2005. Grassroots Environmental Organizations in the United States: A Gramscian Analysis. *Sociological Inquiry* 75 (1): 81–108.

Kempa, M., P. Stenning, and J. Wood. 2004. Policing Communal Spaces: Reconfiguring the Mass Private Property Hypothesis. *British Journal of Criminology* 44 (4): 562–81.

Kerner, O. 1968. *Report of the National Advisory Committee on Civil Disorders* Washington, DC: U.S. Government Printing Office.

King, M. 1997. Policing and Public Order Issues in Canada: Trends for Change. *Policing and Society* 8 (1): 47–76.

– 2004. From Reactive Policing to Crowd Management?: Policing Anti-Globalization Protest in Canada. Paper presented to British Society of Criminology, June 2004.

King, M., and N. Brearley. 1996. *Public Order Policing: Contemporary Perspectives on Strategy and Tactics*. Leicester: Perpetuity Press.

King, M., and Waddington, D. 2004. Coping with Disorder?: The Changing Relationship between Police Public Order Strategy and Practice – A Critical Analysis of the Burnley Riot. *Policing and Society* 14 (2): 118–37.

Klein, N. 2007. *The Shock Doctrine: The Rise of Disaster Capitalism*. London: Allen Lane.

Klockars, C. 1988. The Rhetoric of Community Policing. In *Community Policing: Rhetoric or Reality*, ed. J. Greene and S. Masatrofski, 239–58. New York: Praeger.

Kolbert, E. 2003. The Surge. *The New Yorker*. http://www.newyorker.com/
archive/2003/04/07/030407ta_talk_kolbert (accessed 7 April).

Kraska, P., and L. Cubellis. 1997. Militarizing Mayberry and Beyond: Making
Sense of American Paramilitary Policing. *Justice Quarterly* 14: 607–29.

Kraska, P., and V. Kappeler. 1997. Militarizing the American Police: The Rise
and Normalization of Paramilitary Units. *Social Problems* 44 (1): 1–18.

Krugman, P. 1994. *Rethinking International Trade*. Cambridge: MIT Press.

Kumar, P. 1995. *Union and Workplace Change in Canada*. Kingston: IRC Press.

Kumar, P., and G. Murray. 2002. Canadian Union Strategies in the Context of
Change. *Labor Studies Journal* 26 (4): 1–28.

Kumar, P., and C. Schenk. 2006. Union Renewal and Organizational Change:
A Review of the Literature. In *Paths to Union Renewa: Canadian Experiences*,
ed. P. Kumar and C. Schenk, 29–60. Toronto: Broadview and Garamond
Press.

Labour Canada. 1965–75. *Strikes and Lockouts in Canada*. Ottawa: Government
of Canada.

Laclau, E., and C. Mouffe 1985. *Hegemony and Socialist Strategy:Towards a Radical
Democratic Politics*. London: Verso.

La Fave, W. 1962. The Police and the Non-Enforcement of the Law. *Wisconsin
Law Review* 1: 104–37.

Laidlaw, S. 2000. Pepper Spray Flies at OAS Rally, 41 Arrested at Windsor
Demonstration. *Toronto Star*, 5 June, A01.

Landau, T. 1995. Policing and Security in Four Remote Aboriginal Communities: A Challenge to Coercive Models of Police Work. *Canadian Journal of
Criminology* 38 (1): 1–32.

Langford, T. 1996. Effects of Strike Participation on the Political Consciousness
of Canadian Postal Workers. *Industrial Relations/Relations Industrielles* 51 (3):
563–6.

Lash, C., and J. Urry. 1987. *The End of Organized Capitalism*. London: Oxford
University Press.

Latornell, J. 1993. *Violence on the Picket Line: The Law and Police Response*. Kingston, ON: Industrial Relations Centre, Queen's University.

Lazar, N. 2006. Must Exceptionalism Prove the Rule? An Angle on Emergency
Government in the History of Political Thought. *Politics and Society* 34 (2):
245–75.

Lea, J., and J. Young. 1984. *What Is to Be Done about Law and Order – Crisis in the
Eighties*. Harmondsworth: Penguin.

Leighton, B., and A. Normandeau. 1991. Visions of Community Policing:
Rhetoric and Reality in Canada. *Canadian Journal of Criminology* 33: 485–
522.

Lelievre, S., W.L. Felton, and R.B. Johnson. 1854. *Report of the Commissioners to Inquire into the Conduct of the Police Authorities on the Occasion of the Riot at Chalmer's Church*. Quebec: Rollo Campbell.

Leonardsen, D. 2004. *Japan as a Low-Crime Nation*. Houndsmills: Palgrave.

Leonnig, C. 2007. Police Log Confirms FBI Role in Arrests. *Washington Post*, 3 April, B01.

Levesque, C., and G. Murray 2006. Globalization and Union Renewal: Perspectives from the Quebec Labour Movement. In *Paths to Union Renewal: Canadian Experieences*, ed. P. Kumar and C. Schenk, 113–26. Peterborough, ON: Broadview and Garamond Press.

Lipsig-Mumme, C. 2005. Trade Unions and Labour Relations Systems in Comparative Perspective. In *Union–Management Relations in Canada*, ed. M. Gunderson, 476–93. Toronto: Pearson/Addison Wesley.

Lipton, C. 1968. *The Trade Union Movement of Canada, 1827–1959*. 2nd ed. Montreal: Canadian Social Publications.

Livingstone, D., and J. Mangan. 1996. Introduction: The Changing Context of Class and Gender Relations in Contemporary Canada. In *Recast Dreams: Class and Gender Consciousness in Steeltown*, ed. D. Livingstone and J. Mangan, 1–14. Toronto: Garamond Press.

Loader, I. 2000. Plural Policing and Democratic Governance. *Social and Legal Studies* 9 (3): 323–45.

Loader, I., and N. Walker. 2001. Policing as Public Good: Reconstituting the Connection between Policing and the State. *Theoretical Criminology* 5 (1): 9–35.

– 2007. *Civilizing Security*. Cambridge: Cambridge University Press.

Lopez, S. 2005. Bring Out Yer Dead: Neoliberalism and Crisis of Trade Unionism. *Work and Occupations* 32 (3): 355–9.

Lukes, S. 1975. *Power: A Radical View*. Atlantic Highlands, NJ: Humanities.

Lustgarten, L., and I. Leigh. 1996. *In from the Cold: National Security and Parliamentary Democracy*. New York: Oxford University Press.

Mackay, K. 2002. Solidarity and Symbolic Protest: Lessons Learned for Labour from the Quebec City Summit of the Americas. *Labour/Le Travail* 50: 21–72.

Macleod, R. 1976. *The North-West Mounted Police and Law Enforcement, 1873–1905*. Toronto: University of Toronto Press.

MacNab, A., T. Tache, E. Campbell, and G.F. de Rottenburg. 1855. *Report of the Commissioners appointed to investigate and report upon the best means of re-organizing the Militia of Canada, and providing an efficient and economical system of Public Defence and to report upon the improved system of Police, for the better preservation of the public peace*. Toronto: Public Archives of Ontario.

Maguire, M. 2000. Policing by Risks and Targets: Some Consequences of Intelligence-Led Crime Control. *Policing and Society* 9 (1): 315–36.

Maguire, M., and T. John. 2006 Intelligence-Led Policing, Managerialism and Community Engagement: Competing Priorities and Roles of the National Intelligence Model in the UK. *Policing and Society* 16 (1): 67–85.

Malouf, A., L. Arsenault, and J.P. Brodeur. 1993. *Rapport de l'enquête spéciale tenue sur les désordres qui ont fait suite à la conquête de la Coupe Stanley par le Club Canadien*. Montreal: Gouvernement du Québec.

Manwaring-White, S. 1983. *The Policing Revolution: Police Technology, Democracy and Liberty in Britain*. Totowa, NJ: Barnes and Noble.

Marquis, G. 1993. *Policing Canada's Century: A History of the Canadian Association of Chiefs of Police*. Toronto: University of Toronto Press.

Mathiessen, T. 1997. The Viewer Society:Michel Foucault's 'Panopticon' Revisited. *Theoretical Criminology* 1 (2): 215–34.

Maurutto, P. 2000. Private Policing and Surveillance of Catholics: Anticommunism in Archdiocese of Toronto, 1920–1960. In *Whose National Security? Canadian State Surveillance of Enemies*, ed. G. Kinsman, D. Buse, and M. Steedman, 37–54. Toronto: Between The Lines.

May, J., P. Cloke, and S. Johnsen 2005. Re-phasing Neoliberalism: New Labour and Britain's Crisis of Street Homelessness. *Antipode* 37: 703–30.

McAdam, D. 1999. The Decline of the Civil Rights Movement. In *Waves of Protest: Social Movements since the Sixties*, ed. J. Freeman and V. Johnson, 325–48. Lanham, MD: Rowman and Littlefield.

McBride, S. 1991. Authoritarianism without Hegemony? The Politics of Industrial Relations in Britain. In *Regulating Labour: The State, Neo-conservatism, and Industrial Relations*, ed. L. Haiven, S. McBride, and J. Shields, 118–48. Winnipeg and Toronto: Society for Socialist Studies and Garamond.

– 1992. *'Not Working': State, Unemployment and Neo-conservatism in Canada*. Toronto: University of Toronto Press.

McCarthy, J., and C. McPhail. 1998. The Institutionalization of Protest in the United States. In *The Social Movement Society: Contentious Politics for a New Century*, ed. D. Meyer and S. Tarrow, 83–110. Lanham, MD: Rowman and Littlefield.

McCarthy, J., C. McPhail, and J. Crist. 1999. Institutional Channeling of Protest. In *Social Movements in a Globalizing World*, ed. H. Kriesi, D. della Porta, and D. Rucht, 71–96. Macmillan.

McCleod, R.C. 1976. *The N.W.M.P. and Law Enforcement, 1873–1905*. Toronto: McClelland and Stewart.

McCrorie, A. 1995. PC 1003: Labour, Capital and the State. In *Labor Gains, Labour Pains, 50 Years of PC 1003*, ed. C. Gonick, P. Phillips, and J. Vorst, 15–38. Winnipeg: Society for Socialist Studies and Fernwood.

McDougall, A.K. 1971. *Policing in Ontario: The Occupational Dimension to Provincial–Municipal Relations.* PhD dissertation, University of Toronto.

– 1973. *Perspectives on Policing: Automaton, Henchman, or Servant?* Crimdoc 62. Toronto: Centre of Criminology.

McLeod, D., and B. Detenberg 1999. Framing Effects of Television News Coverage of Social Protest. *Journal of Communication* 49 (3): 3–23.

McPhail, C., D. Schweingruber, and J. McCarthy. 1998. Policing Protest in the U.S.: 1960–1995. In *Policing Protest: The Control of Mass Demonstrations in Western Democracies,* ed. D. della Porta and H. Reiter, 49–69. Minneapolis: University of Minnesota Press.

Mitchell, T., and J. Naylor. 1998. The Prairies: In the Eye of the Storm. In *The Workers' Revolt in Canada 1917–25,* ed. C. Heron, 176–230. Toronto: University of Toronto Press.

Monet, J.C. 1990. Maintien de l'ordre ou création du désordre. In *La manifestation,* ed. P. Favre. Paris: Presses de la Fondation nationale des sciences politiques.

Monjardins, D. 1992. Profession policier. *Informations sociales* 21: 99–107.

Montjardet, D. 1992. Quelques conditions d'un professionnalisme discipliné. *Deviance and Society* 16 (4): 399–403.

Moore, M. 1992. Problem Solving and Community Policing: A Preliminary Assessment of New Strategies of Policing. In *Modern Policing Crime and Justice Volume 15,* ed. Michael Tonry and Norval Morris, 99–158. Chicago: University of Chicago Press.

Morgan, G. 1993. *Imaginization.* Newbury Park, CA: Sage.

Morgan, J. 1987. *Conflict and Order: The Police and Labour Disputes in England and Wales, 1900–1939.* Oxford: Clarendon.

Mouffe, C. 2005. *On the Political.* London: Versa.

Moulton, D. 1974. Ford Windsor 1945. In *On Strike: Six key Labour Struggles in Canada 1919–1949,* ed. I. Abella, 129–61. Toronto: Lorimer.

Murphy, C. 1998. Policing Postmodern Canada. *Canadian Journal of Law and Society* 13 (2): 1–25.

Nakashima, E. 2006. FBI Shows Off Counterterrorism Database. *Washington Post,* 30 August, A06.

'Native Conflicts a Federal Matter, Fantino Complains.' 2007. *The Globe and Mail,* 30 April, A10

Neocleous, M. 2000. Against Security. *Radical Philosophy* (March/April).

Neuman, M. 2005. Victory and Recruitment. *Counterpunch,* 24 June.

Niederhoffer, A. 1967 *Behind the Shield.* New York: Doubleday.

Noakes, J., B. Klocke, and P. Gillham. 2005. Whose Streets? Police and Protester Struggles over Space in Washington, DC, 9–30 September 2001. *Policing and Society* 15 (3): 235–54.

Noel, A., and K. Gardner. 1990. The Gainers Strike: Capitalist Offensive, Militancy and the Politics of Industrial Relations in Canada. *Studies in Political Economy* 31 (Spring): 31–65.

Normandeau, A., and B. Leighton 1990. *A Vision of the Future of Policing in Canada: Police Challenge 2000.* Ottawa: Ministry of the Solicitor General.

Northorp, R. 1975. *Policing a Labour Dispute.* RCMP report. November.

Nozick, R. 1974. *Anarchy, State, and Utopia.* New York: Basic Books.

– 1984. Moral Constraints and Distributive Justice. In *Liberalism and Its Critics,* ed. M. Sandel, 100–22. Albany, NY: New York University Press.

O'Connor, the Honorable, D.R. 2007. *Commision of Inquiry into the Action of Canadian Officials in Relation to Maher Arar.* Ottawa: Queen's Printer

Ogmundsen, R., and M. Doyle. 2002. The Rise and Decline of Canadian Labour, 1960 to 2000: Elites, Power, Ethnicity and Gender. *Canadian Journal of Sociology* 27 (3): 413–35.

O'Grady, J. 1995. The Decline of Collective Bargaining in the Private Sector. In *Hard Lessons,* ed. M. Steedman, P. Suschnigg, and D. Buse, 21–5. Toronto: Dundurn Press.

Oliver, P.E., and G.M. Maney. 2000. Political Processes and Local Newspaper Coverage of Protest Events: from Selection Bias to Triadic Interactions. *American Journal of Sociology* 106 (2): 463–505.

Oliver, P.E., and D.J. Myers. 1999. How Events Enter the Public Sphere: Conflict, Location, and Sponsorship in Local Newspaper Coverage of Public Events. *American Journal of Sociology* 105 (1): 38–87.

Olsen, M. 1968. Perceived Legitimacy of Social Protest Actions. *Social Problems* 15 (Winter): 297–310.

O'Malley, P. 1992. Risk, Power and Crime Prevention. *Economy and Society* 21: 252–75.

– 1997. Policing, Politics and Post Modernity. *Social and Legal Studies* 6 (3): 363–81.

– 1999. Volatile and Contradictory Punishments. *Theoretical Criminology* 3 (2): 175–96.

– 2005. Converging Corporatization? Police Management, Police Unionism and the Transfer of Business Principles. In *Law, Economic Incentives and the Public Services Culture,* ed. Tony Prosser , Pat O'Malley, Colin Scott, Morag McDermont, Peter Vincent-Jones, Mike Feintuck, and Dave Cowan. CMPO Working Paper series 05/129. Bristol: Centre for Management and Public Organization.

O'Malley, P., and B. Palmer. 1996. Post-Keynesian Policing. *Economy and Society* 25 (2): 137–55.

O'Neil, P. 2003. RCMP Accused of Harsh Tactics: Police Broke Law at 2001 Summit, says Report. *Calgary Herald*, 13 November, A4.

Ontario. 1989. *Report of the Race Relations and Policing Task Force*. Clare Lewis, Chair. Toronto: Queen's Printer.

Ontario Provincial Police (OPP). 1972. *Crowd Control Manual*. Toronto: OPP, Planning and Research Branch.

– 1981. *Crowd Control Training*. Archives of Ontario, RG 4-2 63.3.

Oppal, Justice W.T. 1994. *Closing the Gap: Policing and the Community. Commission of Inquiry Report into Policing in British Columbia*. Victoria: Ministry of Attorney General.

O'Reilly, C., and G. Ellison. 2006. Eye Spy Private High: Re-conceptualizing High Policing Theory. *British Journal of Criminology* 46: 641–60.

Osborne, D., and T. Gaebler. 1993. *Reinventing Government*. New York: Plume.

Ottawa Police Service (OPS). 2002. *An Agenda for Excellence for Major Events: Police and Community Challenges*. Ottawa: OPS.

Palmer, B. 1987a. *Solidarity; The Rise and Fall of an Opposition in British Columbia*. Vancouver: New Star Books.

Palmer, B. 1987b. Labour Protest and Organization in Nineteenth Century Canada. *Labour/Le Travail* 20: 61–84.

– 1992. *Working Class Experience: Rethinking the History of Canadian Labour, 1800–1991*. 2nd ed. Toronto: McClelland and Stewart.

– 2003. Repression and Dissent: The OCAP Trials. *Canadian Dimension* (May/June): 12–15.

Panitch, L. 1976. Wage and Price Controls. *The Red Menace*. Ottawa Committee for Labour Action 1 (1): 1.

Panitch, L., and D. Swartz. 1993. *The Assault on Trade Union Freedoms: From Wage Controls to Social Contract*. Toronto: Garamond.

– 2003. *From Consent to Coercion: The Assault on Trade Union Freedoms*. Aurora, ON: Garamond Press.

Parnaby, A., and G. Kealey. 2003. The Origins of Political Policing in Canada: Class, Law and the Burden of Empire. *Osgoode Hall Law Journal* 41 (2/3): 211–40.

Parrot, J-C. 2005. *My Unions, My Life: Jean-Claude Parrot and the Canadian Union of Postal Workers*. Halifax: Fernwood.

Peck, J., and A. Tickell. 2002. Neoliberalizing Spaces. *Antipode* 34 (3): 380–404.

Pedersen, V. 2003. In Search of Monsters to Destroy? The Liberal American Security Paradox and a Republican Way Out. *International Relations* 17 (2): 213–32.

Peirce, J. 2000. *Canadian Industrial Relations*. Scarborough, ON: Prentice-Hall.

Pentland, H. Clare. 1981. *Labour and Capital in Canada, 1650–1860*. Toronto: Lorimer.

Perez, A., K. Berg, and D. Myers. 2003. Police and Riots: 1967–1969. *Journal of Black Studies* 34 (2): 153–82.

Peters, J. 2002. *A Fine Balance: Canadian Unions Confront Globalization*. Toronto: Canadian Centre for Policy Alternatives.

Phillips, C. 2004. *Six Questions of Socrates: A Modern-Day Journey of Discovery through World Philosophy*. London: Norton.

Piazza, J. 2005. Globalizing Quiescence: Globalization, Union Density and Strikes in 15 Industrialized Countries. *Economic and Industrial Democracy* 26 (2): 289–314.

Piliavin, I., and S. Briar. 1964. Police Encounters with Juveniles. *American Journal of Sociology* 70: 206–14.

Piven, F., and R. Cloward. 1971. *Regulating the Poor: The Functions of Public Welfare*. New York: Pantheon.

Platt, T., J. Fruppier, G. Ray, R. Schauffler, L. Trujillo, and L. Cooper. 1982. *The Iron Fist and the Velvet Glove: An Analysis of the U.S. Police*. San Francisco: Synthesis.

Police Chief Defends Officers' Use of Force to Subdue Crowd. 2003. *Times-Colonist* (Victoria), 19 November, C2.

Police Infiltrate Protests. 2005. *New York Times*, 22 December, B1.

Price, J. 1995. Post-PC 1003: A Return to Coercion or New Directions for Labour? In *Labour Gains, Labour Pains, 50 Years of PC 1003*, ed. C. Gonick, P. Phillips, and J. Vorst. Winnipeg: Society for Socialist Studies and Fernwood.

Pue, W. 2005. *Trespass and Expressive Rights*. Ontario: Ipperwash Inquiry.

Pugliese, D., and Jim Bronskill. 2001. The Criminalization of Dissent. *The Ottawa Citizen*, 18 August, A1.

Rand, I. 1968. *Report of the Royal Commission of Inquiry in Labour Disputes*. Toronto: Queen's Printer.

Rapaport, D. 1999. *No Justice, No Peace: The 1996 OPSEU Strike against the Harris Government in Ontario*. Montreal and Kingston: McGill-Queen's University Press.

Raz, J. 1990. *Authority: Readings in Social and Political Theory*. New York: New York University Press.

Redekop, V. 2002. *From Violence to Blessing: How an Understanding of Deep Rooted Conflict Can Open Paths to Reconciliation*. Ottawa: Novalis.

Reiner, R. 1998. Policing Protest and Disorder in Britain. In *Policing Protest: The Control of Mass Demonstrations in Western Democracies*, ed. D. della Porta and H. Reiter, 1–35. Minneapolis: University of Minnesota Press.

– 2000. *The Politics of the Police*. 3rd ed. Oxford University Press.

Reiss, A.J., Jr. 1971. *The Police and the Public*. New Haven: Yale University Press.

Rennie, G. 2000. Brutality Blasted: OAS Security Overreacted. *The Windsor Star*, 6 June, 1–2.

Rifkin, J. 1994. *The End of Work: The Decline of the Global Labour Force and the Dawn of the Post-Market Era*. New York: Putnam.

Rigakos, G. 2002. *The New Parapolice: Risk Markets and Commodi•ed Social Control*. Toronto: University of Toronto Press.

Roach, K. 2003. The Dangers of a Charter-Proof and Crime-Based Response to Terrorism. In *The Security of Freedom: Essays on Canada's Anti-terrorism Bill*, ed. R. Daniels, P. Macklem, and K. Roach, 131–51. Toronto: University of Toronto Press.

– 2004. *The Overview: Four Models of Police-Government Relationships*. Ontario: Ipperwash Inquiry.

Rogers, N. 1984. Serving Toronto the Good. In *Forging a Consensus: Historical Essays on Toronto*, ed. V. Russell. Toronto: University of Toronto Press.

Rose, N. 1996. Governing Advanced Liberal Democracies. In *Foucault and Political Reason: Liberalism, Neoliberalism, and Rationalities of Government*, ed. A. Barry, T. Osborne, and N. Rose, 37–64. Chicago: University of Chicago Press.

Rose, N., and P. Miller. 1992. Political Power Beyond the State. *British Journal of Sociology* 43 (2): 175–205.

Royal Canadian Mounted Police. 1971. *Manual of Tactical Training*. RCMP.

– 1983. *Vancouver Detachment Public Order Report*. Vancouver: RCMP.

– 2001. *Commissioner's Response to Interim Report Prepared by the Commission for Public Complaints Against the RCMP* (CPC). Ottawa: RCMP.

Rubinstein, J. 1973. *City Police*. New York: Farrar, Strauss and Giroux.

Russell, B. 1990. *Back to Work: Labour, State and Industrial Relations in Canada*. Scarborough, ON: Nelson.

– 1991. Assaults without Defeat: Contemporary Industrial Relations and the Canadian Labour Movement. In *Regulating Labour: The State, Neo-Conservatism and Industrial Relations*, ed. L. Haiven, S. McBride, and J. Shields, 14–44. Toronto: Society for Socialist Studies and Garamond Press.

– 1995. Labour's Magna Carta? Wagnerism in Canada at Fifty. In *Labour Gains, Labour Pains, 50 Years of PC 1003*, ed. C. Gonick, P. Phillips, and J. Vorst, 177–92. Winnipeg: Society for Socialist Studies and Fernwood.

– 1999. *More with Less: Work Reorganization in the Canadian Mining Industry*. Toronto: University of Toronto Press.

Sallot, J., R. Seguin, and C. Freeze 2001. Fortress Quebec Is Breached; Activists Topple Riot Fence Delaying Summit Opening. *The Globe and Mail*, 21 April, 1.

Sangster, Joan. 2004. We No Longer Respect the Law: The Tilco Strike, Labour Injunctions and the State. *Labour/Le Travail* 53: 47–88.

Scarman, Rt. Hon. the Lord. 1981. *The Brixton Disorders 10–12 April 1981.* Report of an Inquiry by the Rt. Hon. The Lord Scarman, O.B.E. Cmnd 8247. London: HMSO.

Schenk. C. 1995. Fifty Years after PC 1003; The Need for New Directions. In *Labour Gains, Labour Pains, 50 Years of PC 1003*, ed. C. Gonick, P. Phillips, and J. Vorst, 193–214. Winnipeg: Society for Socialist Studies and Fernwood.

Scott, J., and J. Meyer. 1994. *Institutional Environments and Organization: Structural Complexity and Individualism.* Thousand Oaks, CA: Sage.

Schweingruber, D. 2000. Mob Sociology and Escalated Force: Sociology's Contribution to Repressive Police Tactics. *The Sociological Quarterly* 41 (3): 371–89.

Scranton, W. 1970. *Report on the National Commission on Campus Unrest.* Washington, DC: U.S. Government Printing Office.

Scraton, P. 1985. *The State of the Police: Is Law and Order Out of Control?* London: Pluto Press.

Scruton, R. 2003. *The West and the Rest: Globalisation and the Terrorist Threat.* New York: Continuum.

Seattle Police. 1971. *Training Bulletin.* 1 February.

Senge, Peter. 1990. *The Fifth Discipline: The Art and Practice of the Learning Organization.* New York: Doubleday.

Shaw, L. 1973. The Role of Clothing in the Criminal Justice System. *Journal of Police Science and Administration* 1 (4): 414–20.

Shearing, C. 1981. Deviance and Conformity in the Reproduction of Order. In *Organizational Police Deviance*, ed. C. Shearing, 29–47. Toronto: Butterworths.
– 2004. Thoughts on Sovereignty. *Policing and Society* 14 (1): 5–12.

Shearing, C., and J. Wood. 2003. Nodal Governance, Democracy, and the New 'Denizens.' *Journal of the Law and Society* 30 (3): 400–19.

Sheptycki, J. 2002. *In Search or Transnational Policing.* Great Britain: Ashgate.

Shields, J. 1990. Building a New Hegemony in British Columbia. In *Regulating Labour: The State, Neo-Conservatism and Industrial Relations*, ed. L. Haiven, S. McBride, and J. Shields, 45–78. Toronto: Society for Socialist Studies and Garamond Press.

Shorter, E., and C. Tilly. 1971. Le déclin de la grève violente en France de 1890 à 1935. *Le Mouvement Social* 79 (July–September): 95–118.

Shulz, D. 1987. Holdups, Hobos, and the Homeless: Brief History of the Railroad Police in North America. *Police Studies* 19 (2): 90–5.

Silver, Allan. 1967. 'The Demand for Order in Civil Society: A Review of Some Themes in the History of Urban Crime, Police and Riot.' In *The Police: Six Sociological Essays*, ed. D. Bordua, 1–24. New York: Wiley.

Simon, J. 1997. Governing through Crime. In *The Crime Conundrum: Essays on Criminal Justice*, ed. L. Friedman and G.Fisher, 171–89. New York: Westview Press.

– 1998. The Ideological Effects of Actuarial Practices. *Law and Society Review* 22 (4): 771–800.

Skolnick, J. 1966. *Justice Without Trial*. New York: Wiley.

Snyder, D., and C. Tilly. 1974. Hardship and Collective Violence in France. *America Sociological Review* 37 (October): 520–32.

Solski, M., and J. Smaller. 1984. *Mine Mill: The History of the International Union of Mine, Mill and Smelter Workers in Canada since 1985*. Ottawa: Steel Rail.

Spierenburg, P. 1984. *The Spectacle of Suffering: Executions and the Evolution of Repression*. Cambridge: Cambridge University Press.

Spitzer, S., and A. Scull. 1977. Privatization and Capitalist Development: The Case of the Private Police. *Social Problems* 25 (1): 18–29.

Starek, Paul. 1970. Strike Action Calls for Controlled Reaction. *Police Gazette*, March, 1–5.

Stenning, P. 1981: *The Legal Status of the Police*. Ottawa: Minister of Supply and Service.

Stinson, J., and M. Ballantyne 2006. Union Renewal and CUPE. In *Paths to Union Renewal: Canadian Experiences*, ed. P. Kumar and C. Schenk, 145–60. Peterborough, ON: Broadview Press and Garamond Press.

Storey, R. 1979. *Unions, Workers and Steel; The Blurring of the Picket Lines*. Toronto: University of Toronto.

Sung, Hung-en. 2006. Democracy and Criminal Justice in Cross National Perspective: From Crime Control to Due Process. *The Annals of the American Academy of Political and Social Science* 605 (1): 311–37.

Suskind, R. 2006. *The One Percent Doctrine: Deep Inside America's Pursuit of Its Enemies since 911*. New York: Simon and Schuster.

Sykes, R., and J. Clark. 1975. A Theory of Defence Exchange in Police–Civilian Encounters. *American Journal of Sociology* 81 (3): 584–600.

Task Force on Policing in Ontario. 1974. *Task Force on Policing in Ontario: The Police Are the Public and the Public Are the Police*. Toronto: Queen's Printer.

T'Hart, P., and B. Pijnenburg. 1989. The Heizel Stadium Tragedy. Coping with Crises. The Management of Disasters. In *Riots and Terrorism*, ed. U. Rosenthal, M.T. Charles, and P. T'Hart, 197–224. Springfield: C.C. Thomas.

Tilly, C. 1985. War Making and State Making as Organized Crime. In *Bringing the State Back*, ed. Peter Evans, Dietrich Rueschemeyer, and Theda Skocpol, 169–91. Cambridge: Cambridge University Press.

– 2004. Trust and Rule. *Theory and Society* 33: 1–30.

Tittle, Charles R. 1995. *Control Balance: Toward a General Theory of Deviance*. Boulder, CO: Westview.

Toronto Police Service. 2001–2. Monthly Reports: Public Safety Unit: Industrial Liaison Section.

Torrance, J. 1986. *Public Violence in Canada*. Montreal and Kingston: McGill-Queen's University Press.

Tribe, L. 2000. *American Constitutional Law*. 3rd ed. Vol. 1. New York: Foundation Press.

Trojanowicz, Robert, and B. Bucqueroux. 1990. *An Evaluation of the Neighbourbood Foot Patrol Program in Flint, Michigan*. East Lansing: Michigan State University.

Trudeau, P. 1974 *Asbestos Strike*. Toronto: J. Lewis and Samuel.

Turk, A., 1982. *Political Criminality: The Defiance and Defense of Authority*. Beverley Hills: Sage.

Turner, R.H. 1968. The Public Perception of Protest. *American Sociological Review* 34: 815–31.

Tyler, T. 2007. Top Court Protects Bargaining. *Toronto Star*, 9 June, B1–2.

Uglow, S. 1988. *Policing Liberal Society*. New York: Oxford University Press.

Unger, R. 1986. *Critical Legal Studies Movement*. Cambridge: Harvard University Press.

United States. 1967. *The Challenge of Crime in a Free Society: A Report*. President's Commission on Law Enforcement and Administration of Justice. Washington, DC: U.S. Government Printing Office.

– 1973. National Advisory Commission on Criminal Justice Standards and Goals. *Report on Police*. Washington, DC: U.S. Government Printing Office.

United States Senate. 1976. *Final Report of the Select Committee to Study Governmental Operations with Respect to Intelligence Activities*. United States Senate, 94th Congress, 2nd Session.

Valverde, M. 2007. Police, Sovereignty and Law: Foucauldian Reflections. *Economy and Society* 32 (2): 234–52.

– 2008, forthcoming. Police, Sovereignty, and Law: Foucauldian Reflections. In *Police and the Liberal State*, ed. M. Drubber and M. Valverde. Stanford: Stanford University Press.

Vancouver Police Department. 1983. *Labour Management Dispute Policy*. 10 May. Vancouver: VPD.

– 1995. *Restricted. Review of the Stanley Cup Riot, June 14, 1994*. Vancouver: VPD.

Vannini, I. 1971. *Report of the Royal Commission of Inquiry in Relation to the Conduct of the Public and the Metropolitan Toronto Police*. Toronto.

Vickers, K. 2004. Presentation to Ipperwash Research Advisory Committee. Toronto, 5 October.

Vitale, A. 2005. From Negotiated Management to Command and Control: How the New York Police Department Polices Protests. *Policing and Society* 15 (3): 283–384.

Vogler, R. 1991. *Reading the Riot Act.* Philadelphia: Milton Keynes: Open University Press.

Waddington, D. 1992. *Contemporary Issues in Public Disorder.* London: Routledge.

Waddington, D., K. Jones, and C. Critcher. 1989. *Flashpoints: Studies in Public Disorder.* London: Routledge and Kegan Paul.

Waddington, D., and M. King. 2005. The Disorderly Crowd: From Classical Psychological Reductionism to Social-Contextual Theory: The Impact on Public Order Policing Strategies. *The Howard Journal* 44 (5): 490–503.

Waddington, P. 1993. Dying in a Ditch: The Use of Police Powers in Public Order. *International Journal of the Sociology of Law* 21: 335–53.

– 1994a. *Liberty and Order: Policing Public Order.* London: UCL Press.

– 1994b. Coercion and Accommodation: Policing Public Order after the *Public Order Act. British Journal of Sociology* 45 (3): 367–85.

– 1998. Controlling Protest in Contemporary Historical and Comparative Perspective. In *Policing Protest: The Control of Mass Demonstrations in Western Democracies,* ed. D. della Porta and H. Reiter, 117–42. Minneapolis: University of Minnesota Press.

Walker, S. 1977. *A Critical History of Police Reform.* Lexington, MA: D.C. Heath.

Walmart Accused of Infiltrating Anti-Wal-Mart Group. 2007. *Democracy Now!* 5 April. http://www.democracynow.org/2007/4/5/headlines#6 (accessed 2 September 2008).

Walter, E. 1969. *Terror and Resistance: A Study of Political Violence.* London: Oxford University Press.

Warwyk, W. 2004. *The Collection and Use of Intelligence in Policing Public Order Events.* Ontario: Ipperwash Inquiry.

Weitzer, R. 1995. *Policing under Fire: Ethnic Conflict and Police–Community Relations in Northern Ireland.* Albany, NY: State University of New York Press.

Weiss, R. 1986. Private Detective Agencies and Labour Discipline in the United States, 1855–1946. *The Historical Journal* 29 (1): 87–107.

Wells, D. 1997. When Push Comes to Shove: Competitiveness, Job Security and Labour–Management Cooperation in Canada. *Economic and Industrial Democracy* 18 (2): 176–200.

Westley, W. 1970. *Violence and the Police: A Sociological Study of Law, Custom, and Morality.* Cambridge, MA: MIT Press.

White, J. 1991. The State and Industrial Relations in a Neo-Conservative Era: A Thematic Commentary. In *Regulating Labour: The State, Neo-Conservatism, and Industrial Relations,* ed. L. Haiven, S. McBride and J. Shields, 198–221. Winnipeg and Toronto: Socialist Studies and Garamond Press.

Wiles, P., 1999. Policing Late Modernity in Britain. In *Police et sécurité: Contrôle social et interaction public/privé – Policing and Security: Social Control and the Public–Private Divide*, ed. J. Shapland and L. van Outrive, 139–53. Montreal: L'Harmattan.

Williamson, D. 2002. Stop Scabs, Cops Urged: CAW Says Police Must Bar Replacement Workers at International Plant. *Windsor Star*, 9 July, A3.

Willis, A. 2001. Public Order Policing in the UK: A Fading Star? *Police Practice and Research: An International Journal* 2 (1–2): 15–26.

Wilsnack, R. 1980. Information Control: A Conceptual Framework for Sociological Analysis. *Urban Life* 8 (4): 467–99.

Wilson, J. 1968. *Varieties of Police Behavior: The Management of Law and Order in Eight Communities*. Harvard: Harvard University Press.

Windsor Peace Coalition. 2001. *Criminalizing Dissent*. Windsor Peace Coalition

Windsor Police Service (WPS). 1989. *Emergency Service Unit Policy and Procedures Manual*. Windsor, ON: WPS

– 1984–91. *Annual Report*. Windsor, ON: WPS.

Winter, M. 1998. Police Philosophy and Protest Policing in the Federal Republic of Germany, 1960–1990. In *Policing Protest: The Control of Mass Demonstrations in Western Democracies*, ed. D. della Porta and H. Reiter, 188–212. Minneapolis: University of Minnesota Press.

Wisler, D., and H. Kriesi. 1998. Public Order, Protest Cycles, and Political Process: Two Swiss Cities Compared. In *Policing Protest: The Control of Mass Demonstrations in Western Democracies*, ed. D. della Porta and H. Reiter, 91–116. Minneapolis: University of Minnesota Press.

Wood, L. 2007. Breaking the Wave: Repression, Identity and Seattle Tactics. *Mobilization: The International Quarterly* 12 (4): 377–88.

Woods, H. 1969. *The Woods Report on Canadian Industrial Relations; Recommendations and Observations*. Ottawa: CCH Canadian Ltd.

Yates, Charlotte. 1993. *From Plant to Politics: The Autoworkers Union in Postwar Canada*. Philadelphia: Temple University Press.

– 2000. Staying the Decline in Union Membership: Union Organizing in Ontario, 1985–99. *Industrial Relations/Relations Industrielles* 55 (4): 640–74.

Young, A. 2004. Sweeping, Obtuse Laws Can Be Instruments of Oppression. *Toronto Star*, August.

Young, J. 1999. *The Exclusive Society*. London: Sage.

Zaccardelli, G. 2001. *Commissioner's Response to the Interim APEC Report*. RCMP. http://www.rcmp-grc.gc.ca/news/apec_comm_e.htm.

Zwelling, M. 1972. *The Strikebreakers: The Report of the Strikebreaking Committee of the Ontario Federation of Labour and the Labour Council of Metropolitan Toronto*. Toronto: New Press.

Index

Abernathy, G., 209
Act for the Preservation of Peace Near Public Works, 60
ADM (food processing company), 119–20
American Civil Liberties Union (ACLU), 104
American Civil War, 59, 61
American Technology, 204
anarchists, 47, 89, 219, 253, 258
animal rights protest, 46
anti-capitalist radicalism, 46, 95
anti-globalization protests, 18, 34, 232–3; barricaded areas, 235, 238, 241–2, 245–6, 251–2, 255; colour coding of protesters, 253–5; common-cause with labour, 293–4; cost of policing for, 238, 244, 247; hybrid strategies of policing or intelligent control, 275–7; immigration strategies by police, 240; institutionalization of activists, 248–9; intelligence by protesters, 252–3; intelligence strategies used, 251–6; intelligence strategies used (G8 2002), 247–8; intelligence strategies used (OAS), 239–41; intelligence strategies used (Quebec Summit), 244–5; lessons learned (G8 2002), 249, 308n4; lessons learned (OAS Windsor), 243–4; lessons learned (Quebec Summit), 246–7; and limits to liaison strategies, 141, 251, 290–1; police perception of, 251; Seattle 1999, 146, 236–7, 250; as security rituals, 300; and type of public order policing, 46–7, 304n10; use of coercion by police, 243–4; use of force, 218–19. *See also* Asia-Pacific Economic Cooperation conference demonstration (BC); protests, large-scale
anti-poverty activists, 47, 130, 169, 217, 289
anti-war groups, 80, 97, 98–100
APEC. *See* Asia-Pacific Economic Cooperation conference demonstration (BC)
Aramark Canada Ltd. v. Keating, 173
Arar, Maher, 205
arrests: in APEC demonstration, 191, 233–4, 237; at Burnt Church, 228–9; at Caledonia, 230; by colour coding,